Another Modernity, a Different Rationality

D0277981

Scott Lash

Another
Modernity
A Different
Rationality

BLACKWELL
Publishers

First published 1999

2 4 6 8 10 9 7 5 3 1

Blackwell Publishers Ltd
108 Cowley Road
Oxford OX4 1JF
UK

Blackwell Publishers Inc.
350 Main Street
Malden, Massachusetts 02148
USA

British Library Cataloguing in Publication Data

A CIP catalogue record for this book is available from the British Library.

Library of Congress Cataloging-in-Publication Data

[applied for]

ISBN 0-631-15939-8 (hbk)
ISBN 0-631-16499-5 (pbk)

Typeset in 10.5 on 12pt Baskerville
by Best-set Typesetter Ltd., Hong Kong
Printed in Great Britain by TJ International, Padstow, Cornwall

This book is printed on acid-free paper

Contents

Acknowledgements

This book would have never been written without the generosity of the Humboldt Foundation, which relieved me of nearly two years of teaching duties, between 1986 and 1992. The book was fundamentally conceived during those years. I am indebted to discussions over those years in Berlin with Ulrich Beck, Helmut Berking, Ralf Rogowsky and Hermann Schwengel, and to discussions at Lancaster University with Mick Dillon, Alistair Black, Nicky Chu, Jonatas Ferreira, Paul Morris and Richard Roberts. Drafts of chapters were read and commented on by Lancaster University friends Larry Ray, Dan Shapiro, Rob Shields and John Urry. Other colleagues commenting on draft chapters include Nigel Thrift and Mike Shapiro. I am grateful to the Blackwell readers – Howard Caygill and Tim Luke – who provided lengthy comments and criticisms of the whole book. I am grateful for many long discussions with friends at *Theory, Culture and Society*, in particular with Mike Featherstone and Roy Boyne. I am especially grateful for innumerable conversations over the past decade on all the themes of this book with Celia Lury.

1

Introduction

This is a book in cultural theory. It is just as much a book in sociology. My apologies to those among cultural theorists who disregard sociality, who dismiss the importance of forms of social life. My apologies as well to those among the sociologists, whether of low, middle or high range, who pay scant attention to culture – who neglect the cultural dimension altogether – in favour of the calculated and calculating rationality of actors, systems or massive matrices of quantitative data. These sorts of cultural theorists and sociologists will not find a lot in this book to please them. Indeed, it is a major theme of this book that both cultural theory and sociology have in major part got it wrong.

This book is about modernity, a theme that perhaps more than any other theme has consistently been at stake in both sociology and cultural theory. Modernity has indeed been a stake, an object of contestation: an object to be won in a war of interpretations by both sociology and cultural theory. Sociology and social science more generally have consistently understood modernity in terms of rationality, in terms of the rationality of Cartesian space and Newtonian time handed down from the Enlightenment: from nineteenth-century French positivism down through most currents of early and late twentieth-century sociology. As a stake for sociology, modernity is thus the 'high modernity' of the Enlightenment. For cultural theory modernity has been a radically different stake. It has been a stake claimed by cultural theory by interpretation through deconstruction. Cultural theory has shown how the modernity of dominant social and human science is inscribed in a rationality of 'the same'. This rationality of the same is a logic of a constitutive and constituting inside, a constitutive and constituting 'subject', which excludes, indeed extrudes, all otherness to the outside, where it is to be grasped and studied and controlled as an object. Cultural theory thus interprets modernity through its deconstruction: it rejects the rationality of the same for what amounts to an anti-rationality of the other.

For cultural theory, sociology will have constructed modernity in terms of a rationality of the same. For sociology, cultural theory will have deconstructed modernity, and abandoned rationality altogether for a problematic of the other. This book intends to contest both the construction of high modernity as a rationality of the same and the deconstruction of modernity for an anti-rationality of the other. This book wants neither to praise high modernity nor to deconstruct it. It wants instead to take a third route and speak of *another* modernity. It wants neither to hypostatize rationality nor to reject it. It wants instead to speak of a *different* rationality. This book is about another modernity, inscribed in a different rationality.

Enlightenment versus *the* Enlightenment: Reflexivity and Difference

This book is a set of explorations into this other modernity, a set of attempts in a number of spheres to identify this different rationality. In this sense the book partakes of the 'reflexive' turn in both sociology and cultural theory. It was to this reflexive turn that Michel Foucault was gesturing in his famous essay on Kant and enlightenment. Kant's own late and great essay *Was ist Aufklarung?* was significantly titled not 'what is *the* Enlightenment', but instead simply 'what is enlightenment'.[1] The distinction between high modernity and the other modernity that is the subject of this book is also the distinction between the Enlightenment on the one hand and enlightenment on the other. It is the distinction between the rationality of the same of the Enlightenment and the different rationality of enlightenment. *The* Enlightenment is very much of a piece with Kant's idea of 'pure' reason, with the logical categories, the logic of the same, of pure reason. For Kant, pure reason was also instrumental reason, the specific way that human beings, in their animal nature, dealt with the environment. Here Kant spoke of judgements of pure reason. These judgements would subsume a particular under a universal, the *a priori* categories of reason. This is what Kant called 'determinate judgement'. In determinate judgement one judges under fixed rules, under rules already fixed by the categories of logic. Determinate judgement is a question of cognitive reason: a way that reason works in cognizing the world in the natural sciences. Kantian determinate judgement is the way we understand the world through the prism of *the* Enlightenment, a problematic handed down through the various positivisms of social science.

But Kant also spoke of enlightenment. Enlightenment is based not on determinate judgement but on 'reflective judgement'. If determinate judgement meant that a given case had to be subsumed under an already given, a determinate rule, then reflective, or for our purposes 'reflexive', judgement meant that the rule had to be found. It meant that in judgement we must reflect and find the rule under which a particular case is to be grasped. If determinate judgement of the Enlightenment is a question largely of cognition, then reflective judgement is very importantly a question of *aesthetics*. Kant's determinate judgements refer to the cognition of the first critique the *Critique of Pure Reason*, while he developed the idea of reflective judgement in his third critique, *The Critique of Judgement*, which primarily addressed the problem of not cognitive but *aesthetic* judgements. Reflective or reflexive judgements are aesthetic in another important sense. In determinate judgement of cognitive reason, we subsume the particular under the universal. In reflexive judgement, even when we find the rule, the particular cannot be subsumed under the universal. Indeed, the rule at issue itself is not a universal. The rule is instead another particular. This is also similar to how we judge works of art. We judge art not through logic but analogically, through analogy. We judge art not only through cognition but through much more particular structures of feeling. We will see throughout this book that the other modernity is a largely *aesthetic* modernity, and that its rationality, its different rationality, is less a logical than an analogical rationality.

The reflexive turn in both sociology and cultural theory takes its point of departure effectively from this sort of reflexive judgement. Sociology, and in particular European sociology, thus makes the distinction between simple and 'reflexive' modernity. Here in simple modernity social actors come under the sway of pre-given rules, whether in the norms of modern institutions and organizations like mass trade unions and political parties or large hierarchical firms, or the institutions of the welfare state, and the church and family.[2] In reflexive modernity, in contradistinction, individuals must find the rules to use to encounter specific situations. They must innovate rules in a bricolage of their own identities, a process is as dependent on analogic reason as on the rules of logic. In reflexive modernity one can never quite know, never quite get a grasp on objects of knowledge. The programmes of social engineering of simple modernity have brought with them their own side-effects, their own unintended consequences. It is these unintended consequences that set the stage for reflexive modernity. Contemporary risk societies are thus societies in which ever more individuals are forced into situations of rule-finding reflexive judgement. They are societies in which the impossibility of subsumption of the particular by the pre-given universal is taken for given. Living with risk, living with ambivalence and contingency is forced upon us with the relative decline of institutions and organizations in this age of reflective judgement. In this other modernity, high modernity's principle of rationality becomes a principle of reflexivity. Indeed, the different rationality of the other modernity at stake in this book is reflexivity. The different rationality in *Another Modernity, a Different Rationality*, is reflexivity. The second and importantly aesthetic modernity is not anti-rational or rational but has a principle of rationality based on reflexivity.

If the essence of the second modernity is captured by sociology through reflexivity, for cultural theory it is found in the idea of 'difference'. Difference must not be thought in terms of the binary identity and difference. Difference is not the opposite of identity. It is instead the third term that is neither presence nor absence. Difference in cultural theory means not the other as opposed to the same, but a third term that is neither same nor other, a middle term that bridges, that constitutes a margin between presence and absence, same and other, inside and outside.[3] Difference also importantly resides in Kant's third aesthetic critique. The first critique, *The Critique of Pure Reason*, deals with the realm of the same, while practical or moral reason of the second critique deals with the realm of the other. The theoretical reason of the first critique takes place through the concepts of natural science in the realm of necessity, while 'pure practical' or moral reason of the second occupies the sphere of freedom. If the logical concepts of the first critique's pure reason constitute the same and the 'inside', the second critique's ideas of pure practical reason – God, freedom, infinity, the thing-in-itself, the moral imperative – occupy the fully indeterminate realm of the other, of the intangible outside. Kant's book on pure reason was a critique largely in that it wanted to draw the limits of the island of necessity of cognitive reason, to make space for the 'sea of freedom' outside that island.

So the first cognitive and second moral-practical critiques stand in binary opposition to each other as same and other, inside and outside, necessity and freedom, presence and absence. In the *third* critique Kant recognized the unsatisfactory nature of this juxtaposition. He became dissatisfied with the notion of freedom of the second critique, of its assumptions of a fully indeterminate reason. He became aware of the impossibility of application of a fully indeterminate rule. Hence his third critique constructed a bridge between presence and absence, same and other. This is reflective judgement.[4] Neither determinate, nor fully indeterminate, but partly determinate in that we have to search for the rule. This bridging space of reflective judgement is the space of difference: it is the third space, the margin between same and other. For cultural theory this third space of difference is constitutive of both presence and absence. Difference is more primordial than either presence or absence. Its ethos is neither irrationality nor anti-rationality, but instead another rationality. We understand, then, this other and second modernity of Kantian enlightenment and aesthetic judgement sociologically as reflexivity and culturally as difference: in both cases a broken middle, an aporetic space of ambivalence and undecidability in which everything is at stake.

The Ground

There is, however, something unsatisfactory about both sociological and cultural explorations into this other and second modernity. There is something inadequate, something not quite there. There is something that just too quickly dissolves solidity into air.[5] Simple high or Enlightenment modernity is thus found by sociology to be too foundational. It is rejected for the anti-foundational undecidability of reflexive modernity in which we are free to construct our own biographies.[6] High modernity's epistemological realism – in which subject encounters a fixed object as if a mirror of nature – is also encountered as a foundational, and dismantled for a thoroughgoing constructionism in which subject constitutes object according to its own material and ideal interests.[7] Similarly, high modernity's foundations are deconstructed by cultural theory for the free play, the 'anything goes', of the signifier. Pictorial realism based in Renaissance perspective is rejected for decentred and anarchic notions of the field of vision. Its Newtonian temporality of homogeneous time of cause and effect and productive labour is displaced by a fluid and shifting set of heterogeneous temporalities, by the anarchy of 'the event'.

What this anti-foundational critique of sociological construction and cultural deconstruction ignores is an entire and largely forgotten dimension of the second modernity: and this is the dimension of *the ground*. The critique from the ground views high modernity as not foundational enough. This grounded and parallel critique began at about the same time as the anti-foundational critique: both originating in Romanticism. This parallel critique is levelled, for example, from the ground of community or Gemeinschaft. Here the empty norms of high modern Gesellschaft or society are rejected for the grounded and substantive practices of community. Here Gesellschaft (the social) is seen as insufficiently grounded, as already too anti-foundational, already too abstract. It is levelled from the ground of tradition. Thus Newtonian time is not dissolved into the further abstraction and groundlessness of the event, but instead relocated in the past, in history, in tradition, in the cyclical time of nature. Here modernity is already too future-oriented, too forgetful of the generations, of myth and of origins. This second, grounded dimension of the other modernity is indeed modern, and not traditional. Only in modernity, and indeed after one or two centuries of high modernity, was it possible to achieve the sort of distance on tradition, on community, on place, to allow it to enter meaningfully into discourse.

This ground – which alternately takes the form of community, history, tradition, the symbolic, place, the material, language, life-world, the gift, Sittlichkeit, the political, the religious, forms of life, memory, nature, the

monument, the path, fecundity, the tale, habitus, the body – is just as
important a dimension of the second modernity as groundlessness. It has,
however, been too much forgotten by cultural theory and reflexive sociology. It is perhaps the most central task of this book to retrieve this ground.
To work through the second modernity not just as a deconstructive
'hermeneutics of suspicion', but also as a hermeneutics of *retrieval*.[8] To
retrieve this ground that is more real than realism and has nothing at all
to do with the hyper-real. This book is largely an exercise in such
a hermeneutics of retrieval. To retrieve this ground, whose radical
materiality is much more primordial than interests: this ground which is
not eternally constructed or deconstructed, but into which we are thrown,
consisting not of structures but of forms of life, ever already there. The
other modernity, with its different rationality, is a question of the groundless ground. It is a simultaneous movement of deconstruction and retrieval.
It retrieves and deconstructs at the same time. It is also a grounded space
of a certain consistency. Modernity's fate is eternally to retrieve and eternally to deconstruct the ground. Modernity's fate is that it is a *groundless*
ground, but also a groundless *ground*.

   This groundless ground is a lot more than a series of debates in the world
of theory. All sorts of activities in our everyday lives proceed in the cultural,
in the sensibility of this other, second modernity. Subcultures, for example,
and electronic communities, new collectivities in politics, intimate relations, individual and collective memory, material culture, the reinvention
of tradition, our experience with nature, diasporas and ethnicity all involve the cultural ambience of the groundless ground. All involve the
groundedness, the middle, as much as the groundlessness. There is a
notable absence of consideration of the ground in both sociology and
cultural theory. This book is an attempt to remedy this. The ground is at
the very centre of the second modernity.

The Groundless Ground

This book consists of a set of explorations, a set of inquiries in this other and
second modernity. It looks for the trace of this second modernity in five
arenas or regions of inquiry: *space, society, experience, judgement* and *the object*. In
each we first we consider high modernity and its deconstruction; then in this
context we attempt to retrieve the ground, the missing ground. In each we
attempt to retrieve the ground, the forgotten dimension in the different rationality of our other modernity. Chapters 2 to 4, on *space*, on cultural
geographies, address how modernist architecture emerged from and against
the classical and humanist tradition. Here we look at modernist architecture
not merely as a set of experiments in the abstraction of forms, but also in

terms of a technics, in terms of a characteristically architectural (as distinct from decorative) and even engineering-like concern with the building materials themselves. Then we consider its deconstruction, its undoing in the 'simulated humanism' of the postmodern architects. And finally we turn to the grounded notion of space, understanding the city as labyrinth, in a production of space that is at once oriental and gothic, in which our bodies weave a tactile and ultimately material web of spatial relations.

In chapters 5 and 6 on *society* we have followed a similar method in explorations in the emergence of classical sociological theory. We look at its rise in the critique of humanism, in the rationalist abstraction of sociological positivism. Here the notion of 'life' plays a particularly important role. On the one hand the metaphor of the organism pervades the most unreconstructed positivism, in which the social body is conceived in terms of the normal and the pathological. But the life paradigm structures not just positivist system thinking, but also organicist vitalism, the *Lebensphilosophie* that stood as hermeneutic opponent to positivism. Thus the late Durkheim's notion of the symbolic and Simmel's of life stood opposed to positivism's systems. Whereas positivism saw values as epiphenomenal and determined by social facts, the new hermeneutics saw those very special social facts, those 'total social facts' that are indeed values, as constitutive of system itself. Thus Durkheim's symbolic and Simmel's 'life' were values structuring our 'primitive classifications', structuring today's elementary forms of religious life.

Parts I and II consider the emergence of modernism – in architecture-urbanism and in sociology – from classical humanism. Here a pre-differentiated humanism – whether classical or Renaissance – develops into a modernism based on a machinic or systemic model. In pre-modernist humanism, humans circulate freely with non-humans, as architectural columns are models of man, as nature is seen to be filled with signs, as semiotic and hermeneutic as humanity. With the rise of architectural-urbanistic and sociological modernism (positivism), a humanistic episteme yields to a machinic episteme. Then in both spatial and sociological realms, in response to high modernist mechanism, a deconstructive response emerges. In architecture through the complexity and simulated historicism of literally postmodernist architecture, in sociology through notions of contingency, ambivalence, fleetingness, the stranger built into the work of thinkers like Simmel. In both spatial and sociological paradigms a critique from the viewpoint of the ground also emerges: in the former through the emergence of paths, labyrinths, the retrieval of gothic and non-Western spatial forms, in the latter through the rehabilitation of the symbolic; both as a source or raw material for the classifications of everyday life and in tandem with a notion of life to be pitted against the technological rationality of system.

One side of the *condition moderne*, in *space* and in *society*, has then taken the form of mechanism. The other side of mechanism is of course subjectivity. And the other side of modernity, this subjectivity, plays itself out in experiencing and judging. Parts III and IV for their part focus on modernity not in terms of mechanism and the critique of mechanism (system), but from the point of view of experiencing and judging subjectivity. They are about experience and judgement. Chapters 7 and 8 address *experience* in the critique of phenomenology. Here we see how the notion of difference and deconstruction was initially forged in Derrida's critique of Husserl's concept of the sign. Derrida here does evoke the ground in his foregrounding of the notion of index. My more general argument, however, is that deconstruction in its broader picture pays insufficient attention to the ground and hence misses a large part of the story of the other modernity. The ground instead is found in another critique of transcendental phenomenology, in the intersubjectivity of community described by Alfred Schutz's life world phenomenology. It is found in an ultimately bodily being-in-the-world in the work of Paul Ricoeur.

Chapters 9 and 10 on *judgement* are explorations into aesthetic experience. We begin with serious considerations of the nature of judgement in Kant. We note that unlike the universality of cognitive reason, subjectivity in aesthetic experience is inscribed not in universality but in singularity. We then inquire into the nature of the object of aesthetic judgement. We note that this object cannot be known or used as resources, means or instruments like objects of cognitive reason. Objects of aesthetic experience are instead themselves grounds, media, middle, comprised of a materiality that bridges the space between same and other, inside and outside, necessity and freedom. We then consider – via a discussion of Hans Georg Gadamer's reflections on art – the further grounding of experience in tradition via notions of permanence, memory and the monument.

Aesthetic judgements for Kant take shape in the bridge, the aporetic and undecidable limit that spans the division between the 'restricted economy' of theoretical reason, on the one hand, and the 'general economy' of moral-practical reason, on the other.[9] This said, aesthetic judgements then divide into judgements of the 'beautiful' and judgements of the 'sublime'. Judgements of the beautiful then tend to be once again subsumed into the restricted economy of determinate reason, while judgements of the sublime shift out into the general economy of freedom, infinity and the outside. This is the subject matter of chapter 10, which classically understands Western culture in terms of a Judaeo-Greek paradigmatic. Here the 'Hellenic' is the idiom of the beautiful, theoretical reason, the figural, iconicity, the eye, while the 'Judaic' is the culture of the sublime, the super-egoic commands of moral reason, the discursive symbolism of the voice. Here again we search for a middle, a new bridging and limiting third space, a ground. We look for it in a logic that is neither Jewish discourse nor Greek figure, but what Gilles Deleuze called a logic of *sensation*.[10] Sensation is the ground that bridges figure and discourse, a logic of not icon or symbol but index, of not eye or ear but tactility and the hand, a logic that is more pagan than either Hellenic or Hebraic.[11]

In our explorations in space, society, experience and judgement, our explorations into the structure and agency of the second, the other modernity, we are engaged in a search for the ground, the ground that challenges the groundlessness of both high modernist abstraction and deconstruction. We search for this ground in the urban materiality of place, the semiotic index, in allegory, in Lacan's real. This ground does involve 'tradition'. But it is not traditional in the orthodox sense of Gemeinschaft, nor is it constructed. It is already built, already given. It is not 'beyond' the abstract totality of Cartesio-Newtonian time-space. Instead of beyond or exterior to the totality, it is somehow 'underneath' both the high modernist totality and the deconstructed and contingent exterior. It is underneath as a condition of the possibility of both our cognitive finitude and our ethical infinitude. But it is underneath less in a sense of being 'primordial', than in being merely 'basic'. It is underneath in the sense of constituting our turn-of-the-twenty-first-century primitive classifications, in the sense of being our catacombs,[12] today's Romanesque truth of Heliocentric protestations. This underneath is dirty, the ground is dirty, in the sense that *poètes maudits* and *part maudite* are not just accursed, but also degenerate, unregenerate, pernicious, unwashed.

It is also a grounded space of a certain grain, a certain consistency. Hegel in *The Philosophy of Right*[13] never tired of criticizing Kant's moral imperative for its groundlessness, its inapplicability. His solution is to ground such abstract morality in the concrete practices of Sittlichkeit, or ethical life. There is a grain to this sphere, this middle, this medium – what Gillian Rose refers to as the now 'broken middle'[14] – that, for example, transforms abstract morality into practical ethics. Sittlichkeit here, ethical life, is neither the necessity of pure reason nor the freedom of the moral imperative. Sittlichkeit is a bridge between the egoism and necessity of utilitarian pursuits and the freedom and infinity of the moral imperative. Sittlichkeit, ethical life, community, is thus the bridge here, the space of difference, the third space, the middle, the medium of the ungrounded ground. In his critique of judgement Kant suggests that space of difference can also be found in art, in aesthetic experience. Now it is the work of art which provides the medium for experience that bridges the limit between the same and the other. The grain, the materiality, of the work of art provides such a middle.

One can multiply the examples of this middle, from the work process, to the materiality of language, to the locality of place, to the mediation of gift-giving. The notion of *difference* in cultural theory is this space. The problem is that cultural theory and reflexive sociology forget this medium and move right out into the realm of the other, the realm of freedom. That cultural theory moves straight out of the same and into the other, from presence into absence, from totality towards infinity, from being towards nothingness. Ignored is the middle, the broken middle, that is not means or resource but medium. For Rose as for Hegel, this middle was the law and ultimately Christ. For Rose, Christ is the broken middle, for John Milbank, the 'eternally deconstructed'.[15] Christ is at the same time the ground (the medium, the material) and the eternally deconstructed. Modernity's fate is eternally to retrieve and eternally to deconstruct the ground. Modernity's fate is that it is a *groundless ground*.

At their best, both sociology and cultural theory potentially proffer a notion of the groundless ground, a theory of the other modernity. At their best, both the sociological theory of reflexivity and the cultural theory of difference are like Kant's third critique. In neither do we get just the simple opposition of positivism's same and nihilism's other, in neither the simple counterposition of necessity and freedom, rules and anarchy, the lightness of norms and the dark void of existential angst. Both instead presume a third space, a space of reflexivity which does not deny the rules of sociality, but which understands social activity in terms of finding the rules. A space of difference which is the limit condition of both same and other.

Exploding Difference: from Second Modernity to Global Information Culture

Classical sociological theory – Weber and Durkheim, for example – has traditionally worked from a notion of theodicy.[16] In theology, theodicies are religious ways of accounting for suffering and death. Theodicies are answers to Job's question: if there is a God then why do we suffer so much? In theodicies there is the inexplicable, death and suffering on the 'outside', and a set of religious rites, rituals and prescriptions accounting for such suffering on the 'inside'. In sociology there is also on the outside death and suffering (the existential and military enemy) and on the inside a set of symbols, a conscience collective, a set of more or less elementary, more or less advanced forms of religious life. In sociology, thus, Durkheim's symbolic itself is the answer of the same to death and suffering in the realm of the other.[17] In late modernity, however, this symbolic is individualized, the conscience collective coming to constitute a series of atomized *consciences individuelles*. Now the individual, the individual being-in-the-world, is facing death and suffering all on his or her own. Now there is individual Dasein on the inside and death on the outside. Heidegger's *Being and Time* in fact addresses beings as much or more than being: it addresses especially those very special (human) beings called Dasein. *Being and Time* is about the being of Dasein, the being of subjectivity as constituted on the horizon of time. Time here most importantly is death and Dasein is constituted as a being towards death.[18] Again we have the inside and outside, same and other. Dasein as the same, as inside, is constituted against the horizon of time or death as outside, as other.

Here is where the theory of difference can intervene. Derrida, in speaking of the gift in his book *Given Time*, says 'es gibt Sein' and 'es gibt Zeit'.[19] It gives being and it gives time. What then is this *es*, the it that gives both being and time? This es is of course difference itself: the limit condition, the third space that 'gives' both being and time. Difference is thus primordial, 'older' than both being and time, and the condition of possibility of both same and other. Here both same and other are constituted in this space of difference. This space of difference can also be ground, can have a materiality. Its signifying substance is not so much symbol or iconic as indexical and tactile, the most material and grounded sort of signification. The space of difference, the limit condition, is also an 'invagination', grounded in sensation. Difference has a grain, the grain of desire, of the material and sensory, the grain of sociality, the radical empiricism of tradition and community. It partakes of the critique from the concrete of high modern abstraction. It is singular, particular. Yet through its temporal deferral of meaning, through the ungraspability of its object, through its constant movement and transitory nature, this ground is at the same time groundless. The space of difference, like the reflexive contingency of the risk society, is the groundless ground. It is the space of the second, reflexive modernity and its different rationality.

But what happens with the shift to the global information culture? What happens in a multimediatized cultural space of not difference or perplexity or ambivalence, but instead of *indifference*. Following the era of difference, as the boundary, the fold between same and other, the era of *in*difference heralds the explosion of the boundary, of the margin, the invaginated fold, of difference, of ambivalence. The explosion yields an indifference between inside and outside, it is the explosion of any limit between restricted and general economies. Now no longer does 'technology' constitute the space of the same, of presence, and death the space of the other or absence. Desire is no longer in the space of lack, hence undecidability – thus constituting the ego's same and superego's other. But technology, death and desire themselves become signals, become bits, become units of information on the horizon of the electromagnetic field, alongside other informational units human and non-human, units of desire, microbes, units of genetic information and the like, caught up in the swirling vortex of indifference.

Now no longer is it a question of *es gibt* but of *es denkt*, i.e. it thinks. We are in an age of the inhuman, the post-human and non-human, of biotechnology and nanotechnology. If the symbolic was once collective and the individual, the age of information explodes the symbolic, breaking it into fragments, the objects we track in cities, or track in life on the screen. The imaginary too is fragmented, leaving only the *es*, the real, and the real no longer is a desiring, but now itself a thinking 'substance'. Es denkt, it thinks: the era of speed is the era of thinking, calculating, information-rich and design-intensive non-humans. When things and animals and the un-conscious also think, the human in its singularity is no longer privileged. The perplexity, the undecidability of human subjectivity, is no longer decisive. Aporias recede into relative insignificance, undecidability no longer matters. There is nothing more at stake. The age of difference was also the risk society. Risk takes place in that same space of difference, the partial determinacy, the *'riskante Freiheit'*, the need to cobble together what is a partly indeterminate life history. But what happens when that space of difference explodes, when that margin, that third space, vanishes into air? When all the fears and dangers of the risk society become realized in apocalypse, in disaster, in catastrophe? What happens when difference turns into indifference, when risk turns into apocalypse or disaster? What happens when the greatest fears of the politics of insecurity are realized: when we are living in the vortex of disaster?

What happens to symbolic or imaginary in this age of the negative horizon, in our apocalyptic and post-apocalyptic culture? Both symbolic and imaginary are exploded into fragments and disseminated outside of the subject into the space of indifference in which they attach to a set of humans and non-humans, to objects of consumer culture, to images, to thinking machines, to machines that design. All that is left is a body without organs,[20] a body that thinks, a machinic body that thinks, that symbolizes, that imagines. The individual, the human along with the symbolic, does not implode, but like the heads in David Cronenberg's *Scanners* explodes, spew-ing microbes, non-humans, information, units of desire, death, images, symbols, semen and the like out into what is now the space of indifference.

This is the context of part V of this book. Part V radically changes register. It deals not with the second or even the first modernity at all. Part V of this book, on 'the object', addresses the explosive threat from the *global information culture* to the other modernity and its different rationality. The space of difference, a boundary around the organic totalities of the hu-mans, nations, firms and welfare states, is under threat from the post-nationalism and non-humans of the global information culture. Let me be clear that the global information culture is *not* a third modernity. It is not at all 'modernism in the streets'. Daniel Bell in his seminal *Cultural Contradic-tions of Capitalism* followed mediaeval Arab scholar Ibn Khaldun in understanding modernity in terms of a logic of civilizations.[21] A logic in which every civilization experiences a rise and decline and in which characteristic symbolic structures accompany the rise and other symbolic structures the decline. For Bell in this context, the first or high modernity of the Enlightenment accompanied the rise of Western Civilization and the second, aesthetic modernity its decline. Jonathan Friedman has superimposed this cultural logic on to the rise and decline of world systems, of largely political-economic world systems.[22] The second modernity has exercised its cultural logic still in the context of a world system based on the nation-state, on manufacturing industry and on an institutional set of structures comprising the social or society. The emergence of a new, less Western-centric world system describes a shift from the national to the global, from the manufacturing to the information industries and from the social to the cultural.[23]

At issue is thus a formation vastly different from 'modernism in the streets'. And I at least for my part can no longer get a great deal of intellectual mileage from the notion of postmodern. Yes post-national, yes importantly post-human, eventually with the diasporization of the West, the rise of the East and the emergence of the speed capitalism of what the World Bank calls the 'New Big Five' – Brazil, China, Russia, India, Indonesia – perhaps even the eclipse of the dominance of Western civilization as we know it. But none the less, the new world (dis)order of the global information culture is vastly different from either modernity. Both first and second modernities operated from a certain principle of transcendence, a certain dualism, either of subject and object in the first modernity or the aporetic and ontological difference between necessity and freedom, same and other, of the second modernity. The global information culture explodes the dualisms and the space of difference that separates them. The aporetic difference of the second modernity is not dialectically reconciled or superseded in the information era as much as exploded. Talcott Parsons in *The Structure of Social Action*,[24] drawing on Weber and Durkheim, recognized in tribal societies a symbolic order of immanence. This stood in contrast to the logic of transcendence of both the traditional legitimation of the world religions and, in another register, of modernity. The global information culture is once again a culture not of transcendence but of immanence. A culture in which subjects, objects, texts and being itself figure only as entities of an indifferent ontological substance in the plane of the assemblages, the actor-networks of today. The global information culture in this sense is perhaps less postmodern than *pre*-traditional. According to Bell's schema, if the first modernity follows a logic of *technology* and the second a logic of *culture* seen in contradistinction from technology,[25] then the global information order operates from the indifference of a *technological culture*.

Thus chapters 11 to 13 consider the rise of the *object*, of the non-human in the work of Bruno Latour, Paul Virilio and Walter Benjamin. If, in comparison with high modernity, subjectivity in the second modernity became finite with its situatedness in the world, then in the age of indifference and the object subjectivity becomes *really* finite and takes its place as an equal alongside animals, things, machines, nature and other objects. As subjectivity, relatively speaking, experiences a decline in power and rights, things and objects take on new powers, acquire new rights. Natural rights become the rights of nature: non-human rights. Hence Latour speaks of a 'parliament of things', Virilio the historicity of the projectile and the wall. With the symbolic in fragments, circulating in a global economy of signs and space, for Walter Benjamin things take on powers of locution, become talking things.

The rise of the global information culture, of what Manuel Castells calls *The Network Society*, for all the hype is increasingly much more a question of fact than value.[26] It seems to be irreversible. It cannot be wished away no matter how great the longing for a much kinder age of mass trade unions, socialist parties, a formidable welfare state, full employment, comparative income and wealth equality, and the now seemingly gemütlich charms of print culture and the first media age.[27] Given the great destruction involved in the rise of information culture, there is no denying the space of innovation it opens up, the space of experimentation, the 'lines of flight', for the techno-scientists and techno-artists in today's rapidly expanding digital economy. This book is written in a spirit of affirmation of this neo-world order of technological culture: in affirmation of an age in which the restricted economy is exploded into the excess of the general economy. But at the same time this book is also written in another spirit. A spirit which at the same time warns us that we ignore, that we forget, the legacy of the second modernity, and especially the ground, the broken middle of the second modernity, at our peril. The second modernity, as index, as haptic space, as the tactile culture, as community, as memory, is in many respects in the midst of the global information culture still with us. It is with us, and will be with us for a long time, in the interstices, the sometimes vast and sometimes intimate spaces left more or less untouched by the new millennium's information and communication flows. The second modernity, the groundless ground, is still with us as 'raw material' that is *de facto* or potentially reconfigured by the information networks of the second media age. Most important, it is still with us as memory. Walter Benjamin's *angelus novus* thus writes as dragged into the future at a great pace, while firmly directing his gaze on the past, while looking backwards. Today's *angelus novus* writes moving into the simulations, the database, the archive of technological culture, with an eye to the twin ghosts of Marx and Hamlet (in the age of the *Hamletmaschine*) looking over his shoulder. The second modernity is thus also today a spectre, haunting the network society. The second modernity is memory, monument, tradition, the memorial. Institutions can take two forms. They can be abstract, sometimes expert systems of normativity and normalization. Or they can incorporate memory, can embody tradition. For this writer sociology as an institution is very much understood in the second sense. Thus this book, while a book in cultural theory, is written with the spectres of Durkheim, Weber and Marx prominently in the background, as key figures of the horizon. This book, a work in the spirit of affirmation of technological culture, is also and at the same time a work of mourning.

Part I

Space

2

The First Modernity: Humans and Machines

This chapter consists of a set of explorations into modernism in architecture and urbanism. The aim is to begin to establish a framework of the first modernity as a benchmark for the rest of the book. To look for this in architecture and lived space would seem to be most useful for sociologists and students of culture. This is because in architecture and urbanism, modernism 'descends', as it were, from the realm of representation to occupy the space of everyday life. The emergence of the modern, of the first modernity, comes last of all to architecture and lived space. High modernity emerges in religion and painting in the fifteenth and sixteenth centuries, in philosophy in the seventeenth century, in the novel in the eighteenth and early nineteenth centuries. But in terms of lived urban space modernity descends fully into the social on any kind of significant scale only well into the twentieth century. At issue is the modern no longer only as narratives and other representations of disembodied culture. Now modernist culture goes three-dimensionally into the culture of everyday life, visual, aural and as tactile as the chair you sit on. No longer is modernity just a question of representations – in thought, ethics, the arts, it is now pervasive in every aspect of life. Only in the twentieth century do these high modernist principles pervade everyday life, in the factory, in the applied positivist social statistics and their concomitant lived classical welfare state, in the houses we live in.

As in representational forms of culture, the first modernity in architecture and urbanism works from a principle of abstraction. This abstraction in all spheres of culture is principally of subject and object. This is similar to subject–object relations in modernist epistemology, ethics, literature and painting. There is a relation of abstract, disembedded subject with abstract, disembedded object. The major difference is that as high modernism descends into the streets, both subjects and objects are no longer individual (as they were in high modernist epistemology and aesthetics) but collective. The collective subjects are the increasingly urbanized masses, and especially the working class. The collective objects, when assembled together, come more and more to take on the character of the machinic: they are machines, they are technology. They are no longer represented objects – like the objects of science and aesthetics. They are instead lived objects. These machines are lived objects in both the home and the factory. Thus Le Corbusier's *machine à habiter* is joined by Charlie Chaplin's *machine à travailler*.

Although subject–object thinking and abstraction are predominant in all sorts of high modern urbanism, some focus more on subjects and others on objects, on structures or machines. In this chapter we will look at subject- or human-centred modernism in the garden city idea and functionalism. Functionalism was the most socially oriented of the modernisms. It not only proffered a built environment for the working class as collective consumer, but as we shall see was based on the reorganization of the building trades themselves, i.e. on the working class as collective producer. Then we will turn to the more object-centred or machinic visions. Here buildings were not addressed to either individual or collective social agent, but were more or less self-referential. We will address two types of such object- or machine-centred configurations. The first we will call 'structuralism', and this is perhaps typified in the work of Mies van der Rohe. The other is 'formalism', as typified by Le Corbusier. In structuralism we will see that a building's form should express its structure. Structuralism works from a 'tectonic' principle with a very strong engineering dimension, in which the built environment expresses the materials, glass, steel, stone, concrete of which it is comprised. Formalism works from a 'stereotonic' principle of the relation of the elements of a building to one another. Its aestheticist credo will define architecture as 'the magnificent, knowledgeable and correct play of volumes under light'.

Both human-centred and machine-centred modernisms, we shall see, emerged from a break with the classicism of the beaux-arts tradition. Both intuitively rejected the Academicians of beaux-arts for an initial attachment to the artisan, to craft traditions. Both also rejected the focus on culture and on classical form of the beaux-arts for naturalism and organicism. But both ultimately, we shall see, reverted to the subject–object, human–machine dualism that is constitutive of the first modernity.

Garden City and Functionalism

The garden city idea was only the definitive crystallization of a tradition of modern urban planning which had begun some forty to fifty years earlier. Modern planning was effectively 'anti-urbanist' from the start. Its roots are not so much in the grids emerging at the beginning of the nineteenth century in, for example, New York. Planning instead lay not in 'grid' assumptions but in 'green' assumptions, and developed as a reaction to the crowding into slums of the working classes of the mid and late nineteenth centuries. The earlier advocates of the grid gave priority to circulation; for the 'greens', the priority was space, light, fresh air and parks for the urban masses. Modern planning was born along rather similar lines yet independently in Bismarck's Germany, on the one hand, whose central figures were Baumeister and Camillo Sitte, and in *laissez-faire* America, on the other, in the mid nineteenth-century Park Movement.[1] The American Park Movement began in New York City in the 1840s. Leader Frederick Law Olmstead was appointed Head of New York's newly formed park commission in 1857. For Olmstead the enemy was a coalition of city government at Tamany Hall and private speculators. Central Park, designed by Olmstead in the English picturesque tradition, opened in 1862. He was subsequently pivotal in the Park Movement in Boston and designed the campuses for Columbia and the University of California at Berkeley, themselves serving as green utopia models for Lewis Mumford and twentieth-century planners.[2] As important was architect James Burnham's City Beautiful Movement, developing from the Columbia Exhibition in Chicago in 1893. The World Fair featured a massive display of beaux-arts buildings on the Chicago Lakefront, commissioned by Burnham and laid out in a landscape – describable perhaps as 'monumental kitsch' – by Olmstead. The City Beautiful Movement, less critical of capitalism than the Park Movement, worked closely with business. The 1893 Exposition was correspondingly a celebration of America's new expansionist identity. The idea for Burnham's Chicago plan of 1907 was developed by businessmen from the Commercial Club of Chicago.[3]

The garden city idea, of course, is British. It makes sense in the context of this chapter to build from a distinction between, on the one hand, American and French modernism that has been largely aestheticist in character, and British and German modernism that is social-critical in character. The Franco-American tradition is more likely to be formalist and 'stereotonic', while the Anglo-German tradition is more likely to be structuralist and 'tectonic'.[4] Founding leader of the garden city movement Patrick Geddes worked with sociologists at the University of Chicago, collecting data on daily life in the city. Geddes, influenced by French social theorist Frederick Le Play, advocated planning on a regional level and community participation in decision-making. He was a central figure in the first US National Conference of City Planning in Washington DC in 1909, and organized the benchmark Town Planning Conference and Exhibition at the Royal Institute of British Architecture in London the following year, in which Burnham, the two other leaders of the British movement,

Ebenezer Howard and Raymond Unwin, and German planning theorist Joseph Stubben participated.[5] The idea of the garden city was initially discovered and developed in Howard's *Garden Cities of Tomorrow*, published in 1902. Influenced by Morris and Ruskin, Howard's urbanist critique of capitalist modernization advocated a return to the craft standards and ethical codes of the mediaeval guilds. In his towns housing was to be collectively owned through the municipality. His towns paradoxically owed a lot to the experience of company towns. His garden cities were to be economically self-sufficient units of 30,000 people surrounded by green belts.[6]

Raymond Unwin, author of a scholarly yet widely read book on medi-aeval guilds in London, designed the first actually realized garden city in 1902–3 and laid the plans for Hampstead Garden from 1905. Unwin's 'satellite towns' were not functionally differentiated in the sense that sub-urbs brought about the differentiation of functions (production, residential, commercial etc.) within an urban agglomeration. Each of the satellite towns was itself to take on all the functions. Yet within each satellite town, zoning created rather strict functional differentiation. Unwin's satellite towns featured an outer circular road, criss-crossed by six broad boul-evards. The town centre was made up of public buildings surrounded by four-and-a-half acres of park, around which were glass-enclosed winter gardens and a commercial centre. Along the circular boulevard and in its vicinity were residences, schools and playing fields for children. The outer ring, beyond the circular contained factories and warehouses, with an agricultural belt was found still further out. The British movement was quick to take institutional form. The British National Housing Reform Council was founded in 1900 and the Housing and Town Planning Act passed in 1909.[7]

The garden city idea was influential in America during the 1920s, with the establishment of the Regional Planning Associations. Prime movers here were Progressives such as Stuart Chase and Lewis Mumford. Ameri-can Progressivism was a social-liberal movement of the often rural and Protestant, college-educated new middle classes. Whether urban or rural, they opposed urban poverty and the corrupt, often Catholic-run, big city town halls.[8] Regional Planning Commissions were formed in several cities in the 1920s and 1930s. In New York, where a prominent role was played by the business community, the plan instituted more rigorous zoning, encouraging tertiary concentration in central city skyscrapers. Progressives were much more active in urban and regional planning in Franklin D. Roosevelt's New Deal administrations. Their garden city anti-urbanism was evident in the National Recovery Act's policy of industrial decentrali-zation: for example, in the Tennessee Valley Authority. It was also the context for Frank Lloyd Wright's Broadacre City plans of 1935. Unlike in

Britain, American social urbanism could not successfully put its ideas into practice. The Resettlement Administration failed in its attempt to create green belt towns, as did the attempt to pass a Housing Act in 1937.[9]

It is instructive to consider at closer range the ideas of Mumford, exemplar of the garden city idea in the USA, who was the most influential urban and architecture critic in the country for a period of several decades. Mumford's garden city was intended to combine the enduring values of the village with the diversity of the city. Influenced by Chicago sociologist Charles Cooley's theory of primary groups and secondary associations, Mumford wanted to divide his garden city into six unzoned, cellular wards. The wards would serve as primary groups, the town of 32,000 as a space for secondary associations. For Mumford the Regional Planning Association's ideas were best realized in the town of Radburn, New Jersey. Here neighbourhoods were based on 'superblocks' with interior walkways which separated circulation into walkers and drivers. Superblocks had cul-de-sacs and few cross streets. A continuous inner park bound the superblocks together.[10] Mumford held that 'most of the fresh forms of domestic architecture and planning grew out of the suburbs'. Not for him Rem Koolhaas's visions of complexity and delirium in New York. Mumford's Manhattan utopia was one instead in which 'the great volcanic palisade of buildings in downtown and midtown Manhattan would give way to whole quarters in which the tall structures – none of them over fifteen storeys – would be widely spaced and placed on the mass transit routes and stops'. For Mumford, a 'basic pattern of order is essential to the full enjoyment of the city, particularly in our own age, in which a multitude of sensual and symbolic stimuli – print, sounds, images – at every hour of the day would produce confusion if the general background were equally confused'.[11]

Functionalist doctrine in architecture and planning is relatively unconcerned with form. Its basic proposition is that the built environment, materially conceived, must function for social actors, and in particular for collective social actors. In contrast to what we have described as Franco-American formalism, functionalism is English in its roots (in Morris and Ruskin) and German in its systematic elaboration in the Weimar Republic. This formalist/functionalist distinction pitted two central theorists of the modern movement against one another. For Nicholas Pevsner, a German residing in England, modernism was functional, and was largely Anglo-German, as the subtitle of his influential *Pioneers of Modern Design, from William Morris to Walter Gropius* indicates. The other major theorist was Sigfried Gideon, Swiss and close to formalist Le Corbusier, who proffered a formalist doctrine.[12] Philip Johnson thus distinguishes the functionalist, 'modern movement' from the more formalist, 'International Style'. The modern movement was the name for the new architecture in Britain, the

International Style the name in America. What America received in the famous 1932 MOMA (Museum of Modern Art) Exhibition that Johnson and his colleagues organized was not social, or functionalist or a 'movement' at all, but a *style*, the International Style, based on the formalist work of van der Rohe and Le Corbusier.[13]

Thus the two main factions in the CIAM (Congrès Internationaux d'Architecture Moderne) were led by Le Corbusier and the German functionalists. These latter were led by heavily politicized and anti-aestheticist architects such as Ernst May, Mart Stamm and Hannes Meyer. The two factions had rather opposite explanations of the contemporaneous crisis in architecture. For Le Corbusier and Gideon this crisis was within the realm of architecture: its enemy the beaux-arts. In fact Le Corbusier's projects had been rejected in favour of beaux-arts proponents both in the League of Nations competition (1926–9) and for the Palace of Soviets. For the Germans the main contradiction was social, between capital and labour. The functionalists criticized Le Corbusier's work as too 'individualistic', 'aestheticist' and 'uninhabitable'. In contradistinction they proposed an 'objectivist' (Sachlichkeit) urbanism of 'pure technique to organize the functions of collective living'.[14] The problem for them had nothing to do with form, but with 'finding the optimal use for the technical knowledge of building'. For them the crisis of urbanism was due not to architectonic errors, but to the disorganization of the building trades. At the founding international conference in Switzerland in 1928, Le Corbusier and his followers dominated; at the second in Frankfurt in 1929, Le Corbusier was in South America and the Germans dominated; by the time of the third conference in 1930, the Germans, Meyer, May, Stamm and Hans Schmidt, had emigrated to work in the USSR.[15]

There were three separate, yet closely interrelated, strands of German Weimar functionalism: the Werkbund, the Bauhaus and the actual experience of council house building in the middle 1920s. In each case functionalism was as much concerned with the 'supply side' of the organization of the building enterprise as with the 'demand side'. The Werkbund was founded in 1907. In opposition to the academy, the Werkbund challenged the distinction between (academic) architecture and the crafts of building and design. In its first decade the Werkbund self-consciously promoted the German and particularist notion of *Kultur* against the cosmopolitan universalism of *Zivilisation*. The model for Germanic Kultur came, however, from England, from the arts and crafts movement, from a Gothic notion of guilds working in harmony with each other and with the urban fabric. After the First World War technological advance became acceptable, although a sort of 'ideology of labour' remained.[16] The Werkbund was closely associated with industrialist leader Walther Rathenau and his architect Peter Behrens. These two men were part of the Deutsche Demokratische Partei, led by Werkbund supporter Friedrich Naumann, which supported not a free market, but a neo-corporatist (with trade unions as a full partner) solution to Weimar's economic problems. On the 'demand side', the Werkbund advocated a garden city like anti-urbanism, a *Wohnkultur* (mostly the problem of working-class housing) based on the English model of private housing. Mies van der Rohe took over the leadership of the Werkbund from 1921 and through it organized the construction of the Wiessenhof Siedlung (council houses) in 1927.[17]

Walter Gropius and Bruno Taut at the Bauhaus in the early 1920s advocated 'community-type' solutions for problems of both consumption and production. For them buildings were to symbolize contemporary meanings ('Soziale Gedanke'), and art to endow the community with spiritual signification. Thus Taut's early work and the Weimar Bauhaus building itself have been described as 'a sculptural arrangement of masses and planes in space'. But the later work of the Bauhaus architects is conspicuous for its very absence of any complex patterns or massing and its reduction to an architecture of a pure Sachlichkeit of material functions.[18] As regards production, in the early post-war years Gropius's metaphor for social meaningfulness was the mediaeval cathedral and the craft guild which built it. Gropius largely blurred the arts/crafts distinction and a large number of craftsmen taught at the Bauhaus. Later, under the influence of de Stijl and Constructivism, a new tack was taken. Laszlo Moholy-Nagy, influenced by Russian constructivism, took over the school's foundation course in 1922–3 from craft teachers. Now came the advocacy of standardized design; talk was more of the machine than of revolution; and functionalist discourse became pervasive. In 1925 the new right-wing government of Thuringia closed down the Weimar Bauhaus, objecting to Bauhaus advocacy of putative French rationalism against traditional Germanic Kultur.[19]

Most significant for Weimar functionalism was the large-scale construction of the Siedlungen (council estates) in the big cities. Crucial was the organization of the production process. Martin Wagner, Stadtbaurat (City Building Councillor), organized Berlin's Sozialbauhütte in 1919. The Bauhütte mimed the mediaeval crafts, but provided mechanisms for worker participation in management through the building unions. In 1927 the Bauhütte became part of the Verband sozialer Baubetriebe (the Association of Social Building Establishments), comprising producer co-ops and consumer co-ops. The production co-ops were institutionally situated in DEWOG, a joint-stock company controlled by the German national trade union confederation.[20] Actual building in Berlin and the rest of Germany only began on any kind of scale with the resolution of the economic and currency crisis in 1924. This was the year that Wagner founded the Gehag[21] (Gemeinnützige Heimstattenaktiengesellschaft; the Cooperative Home Building Joint Stock Company) under the directorship of Taut. It was the Gehag and Taut that carried out most of the building in Berlin. The Gehag needed finance to buy the land, mostly on the outskirts of Berlin. The majority of this capital came from the trade union confederation and from the Verband sozialer Baubetriebe. A substantial amount came from the city's Wohnungsfürsorgsgesellschaften (housing assistance association), whose resources were substantially increased from funds made available by the new property tax.[22] The Gehag did build extensively, but primarily in the outskirts of the city, while business interests dominated building in the city centre.

In Frankfurt the large-scale council house building programme carried out by Weimar Stadtbaurat Ernst May already had solid foundations before the war. In this case municipalization came partly in response to demands made by the social-conservative *Verein für Sozialpolitik*, whose wider German membership included Max Weber and a number of distinguished university professors. As early as 1890 a municipal building company was created that established a land tax enabling the building company to acquire land. Newly acquired land was rationalized through redivision into lots, and buildable land was organized on a communal level.[23] Influenced by Unwin's Trabantenstadt (satellite city) idea, May – controller of the largest building company in Frankfurt – wanted the city divided into semi-autonomous nuclei. What he got, and what Berlin got, was working-class suburbs. Lewis Mumford, none the less, enthused that May's Romerstadt Siedlungen were 'prophetic of a new civilization'. May's effective anti-urbanism was not shared by late nineteenth-century German critics Baumeister and Eberstadt, who celebrated the *Großstadt*, and thought that distortions could be mitigated through zoning. Berlin Stadtbaurat Wagner too was no garden city advocate: he was proud of and wanted to preserve Berlin's status as a world city. Wagner wanted to improve Berlin's historic centre: the historic competitions for the Friedrichstraße skyscraper and the redesign of Alexanderplatz took place during his reign. Ultimately no radical rezoning or new differentiation of functions was carried out in the Weimar Republic. Some of this zoning had already taken place in the second half of the nineteenth century. Instead what was achieved was the construction of 'little rationalist utopias on the [cities'] outskirts'.[24]

Structuralism

Structuralism, it seems to me, is architecture in which form expresses the structure of buildings: it is an architecture of the primacy of the building materials. If formalism is 'stereotonic' on a fine arts model, then structuralism is 'tectonic' and on an engineering model. Structuralist architecture features the facticity of the new industrial materials: cast iron, steel, glass and concrete. Most of the early examples of structuralism were the work of engineers. Engineers used cast iron in New York in the 1840s to construct commercial buildings whose fronts were assembled from pre-fabricated iron elements, in Manhattan's Cast Iron District. Their British counterparts built cast iron bridges in London in the first half of the nineteenth century. The 1851 International Exposition in London saw the construction of James Paxton's famous glass and iron Crystal Palace, and the World Fair two years later saw its New York clone by James Bogardus.[25] American John Roebling, who built the first cable suspension bridge in 1846, originally conceived the idea for the awesome Brooklyn Bridge (1871–2). If this burgeoning modernist built environment was 'tectonic' and hence materials-based, its tactile nature was a lot different from architecture past. The 'ancient' material, stone, underlay a built environment that was massive and protective, the new materials an environment 'light, aerial, open to sunlight, an architecture of voids rather than solids'. The advantage of steel, a new material, 'was to span and enclose space, to remove the bulkiness of load bearing walls and stone columns'.[26]

The new materials began significantly to underwrite the transformation of the city *per se*, with the emergence of urban tertiarization, as the new middle class swelled into the city, in the 1880s. Now the architects picked up the baton from the engineers in the Chicago Commercial Style. Two conditions were necessary for this. First, Chicago rose to prominence as a commercial centre: its population doubled to one million from 1880 to 1900. Second, and this speeded the emigration of talented young architects from all corners – including Wright, Sullivan and many others – to Chicago, was the Great Chicago Fire of 1871, razing the city's centre. Sigfried Kracauer implied that Berlin was the first city of modernity, in that – especially compared to cities with 'ancient' pasts like Paris – it was 'cleaned up' and somehow 'cleaned out'.[27] This surely is correct when comparison is made with European cities and even with New York and Boston. Chicago was literally 'cleaned up' by the fire, after which the employment-seeking stream of proto-modernist architects flooded in; and then literally 'cleaned out' by the subsequent zoning ordinances. In this, Chicago arguably set the precedent for tertiary concentration, as this so to speak 'zoning through disaster' drove homeless centre city dwellers to the outskirts and factories to along the edge of the Chicago River. The new centre of tertiary concentration was subsequently given the finishing touches of clear and distinct definition by the construction of the elevated metropolitan transport line whose 'loop'-like shape gave to the city's centre its enduring name.[28]

The Chicago Commercial Style was based on steel structure, on steel beams projecting from steel pillars to support the weight of the facade. These buildings could be tall due to the new elevator technology. The new buildings used windows differently: as the illumination of rooms displaced the classical imperative of the symmetrical facade. Compared to other cities, still dominated by the beaux-arts, Chicago's buildings were pretty much straight up and down with very little ornament. The 'father' of the Chicago Commercial Style was William Le Baron Jenney, in whose office were trained future master builders Louis Sullivan, Daniel Burnham, William Holabird and Kevin Roche. Jenney built what was arguably the world's first steel skyscraper in his Home Life Insurance Building (1883–6). His Leiter Building of 1889–91 was a benchmark in 'pure structure'. Chicago is even today the archetypal modernist city in its notable paucity (more visible even than in San Francisco and Los Angeles) of historicist architecture. This consequence was not necessarily the intention of its architects.[29] Take, for example, John Wellborn Root and Burnham's classic and still standing Monadnock Building. The Monadnock is one of the world's tallest (at 15 storeys) masonry buildings. Its innovative use of bay windows to maximize light and its unadorned facade were applauded by Montague Schuyler, leading contemporary architecture critic, as a 'master-piece of structural sincerity'. But the idea for a fully unornamented building came not from the architects, but from their businessmen clients. What a number of prominent American businessmen wanted was to construct their headquarters in New York in expensive historicist styles and their less prestigious commercial offices in Chicago in a no-nonsense purely func-tional style that looked to have been built by engineers.

Structuralism's representative among the self-conscious modernist avant-garde of the 1920s was Mies van der Rohe. His tectonic sense, his almost tactile feeling for the materials, may well have stemmed from his early years – from his contact with his father, an Aachen stonemason; and from his training – not in the academy or in any formal institution – but in a trades school, followed by his apprenticeship to local architects and designers. Mies was from 1926 the Vice President of the Deutscher Werkbund, an anti-Academic institution, originally established to help German industrial design catch up to its English competitors. His early buildings were steel frames with glass and brick infill. He appreciated craftsmanlike brick as a material, admiring its use in the nineteenth-century German factory vernacular style of the *Fachwerkbauen*.[30] Van der Rohe's architectonic called attention to the materiality of the elements of the building. He promoted a concept of the wall which called attention neither to the wall's function as enclosing the space of a cubic room, nor to it as a load-bearing element.[31] Neither of these functions was necessary, due to steel structures, so in, for example, the Barcelona Pavilion, Mies slid the wall out from beneath the ceiling, and disarticulated it from weight-bearing steel beams. The result was the free-standing wall, extending out into a building's landscape.[32] Steel was in his 'skyscrapers, [to be] revealed in their bold structural pattern during construction'.[33] In the use of glass Mies was influenced by Gropius's *Faguswerke*, Taut's *Glashaus* and German expressionism. The liberal use of glass walls was the best way, not to maximize lighting, but to reveal as much structure as possible. The qualities of glass as a material permit not 'the play of light and shadow as in ordinary buildings . . . but the play of reflections; it also permits a particular massing of the building as viewed from the street'. Mies used geometrically massed glass in his projects for the Berlin skyscraper competitions of 1921 and 1922; in the second case the glass buildings were to be curved. For him glass as a material was 'not empty, but, in its prismatic articulation, deep and rich in reflections of the severity of its curved surfaces'.[34]

What did 'structure' mean on a more general level for Van der Rohe? According to Bläser, Van der Rohe's 'architecture has nothing to do with the discovery of new forms or with personal inclinations. Real architecture (*Baukunst*) is always objective and is the expression of the inner structures of the epoch out of which it grows.' In the industrial era, construction itself is the 'guarantor' of the contemporary 'Zeitgeist'; hence the centrality of 'principles of construction, so that the form of a building is the complete expression of its structure'.[35] Mies himself gives the following apparently elliptical definition: 'Struktur ist ein konstruierter Zusammenhang, eine sinnvoll in allen Einzelheiten durchgedachte konstruktive Gestalt.'[36] This defies translation, but may approximately be rendered as 'Structure is a constructed coherent relationship, a constructed form which thinks meaning through each of its details.' Philip Johnson's three Miesian principles of architecture add clarity to Mies's obscure formulation, and articulate modernism's reception in America. They are: (a) the 'ordering force' is no longer, as in premodern architecture, axial symmetry, but 'the regularity of skeleton structure'; (b) exteriors are no longer 'heavy solids, obedient to gravity', but 'weightless, non-supporting skins'; (c) the use of 'structural detail in place of applied ornament'.[37]

Let us think then in terms of 'stereotonic' formalism and 'tectonic' structuralism as two polar-opposite ideal types. Thus gothic architecture is structural while Renaissance and classical architecture is formal. Structuralism involves a 'tactile' principle, while the formal and 'stereotonic' operates from what Martin Jay calls a principle of 'vision'.[38] Proto-modernist forebears of the structural principle are Ruskin and Morris: their formalist counterparts are, we shall see, Behrens and Sullivan. In painting, structuralism is like expressionism and formalism is like cubism. Structuralism builds gothic-like towers, while formalism builds 'blocks'; structuralism is vertical, formalism horizontal; structuralism is to the arts and crafts and to Kultur what formalism is to more abstract architecture and Zivilisation; structuralism relates to materials as formalism relates to space; formalism in German is *Architektur*, while structuralism, more idiomatically, is *Baukunst*. Whereas, say, Gothic structuralism is addressed to a Christian principle, its Miesian counterpart is quite substantially *self-referential*. Architecture must become an autonomous practice. This principled ordering in architecture may have been foreshadowed by Mies's Thomist education, fostering a belief in a higher ordered reality. Thus his supremely Thomist utterance: 'We must have order, allocating to each thing its proper place and giving to each thing its due according to its nature.'[39] Mies worked for Peter Behrens and shared the latter's enthusiasm for the classicism of Schinkel. The Kroller house, for example, built by the 26-year-old Mies in 1912 was Schinkelesque in its use of horizontal space. He followed Schinkel in attaching wings to the main structural, and in pyramidal massing. Mies's early work more generally is characterized never by monumentality, always by classic serenity. Surely formalist is the influence of Theo van Doesberg and de Stijl on the Mies-led Novembergruppe in the early 1920s. Thus the project for the Friedrichstraße skyscraper, following clues from de Stijl, had no cornices, only uninterrupted glass walls.[40]

Whereas Mies saw glass as dissolving the distinction between the inner and the outer,[41] Richard Sennett has argued that glass in tall buildings means we on the inside cannot hear or participate in outside events, and 'isolation is magnified'.[42] This, he continues, is only the logical extension of the nineteenth-century Romantic cult of the subject. Here the autonomous art or architecture corresponds to 'an inner order'. This 'order', argues Sennett, entails inviolable rules which have their own 'rights against man', destroying our 'sense of materiality, of the sensual, of the physical in the built environment'.[43] This autonomist logic in Mies's architecture may be a clue to his depoliticization. When Mies came to the Bauhaus in 1930 he was no longer the left activist leader of the post-war Novembergruppe. Indeed, when the Nazis came to power and attempted to close the Bauhaus in 1933, Mies intervened, paying a personal visit to Alfred Rosenberg. He argued with Rosenberg and later to Berlin Gestapo leaders in Alexanderplatz that architecture in general and the work of the Bauhaus in particular was in principle apolitical and aesthetic, though it had technical uses. For his part Rosenberg, a graduate architect, and previous applicant for a post with Behrens, saw architecture as eminently political. Although the Berlin party authorities decided not to close the Bauhaus, it folded none the less due to lack of funds.[44]

Formalism

The Classical in the Modern: Sullivan and Others

In functionalism, we saw, architecture is a set of material elements functioning as 'use-values' to human beings. In classicism architecture is a set of signifying, hence cultural, elements functioning to produce meanings. Formalism, for its part, is like classicism in that architecture is taken primarily as a set of cultural elements. In classicism this meaning is addressed to human beings, in formalism the discourse is self-referential; that is, it is addressed to discourse itself. Formalism, primarily identified with Le Corbusier, has major forebears in Louis Sullivan and Peter Behrens. Formalism, conceived in rupture with the beaux-arts tradition, may instead have been, I want to argue, the logical extension of the anti-historical aestheticism that the beaux-arts academicians began.

Sullivan, who personally was responsible for the dictum of 'form follows function', may have been the first modernist-formalist. Correspondingly, he was adopted by critics of the 1920s and 1930s as a precursor of the modern movement, and in particular of functionalism. We have seen above that functionalists were not exercised by the relationship between material function and form, but by material function as use values for (working-class) communities. Another generation of commentators in the 1980s have given us a 'postmodern' Sullivan. Hence De Witt casts him (and Sullivan was trained at the Parisian Academy), in an American beaux-arts lineage extending from Cass Gilbert, Richard Morris Hunt and Henry Hobson Richardson of the previous generation, through Burnham and Sullivan, and even on to Frank Lloyd Wright.[45] Or, alternatively, he is cast as an ecological critic of modernity, as a 'romantic and a transcendentalist', whose buildings' rounded corners are 'living membranes', wanting 'to achieve through art a communion in the cosmos, a union with nature'.[46] It seems to me instead that Sullivan may have been a formalist, who, unlike structuralists, was concerned with building a language of architecture: that he developed two languages of architecture, one of structure and another of ornament.

Sullivan's language of structures bore important resemblances to classicism. Although he worked with Chicago Commercial Style architects, his buildings were less expressive of skeleton steel lattices and contained more masonry and less window than the Chicagoans. The ratio of window to wall on outer facades was closer to contemporaneous beaux-arts buildings and to, say, the later 1980s buildings of Michael Graves than to Chicago or International Style. The substantial, weighty blocks that Sullivan built were influenced by Henry Hobson Richardson's work, particularly his Marshall Field Wholesale store. This heavy Romanesque structure was built before the dominance of late nineteenth-century Renaissance style. The bulldog-like blocks featured 'layers of heavy Romanesque', incredible weightiness, assertiveness, large simplicity, made of 'rugged quarry faced granite' and comprising an 'ascent of stacked arches'.[47] And Sullivan's was indeed, in its cubic, solid quality, an architecture not of 'towers' but of 'blocks'. With their two-storey bases and overembellished cornices, his constructions 'preserved the blocky quality of the Renaissance palace', polar opposite to the verticality of the New York's Gothic towers. This prevalence of blocks in Chicago was partly a reaction against the chaos of the previously dominant Victorian buildings. Unlike in New York, less expensive land in Chicago's city centre came on the market typically in large block-like plots.[48] Even today's visitor will note that characteristically classic Chicago hotels like the Hilton and the Palmer House take up entire city blocks. Finally, towers were expensive to build: and New York's corporate clients with almost unbounded resources were thin on the ground in Chicago. Thus Sullivan was not notably a skyscraper architect: even his successful towers for the Schiller and Auditorium buildings in Chicago were viewed as 'elongated blocks'. But to cast him as a traditionalist would be to miss what is fundamentally modern in his work. The Chicago style did indeed have an influence on Sullivan. His Wainwright and Guaranty Buildings, for example, do, like in classicism, have base, shaft and capital structures. The shaft is very regular indeed, and apart from the vertical masonry piers, is pretty much – especially in comparison to the New York tall buildings – straight up and down. These buildings have twice as many masonry piers as are necessary to express the buildings' steel columns. But the piers themselves, in their verticality, emphasize 'soaringness' and 'proud loftiness'.[49] And this is quintessentially modern. It is as if the thrusting verticality of the piers bursts through the block-like and Renaissance integument of Sullivan's buildings, as if the classical balance of the structures is disrupted by soaring self-infinitization of modernity.

Sullivan's use of ornament, though profuse and often excessive, is also I think modern. Sullivan was influenced by Owen Jones's distinction in the *Grammar of Ornament* between 'historical' and 'natural' ornament. Jugendstil (art nouveau) also made this distinction: drawing on William Morris, art nouveau practitioners understood natural ornament, which they used, as modern in comparison with the traditional use of his historical ornament.[50] But Sullivan's ornamentation fundamentally was not like Jugendstil. Instead of Jugendstil's discrete ornamental elements, Sullivan gave us a sort of matted superimposition. His ornament was plain in contrast to Jugendstil's exoticism. Whereas art nouveau ornamentation was, like its crystalline deco successor, fundamentally decorative, Sullivan's was fully serious and laden with meaning. This lay in the assumptions that Sullivan shared with American Transcendentalist philosophers Henry David Thoreau and Ralph Waldo Emerson, for whom nature was hypostatized as a sacred realm, whose abundance was infinite.[51] Hence the infinity evoked in not just the structure but the embellishment of Sullivan's tall buildings. Sullivan's favourite material for ornamentation was terra cotta, a baked clay which is quite ductile before firing. He used terra cotta for the spandrals and cornice in the Wainwright building, while the Guaranty Building, perhaps an orgy of self-indulgence, was completely clad in the material.[52] Sullivan's ornamentation is characterized at the same time by 'order' and 'intricacy'. The order lies in the geometrical surface patterns, the geometric shapes abstracted, as Jones suggested, from specific paths. The order is also in his method of ornamentation, which provided for systematic subdivision of the building facade. The intricacy was involved in the sheer amount of ornamentation, in the cornices, in his incessant use of loggia. Critic Montague Schuyler criticized Sullivan for what he saw as amounting to an 'orientalism' in design. And indeed such design resembled what Jones called 'Saracenic ornament', in its polychromy, its use of melding colour, its extensive subdivision of the field, its intricate surface pattern. This intricacy of Near Eastern ornament, in its sense of infinity, addresses 'the sublime'.[53] The other side of the modernism of order of Picasso, Schönberg or Russian constructivism is 'the sublime', in, for example, expressionism and art nouveau.[54] Sullivan's structure and ornament eminently signifies both the balance and systematic combination of the former and the self-infinitization of the latter.

I have written of formalism in architecture as 'stereotonic', and the structuralist focus on the materials as 'tectonic'. What do these terms mean? Jacob Burckhardt spoke of two and only two great 'organic styles', which together established the tectonic as architectural standard. These were the peripteral temple of the Greeks, and the multi-aisled, complete with front tower, Gothic cathedral. In comparison, Roman architecture, as well as Romanesque, Byzantine and Renaissance structures, diverged from the tectonic norm with their characteristically 'stereotonic' emphasis on space. The tectonic dominance of solids stands in contrast to the stereotonic dominance of cubic and planar components. In the tectonic the orders, vaults and craftwork are of greater significance than spatial organization. Stereotonic building is somehow 'totalizing' in the Aristotelian sense of the whole preceding the parts. The tectonic comprises 'organic membered structures' and the stereotonic 'crystalline mechanical wholes'.

According to Alois Riegl, the *Kunstwollen* of modernity is stereotonic, in its 'absolute clarification of spatial form to mathematical precision'.[55] Peter Behrens, sometime employer of the young Gropius, Le Corbusier and van der Rohe, was a follower of Riegl. There is irony in this, because Behrens, best known for factory architecture at Walter Rathenau's AEG, would seem to be an advocate of engineering, materials and tectonic building. In fact he was opposed to the engineering principle and tectonics right down the line. Whereas previous German factory architecture, built by engineers, worked from a technical programme based on the ferro-vitreous wide span frame, Behrens operated from a formal, almost classicist, programme. In contrast to the lightness of most factories, Behrens wanted to give the AEG buildings 'corporeality', which he did with the use of substantial concrete walls in place of the normal factory brick infill. Equally classical in influence was the anthropomorphism of 'the entabulature like beam in the front element, which establishes', said Behrens, 'a corporeality, a body resting on the principle members of the side elevation and on the structural mullions of the window at the front'.[56] Even the subsequent, less fully worked out, AEG buildings comprised independent masonry construction for weightiness. Behrens opposed 'culture', architecture and the stereotonic to engineering, which he viewed in terms of 'nature'. His architecture, like Sullivan's, gave priority not to a material goal but to cultural aims: his buildings were things ordinary men 'should live up to'. Like Sullivan's, Behrens's modernity did not break with history, but proposed historical continuity and the universalism of substantial classical elements. Behrens was 'the prophet of a new classicism destined to re-interpret the energies of contemporary life in terms of the eternal verities'.[57]

Frank Lloyd Wright's work also shares important properties with formalism. For Wright the crucial client was an aestheticist-oriented upper middle-class audience for single family houses.[58] Wright was surely more tectonic in orientation than Sullivan and Behrens, and in this sense bears comparison with van der Rohe. The difference was for him that the crucial materials were not industrial but natural. Wright's idea of nature was more concrete than the abstract notions of Sullivan. Wright used natural finishes and earth colours in both facades and interiors. His concept of site included the exterior which at the same time virtually formed part of the interior, with huge glass windows making the insides extend into outsides. The same materials used for floors on the inside extended into patios on the outside. Wright's sense of 'place' extended to the importance of living plants on the inside. Yet Wright championed the formal and often complex combination of geometric elements. This was a formalism of planes, in contrast to Le Corbusier's volumes. Wright was master of the horizontal, of the low pitched and broad roof – allusion was to huts and log cabins. His 'horizontal bands' of windows were 'glass walls forming the skin of the building'.[59]

Le Corbusier

Le Corbusier was born Charles-Edouard Jeanneret in La Chaux-de-Fonds in the Swiss Jura in 1887. Though accepted at the Ecole de Beaux-Arts, he never matriculated and instead undertook education at his local art school in the new *cours spécial et supérieur de composition décorative*. Central here was ornamentation in the work of Ruskin, Jones and Eugène Grasset. Le Corbusier studied directly from nature in the local region, using Jones's method of working in geometrical abstraction from the flora,[60] in which the 'principles of natural structure were to be extracted from a direct, discriminating study of natural phenomena'. Le Corbusier learned that 'it was the grouping of forms in nature, their structural relations that mattered, and the architectural or decorative should start from an abstract study of basic geometric figures, to arrive at principles of harmony'.[61] This *Naturphilosophie*, in which nature was the privileged site of rationality and order, was to change with time. After the First World War, as a force behind the journal *Esprit Nouveau*, itself proffering a critical extension of cubist principles, rationality came to be sited in both humanity and nature. Le Corbusier wrote, 'one of the highest pleasures of the human species is to perceive order in nature': indeed, the 'work of art' was a 'masterpiece of human nature'.[62] On this view it was culture that now colonized nature. Thus planting was not a geometrical reinforcement of architecture, but 'a natural counterfoil to architectural symmetries'.[63] And his villas were 'geometric containers' whose 'violent frontality' excludes nature. This 'purist' philosophy understood the cleavage of culture and nature as opposing 'geometric order' to 'sublime chaos'. The young Le Corbusier thus contrasted the culture of urban vehicle circulation with the natural 'law of the donkey'.[64]

Whereas in van der Rohe's structural expressionism the material structure or referent (the real) 'causes', so to speak, the form or 'signifier', in formalism the real or referent declines in importance. Instead the appropriate model is structural linguistics, where it is the relationship between signifiers that makes meaning possible.[65] What, then, were the 'signifiers' or linguistic elements in Le Corbusier's langue? 'Linguistic competence' was perhaps above all grounded in a matrix of 'volumes': here architecture was 'the magnificent, knowledgeable and correct play of volumes under light', featuring the 'hierarchy of clear intentions in the plan, regulation of proportions in the elevation and use of primary masses'. This is an effectively sculptural architecture and Le Corbusier's paintings as a systematic Purist were indeed sculptural.[66] In the paintings too, the object is a volume formed by light. Le Corbusier painted geometrically simplified three-dimensional still lives of 'object-types'. In his Purist buildings of the 1920s the facade is a 'frontally composed screen through which light passes to model the surfaces of the austere but richly sculpted interiors'.[67] What, then, counts as 'volumes' in Le Corbusier's architectural syntax? First, the spaces of the interior, in which the living room functioned as pivot to structure other living spaces. Second, the volume of elements in the interior, the rich layout of geometric parts, of fireplaces, flues, stairs and ramps. Third, the volumes of the exterior, based on the square plan as 'pure and natural form'.[68]

The house is a 'machine à habiter'. The elements of this machine à habiter were, in the first place, material, like the components of a car, the headlamps and the radiator. This idea of elements in a functioning machine-like system is suggested by the five points of the new architecture which Le Corbusier promulgated in 1925. These were: (a) the concrete pilots on which the house was propped up; (b) the free plan, allowing the separation of structures from the walls; (c) the free facade; (d) the horizontal strip window; (e) the roof garden. Le Corbusier developed a series of 'cells', or basic units of housing structure, that were to be mass produced. He was familiar with the ideas of Frederick W. Taylor, and his structure developed in 1922 was called Citrohan 2 after the automobile.[69] This architectural Fordism was extended in prefabricated two-storey housing cells into six to twelve storey apartment blocks for residents.[70] But these machinic elements were also signifying elements: not just a set of 'monofunctional tools' but 'a masterly, correct and magnificent play of interacting poetic operators', so that the machine à habiter was also a 'machine à émouvoir'.[71] Le Corbusier wrote that the 'house is . . . a machine for living in . . . But it is secondly, a place intended for meditation and thirdly, a place where beauty exists and brings to the soul that calm which is indispensable.' These material elements, which Le Corbusier conceived like his sculptural paintings as 'objet-types', had ideal functions. Windows, for example, were 'to illuminate walls'.[72] Sullivan's and Behrens's formalism, like classicism, produced meaning for human beings. In Le Corbusier's work, however, the aesthetic value lies in the harmonic relations of the parts and the experimentation with the architectural elements. It is ultimately aestheticist. Philip Johnson compared it with Mies. For van der Rohe, he noted, the 'corner reveals both structure and connection', while for Le Corbusier 'the notion of the skin neutralizes the corner as it wraps around it and, in its suggestion of containment, gives character to the space inside and creates a dialogue between the internal spaces and the surface'.[73]

Modernism began as a critique of beaux-arts aestheticism, and of the autonomy of the aesthetic. Instead beaux-arts training was to be forgone for more practical training (van der Rohe, Le Corbusier); the 'arts' were to be grounded in the crafts, both in the latter's 'tectonic' qualities, i.e. feeling for the materials, and the idea of craft guilds as making up part of everyday life; finally, the aims of modernism were not to be purely aesthetic but social. The logic of cultural modernization made this impossible.[74] Instead, far from negating beaux-arts practices, the modernists only aggravated and extended tendencies which were already present in the beaux-arts. If the academy began the break with history and collective memory in its adoption of histori*cism*, then the modernist negated even these remnants of connection with the past. If the beaux-arts sacrificed the humanist project of architectural meaningfulness in everyday life on the altar of aestheticism, the self-referentiality of modernism, in structuralism but especially in formalism, was the fulfilment of this aestheticist project.

Modernist Humanism?

Does this mean that a 'modernist humanism' is impossible? Theodor Adorno in a lecture given to the Deutscher Werkbund in 1965 was agnostic. Adorno's putative 'aesthetic rationality' entails a tectonic working through the possibilities of the aesthetic materials. It stresses the 'facticity' of the materials. In the 1965 lecture Adorno endorsed the *Sachlichkeit*, the 'objectivism' of Adolf Loos and Karl Kraus, while at the same time warning the Werkbund audience against the anti-art orientation implicit in Loos's imperative of the restrictedly technical use of architectural materials. Adorno's facticity is also 'stereotonic', pointing to Schönberg and Le Corbusier, whose 'architectonic imagination involves the ability to articulate space purposely'.[75] Yet for Adorno purely aetheticist practices are both undesirable and impossible. Commodification, for example, causes distortions to any pure aesthetic. And the 'facticity' of the materials is 'never given in nature', but is always historical and social. 'History', Adorno states, 'is accumulated in them [the materials], and spirit permeates them.' It is impossible, Adorno concludes, fully to separate art from purposes. Even high art, he notes, is used for purposes of sociability.[76] The centrality of history and collective purposes points to a sort of modernist humanism, which, for Adorno, must lie in architecture's utopian dimension. Functionalism in housing, he notes, relates to man as he should be, but an effective utopian dimension must also relate to humans and society as they are. The unconscious itself in modernity works through an imagery of mechanical figures such as trains, planes and automobiles, through which, Adorno continues, 'by means of the mimetic impulse, the living being equates himself with the objects in his surroundings'.[77] What Adorno is pointing to is an architecture that can work as a critique of commodification. This is a negative dialectic, largely a critique of the universal from the particular, in this case a critique of a bad universal, the commodity through the history and sociality that comprise the finality of the material and built environment. The built environment as critique then itself starts to pervade the horizon, the political unconscious of its inhabitants.[78]

Another sort of modernist humanism finds echoes in Lewis Mumford. Mumford's periodization of urban forms is based on a principle or 'dominant' which in each age 'generates the plan' for its cities. The mediaeval dominant, for example, was 'the institution of the city' (church, guild etc.); in the baroque it was 'the mind of the absolute king', in the modern, the market.[79] This dominant is embodied, according to Mumford, in an age's monuments. For Mumford commodification and repressive states block any attempt to create the monuments of a genuine modernist built environment.[80] Indeed, the negative effects of modernization set in with the baroque cities of the absolutist kings. The commercial city only extended this process, the difference being that the 'principle' of modernization passed from the absolutist monarch to the market. Baroque culture bequeathed to us not just the long, wide, straight tree-lined avenues, but also in place of the Renaissance and mediaeval square, the roundabout, whose origins were in royal hunting parks. This was a military aesthetics, visible in particular in cities like Berlin, where both roundabouts and wide boulevards permitted the disposition and movement of troops.[81] The baroque was also responsible for opening up the 'closed' Renaissance square into a space dominated by monuments and symmetrically flanked by public buildings.

Attempts were made to extend effectively this baroque principle into the modern itself in, for example, James Burnham's plan for Chicago of 1893, with its parks, parkways and diagonals. Equally, the French engineer Charles L'Enfant's plan for Washington DC began with the principal public buildings and then organized the street system around them. The plan was never realized, but Washington was and is still left with unusually wide avenues and still partly baroque assumptions, 'done over in classical republican symbols'.[82] Although the corridor avenue, characteristic of the commercial city, became dominant in most US cities – for example, in New York and Chicago (though not in Boston and Washington) – the roundabout has remained salient in European metropoles (Paris, London, Berlin). In the commercial city the market was, so to speak, transformed 'from a protected component of the mediaeval town to an expanding institution that thrust its methods and goals into every other part of the city'. This 'commercial plan' featured the 'speculative ground plan', in which the fundamental unit of residence is no longer the neighbourhood, street or precinct, but the individual building lot.[83] These rectangular square blocks also permitted the extension of buildings, as peasants flooded into cities to be converted into workers, deep into the interior of the block. Hence the Berlin phenomenon of multiple *Hinterhöfe* (rear courtyards), three and four deep, with the poorest proletarian families getting little air and light. The American didn't need Hinterhöfe, but just extended the lengths of the buildings back from the front lot so the windows of one neighbour were separated only by feet from those of the apartment building next door. Just as little sun and air was the result in the American tenements. The commercial city also gave us 'corridor avenues' which, unlike baroque avenues, don't all converge on palaces, don't all lead to monuments, but run in endless straight bands (e.g. Chicago's Western Avenue is some 25 miles long without interruption), which criss-cross the city at intervals of a half-mile. Circulation here is not for the sake of military or monuments, but for the sake of the circulation of commodities or for the sake of pure circulation (movement) itself.

In place of this modernist nightmare of instrumental rationality, Mumford proposes a humanist modernism. There are, he states, three sources of such a built environment. These correspond to outer nature, social nature and psychic nature. These are: (a) nature, the environment, more or less in Frank Lloyd Wright's concrete sense of nature; (b) institutional and community needs and values (these for Mumford are not a question of the social just as technological development, but as a process of history and historical culture); (c) the human psyche. This is an evolving human psyche, and hence is itself historical; in this humanism development is not just a matter of mechanical progress, but an 'organic order', 'based on variety, complexity, balance and stability', which comes about through adaptation, in 'ever more complex transformations'.[84] Others, in contrast, would argue that such a modernist humanism would be a contradiction in terms. Peter Eisenman, drawing on Foucault, has argued that it is, that the modern is somehow the age of the end of man. That the modern is somehow inherently 'structuralist' in the same sense that the ancient and more recent periods which have looked to the ancient for universals are somehow inherently humanist.[85] On this view, the modern is to system what the ancient is to action or social agency, and the modern is to 'first principles' what the ancient is to 'anthropomorphism'. If the built environment is seen as a functioning system of made up material and cultural elements, then there are two possibilities. Either the system can function for the material and cultural needs of human beings, or it can have as priority its own reproduction. This sort of system/agency relationship holds not just for architecture but for social theories. In this sense Eisenman is right in arguing that the technicist functionalism of the Weimar architects was the last vestige of (ancient) humanism. Eisenman celebrates the predominance of structure and system in the modern.

Conclusions

Functionalism and structuralism on the one hand, formalism on the other. Logique on the one hand, technik on the other. The Anglo-German tectonic tradition, with its focus on the materials on the one hand, the Franco-American stereotonic tradition with its focus on the combination of forms on the other. These are the complexities of modernism in the built environment. These are the two parts, the two dialectical halves of modernist spatial formation. On the one hand the tectonic materialism of solids, of the expression of structure, on the other hand the stereotonic dominance of spaces, planes, geometry. Both tectonic and stereotonic paradigms were born of a reaction to the beaux-arts and classicism in the broadest sense of the word. Both, in a first movement, reached out to the crafts and back to organicist notions of nature, but then, in a second movement, shifted fast forward into a problematics of mass production and machinism. Indeed, the dialectic fusion, or even supersession, of the tectonic and the stereotonic, of technik and logique, is the machine. The machine à habiter.

Any phenomenological reduction of this high modernity, of the first, not the other, modernity, would find its essence to be the machinic. High modernity in this sense is not narrative. It is not even the disembodied cogito of the Cartesian 'I'. It is instead machinic. Identity and self-identity in modernity is not narrative but machinic. The reality, largely lived in traditional societies – including the experience of all the senses – is largely natural. In modern societies we can speak of a machinic reality. In contemporary global informational culture – and the shift to installation art in the fine arts is symptomatic of this – we are heading it seems to a parallel and virtual reality. In none of these formations is narrative necessarily decisive or dominant for identity formation, for cultural orientation in the world. What is decisive is a particular sort of spatio-temporality. There was something of the heaviness, of solidity of blocks in the pre-modern architecture, captured in Romanesque and neo-classical buildings. The blocks, the massed solids, were political defenders of the city from the outside and symbolically unified its populace on the inside. Identity and cosmology in, say, religion had as much to do with this lived symbolic and material space as it did with biblical narratives. In comparison to classical solids, modernism has light structures. It has not massed blocks, but geometric planes. Modernism soars. The light materials, no longer load-bearing – glass, steel, aluminium – capture and mime the movement, the pace, the circulation of urbanism itself, which begins to spell the beginning of the end for architecture and the cité. Massed solids indeed do melt into air, into forms and geometrical patterns of light and planes in architectural modernism. The city and the buildings capture the space and the time of contemporaneous experience. They engrave the modern habitus. Being is no longer solidly in the world in modernity. There is instead an (unbearable) lightness of being, as the horizon desolidifies into planes and movement.

What about human beings? The first modernity is on the one hand the space and place of the machinic. It is on the other that of a distinctly human habitus, that encounters this contrasting machinic spatio-temporality. On the one hand, humans, on the other machines; on the one hand the human, on the other the machinic. Thus it makes sense to speak of modernist humanisms, in which the machines function for individual and collective social actors. But is this still the case in the turn of the twenty-first century's emerging global information culture? What happens when we move into an ambience of what the MIT Media Lab calls 'things that think'? What happens when we can no longer so easily cordon off the human on the one hand and the machinic on the other? What happens in an age in which humans travelling in machines on the background of time are superseded by objects travelling in electromagnetic fields on a background of speed? What happens with the collapse of the material and immaterial, of time and space? As the time of humans accedes to the speed of the non-humans? What happens to our spatio-temporal orientation, what happens to our culture when architecture and urbanism come under challenge? These sorts of issues are addressed in part V of this book. For the moment, having set up a working model of the first modernity, let us begin to explore its challenge and deconstruction by the other modernity. Let us turn to its deconstruction in postmodern architecture's simulated humanism.

3

Simulated Humanism: Postmodern Architecture

The notion of humanism is ever present in parts I and II of this book. Let me explain what I mean by humanism. The beaux-arts classicism of the academy for me is humanist. The modernism that grew out of it and in reaction to it is not humanist. Modernism, in architecture and urbanism, operates through a dualism of humans and machines. Some architects, planners and critics focus on the humans, and especially the collective humans, the collective subjects – in chapter 2 epitomized in functionalists such as Hannes Meyer and garden city enthusiasts such as Mumford. Some of these, including expecially Mumford, did attempt to preserve aspects of the integralism of classic humanism. But most did not. Most succumbed to a logic of social utilitarianism, in which humans beings, abstracted from the full richness of their meaningful activities, are seen as benefit-maximizing animals. With such a dualism of people and machines, humanism in any meaningful sense is impossible.

Let me suggest further what might be humanism. Beaux-arts training was humanist, though in a slightly sterile sense. The rise of the first modernity (as we shall see in chapters 5 and 6) in the social sciences constitutes a fundamental break with the humanist university. There is a strong humanist reaction to this development of social science positivism. Where else do we find humanism? In the Renaissance – with the comparative absence of sharp differentiation between art, science and ethics – but not in the Enlightenment. Grotius, Pufendorf, Alberti and Vitruvius were humanists. Descartes and Hobbes were not, already dealing in the logic of abstraction and opposition of subject and object. In *Les mots et les choses* Foucault speaks of a Renaissance episteme before the Enlightenment in which rhetoric was integral to things, in which words and things coexisted. The humanist assumptions of the Renaissance for Foucault stand in contrast to the Enlightenment's grammaire générale and natural history, in which a logic of 'classification' brought words into a dualist relation to things, into a separated realm from things. Now rhetoric disappears as words are clear and distinct, and used to classify things. Indeed, Foucault can characterize the entire modern episteme's principle as *représenter*.[1]

Humanism thrives where there are no sharp dualisms. The transcendence of the absolutist state and of the world religions is inimical to humanism. It works better in small city states: in the Greek polis in antiquity, in Italian Renaissance city states, in the Bildungsbürgertum of Goethe's Weimar before Prussification. This happy sort of humanism is prevalent in Horkheimer and Adorno's *Dialectic of Enlightenment*, which was intended as a dialectic of *the* Enlightenment. Here moving out of the dual dictatorship of Church and absolutist king, enlightenment meant some sort of harmonic relation of human beings with what the Critical Theorists called 'outer nature', 'inner nature' and 'social nature', the last entailing an integral relationship with the past. This was the initial humanist promise of enlightenment, later destroyed through the re-establishment of dualisms through the immanent contradictions of enlightenment's very dialectic.

By humanism I do not mean the 'problematic of the subject'. I do not mean humanism as opposed to structuralism. To speak of structure and agency, or structure and action, is already to depart from humanism. Structure/action dualism in sociology is very similar to the human/machine dualism in modernist architecture discussed in chapter 2. Humanism cannot think in such dualisms, in which the actor is often reduced – especially in rational choice theory, but also in Weber's or Parsons's action types – to a sort of means–ends rationality, abstracting from the richness of meaningful human activities.[2] Much more humanist than this is Alasdair MacIntyre's Aristotelian account of the virtues and communities of practice.[3] Also humanist is Foucault's work on sexuality in antiquity, in Hellenic times where there is a much more harmonic notion of human practices,[4] as distinct from the radical dualisms that for him characterize modern sexuality. The 'ground' in the second modernity – which I shall develop especially in chapter 4 and in chapters 7, 8 and 10 – retrieves important dimensions of such a humanism.

Humanism does not mean the organicist immanence of man and nature. The pre-traditional, so-called primitive societies described by Durkheim in *The Elementary Forms* are not humanist.[5] There is instead here the indistinction of what Weber saw as the 'plurality of gods and demons'.[6] These immanentist religions were pre-humanist. Humanism works better in the presence, not so much of organicist and fully integralist indistinction, but instead of the mild distinction and harmony of humans and nature. It works best in situations not of radical immanence but of mild transcendence, mild dualism. Humanism comprises elements of tradition and elements of modernity. It can survive in the presence of not overly harsh world religions. It needs a certain measure of representational culture as in the Renaissance or Classical Athens. Humanism is also not prevalent in the de-differentiation, the indifference of turn of the twenty-first century global information culture, in which the machinic becomes ideational and human beings become increasingly attached to their (information) machines. There will be some extended discussion of humanism in terms of the built environment in this chapter and chapter 4. In chapter 5 we will discuss how sociology itself emerged out of humanism in the university.

Postmodern architecture, which we will address in this chapter, works from a principle of simulation of humanism. By postmodern here I do not mean the global information culture which we will address in chapters 11 to 13. I mean the architecture that the architects and the critics call postmodern. Postmodernism is a term that has now passed into the general vernacular. It has not so much of the global sweep and power of the shift to the indifference of the global information culture. But it refers more to the playful mix and match of high and popular culture, to fragmented identities, to buildings and plays and TV shows. In this sense the shift to the global information culture is epochal and 'heavy'. Postmodern culture is playful and 'light'. This chapter is none the less worth reading for those with more serious scholarly concerns. First, because of the treatment of humanism (and its simulation). Second, because the section on complexity below does treat aspects of vernacular, does begin to address the ground of the second modernity.

The second modernity, as I said in chapter 1, involves at the same time deconstruction and grounding. The problem for me in this context is that there has been too much deconstruction, too much melting of all that is solid, and too little grounding. Postmodern architecture itself exemplifies this focus on only the deconstructive moment. Postmodern architecture, we shall see just below, is deconstructive in a double movement. In a first movement it is an anti-foundational critique of the first modernity in architecture. In a second movement it simulates the humanism just described. It does not incorporate humanism. Its humanism is not through incorporation but only through reference. Its humanism is only as simulation.

Postmodern architecture differs from its modernist counterpart in five analytically distinct yet integrally interrelated ways. First, modernism assumes a decisive place for an avant-garde. Postmodernism assumes convention in place of an avant-garde. Second, whereas modernism wanted to break with history, postmodernism wants to restore the historical scene. Third, postmodernism counterposes humanism to modernist structuralism or formalism. Fourth, whereas modernism is based on a single governing principle or 'simplicity', postmodernism advocates a plurality of principles or 'complexity'. This holds on the one hand for complexity between buildings in an urban setting ('typology'), and, on the other, for complexity within a single building ('eclecticism'). Fifth, whereas modernism assumes autonomy or abstraction from the everyday, post-modernism wants to draw on the vernacular of the everyday. In each case, however, this turns out to be a simulation. Postmodern spatial forms are thus a matter of *simulated* avant-gardes, *simulated* history and *simulated* humanism. This chapter seriously considers some of the original and sharpest formulations of this 'critique through simulation' in order to throw some light on the other modernity in urban space and begin to obtain some conceptual purchase on our spatial sensibility in the global information society today.

Avant-gardes

Robert Stern has spoken of 'traditional postmodernism', a category which is set up in opposition to the 'self-reference' of avant-gardes. Such a postmodernism is 'true to history' and 're-integrates with earlier strains of Western humanism'. It breaks with the 'materialism' of the avant-gardes in favour of 'visual pleasure and symbolic power'. Stern advances several reasons for the postmodernist opposition to avant-gardes. 'Avant-gardes', he has written, 'are no longer the exclusive defenders of the holy grail of insight.' It is just as likely, he maintains, in the era of high modernism that the frequent shifts in sensibility had more to do with the exhaustion of previous styles than with any real substantive progress.[7] Moreover, central tenets for contemporary architecture are public responsibility, communication of architects with the public and a built environment which favours the communication of members of the public with one another. This sort of responsibility to the public rules out the autonomy of the author/architect which is necessary for the existence of avant-gardes. How can the architect play an avant-garde role, proceeding according to the dictates of first principles, when he or she is responsive to the public? Further, Stern wants postmodernism to have its own 'grammar', to not fall into the traps of 'revivalism' or the 'merely picturesque'. Thus he advocates an architecture of 'semantics' and not 'syntax'. But an architecture of 'syntax' is necessary if avant-garde experiments with materials and forms are to be carried out. The avant-garde and modernist dialectic of 'is' and 'ought', Stern concludes resolutely, if somewhat cryptically, is being replaced by the postmodernist 'resolution', or 'at least recognition', of the 'is' and 'was'.[8]

What Stern has underscored implicitly in this last sentence is that in contradistinction to the particularism of the 'is', there are two places for architecture to look for universals. The first, asociated with the modern avant-garde, is to look in the first principles of the 'ought'. The second is to be 'ancient' or postmodern and look for these universals in history or the 'was'. Leon Krier's classical revivalism has opposed high modernism's search for universals in first principles. He endorses a universalism of beautiful forms, perceivable through the horizon of a given social or cultural order. For Krier the incessant change bequeathed to us from avant-gardes is incompatible with any possibility of universals, and instead winds up in the proliferation of kitsch. 'The barbarous profusion of innovations culminates in the kitsch which perverts every level of life and culture.'[9] For Krier, an Austrian, 'kitsch' evokes avant-gardes, commodification and Americanism, while 'art' is 'Europeanism with a vengeance'. The kitsch of the avant-gardes is a 'deceived promise', and the 'fundamental basis of the never ceasing production and consumption process', whereas art 'represents a basically static and undynamic moment'.[10] Krier's answer to kitsch and avant-gardes is historical. He preaches the reconstitution of 'collective memory', for architects, for workers in the building trades and for 'consumers' of the built environment in the wider public. He takes as axiomatic that 'all pleasant living rests on memory, every intelligent activity is a perpetual recovery of past experience. [Memory] is the basis for all human life and culture.' The collective memory of the European popular classes, to the extent that it persists, makes possible still today the appreciation of classical architecture. In general, then, if urbanism is to be art, we must 'rediscover the forgotten language of the city', the universal validity of its elements, 'the quarter, the street, the square', 'that achieved formal perfection in the eighteenth century'.[11]

For Krier the solution is to be found in the crafts. Van der Rohe, the Deutscher Werkbund, the Bauhaus and the Weimar socialist architects wanted to use the crafts against the academy in their avant-gardes. Krier, the advocate of the past, wants to use the crafts *against* the avant-garde, already institutionalized and routinized in today's academy. The root of the problem for him is capitalist industrialization and its concomitant division of labour, which has destroyed the crafts, themselves the basis of architecture. What the avant-gardes are building, claims Krier, is 'packaging' and not architecture. Real architecture, he continues, is based on a principle of 'construction', and 'construction' is grounded in the crafts. The craft structure thus represented a 'vast building of popular knowledge carried through time by the collective memory'.[12]

For Krier, not only did capitalist industrialization, helped by the avant-gardes, destroy any aesthetic possibilities for the built environment; it at the same time destroyed the previously existing public sphere. Habermas views the public sphere as only possible if modernity's 'unvollendete Projekt' is completed; Krier in direct contrariety would see the completion of the modern project as the condition for the destruction of Offentlichkeit's few remaining possibilities. For him, the classical street and the square 'represent the only and necessary models for the reconstruction of a public realm'. What then is to be the agency of Krier's utopic promise of 'forward to the past'? It is the urban social movements that have struggled for a 'decentralized and self-governed city'. The models here are the anti-zoning movements in Brussels (which also included artisan training for local youths), Bologna and Berlin. Krier's aim has been to 'define a movement in which intellectuals who struggle for neighbourhoods on a daily basis and others who work in architecture gather together in the context of political and social pre-occupations outside of any spirit of an avant-garde aesthetic'.[13] Robert Venturi, in other respects an opponent of Krier, echoes this call for the power of local people against avant-gardes, partly because 'we like being conventional and being conventional is in a sense relying on history'.[14] In several respects, postmodernism is indeed an 'avant-garde leading from the rear'.

History

If the paradigm setting event for the American reception of architectural modernism was The International Style exhibition hosted at the Museum of Modern Art by Johnson, Barr and Hitchcock in 1932, then the equivalent for postmodernism was the Ecole de Beaux-Arts Exhibition hosted at the MOMA in 1977. The major difference is that US lateness in the reception of modernism meant the 1932 exhibition had limited significance, while the 1977 counterpart was a major introduction of postmodernism, not just to America but to the world. The point of course was the beaux-arts' poignant affinity with the postmodern sensibility. This was partly because modernism, from which the late 1970s audience suddenly felt so sharply estranged, was formulated as a challenge to the academy. Moreover, the late twentieth-century middle class felt estranged from the 'white' and seemingly sterile world of the modernist architects. If modernism's origins involved an avant-garde of producers, eminently non-avant-garde postmodernism has responded to already pre-existing tastes of consumers. And the latter felt so at home in the 'brown', beaux-arts aesthetic of nineteenth-century bourgeois kitsch.

The Ecole de Beaux-Arts was the academy for art and architecture established in Paris. Here art, architecture and sculpture were taught in a decidedly humanist vein. Previously instruction was regulated by a professional-guild structure itself with mediaeval origins. The context of beaux-arts humanism was the already existing differentiation of the fine arts into specialist disciplines. It was based, moreover, on the separation of arts and crafts. It was an elite that was educated at the Ecole, whose instruction was overwhelmingly classical in content. This was partly due to its location in France. As other academies were established – notably in cities less partial to classicism, like Berlin, Vienna and London – they took many of their cues from Paris. The Beaux-Arts taught not only the classical style: its graduates partook broadly of nineteenth-century historicism. But Beaux-Arts historicism, unlike postmodern eclecticism, did not involve mixing styles in one building. Training at the Ecole was initially decidedly stereotonic: students learned little of the construction, technology or engineering side of architecture. In the late eighteenth and early nineteenth centuries, the academy was dominated by the Renaissance and neo-Platonist precepts of Charles Nicholas Ledoux and Etienne-Louis Boullée. This architecture featured the 'idea' and ideal harmonic proportions. There is evidence that this changed over the course of the nineteenth century. In the late nineteenth century, however, in some ways parallel with Ruskin's Arts and Crafts influence in Britain, the Ecole became more concerned with the material side of architecture and design. Now Labrouste, whose Bibliotheque Ste Geneviève is 'deeply structural', was a guiding force and there was a new focus on the reality of the building materials.[15]

Any further evolution towards modernism in the academy was limited, however. Modernist movements constituted themselves in opposition to the academy. Impressionist painters, for example, whose paintings were rejected for exhibition at the academy-dominated annual Paris Salon, instead exhibited at the Salon des Refusés. The Vienna Secession movement rose up in dispute against the academy's classicism and historicism, as did the Secession movement a few years subsequently in Berlin.[16] The high, lofty idealism of the beaux-arts was not palatable to modernist 'materialism'. The Ecole de Beaux-Arts had not even the vaguest idea or interest in planning, and designed only isolated buildings. The Beaux-Arts architects seemed to have greatest concern with the grandeur of the entry to buildings, with 'the sequential set of spaces and forms which surrounded the process of entering a building', in which 'mountainous steps lead to grand halls which then prove to have been only foyers for the climactic spaces which follow'. For their part the modernists were concerned with not the lofty but the most mundane of activities, with working in factories, with kitchens and bathrooms.[17] At stake was a transition from neo-Platonic idealism to the brute facticity of everyday life. Beaux-Arts buildings were to be built by craftsmen, but designed by architects, viewed almost as sculptors and radically separated from the crafts and engineering. The modernists wanted the architects to be more like craftsmen. Their romance of technology and the new belief in mass production of prefabricated units from the 1920s was also the celebration of the engineer.

Was beaux-arts architecture historical or historic*ist*? Colquhoun underlines the distinction between historical and historicist, noting that historical architecture entails the search for universals, for 'immutable laws' or, as in Vitruvius, for 'natural laws'. Historicism, to the contrary, is grounded in a Rankean or Crocean relativism. In its fidelity to Ledoux's eighteenth-century classical tenets, in which 'the rules of architecture could be deduced from a few self-evident axioms based on our observation of nature', the Ecole was historical. Towards the end of the nineteenth century and in the early twentieth century it became increasingly historicist. In this emergent neo-Platonism, churches, for example, were gothic and public buildings fashioned in classical or Renaissance style. Now historical styles became the ideal emblems of the cultures which produced them.[18] And if Mumford is right that an age can only properly realize its own Weltanschauung in architecture, then such historicism must be shallow and meaningless.

Yet the variety of building forms made the beaux-arts practitioners masters of typology. Instead of more modernist sameness, we can learn from the beaux-arts' sensitive treatment of building typologies and 'urban morphologies'. Modernism, argued Denise Scott Brown, achieved aesthetic control through 'total design and aesthetic zoning', the beaux-arts through typology, 'orders, massing and axial planning'.[19] Previous ages, however, registered achievements in typology and morphology without historicism. It should be possible, thus, to reject historicism while learning from their typology. Indeed, the American achievement of beaux-arts architects well into the twentieth century should be distinguished from the staleness of many of its European products. The classic skyscrapers of McKim Mead and White, of Cass Gilbert, the Chrysler Building and Chicago's Board of Trade were beaux-arts products. It is these buildings, rejected by Le Corbusier's and Mumford's austerity, that surrealists Chirico and Dali and the contemporary sensibility have thrilled to.

The late twentieth-century sensibility has been drawn to the beaux-arts towers in much the same way that it has to art deco. The latter was in fact the beaux-arts' answer to cubism: the adaptation of beaux-arts decorative systems to the principles of cubism. What deco does is to propound, and at the same time destroy, modernist first principles. As modernist ornamentation (or decoration) art deco is a contradiction in terms. Modernism applies first principles to the systematic working through of possibilities in the materials, steel, glass, concrete, volumes and planes. Ornamentation wholly ignores the materials. Art deco was thus the depthless (and commercially popular) appearance of such first principles. Postmodern architecture uses two types of 'vernacular' materials: one from folk culture, such as traditional Lancashire limestone;[20] the other from popular culture, such as billboards or neon. Folk culture is indisputably localist and particularist in comparison with the universalism of modernist (and humanist) high culture. Popular culture is international and universal: it is universal without being universalist. It is everywhere, but it has nothing to do with either humanist or modernist universalism of first principles. Popular culture violates any kind of universalism by being purposely transitory, by being 'throw-away', by being purposely meaningless and decorative. Art deco is perhaps the first appearance of such popular-culture or commercial vernacular. Thus the extraordinary popularity of the very early (well before the 1925 Paris Exhibition des Arts Décoratifs) designs of Josef Hoffmann and Golo Moser. This furniture and interior design were less a reaction to cubism than the reworking of art nouveau through the prism of geometry. Art deco, like New York's gothic skycrapers, gives form to the depthless: it partakes of an effectively comic book aesthetic.

The beaux-arts influence in America was great, perhaps because of the absence of a proper humanist tradition. It dominated the US academy well into the 1930s. In the 1930s Gropius brought Harvard into modernist academicism, which then came to dominate architectural instruction throughout the country. Princeton, however, kept an important place for the beaux-arts in its curriculum until much later. Louis Kahn belongs to the Princeton tradition. Kahn's younger colleague, Robert Venturi, studied at Princeton in the 1940s. European modernism, for its part, originated very much outside the academy as a critique of the beaux-arts.[21] Modernism and postmodernism in America have been academic movements. The European (including British) critique of modernism has come largely from popular sources, from urban social movements, from the streets, in support of local, folk vernacular materials. In America it has come from elites, from the MOMA and the universities, especially Princeton – where Graves, Eisenman and Anthony Vidler have taught. Nineteenth-century beaux-arts historicism, notes Colquhoun, placed great value on historical knowledge. The historical ignorance of late twentieth-century postmodern buildings is able only to signify the 'pastness' of the past. Beaux-arts buildings, although they used decoration, at least developed their form from a structural plan.[22] Postmodernism's 'decorated sheds' often forgo even this.

Humanism

Humanism in architecture and urbanism is anthropomorphic, anthropocentric, anthropometric and foundational. Humanism is anthropomorphic in the sense that it stands in a mimetic position in regard to man.[23] Whereas modern architecture, argues Eisenman, is real itself, humanist architecture 'represents the real'. This is a literal mimesis is in which buildings have wings; in which the base, shaft and capital of orders reproduce the foot, body and head of man.[24] Humanist architecture's anthropomorphism entails an aesthetics of beauty, whose valuation of proportions and symmetry is based on the human body. Modernist machinism destroys this.

Humanism is anthropocentric. The humanist built environment must function for man, both materially and culturally, in its buildings and public space around buildings. Space works anthropocentrically when it, through its symbolic and material qualities, promotes collective identity formation. This is the non-rational and symbolic condition of possibility of ultimately rational interaction. An anthropocentric built environment must operate not only syntactically but also semantically. Baroque and gothic architecture are semantic but not humanist. Humanist architecture must address man, and address man with a purpose. Charles Moore writes: 'the psychic spaces and the shape of buildings should assist the human memory in restructuring connections through time and space so that those of us who lead lives complicatedly divorced from a single place in which we can find roots, can have, through the channels of our minds and our memories, through the agency of building, something like those roots re-established'.[25] Moore is proposing that the built environment assist us in shifting our attention from 'is' to 'ought'. Only the 'ought' in this context is a 'was'.

Humanist architecture is anthropometric. Its mediating elements must make space usable and comprehensible to people. For example, Aldo Rossi's neo-classical constructions might be usable to the European 'who has a sense of historical traditional culture'. They would be less so to Americans. The latter, Robert Stern notes, need buildings which actually tell them how to use space.[26] Larger and public spaces must be anthropometric. Too large a scale – for example, the very large squares of Chicago's Civic Centre or eastern Berlin's Alexanderplatz – effectively 'kill' public space. The scale is simply daunting. They must be brought down to human size. And for this mediators are necessary. Thus the attraction of closed squares with outdoor cafes and amateur musicians. Or Manhattan's ubiquitous street basketball courts. Symbolic elements of architecture must also be brought down to scale, so to speak 'anthropometrized'. Thus monumental buildings can use 'classical elements, e.g. painting, sculpture, mosaics and mouldings of some variety to reduce the scale of their compositions and to give a sense of humanity to the whole'.[27] The humanist built environment is finally both foundational and universalist. Universalism here refers to the spatio-temporal value of urban forms. Humanist architecture looks to the past and to 'man' as a measure of validity that holds for all temporal and geographic locations. Foundationalism implies historical rootedness as well as rootedness in a grounded particularity. Humanist architecture is rooted in both.

The postmodern architects have fallen short on these humanist criteria that they espouse in their arguments against the moderns. Postmodern playfulness lays no claims to universalism. Postmoderns take history far less seriously than their Renaissance and classical predecessors. To the static notion of time presumed by the postmodern Weltanschauung it makes little sense to study the past. Postmodernism also falls short in the dimension of foundationalism. The eighteenth-century Enlightenment had already witnessed the sweeping away of foundations of the ethos of everyday forms of life. Postmodern yearning to re-establish these foundations would seem to contradict the equally strongly held assumptions of the ephemeral nature of contemporary consumer culture.

Complexity

'Complexity', according to Venturi, entails that the structural composition of a building is not subordinated to a single compositional principle. Instead, he insists, a plurality of logics should give a building its cultural significance. What this means is that architects practise not 'deduction' but 'accommodation': that they practise accommodation with the client, the building's users and its surrounding urban morphology.[28] Eclecticism grows out of this accommodation. Complexity means more than one logic either in architecture or in urbanism. Krier, for example, has written that industrialization has destroyed the 'social, typological and morphological complexity of the historic urban centres'.[29] Industrialization entails zoning, and zoning, apart from giving us a 'repetitive and confusing' urban experience, leaves architects with very limited typological programmes. Type must conform to programme and typological complexity is hereby reduced. For Krier, the 'modern movement' began in late eighteenth-century England, in which even Georgian London is a product of zoning. A complex typology is necessary for urban legibility. Building typology must be subject not to zoning, but 'to the constraints of urban morphology', whose imperative is optimizing conditions of existence for a public realm. Prior to the 'ritualization of zoning', notes Krier, 'there is an immediate relationship between programme and building type' and 'a very strong relationship of the building to the public realm (urban morphology)'. Industrialization and zoning lead to the 'collapse of type' in which every building 'in the city is viewed as an isolated object'.[30]

According to Hegel's *Logic*, 'contradiction' presupposes the existence of (a) two opposing principles and (b) a pre-existing totality within which these principles exist.[31] Venturi programmatically rules out totality or a single organizing logic, and has a very different notion indeed of contradiction. Contradiction for him is not the eclectic coexistence of several styles in the same building, but the opposition between programme and type. He disagrees with Krier's conventional assumption that type follows from programme, whether that programme be governed by material or ideal purposes. For Venturi, form should float entirely free from and even contradict function. When Venturi speaks of 'form' or type as contradicting programme, plan, structure or function, he mostly means ornament. Venturi wants the facade to tell us very *little* about a building's structure or function. He champions mediaeval architecture, in which the 'front piece of a cathedral is 'a billboard with a building behind it'. Venturi makes no bows in the direction of humanism and classicism, for which 'structural ornament reinforces rather than contradicts the substance of structure and space'.[32] Venturi's buildings are 'decorated sheds', in which a straightforward modernist plan for the inside may contradict the anything-goes on the outside.

This notion of decorated shed implies that there can be no language of postmodern architecture. Venturi tacitly admits this. If architecture is largely ornamental, ornament not meaningful and language's main function the production of meaning through statements, then Venturi's shed has no architectural language. If architecture is 'accommodation' to popular tastes, then it cannot attain the internal consistency of language. Thus Tafuri wrote of 'the radical devaluation of language' in Venturi's 'billboard world', in which architecture is 'reduced to a mass medium' that promises no 'effort to restructure the urban system, [but instead] a disenchanted acceptance of reality, bordering on extreme cynicism'.[33] Philip Johnson is equally critical. He admits that his own New York AT&T Building is not only a 'duck' (i.e. in which form expresses structure), but also a 'decorated shed', in which an International Style plan is contradicted by a base laid out as open colonnade, a shaft taken from Raymond Hood's classical 1920s New York skyscrapers and a capital with cornice and broken pediment. Yet the postmodernists, he argues, have 'no new sense of plan', develop 'no new space in the section'. In their absence of language, they can make 'no positive statement'.[34]

Venturi's notion of 'contradiction' and decorated shed rules out architectural language. A language of postmodern architecture would need to keep the complexity, while dropping the contradiction. This complexity without contradiction would be dear to the hearts of classicists such as Rossi and Krier. Yet their revivalism precludes constituting a new language. Such a language may, however, have begun to emerge in the work of architects like Michael Graves. Like Peter Eisenman, Graves's roots were in the early 1960s Le Corbusier revival. For the young Graves and Eisenman, Le Corbusier was not formalist enough: function had instead to be fully 'absorbed into form'. These architects wanted neither decorated sheds nor ornament, but like Corbusier worked with volumes, spaces and structural elements. In both the stereotonic dominated the tectonic: the 'ideal completely dominated the pragmatic'.[35] Architecture's materiality was heavily outweighed by its cultural and aesthetic significance.

In contrast to Venturi's 'Europeanist', vernacular postmodernism, Graves's *modus operandi* has been thoroughly American. Architecture for Graves is elite and intellectual, and in no respect populist or popular: the idea is to communicate with individuals and not with social classes. Clients in the USA are less likely than in Europe to be public bodies, say local councils or working-class organizations, and more likely to be either heads of corporations or individuals building single family houses. Thus in the USA the architect is more often cast as the 'arbiter of taste'. Thus American modernism has been less functional than the European norm, with more play of volumes and planes. Finally, in the American tradition houses tend to open up on to nature: a tradition set by the nineteenth-century veranda and pursued in the innovation of bay windows.[36]

Graves's early work, like Eisenman's, was very much rooted in this Corbusian framework. Into the 1970s, while Eisenman continued to develop his formalism, Graves's work took on a new semantic quality. Yet even Graves's early buildings reveal a more pronounced 'painterly' quality than Le Corbusier's. Even these buildings show the beginnings of a language of complexity. In these buildings, Graves begins with the neutral grid of the 'three-dimensional cage' which he 'pictorially' reconstructs so that 'the plan is thought of as possessing figural qualities'. These plans differ from Le Corbusier's 'muscular, vertebral sense of order'; they have instead 'multiple centres, complex spatial subdivisions and gentle inflections', 'almost endless elaboration and half-statement'.[37] Graves's later work continues these explorations. He begins to use classical ornamentation, sometimes eclectically, sometimes consistently. For example, his windows and doors come to have architraves and pediments. He puts in columns with bases, shafts and capitols. His work becomes much more tectonic, consisting of solids as much as spaces, taking on a block-like quality. Windows become relatively small, while walls take on opacity. This work is sculptural, as thickly hedged garden walls grow right out of the walls of the house.[38] The work takes on a semantic quality, an anthropomorphism.[39]

Vernacular

Robert Venturi occupies a position that is polar opposite to Graves. Where Graves's assumptions embody the concept of architect as creative 'auteur', Venturi wants to give aesthetic power to the client. Where Graves's work is elitist, Venturi's tries to be populist. Where Graves is concerned with universals and humanism, Venturi is concerned with the particular and vernacular. Where Graves's architecture communicates with the individual, Venturi's is intended also to communicate with social collectivities. Venturi's *Complexity and Contradiction* gave postmodernism a discourse of pluralism and the decorated shed. *Learning from Las Vegas*, published with Denise Scott-Brown seven years later, dealt with semantics and in particular with vernacular. But whereas the European critique of modernity has often proceeded via the vernacular of local, traditional and folk cultures, the 'commercial vernacular' proffered by Venturi and Scott-Brown came from popular culture.

Venturi and Scott-Brown's vernacular architecture presupposes the collapse of architecture as an autonomous practice. They argue with Victor Hugo that 'architecture will be killed by the word'. In previous historical periods, it was the popular forces that gave architecture its vitality. The closing decades of the twentieth century provided unfruitful grounds for such autonomy. Architects are now less important as creators; influenced by pop art they argue now is not 'the time for an heroic age in architecture'.[40] Indeed, for Venturi and Scott-Brown architecture can at no historical time be really autonomous. There are no 'autonomous discourses and architecture is [necessarily] embedded in a global ideology from which there is no escape'.[41] Commercial vernacular presumes that architecture has a double meaning, one for the popular classes, another for culture cognoscenti. Often the intention of Venturi and John Rauch's work has been genuinely social – for example, Guild House, built in 1964 for working-class residents and designed not to be pretty, but to give a neutral background to life in a semi-industrial area; to fit in with the latter in its brick and arrangement of windows.[42]

Three sources, notes Scott-Brown, have been fundamental in the challenge to the modernist built environment: the urban social movements, the social planners' critique of urban renewal and the architects, both in the schools and in practice. Yet only a few American architects 'place any value in social knowledge'.[43] The American devaluation of the social was exemplified in the MOMA's use of the beaux-arts exhibition to symbolize its engagement with postmodernism. The social side of postmodernism, for Scott-Brown, is seen both in the commercial signification of Las Vegas and in the local 'taste cultures' that sociologist Herbert Gans has written about. Architecture must be made legible to the popular classes. Thus Venturi and his associates are 'urbanists', 'architects and planners' and 'ameliorists'. In agreement with more recent notions of planning, they hold that architecture must work to a plurality of local tastes: 'If you're working for the planning commission on aesthetic regulation, you cannot say, "I'm going to abolish popular culture on South Street".'[44]

Vernacular architecture entails a semantically loaded built environment. Vernacular provides mediators between architectural universals and the popular classes, making these universals legible. Thus local deities were the vernacular that translated abstract precepts of Christianity into the 'common sense' of local peasantries. Venturi and his colleagues have aspired to be postmodern 'organic intellectuals', to help to 're-establish intellectual ties with the world around us'.[45] At times they have tried to semanticize architecture by means of contradiction. In their addition to the Oberlin Art Museum, a modern plan is added to a Renaissance building, and then dressed in commercial vernacular to resemble an American 1940s gymnasium. We start with a 'plan', Venturi explains, 'with a distinct order and with several cross axes, which is initially symmetrical and has a sense of unity', then we 'break the order and modify the unity'.[46]

For Charles Moore these attempts are successful. He argues that Venturi 'finds strength in the familiar and sees in the ordinary the images to make buildings of compelling power'.[47] Critic Colin Rowe has disagreed and written that 'the ironic juxtaposition of things taken out of context' does not add up to the 'positive myth' necessary for a semantically charged architecture. He suggests that postmodernists should attempt to use 'Main Street and Las Vegas as an adequate base for a continuing mythic structure'.[48] If Rowe is right, the absence of such a 'positive myth' makes semanticization impossible. In the absence of any chances for meaning, then even at its most effective, the best that such architecture can achieve is the effect of 'delirium' or an ironic frisson in its public. If Moore is right, however, then Venturi's vernacular has successfully served as a mediator of meanings to the wider public. Yet Venturi's semantics does not mediate universalist, humanist meanings to local popular cultures. It may instead be a vernacular which mediates the meanings of meaninglessness, the semantics of the already desemanticized.

Conclusions

As a movement, postmodernism in architecture is a thing of the past. As a presence at the end of the 1990s in our everyday lives it is ubiquitous: in ever more historicist towers, shopping malls, universities, local council architecture. Whether commercial vernacular or historicist, postmodern architecture has aimed at the deconstruction of high modernist urban space. It has challenged the machine à habiter and zoning in the name of complexity and semantics. If the functioning parts of both the domestic machine and the urban machine are a language, it is one with syntax and no semantics or meaning. Moving from simplicity to complexity is at the same time a move from the abstract to the concrete, and hence opens up the possibility of legibility, of some kind of meaningful mapping. We note here that postmodern architecture has challenged not the univocality, but the absence altogether of vocality in modernism's boxes and grids.

Now whereas classical and humanist complexity was legible and more or less univocal, there is a multivocality to postmodern complexity. Even when humanist and classicist ideals are in mind the result is a sort of either eclectic or simulated humanism/classicism. The result is thus a multivocality, a constant shifting of meaning. The result is an architecture of différance, in literally Derrida's sense of multivocality and shifting, deferral of meaning. Postmodernist space is thus the space of difference, Ed Soja's 'third space'.[49] This is neither the space of the same, nor the easily categorizable space of the other, but a space of ambiguity, of difference, constituted between the live zones and dead zones, between the wild and tame zones of the contemporary city. It is the space of the lumpen bourgeois, irregularly employed techno-artists in Los Angeles multimedia industry. The space of ethnic entrepreneurs, their small firms filling up the margins in Los Angeles, not identifiable as either black or white.

But does this architecture and urbanism of difference have a continued purchase on the contemporary cultural sensibility in the digital and global age? Or is it only the other side of high modernism's machinism? The other side of high modernist narrative is its deconstruction through textual difference, just as the other side of high modernism's machinism is its deconstruction through third spaces of urban difference. Might not today's cultural and spatial sensibility be a matter of a total displacement of debate from narrative/machinism and their deconstructions? Might not our spatio-temporal and ultimately cultural orientations be sited somewhere else? What happens if the space of difference explodes to become general-ized indifference?

What happens when the permeability of the city's and the nation's zones becomes such that it is no longer possible to speak of a third, frontier, space? Complexity then takes on a different complexion. For Rem Koolhaas, in his construction of a mini-city around Lille's TGV station,[50] complexity is connected not so much with architectural typology and morphology as with speed. With the speed of people moving at pace through convention halls and shopping areas, and from one mode of transport to another. Speed supersedes space as indifference supersedes difference. The location of Koolhaas's construction is nowhere, it might be anywhere. The complexity of movement in international airports, themselves interchangeable, is indifferent. Just like zeros and ones are indifferent.

Postmodern architecture and difference contest modernism's machinic absence of memory with the reconstruction of collective memory, itself a basis for the legibility of the new built environment. Its legibility as univocal brings into play conscious memory, its legibility as multivocal unconscious

memory. But what happens when memory in an age of indifference becomes neither conscious nor unconscious but instead prosthetic?[51] What
happens when memory becomes not ambivalent but *false?* What happens
when memory becomes databases on external hard drives? Machines in
the modern age do not have memory. In the digital age objects that think
do have memory. What are the implications of this for semanticization?
The curious thing is that, unlike its machinic predecessor, postmodernism
and the architecture and urbanism of difference, of the third space, is not
a mix of the tectonic and the stereotonic, but almost exclusively stereotonic.
No feeling here for the materiality of the bridge, the materials of glass and
the spandral.

   In contrast, digital and global space is life on the screen as well as life
in the city. It is once again a tactile space. It is part and parcel of a new
tectonic. An informational tectonic of a new hands-on-ness. Orientation in
the digital/urban space of indifference is no longer a question of legibility,
of readability. It is more a matter of tactility. In the age of the post-human
our orientation in space is perhaps not a lot different from that of non-
humans. Of robotics and other thinking things. Postmodern architecture
and the space of difference are, though deconstructed, a space of logique.
The new digital age and its architectonic, whether virtual or built, is
perhaps more than ever tectonic, more than ever a space of technik.

4

Grounding the City

We have looked in chapter 1 at the technik and logique of the first modernity in architecture and urbanism. In chapter 2 we have examined its deconstruction through postmodernist architecture. This deconstruction is the initial movement of the other modernity: the dissolution of a set of determinate rules into an anti-foundationalism challenging pre-given rules. This is the dimension of difference, of groundlessness, of the other modernity. But there is a second, equally important, though often forgotten, dimension: it is the dimension of the ground. The different rationality of our other, second modernity is at the same time a search for groundlessness and ground, an undercutting at the same time as an uncovering of soil. The second modernity is a configuration of at the same time *routes* and *roots*. The 'routes' deconstruct the order, the universal foundations of the first modernity. The 'roots' retrieve the first modernity's missing ground. This chapter is largely about roots. It is dedicated to the re-establishment of the particular: to the rights of the particular. We will address this ground, these roots, this particular dimension of the second modernity in subsequent chapters in its various forms as life-world, sociality, tradition, memory, sensation, the index, the real. This chapter addresses it through a set of explorations in urban space.

What follows has two objectives. The first is to develop a theoretical framework for grounded urban space. The second is to analyse a series of historical and geographical examples of grounded urban space. In much of the literature, the ground, the particularity of urban space, is subsumed under the notion of 'place'. I will prefer instead to speak of what I will call '*labyrinthine*' social space. Thinking through such grounded urban space resists historical periodization. In contemporary times we encounter it perhaps most often in notions of vernacular, of urban density, that we began to address towards the end of chapter 3.[1]

This said, the first section of the chapter will develop a model of subjective space, which is based on a phenomenological notion of the 'field', contains a specific and limited set of elements, is structured by organizing myths and symbols and through which individual and collective subjects 'produce', so to speak, space. The second section looks at historical labyrinths via considerations of both classical or 'humanist' and gothic models of spatial organization. The third section pursues this ideal-type of labyrinth further in consideration of how space is structured in Japan and how this structure is thoroughly implicated in characteristically Japanese modes of signification and cosmologies. The final section uncovers a certain allegorical density in the heart of the modernist Cartesian grid.

Fields of Mapping: Grids and Labyrinths

In his benchmark article published long ago in *New Left Review*, Fredric Jameson began to develop a concept of 'cognitive mapping'.[2] Mapping, as a notion of cultural orientation, as distinct from legibility moves us away from the abstract and towards the ground. Only, as we shall see, mapping is as much tactile as it is cognitive. But let us begin at the very most abstract level in order to begin to understand how we 'image', how we 'figure' space. And for this I want to turn to Abraham Moles's 'psychology of space'. According to Moles we register space in a 'psychological field'.[3] This heuristic of 'the field' is very common in French social theory. Pierre Bourdieu used to speak of a force field of collective actors, institutions and types of social and cultural capital. Jean-François Lyotard spoke of fields in his *Discours, Figure*, in which he formulated his fundamental critique of Jacques Lacan's conception of the unconscious. Lyotard argued that the unconscious was not structured like a language but instead like a field, in which desire or libido was invested in a sets of images or figures. The mobility of desire was to be fluid in this field, as it moved from investment in one set of images to another. Bourdieu and Lyotard seem to have taken the field heuristic from their generation's teacher, Maurice Merleau-Ponty, for whose phenomenology the body is situated and intentionally related in a 'perceptual field'. The idea of field that I want to develop in terms of spatial orientation has a lot more to do with such a space of perception than with either legibility or cognitive mapping.[4]

Moles's field is not, however, a model for the social or for the unconscious, nor an account of human perception in general. It is a framework in which we experience space. For it he draws on psychologist Kurt Lewin's 'topological field'. This is a space of consciousness with 'gratification poles' which are sources of attraction and repulsion. It is a 'valorized space' whose elements are differentially endowed with meaning. In Lewin's field the distance of the subjects from a value or point in the field was the measure of its significance to the subject.[5] Moles is concerned with the representation of real space, and the field of such representation is the 'mental map' (*carte mentale*). Moles, like Gaston Bachelard in the *Poétique de l'espace*, is concerned with the dimensions of the space registered on the mental map.

Here he distinguishes between: (a) the small space of human gestures, the palm of the hand, the pocket; (b) the 'spaces of life' the room, the apartment, the house; (c) spaces of the human group, e.g. factories, supermarkets; and (d) 'vast spaces', such as cities and deserts.[6] Moles's mental map mediates between real space and the differentially valorized topological field of the conscious mind. Highly valorized spaces in the mental map are given values by the latter,[7] and in this sense charged with meaning. There is thus a sort of 'condensation of the sacred in certain specialized signifiers', a distribution of the sacred in space.[8]

Moles speaks of grids and labyrinths. Here the topological field of the psyche is constructed along the lines of the labyrinth. Grids and labyrinths, he observes, are ways of 'marking space'. Grids provide 'cognitive security', while the labyrinth is the canonical form of constrained space enclosing the exploratory tendency of human beings.[9] Grids are like French gardens, based on the model of the smaller Italian Renaissance gardens, and are examples of Cartesian clarity. Labyrinths are more reminiscent of the English garden, whose gothic disorder is in fact the expression of another order which is hidden from the promeneur.[10] The original labyrinth of Daedalus was not similar to the winding mediaeval street but geometric in structure. Moles defines labyrinths as: (a) complex in nature; (b) structures which construct this situation of the individual 'en errance' (i.e. the lost, wandering, exploring individual); further, (c) the individual has limited knowledge of a visually limited environment; and is thus (d) forced to rely on memory in order to master this environment.[11]

We can begin to fill in Moles's abstract field model of how we 'figure' the city by drawing on Kevin Lynch's *Images of the City*. Lynch was concerned above all with a city's 'legibility' or 'clarity'; that is, with how easy or difficult it was for the individual to gain a sense of orientation in a given city. For him the development of a 'workable' image of a city was a 'learning process' and dependent on three conditions.[12] The first of these is 'identity', i.e. the city must be recognizable as a separate entity, and is similar to Mary Douglas's concept of 'group'. The second is that the spatial pattern internal to the city must be identifiable, rather like Douglas's concept of 'grid'. The third is that the city's elements must have practical or emotional meaning; for example, the Manhattan skyline might connote power, mystery or decadence.[13]

For the sources of variance in clarity of urban images Lynch carried out interviews in Boston, Los Angeles and Jersey City. Counter-intuitively Lynch found that individuals had the clearest cognitive maps of the most labyrinthine of the three cities, Boston. Of the three cities only Boston – unlike also New York and Chicago – never was locked into the gridiron structure. Images of Los Angeles and Jersey City were far less vivid, were comparatively formless. In 'pre-modernist' Boston respondents'

descriptions were largely 'perceptual', with reference to concrete characteristics of the city and its streets. In modernist Los Angeles and Jersey City,
in contrast, descriptions were often 'conceptual' and relied, for example,
on the names of the streets.[14] The sources of 'legibility' or, respectively,
'illegibility', observed Lynch, lay in the comparative clarity of a city's
'image elements'. We shall be drawing on Lynch's typology of image
elements to explore the parameters of space throughout this chapter.
The elements are:

(1) *Paths.* Paths are ways of moving through the city. Mastery of a city's
path structure is necessary for a workable cognitive mapping. Paths
have direction; they have origins and destinations. Paths can be streets,
boulevards, motor ways. Some are one-way.[15] Paths (and other elements)
can serve as 'orientation' points or 'disorientation' points. The freeways in
Los Angeles serve as orientation points. In cities structured by boulevards
and squares such as Berlin or those without a grid such as Boston, motor
ways function as disorientation points.[16] Some paths function primarily
for circulation of vehicles (grid), while others are primarily for pedestrians
(labyrinth). And, further, the directionality of paths is variable, i.e.
some streets are more for living (labyrinth) than for passing through
(grid).

(2) *Districts.* Districts along with paths are the most important elements
for adequate cognitive maps of cities. Districts need a common identifying
character. Many of Lynch's respondents had the clearest images of upper-
class districts. Ethnic group or functional activity, such as banking
or industry or night life, can be identifying characteristics of districts.[17]
Some of the most distinct districts in terms of image are the square mile
of the City of London, the East Village in New York, Berlin's Kreuzberg
and so on. Districts vary in size and shape. For example, for Lynch's
Los Angeles respondents they were often small and linear. Note here
that Lynch's cognitive maps are of entire cities. There is no reason why
adequate maps of more localized areas should not be of equal or greater
importance.

(3) *Nodes.* Nodes are particularly heavily used bits of public space. Lynch
speaks of two types of nodes:

(a) *Junctions.* These are spaces through which people and vehicles
pass, though junctions criss-cross heavily used paths in several directions
at once.[18] Underground urban transport has such junctions, such as Metro
Center in Washington DC, Zoologisches Garten in Berlin or Euston Station in London. Railway stations and central bus stations such as New
York's Port Authority used to be very important as such junction nodes.
Today airports are perhaps most important. Also significant as junctions
are major roundabouts or intersections.

(b) *Concentrations*. These are places where people gather rather than just pass through.[19] This is the space *par excellence* of public culture. Its significance and vividness in cognitive maps stems not just from interaction. The meaning-loadedness of such space also stems from the iconic power of marginal figures of the city, such as addicts, dealers, pimps, gays, prostitutes. The canonic space for such nodes is the square or plaza such as Piazza San Marco in Venice or the square in front of the Centre Pompidou in Paris. Savigny Platz in Berlin functions effectively as such a node, but the 'squares' of Berlin and so many other cities are built for the circulation of military and commercial traffic and thus are more junctions than concentrations. Eastern Berlin's Alexanderplatz attempts but fails to be such a concentration. Some junctions, such as airports, can function as concentration nodes. So can paths: for example, boulevards such as Chicago's Armitage Avenue or the boulevards on Manhattan's Upper West Side; and much narrower streets such as Paris's Rue Mouffetard or 8th Street in Manhattan's East Village.

(4) *Edges*. Edges can either surround the city and thus identify it as a separate entity, such as the way Boston is defined as a peninsula or Chicago's lakefront.[20] In this way they separate the inside and outside of a city ('group'). Or they can make more distinctive the spatial pattern internal to a city (Mary Douglas's 'grid'), examples here being western Berlin's Landwehrkanal and the Chicago River. Edges, we will see below, are particularly heavily charged with meaning in configurations of Japanese space, and especially in the context of smaller scale mental maps such as the district, the block of flats, the individual house or apartment. Sometimes whole cities, Lynch notes in the case of Jersey City's juxtaposition to New York, have self-perceptions of being edges for other spatial agglomerations. At other points edges themselves become nodes. For example, Los Angeles's Wilshire Boulevard was an edge of the city's central district at the time *The Image of the City* went to press in 1960. In the late 1980s it has gained in material and cultural significance to the point at which it, if anything in Los Angeles, has attained the status of node.

(5) *Landmarks*. Lynch speaks mostly here of edifices which help the individual find his or her way about the city.[21] He also confines himself to the exterior of such buildings. I would rather talk about 'monuments' than landmarks. Here I would like to understand 'monuments', along with Lewis Mumford and Aldo Rossi, as buildings which take on a particular symbolic significance in a socially defined epoch. Gothic cathedrals are monuments, as are baroque palaces constructed by absolutist states. Factories and modernist public housing are monuments in the age of industrial capitalism, as are postmodern financial districts and renovated city central areas in the information age. Insides of buildings can have monument properties. In this sense a building or building complex can serve as a

'node'. For example, the atrium in Helmuth Jahn's State of Illinois building is intended to function as a node. So are arcades.

We have now an urban perceptual field whose spaces and elements are differentially charged with significance. We have charted main elements of the field. Let us stress that the meaning with which elements of urban space are charged is not just cognitive, but also affective. What gives vividness to both cognitive and affective dimensions of urban imagery, I would suggest, is 'myth'. Myths are stories, operating in the dimension of time, which give to objects in urban space symbolic power. The power of myth is the power of the past. Particularly important are myths of urban origins – for example, of Apollo building with his own hands the walls of Troy, or mythical contracts as the basis of founding cities, which are often somehow simulacra of God's creation of the world.[22] As are myths of the fall or destruction of cities, of, say, Atlantis or Jerusalem. These myths, when translated into built forms, structure the 'physiological capabilities of perception' or collectivities which are at the same time their conditions of survival.[23] In this sense myths are the very stuff of urban identity. In the premodern city, myth was embedded into the walls and gates of the city – and thus, functioning as symbol of 'group', connoted both urban and Christian identity. Baroque space under absolutism, with its corresponding mythic structure, led to the superimposition of images of the state on to images of the city and the 'statification' (*Verstaatlichung*) of perception and identity.[24]

Further modernization, the destruction of city walls, the disappearance of typology with the homogenization of the appearance of buildings, leads to the further disappearance of the visible city as an object of perception. The upshot of this, maintains Dieter Hoffman-Axthelm, is that the substance of the city (*Stadtsubstanz*) is emptied out and displaced on to images, of the media, of the heritage industry, but also on to the hypostatization of local culture by the urban social movements.[25] Urban imagery is displaced on to a set of secondary and media images of, say, Lou Reed's New York in the 1970s or, in the 1990s, James Ellroy's Los Angeles of *LA Confidential*. Thus myth no longer structures perception in our cities but becomes the object of such perception; cognitive mapping maps not space but images; and urban imagery is constructed not of images of the city but of images of images. Thus far, it seems as if post-industrial political and economic power has been able to make these images function effectively for its own ends. For example, to celebrate the city's 750th birthday the Christian Democratic governed Berlin Senate set up an enormous apparatus of images and celebrations in the summer of 1987. The Berlin left was highly critical of this, but was –argued Hoffmann-Axthelm and his colleagues – too much trapped by the Puritanism of its own ideological assumptions to counter the right's hegemony in this field of images.[26] To remedy this, Hoffmann-

Axthelm and his colleagues set up an alternative exhibition entitled Mythos Berlin. The object of the outdoor *Ausstellung*, which was set up on the grounds of Anhalter Bahnhoff, destroyed by overzealousness planners in the 1950s, was to create such an alternative set of images and myths, especially through the recovering and reinterpretation of Berlin's historical figures and events.[27]

Productions of Space:
the Classical and the Gothic

To engage in such struggle on the terrain of the postmodern field of images is at the same time to engage in the struggle for what Henri Lefebvre calls the 'production of space'. For Lefebvre, space is produced by the organism or the body around itself, as individuals and collectivities of human individuals and animals extend themselves in space, establishing around their bodies symmetries and dissymmetries. The organism does this in order to harness the energies of the environment for its own ends. Space is produced through the organism's marking out of territories and places. The social production of space involves the leaving of traces which are both symbolic or cultural and practical or material. In this, symbolic traces involve the deposit of an 'emotive charge' which is also the deposit of 'memories' or 'myths'.[28] Lefebvre offers two formulae for the production of space: one which leads to the production of grids, or what he calls 'abstract space', 'Cartesian space' or the space of the 'ego'; and another which leads to the production of labyrinths, or 'historic space', 'lived space', the space of the 'body'. The logic of the production of space entails the historical and ontological precedence of concrete 'place', long before the existence of 'the word' or 'logos'. Abstract space is the space of 'the grid', of the word over the real and place, of 'discourse' over 'figure'. Abstract space assumes the hegemony of time over space, presupposes an Augustinian metaphysic in which time is abstracted from concrete space, in which place comes under the sway of a logic of redemption.[29] Such a world view of the primacy of time over space is instantiated in the increasing importance of circulation over space for living brought about through modernization, whether in the Roman network of roads, Haussmanization through the establishment of boulevards or the predominance of nodes as junctures in place of nodes as concentration, as best seen in the decline of the ubiquity of squares and the proliferation of roundabouts.[30]

Lefebvre's own view of time is rather more cyclical than Augustinian or linear. For him systems of lived or historic space are found in primitive, Ancient Greek and Gothic configurations, while abstract space was generated in Roman Antiquity, in the Renaissance and in capitalism.[31]

Hence we have abstraction produced by the state in Roman roads, baroque vistas and monuments (not to mention Stalinist and Third Reich monumentalism) and the creation of nineteenth-century Parisian and Viennese boulevards for the movement of troops. Abstract economic calculation of capitalism completes this with twentieth-century modernism, whose extension is the postmodernism of skyscrapers in 1980s financial districts. Lefebvre instead proposes a bodily mode of spatial orientation through the revenge of his cyclically repressed; a production of space which 'rehabilitates the lateral, the labyrinthine, perhaps the uterine, the feminine'.[32]

Lefebvre has begun to develop the labyrinthine as a ground, the grounded dimension of the other modernity. There are two dominant models of such a labyrinthine utopia. The first is along the lines of the gothic city. This model is the one to which the Jane Jacobs's idea of local urban anti-growth coalitions and movements best corresponds. We will develop it further below. The second is based on Renaissance and eighteenth-century classical humanism. The original labyrinth form is indeed more classical than gothic, its creator Daedalus being the only architect of Greek mythology and, as the inventor of many wondrous works, the 'symbol of humanist architecture'.[33]

Aldo Rossi proffers such a classicist and humanist vision of the labyrinth. He foregrounds the monument. Invariant in all cities are monuments, the city's 'primary element', and housing. For Rossi, the specific 'configuration' of any city is 'based on the relationship of dwelling areas and [these] primary elements'.[34] Rossi sees modernization as a process that erases historical space. Drawing on Maurice Halbwachs, he understands the city and its monuments in terms of the 'collective memory' of its people. Historical – and not 'historicist' – Rossi's city is a 'theatre of human events': its elements are sites of a succession of events.[35] Buildings and spaces take on a 'typology' in an ongoing historical process in which types are given significance as 'repositories of collective memory'.[36] Modernization and industrialization sound the death knell of the historical and humanist city. In Berlin, for example, this process began at mid-nineteenth century with the introduction of functional zoning. The historical and gothic and mixed-function centre of the city was destroyed, and functional specificity set in as the centre was reserved for public monuments. Villas were constructed in the middle-class zones, working-class apartment buildings were constructed in the famous *Mietkaserne* on the periphery and the factories began to move even further out. The adoption of high modernist architecture along with the garden city concept in the Weimar Republic was a continuation of this process of modernization and differentiation, further destroying civic architecture and making any coherent and unified urban imagery impossible. The 1920 plan and new zoning laws featured the devolution of sport and leisure areas to outlying areas, and the supplementing of privately owned working-class apartment blocks by the even more peripheral council estates.[37] In Berlin and elsewhere, functional differentiation meant typological homogenization as the buildings in any given zone came to look more and more alike. Complexity or difference yielded to uniformity.

In contrast, Rossi proffers a humanist, anthropomorphic, vision, largely based on the tenets of Alberti. Rossi follows Alberti in: (a) the rejection of the monumental and the large-scale; (b) the idea of the city as a metaphor for the house of the individual human being; (c) the city as a microcosm of a harmonic and macrocosmic universe; (d) the advocacy of symmetry in the built environment on the model of the symmetry of the human body.[38] Rossi's built environment is also humanist, in that it provides the sort of space which is an ideal backdrop for the most human of activities, so to speak a 'stage set where encounters, gossip, games, fights, jealousies, courtship and displays of pride occur'.[39]

What this entails is further clarified by comparison of the Greek city with the cities of the ancient empires of the oriental despots' hydraulic societies. In the counterposition of 'system' of the despots of the Asiatic Mode of Production and the 'life-world' of Classical Greece, the unifying distinction between the Oriental city and Hellas is that in the former space is functional for the despot and the symbolism of the built environment is basically addressed to the despot, while in Hellas space is functional for, and the built environment speaks to, 'man'. The palace of the sovereign is the only formative element of the oriental city. In the palace quarter of the oriental city are found government offices, law courts and bureaucracy, but these speak directly to the despot's power. These stand in strong relief to the organs of Athenian political life, the boule, the ecclesia and the aeropagus.[40] The temple of the divinity is also a formative element, but it is dependent on the sovereign in a much stricter sense than the Greek case.

In the temple quarter of the oriental city are found the astronomy observatory, the library, schools, the college and theatre. The Greek oracles are in contrast located outside the city. They address not just the despot or leader but also the problems of the citizens. Thus Olympia is oriented towards sport; Cos towards health, around whose place gathered physicians and followers of Hippocrates; and Delphi had a unifying mission. Buildings were not so much connected to power as addressed to social needs. Thus the offspring of Olympia was the gymnasium, an enclosed sports ground with baths that later came to have classrooms, and became established as the forerunner of the famous schools the Lyceum and the Academy. Equally, the gymnasium and the theatre subsequently moved out of the market place in Hellas, while the equivalent institution tended to remain in the temple quarter in the oriental city. Finally, oriental religion turned the symbolic world of the religion of the peasant village upside

down, and located the sacred in an unbridgeable transcendental realm.[41]
The gods of the Greek city, cast in the image of man, both physically and
behaviourally, occupied a realm whose transcendental nature was modulated. The oriental city was a great walled encampment, a 'barbarous
installation which lived off [its] neighbours'. Athens, in contrast, stood in an
organic connection to its surrounding region and came to have walls only
in the later history of the polis. For the Athenian citizen the city was
in essence a political entity; only in Rome is the concept of the city as
a physical place, with corresponding urban problems, developed. The
implicit or potential 'communitas' of inter-urban relations of the Greek
cities disappeared in Rome, where the diocese became the basis of the city
district. This was an offspring of the principal of imperial dominion, whose
vertical relations superseded the horizontal ones of more or less independent cities. This was continued as Rome Christianized and the cities became
bishops' seats.[42]

The gothic city, for its part, is perhaps human in scale, but is decidedly
not humanist. It is an eminently Christian city, as symbolic and material
space are subordinated to a Christian principle. The development of
markets might have been the determining principle in the rebirth of the city
in the Middle Ages, but it surely was not the dominant principle. The
mediaeval European city 'is a collective structure whose main purpose was
the living of a Christian life'.[43] From the twelfth century an immense
building programme covered Europe with a 'white robe of churches'. The
church – in comparison to the Greek city constituting a new type of ecclesia
or assembly – built monasteries, hospitals, alms houses and schools, taking
one-tenth of parishioners' income in its tithe. In England at one point, one
parish church existed for every 100 families. Most towns had two hospitals,
one for lepers, but a city like thirteenth-century Florence had thirty hospitals servicing a population of some 90,000.[44] Sometimes friaries with walled
gardens were built in the towns, but more commonly young men from the
city would go to the monasteries in the countryside, while preaching orders
from the countryside paid visits to the city. The church made itself felt in
the urban economy. Mediaeval fairs, for example, at which substantial
international trade took place, were held three or four times annually at the
times of religious festivals, when pilgrims would flock to the holy shrines.
The religious confraternities of patron saints were forerunners of and
served as a framework for the craft and merchants guilds. The political
weight of the church, and kings trembled before the threat of excommuni-
cation, was symbolized in this very physical visibility.[45]

Yet the gothic city was also labyrinth, was also ground. A simultaneous
principle of horizontality challenged the verticality of the church. This is
particularly apparent in the guild structure of these cities. The guilds had
social insurance functions, including the collective provision of funerals.

Through their patron saint confraternities, they provided a social life for their members. The guilds built chapels, guild halls, grammar schools. On a town's main square the craft guilds would typically build the guild hall and the merchant guilds would build the town hall. The town hall or *Rathaus* reserved its ground floor for the display of market wares, while in its top floor would meet the mayor and the town council. The top floor served also for the administration of justice, and for periodic feasts, marriages and balls for the city's upper classes. Town precincts or districts were arranged according to guilds. Fourteenth-century Venice was divided into six neighbourhoods whose separating edges were canals, according to the city's six guilds. Each precinct, except for the college precinct, had its own guild hall. Houses in the city's winding streets, usually only two or three stories high, served as workshop, store and living space. Beds were in living rooms, in curtained alcoves. Michaelangelo slept with his craftsmen, four to a bed. The town's public culture was also sited in bathhouses – there were twenty-nine of these alone in Frankfurt in 1387 – and around the drinking fountains set up in the public square. A square with guild hall, town hall, cathedral and market was also a place for the gallows and public punishment which particularly attracted large groups in public spaces. The gothic city had already passed its peak with the emergence of absolutism, with the steady ascendancy of the (centralizing) merchant guilds over the craft guilds.

If the market square was the node, and the guilds set the pace in determining districts, edges and monuments, it was perhaps the mediaeval 'paths' that were of greatest significance. Mumford lyrically praised their 'curved', 'organic' character and 'naturalness' in contrast to the paths of baroque absolutism where the 'street drives headlong into the town centre . . . symbolising the collection of public power in a centralised institution or a despotic prince'. Instead the curved, 'organic', mediaeval streets were prefigured by cow paths; their 'organic curves led by a series of irregular rings and devious passages to a central quarter or core'. To understand the mediaeval, gothic city and its architecture, one must gaze, Mumford continues, from the eyes of a procession, often of the guilds and their banners, 'winding' around its streets before 'debouching in the cathedral square'. This is indeed no 'static architecture. The profiles of the buildings, with their steep gables with their sharp roof lines, their pinnacles, their towers, their terraces, ripple and flow, break and solidify, rise and fall, with no less vitality than the structures themselves.'[46] 'The short approaches to the great buildings, the blocked vistas, increase the effects of verticality: one looks not to the right or left over a wide panorama, but skyward. [This] ambulatory enclosure was . . . an organic part of the processual movement . . . the visual movement of the eye is up and down . . . with a feeling of constriction in the narrow streets and of release as one suddenly came out into the parvis or market-place.' In the gothic procession 'spectators were also communicants or participants: they engaged in the spectacle'.[47]

Yet the medieval city, for all its social de-differentiation, self-government and complexity, was surely not a humanist city. Its universities – Bologna was founded in 1100 and Paris in 1150 – reproduced distinguished masters for the guilds,[48] and only emerged from this collective regulation into a developing 'humanistic' orientation in the Renaissance. To Giorgio Vasari, equal of Leone Battista Alberti as a Renaissance art historian, the gothic was 'the monstrous and barbarous *maniera tedesca* (German style)'. It was, Vasari added, the 'invention of the Goths', who 'ruined the ancient buildings and killed the architects in the wars'. The architects 'who were left constructed the buildings in this style. They turned the arches with pointed segments and filled all Italy with these abominations of buildings.'[49] Vasari's humanist critique took gothic architecture to extended task for: the irrational mode of setting up weight-bearing supports; the excess of ornament, particularly around cornices; their confused and disordered appearance; their absence of symmetrical proportion; and their flimsy and insubstantial appearance.[50]

For ancient Greek and Renaissance humanists, man is an integral unity of body and soul, whereas the mediaeval conception of man is just a 'clod of earth, miraculously united with an immortal soul'. It is this very devaluation of the human which explains the absence of distinction in mediaeval scholasticism between the natural sciences and what Erasmus called *studia humanistica*, as well as, as Hennis has argued, the modernist triumph of positivism. It is also this low valuation of the human which explains the absence of concern in mediaeval times (and modern times?) with human history. Because of this absence of significance of the human past, the Middle Ages could not understand the past as somehow distanced from the present. It was only in the Renaissance that Antiquity could be understood as completely detached from the world of contemporaries. The Middle Ages saw man as capable only of animal passions, and Ancient Greece as even worse because of its paganism. Classical themes could not be given classical motifs in mediaeval art. Instead of idealizing, classicizing motifs, classical themes were painted in the images of contemporary courtly manners. Classical motifs were reserved for Christian themes.[51]

The gothic/humanist opposition is particularly clear in the context of the theory of proportions: here ages which highly valuate man foreground anthropomorphic proportions. In Pharonic Egypt, proportions were not anthropomorphic but geometric, as design was preceded by the setting out of finely meshed networks of equal squares, and systematic rules existed for the relative size and place of feet, legs etc. The non-humanism of such art was evident in the absence of portrayal of movement (not to mention the absence of three-quarter views); lunging, for instance, was represented only by moving the feet a bit further apart. This is partly explicable by the fact that such art was not designed for the vision of the human eye, but placed in dark inaccessible tombs. It was created to serve not for this life but for another.[52] In Greece, mimesis contrasted with the Egyptian 'constructionism' the principle of 'anthropometry', as outlined in the writings of Polyclitus, with the principle of geometry. This was humanism in the sense that human beings could be idealized with classical proportions, as could architecture with its clear and distinct orders (in comparison with the confusion of orders in the Gothic), with symmetrical proportions. Greek art also brought beginnings of perspective, the assumption of the human viewing eye, through what Roman thinker Vitruvius called 'eurythmia'. This was a set of optical refinements, of thickenings and foreshortenings, which altered the objective dimensions and made the object 'eurythmic to the sense of sight' of the observer.[53]

Mediaeval painting, with its absence of optical refinement, like Egyptian counterpart systematically suppressed depth. Its Byzantine variant was dependent on an algebraic theory of proportions whose oriental influences included the number mysticism of tenth-century Arabic painting. Gothic painting for its part relied on a 'schematic' theory of proportion, in which systems of lines, triangles and squares were the organizing principles for portraying bodies. In the Renaissance the position of the viewer is fully developed as the human subject. The Renaissance, and not classical antiquity, developed a theory of perspective in which the visual is interpreted as a central projection 'constructible by geometric methods'.[54] The object represented is more fully humanized with the revolution in the representation of movement initiated by Leonardo's investigations into how body dimensions change with movement according to the principle of 'continuing and uniform circular motion'.[55] Further, there is the developing 'humanization' of the painter/architect as an individual creator instead of a member of a craft guild. The valuation of the human form in painting entails the valuation of art itself, which was surely not a principle of Antiquity. Only with the Renaissance does the theory of proportions become a metaphysical principle. Finally, the valuation of heroism in Antiquity is replaced, in, for example, Erasmus, by a doctrine preaching the dignity of man, accepting human limitations; a doctrine advocating 'the unheroic love of tranquillity', ironic scepticism and the acceptance of human free will and responsibility.[56]

Martin Jay has argued with convincing force that vision is a paradigm for modernity. In light of the above, it would seem to me to be just as likely that vision, and the assumption of perspective and the eye of the viewing individual, is the organizing principle, perhaps less of modernism than of humanism. And in this sense the Gothic would be the supreme ideology to counter the culture of vision. The gothic runs counter to the visual regime in its opposition both to symmetry and to light or clarity. Hence the assymetry of the windows on Gothic houses and the three nave cathedral, covered, as Brough describes, 'with cruciform vaults and surrounded by windows with pointed arches and Gothic tracery'.[57] The ideology of darkness is evidenced in the effect of the stained glass, in the hidden staircases, in the crepuscular naves of the churches. The Germans, especially from the eighteenth century, were to reverse the invidious distinctions of Antique and Gothic of the Italian architects and critics, and recreate the Goths as historical heroes and their language as a historical archetype.[58] The *maniera tedesca* in architecture too was revaluated by the Germans as part of the development of their own national awareness. Its corresponding anti-humanism and anti-universalism left, of course, their own historical traces.

The Other Modernity: Lived Space in Japan[59]

The grounded and tactile side of the other modernity is, I think, further exemplified in the Japanese conception of space. In Japan the labyrinthine spatial arrangements are reduplicated in a set of characteristically de-differentiated symbolic structures and modes of signification. Let us consider Japanese spatial organization, with an eye to Lynch's elements of urban space. We will note in advance that it seems above all to be the 'path' and 'edge' which lend to Japanese space its characteristic form. The Japanese path has encountered two historical attempts of subsumption to a foreign imposed grid, first in the Japanese adoption of Chinese civilization in the seventh and eighth centuries CE, and second with the adoption of Western values with the 1868 Mejei Restoration. In both cases the attempts failed. Streets in the grid are linear. This means they connect two points which lie outside of the street at either of its ends. Streets in the grid follow the 'logic of the visitor' (often the Imperial visitor), in that they come from elsewhere and go elsewhere. They follow the Cartesian logic of the directional street. They are organized in connection with a pre-existing, extrinsic reference. Streets in Japanese labyrinthine space are more non-linear. They are streets for pedestrians, who pulled carts until well into the twentieth century, not for vehicles. Streets in the labyrinth follow the 'logic of the dwelling', their point of reference intrinsic.[60]

With the emergence of the Western grid, streets began to follow an extrinsic logic, streets were given names and houses numbers. Names were introduced for Parisian streets in 1729 to enable systematic tax gathering by the state, house numbers by one of Napoleon's artillery generals. Japanese streets often still have no names, and Japanese houses no street numbers. The US occupants after the Second World War attempted without luck to introduce street names in Tokyo. Japanese urban addresses comprise not street names but the names of quarters. To this name are attached three digits, designating not a street number. The first digit stands for the section of the given district, the second for the rectangular block of houses and the third for the individual house in this rectangular block. And the order of this last digit does not follow a linear or even rectangular principle, but instead the chronological order of when the house was built.[61] Hence the ubiquity of fax machines in today's Japan, necessary to send maps to visitors to find places of business.

In ancient Kyoto the Chinese dominance brought a linear supra-local order of public thoroughfares and road systems. The Japanese labyrinthine logic reasserted itself from the twelfth century, by which time the quarter (*machi*) no longer designated a place in the grid, but was named according to local functional activities. During the Tokagawa period the *daimyo* moved en masse to the cities to form a courtier class. The spatial positioning of their houses encourages a multiplication of the number of street angles, cul-de-sacs and T-junctions. Even in contemporary Tokyo, some two-thirds of intersections are not crossroads, but T-junctions.[62] After the Mejeii Restoration, and especially with the US occupation, attempts were made at conversion to orthogonal space. For example, the plan of Obihiro was taken from Washington DC. But still deviations persisted. Japanese streets are for living, and give the impression of depth, movement and complexity. This is not geometric space, but 'cinetic space', in which the experience of moving through counts more than the destination. It is as if one were in a building in which the interior has been extended, deepened step by step, where a room's only link is with the 'room immediately before and the one immediately after'. The Japanese city offers no, or few, perspectives, on the baroque model, but visual abutments which punctuate progression. In the Japanese garden (and tea pavilion) the visitor, unlike in the perspective of the geometric Italian or French garden, must concentrate on a series of successive views.[63] Connections in the Japanese city, as in the Greek city and mediaeval city, are 'horizontal', whether within the city or between cities. Connections in the grid, whether in Asian despotisms, Rome, the baroque or the modern, are vertical and extend from central power to the city.

The square is the paradigmatic form of the node. But the square is conspicuously absent in the traditional Japanese city. The activities normally consigned to the square – market, worship, politics – go on in the street. Paths in Japan function as nodes, and the fête, whose conventional place is the square, becomes a procession. In the occidental city, the collective will and 'the sacred' are embodied in monuments. Not so in Japan. Sacredness and the weight of significance, notes Berque, lies in the *ma*, which is a sort of link between two other entities. Thus paths from one place to another, or 'edges' which connect two spaces, instead of monuments, can be the symbolic bearer of affective charge. In Japan the dwelling has the sort of symbolic weight invested in Western monuments, and the monuments themselves aren't very 'monumental'. In ancient, Sinified Japan, monumentality and geometric palaces were the rule. In Tokyo in the subsequent Edo and Tokugawa Epochs, the royal palace was not at the end of a baroque vista, but was well hidden. Roland Barthes celebrated Tokyo in its anti-monumentality as a city without a centre. In Kyoto the most beautiful monuments are not at the centre but at the city's periphery. Cultic places are enveloped by green belts and thus effectively hidden from the eye. The chateaux of the *daimyo*, unlike in the West, were intended to hypostatize not the collectivity but the *daimyo*'s own power. Assumptions of cyclical natural destruction, basic to Japanese cosmology, foster a view of monuments as temporary structures.[64]

Edges are insubstantial to the point almost of non-existence inside the Japanese house. What internal differentiation there is comes through mobile partitions and not walls. Often the only clue to any sort of separation of rooms is that domestic space other than the kitchen is raised off the ground. Many sleeping in the same room, even when space is plentiful, and taking baths collectively is still a common practice. The absence of any sort of 'group' or edge within the domestic unit is reflected in the blunt directness of address of family members to one another and the notable absence of table manners. The edge, on the other hand, is between the family unit and the outside, and it is drawn not between the house and garden, but between the house and garden on the one hand and its exterior on the other. Upon entering the domestic unit, shoes are taken off. Heavy wood panels shut out the outside at night. The heavy edges of 'group' and weak edges of 'grid' of the domestic unit underscore less demarcated notions of individualism than in the West. The individual represents the home as if by delegation; fathers quit jobs when sons are arrested. This may also lead, Berque argues, to weaker superego development: the sense of moral obligation to total outsiders is relatively underdeveloped. But Japanese edges are not, as in the West, mere separators of space, but, as embodiments of the *ma* – which is a transitional zone between the things that it 'envelopes' – are spaces of sedimented meanings, which they gain reciprocally, defining the entities they, in separating, also bring together. Thus the importance of the *engawa* in Japanese buildings. Japanese apartment buildings are entered through the *genkan*, which delivery boys and others from the anonymous public can enter. But between this outside and the inside of the individual flats is the *engawa*, transitional edge-type space, where only those who live in the building can relax, gossip and variously carry on.[65]

The edge between town and countryside is weak. Like those in Britain, Japanese towns were typically without walls, signalling restricted autonomy from feudal power. Walls are more often found around chateaux. Building density is low in traditional Japanese cities: private dwelling architecture is similar in town and country. Rural social forms persisted and still persist in the city. Japanese rural areas have a high population density and very much a 'man-made' character. The Westerner is thus surprised by the comparatively great environmental damage in the countryside. The crucial and heavy edge is instead between town and country, on the one hand, and forest and mountains, on the other. This is the edge between culture and nature, as forest and mountains are wilder and more savage than in Europe. Here rural areas themselves are the edge between the culture of the city and nature of the wild undeveloped areas.[66]

'Communitas', and not 'dominium', is the principle of the Japanese district. The rural community (*mura*) is centred on the collective use of water, standing in contrast to state governance in the hydraulic societies like China. The *mura* entails strong group boundaries and 'district' consciousness. The worst possible punishment for an individual was to be banished from the local rural community. Village festivals ritualized this by throwing flaming straw dolls, representing the diverse evils, outside of the *mura*. The rural *mura* persisted as units of city organization used as an intermediating unit by state power in Tokugawa Japan. They were partly reproduced in the *chronokai* under the Mejeii Restoration and for industrialization and mobilization for the Second World War. These, like European mediaeval associations, were pan-functional. The paradigmatic organizational form they created later resurfaced in the residents' movements of the 1960s against the growth policies of central government.[67]

This tectonic and labyrinthine spatial imaginary finds its parallels in spoken language. In phonology, syntax and narrative structure, signification in Japan would seem indeed to be de-differentiated. Signification is figural, taking place through the resemblance of the signifier and referent. Hence the Japanese alphabet is less mediatedly tied to the concrete than Phoenician and Cyrillic alphabets. Japanese verbal sounds are more similar to natural sounds than in Western languages, with a pronounced use of onomatopoeia. Thus neurophysiological studies have suggested that among Japanese the areas of the brain register both verbal and natural sounds, while among Western subjects these functions are separated. This is not biologically but culturally acquired, and seems to be partly explicable by the prevalence of vowels (natural sounds are more vowel-like than like consonants) in Japanese. In Japanese the pronoun is relatively rarely used. The abstract subject is thus not differentiated from role and/or place. When teachers address pupils they refer to themselves not as 'I' but as 'teacher' (*sensei*). People are commonly addressed not as 'you' but as their occupation. Place is used metonymically for specific individuals. The husband calls his wife frequently *kanai* (at home) and the wife her husband *uchi-nohito* (person of the home).[68]

In Japanese syntax there is a notable lack of differentiation between subject and predicate. The lover does not say to the beloved, for example, 'I love you', but merely utters a word expressing the sentiment love. The same words render 'I'm cold' and 'it's cold'. 'I run', 'you run' and 'he runs' are all *heshiru*. The speech-act theorist would find little employment in Japan, as there is little speaker/statement distinction. This seeming priority of predicate over subject, of statement over speaker, is perhaps the background for weak notions of predicative logic in Japan. Such logic assumes predicative chaining between subject and action. It assumes, so to speak, that the subject or agency is the 'cause' of the action. Thus in Japanese sentence structure the grammatical subject is often not the existential subject, but the complement of the direct object.[69] There is a weak presence of verbs such as 'to do' and 'to make'. What is valorized here is not the cause (by the subject), but the event itself, 'the spontaneous becoming (of the object)', the 'natural and dynamic'. Japanese literary forms, and especially seventeenth-century Noh theatre, similarly avoid a predicative, causal logic, in which the intentions of the actor are the cause of an event. This has been noted by dramatist Robert Wilson. Wilson writes that his plays attempt to avoid such a predicative logic in which the subjective states of actors are the cause of events. Following Noh theatre, focus is on the event, with gesture (and for him stage design and lighting) as the organizing principle.[70] In place of predicative logic, Japan, notes Berque, proffers a 'topological logic', a 'logic of the field', in which focus is on 'place' and 'perception proceeds in a highly contingent manner'. Here meaning is not found in the subject–predicate relation but in the topological field, and the *ma*, or connection and interval between two adjacent entities on the surface of the field, or of two successive events in time. Meaning is not predicative but 'contextual'. What counts is not predicative successions but contextual affinities.[71]

This collapse of the signifier into the referent, the subject into the predicate, is the cosmological base of Japanese conceptions of nature. In comparison to Western conceptions of nature, whose presumptions have largely been Augustinian and then Newtonian linear time, in Japanese notions of nature there is the comparative prominence of cyclical time. This resembles the cyclical experience of flooding that has historically plagued Japan at least since the very early centuries CE, well after Japan made the transition from mountain dwelling and hunting to settling in the valleys as rice growers. In the early centuries of rice growing, unpredictable and savage flooding wreaked destruction on the homes and livelihoods of the settlers. Destruction of settlements was followed by overgrowth of heavy vegetation, whose significance wandering groups came to appreciate. These cycles of rotting, dissolution and regeneration marked the development of Shinto cosmology, which, in place of the Western and Chinese notion of origins, substituted visions of begetting and becoming. In China man controlled the rivers, hence man and nature were separate and time was a linear sequence of (subjective) causes and effects. In Japanese cosmology, which implodes man and nature, determination is, not a matter of agency, but a succession of 'cataclysmic surgings of nature . . . of events which refuse to be analysed, which imply acceptance of events as they are', in which 'nature looms up to our perception, immediately and prior to all determinants'. This may be related to the comparative absence of landscape painting in Japan in comparison to the West. In landscape painting from sixteenth-century Holland, nature comes to be depicted not as symbol but as referent. Non-Western cosmologies precluded this sort of objectivization of nature involved in landscape painting. In Islamic painting, for example, nature is never figure, always ground. In China, in the fourth century CE, paintings did depict nature as figure, but never representationally, only as symbol. Japanese painting, often following this Chinese example, portrayed a nature symbolizing solitude, melancholy and desolation. It is predominantly in the landscapes of the occident that nature fully becomes separate from the symbolic and hence the subjective, and thus loses its mythical or metaphoric character.[72]

Nature in Japan tends often to be conceived as not an object but a subject with its own causal powers; as an entity that is loaded with meaning for humans. Nature exists both external and internal to humans. The Japanese have a comparative familiarity with nature. Nature tends to be viewed as a companion. Nature in Japan is, on the one hand, primitive and wild, and, on the other, harmonic and refined. The first sort of *nature sauvage*, of forests and unpredictable floods, 'projects itself into culture at all moments': it is 'metaphorically present in culture, it shapes culture'. This nature is the subject of its own proper 'surrection'. It is 'autogenic', 'comes to pass by itself'. The second type of nature is a sort of *nature contrainte*, which is more abstract, less immediate than *nature sauvage*. It operates not as subject and driving causal power, but as a sort of state of being. In seventeenth-century courtier society, this was seen as an escape from savagery, a departure from bestiality. Here the quest for the natural is a quest for refinement, for balance and the 'ludic mastery of desire'. In this sense the tea pavilions and pottery of the late sixteenth century attempted to put some system into nature's contingency. And in a similar vein today's Japanese ecologists argue that the destruction of the environment by business means that humans are about to lose a long-standing partner.[73]

Western urban planning influence is registered in educational manuals during the Mejeii Restoration. The Tanaka governments saw considerable functional separation and zoning. Especially notable now is the absence of greenery in Japanese cities. Tokyo has only 2.0 square metres of greenery per person, in comparison with 8.3 in Paris, 11.4 in Rome and 19.1 in New York City. In pre-industrial times parks in *daimyo*'s residences made Tokyo greener than European cities. Despite such recent Westernization, Tokyo's deep structure is still mid-eighteenth-century Edo. Japanese nature cosmologies allow the semi-wild vegetation which still persists not far from the city centre. The high city in west Tokyo, where the *daimyo* lived, still boasts the irregular plan, standing in relief to the orthogonal low city in the east, always the place of the merchants. Even this latter is not so much one grid, but a decentred mosaic of grids, where intersections operate connectively and not as cross-junctions.[74]

Urban Space and Allegory

If baroque churches are monuments embodying the collective will in the era of the absolutist kings, then skyscrapers are their modern counterparts. Skyscrapers can be the extension of modernization's original horizontal orthogonality into the dimension of the vertical. Chicago is probably the classic city of such a Cartesian skyline. They can also stand in complex contradiction to such orthogonality, to which the New York skyscraper, with its building boom of the 1920s and 1930s, still bears testimony. 'Delirious' New York, as Rem Koolhaas observes, is the city of 'two-dimensional discipline and three-dimensional anarchy'. New York is one of the original cities of the modernist grid, designed by Simon De Witt in 1811 in the shape of twelve avenues running north and south and 155 streets running east and west. The grid, beginning from Houston Street, leaving a labyrinthine southern remainder, was abstractly conceived with little thought of topography or even population. Indeed, in 1853, as New York City built its Crystal Palace in the International Exposition and plans for Central Park emerged, the population had still only expanded to 42nd Street. The grid was promoted as an effort to put order into previously existing chaos, which was not to be long in exacting its spiteful revenge.[75]

This revenge, of course, was in the shape of the skyscrapers. The skyscrapers, built by graduates of Paris's Ecole de Beaux-Arts, were gothic, vertical needles. In modern cities, 'blocks' lend themselves to classical style, while towers are irremediably gothic. Chicago, with its large lots, built 'blocks'. Due to scarcity of land and smallness of lots, New York had no choice but to build towers. Manhattan was made for towers – for Cass

Gilbert's Woolworth's building designed as the world's tallest building in 1913, with 27 floors topped by a 30-storey tower. In its 'interior business', its 'exterior pure spirituality', the Woolworths was 'an automonument to the anti-monumental'. Gilbert was surpassed by Raymond Hood, 1905 Beaux-Arts graduate and paradigm architect of 'Manhattanism'. Hood, winner of first prize with his Gothic submission to the Chicago Tribune skyscraper competition of 1922, was author of the McGraw Hill building, constructed in 1929–33, its exterior in polychrome. Hood's Manhattan was a 'city of towers', a 'forest of free-standing competing needles made accessible by the regular paths of the grid: a practical Luna Park'. To this was added William Van Alen's (1929) Chrysler Building, helping to create a Manhattan imaginary of gothic, 'quasi-nocturnal images' that found its way into magazines, tourist brochures, comic books and the like. In Manhattan is found William Sarris's Empire State Building built in the mid-thirties and the Waldorf-Astoria, occupying the block circumscribed by Park and Lexington, 49th and 50th Streets. The Waldorf was the hotel of excess, the signifier of wealth to an age in which it became the mode for the wealthy to take up residence in hotels, and the subject of a number of Hollywood films.[76]

Unlike in materialist Chicago, the New York towers were primarily cultural. They worked on not the symbolic but the imaginary, as not discourse but figure. Here the indexicality of buildings themselves was doing the signifying. As Salvador Dali intoned, 'What Piranesi invented the ornamental of your Roxy Theatre? And what Gustave Moreau, apoplectic with Prometheus lighted the venomous colours that flutter at the summit of the Chrysler Building?' Dali applauded their 'paranoid-critical method', 'the spontaneous method of irrational knowledge based on the critical and systematic objectifications of delirious associations and interpretations'. De Chirico likened New York's effects to his paintings. And Dali upon a visit in the mid-thirties said, 'New York: Why, why did you create my statue long ago, before I was born?' New York's skyline signifies gothically by night. Hence Ferris's drawings of this cityscape 'created' 'an artificial night that leaves all architectural incidents vague and ambiguous'. Ferris's Manhattan is 'an illuminated night inside a cosmic container . . . a pitch black architectural womb that gives birth to the consecutive stages of the skyscraper in a series of sometimes overlapping precipices'.[77]

Also inscribed in such a gothic tactility and indexicality of darkness are a different type of path, the *Passagen*. According to Johann Geist, the arcade, whose most conspicuous historic precursor may have been the covered bazaar, is a glass-covered, narrow passageway, connecting busy streets, lined on both sides with shops in a city's main commercial district. Arcades are creatures of the era of liberal capitalism. They are born and die

with the nineteenth century. The arcade, first in Paris's Palais Royal –
which provided a promenade for emancipated, post- Revolutionary society
– was the object of speculation by contemporary property developers,
made possible by the rapidly growing market for luxury goods. The
consequence, however, of such private speculation was the provision
of an eminently public good.[78] The arcade, a labyrinth in the womb
of the modern, was in its material use value an arena of public space.
This built-environment public space allowed solely pedestrian traffic.
Its very protectedness and isolation from the external environment
made possible 'a systematic forum for communications free from interruptions'.[79] The arcade promoted not only communicative rationality,
but what William H. Whyte has called 'schmoosing space', space to
meet, gossip, carry on and generally socialize. Whyte in *The Sociology of Small
Public Spaces* shows that people tend to 'schmoose' in narrow places,
in nooks and crannies, in places that are most traversed by other people,
in places where they can sit down and rest and/or take refreshment,
and in places near ongoing activities, entertainment or performance.[80]
The arcade provided all of these. It was lined not only with shops, but
with cafes, restaurants, beer halls, brothels, gambling rooms, meeting
rooms, reading rooms and baths, a veritable paradise of the vanities
and vices.[81]

The public sphere, according to Habermas, declines in the era of
'organized capitalism'. So do the *Passagen*. With the rise of garden city
anti-urbanism, the darkness of arcades became suspect. Zoning laws intervened. Real estate reform prevented construction connecting adjoining
buildings. Arcades stood in violation of the new minimum street frontage
laws. The new ideology of planning opposed enclosures, instead 'punctuat-
ing the city with broad public spaces'. The city as a system of spaces was
replaced by a system of separate entities. The last decades of the twentieth
century have brought a new fascination for arcades. The new classes of
cultural intermediaries, giving a renewed basis to specialized luxury
consumption and fed up with modernist light and abstract space, wanted
the complexity, congestion, shadowiness and enclosure that the arcade
promised.[82]

In Walter Benjamin's *Passagenwerk* modernity is about labyrinths in
grids. Urban space for Benjamin is an arena for the staging of 'micro-
events'.[83] These events, whether cultural ('communicative') events or not,
are impossible without figures of urban space. Such figures can be either
people or objects. They can be objects of design or circumscribe spaces in
the built environment. Benjamin's figures of the urban imaginary are social
actors and objects that are paradigmatic for a particular type of urban
space. For example, the stockbroker, the drug dealer, the punk, the advertising executive are paradigmatic figures of late twentieth-century urban

space, as the leper and the guild master are of the mediaeval cityscape. Benjamin's parade of figures – 'the bohème', 'the provocateur', 'the poet', 'the conspirator', 'the rag picker', 'the littérateur', 'the pimp', 'the prostitute', 'the flâneur', 'the criminal', 'the assassin', 'the apache' – give to urban space its characteristic and labyrinthine complexity. Perhaps the mould for the modernist figures of the *Passagenwerk* is set by the 'bohème', who takes on the shape of any and all of the other figures. Benjamin's bohème, as ideal type, is polar opposite to Habermas's communicatively rational actor. The bohème is not only not given to rational discussion, but 'not given to discussion' full stop. Worse, he is 'cryptic'. The bohème is political. But his politics are the politics of conspiracy, of Napoleon III. He is a believer in the 'metaphysics of the provocateur'. He says 'long live the revolution as I would say long live destruction'. He is not just the Blanquist or nihilist. He is positively devious and also, with Baudelaire, says 'long live the false ideas'. For him revolution, and the barricades, which as 'magic cobblestones rise up to form fortresses', are merely sets of signifiers, are primarily allegory. The professional conspirator is, at the same time, 'the disinherited', 'the brutal, starved, envious, wild Cain who has gone to the cities to consume the sediment of rancour which has accumulated in them and participate in the false ideas'.[84]

Like Koolhaas's skyscrapers in New York by night, Benjamin's (and Baudelaire's) urban conspirator operates in a world of darkness and contingency. Baudelaire's conspirator is not favoured by God (or reason) but by 'fortuna and satan'. Benjamin cites Marx, who saw Napoleon III, 'bohème dorée', as a 'confidence man favoured by fortune'. 'Satan is the father confessor of the conspirators', wrote Baudelaire. Benjamin notes that Baudelaire was not himself a Satanist, but observes that it is to Satan that his verses 'owe their subtle power not to deny loyalty entirely, even in desperate outcries, to that to which understanding and humaneness rebelled against'.[83] The labyrinth in the grid is often presented as existing underneath the streets of the city in sewers, passages of the metropolitan transit underground, underground parking lots and the like in films of the 1980s such as Jean-Jacques Beineix's *Diva* and Luc Besson's *Subway*. And Benjamin and Baudelaire's Satan is 'his highness who has his subterranean dwelling in the vicinity of the boulevard'. Benjamin proffers the urban space not of material, but of communicative events. His figures function like Koolhaas's monuments as signifiers, not in Habermas's discursive communication but, like Sennett's *Public Man* and Whyte's spaces of sociability, in communicative events which are largely figural. This seems very much the polar-opposite counterpart of Habermas's ideal speech situation. For Benjamin, statements are only allowed which deliberately contravene any possibility of validity in regard to the external world. Statements must also contravene any possible conventional or

universal normative tenets. Utterances must, to the greatest possible
degree, strive to contravene expressive validity and should aim for
inauthenticity. Benjamin's archetypes, like Koolhaas's skyscrapers, communicate not through meaning, but through sensation: any discourses
attempting to redeem their validity claims are useless. Benjamin's communicative events are almost always one-way, with the interlocutor deprived
of any right to response.

Benjamin's urban imaginary also comprises objects: for example,
cultural objects, like newspapers. The press as cultural object functions not
only to provide information but as symbol, as part and parcel of the urban
environment. Manhattan is not Manhattan without the sight of the *Village
Voice* on news stands, and Paris not visually Paris without the ubiquity of *Le
Monde*. Benjamin notes that a change occurred in the press at the end of the
1820s. The price of newspapers halved at this time, so no longer could one
afford to read them only in cafes. Circulation boomed, he observes, with a
four-fold increase in subscriptions in Paris from 1824 to 1846. At this point
the press, led by Émile Girardin's *La Presse* and *Constitutionnel*, developed the
feuilleton, soon a basis for boulevard cafes and the new 'cocktail hours'.
Previously literary life had been confined to the periodicals. Further, the
daily newspapers began to carry serialized novels, advertisements and *faits
divers*.[86] Just when the daily newspaper began to reach sufficient citizens to
create a public sphere, it abandoned the principles that would support such
a sphere. Baudelaire saw this corruption in the serialized novels of the
newly rich 'writers as whores': Eugene Sue, Lamartine and Dumas.
Baudelaire himself aspired to such whoredom.

In the discussion of 'the ancients and moderns', Benjamin speaks of the
poet as hero. He speaks in the physical imagery of warrior- type heroism.
Here poetry, like fencing, takes a great physical effort of the poetic will. The
physical existence of the poet/painter, like that of the warrior, is tenuous
and fragile. The poet-hero 'abandons one part of his bourgeois existence
after another, and the street increasingly becomes a place of refuge for
him'. He is the 'apache', as criminal: 'the apache abjures virtues and laws:
he terminates the *contrat social* forever'. Baudelaire offers such a 'poetry of
apachedom' in, for example, 'Le vin de l'assassin'. The poet is the 'apache
in his solitude', the apache in his 'difference', the '*noli me tangere*, an encap-
sulation of the individual in his difference'. Benjamin may speak of ancients
here, but this is not antiquity of humanism. Benjamin's poet succeeds
through physical effort, not the balance, proportion, serenity, love of tranquillity and acceptance of responsibility of ancient humanism. It is instead
a very Nietzschean and physicalist aesthetics of sensation. The antiquity
evoked here by Benjamin is not humanist but epic and pre-Socratic. Also
opposed to Greek humanism is the 'solitude', the 'difference', the very
'privacy' of Benjamin's poet. The ancient poet, in an age prior to the

separation of labour and art, was a public figure, fully rooted in the social. The ancient poet was not like Benjamin's 'a criminal'. The ancient poet chronicled heroism, mostly in war, but was no hero himself. Benjamin's poet, Baudelaire as figure, was then not ancient. He was the ancient in the modern. The antiquity in this modernity was not humanist or classical, it was pre-Socratic, gothic, labyrinthine.[87]

The figures rendered by antique art were public and official, warriors, kings, gods, as were the figures, idealized in the classical manner, by the painters of the nineteenth-century academy. The subject matter of the bohème's poetry was instead private. 'The subjects of private life which are heroic in quite another way. In the spectacle of elegant life – of the thousands of irregular existences led in the basements of a big city by criminals and kept women – as the *Gazette des Tribunaux* and the *Moniteur* demonstrate, we need only to open our eyes to recognise our heroism.' Finally, the antiquity that Baudelaire, through Benjamin's prism, gives us is one of the decrepitude and ruins of the ancient. Baudelaire thought that the modern was equally decrepit and fragile, that Paris too would one day disappear.[88] This notion of transience of an epoch surely is not humanist.

Benjamin's antiquity is not only not humanist, but is no kind of real antiquity at all. It is instead merely an *allegory* for modernity. According to the *Petit Robert*, in 'allegory', each element of the story or painting 'evokes the diverse details of the idea which it attempts to express'. The dictionary cites Thibaudet as an illustration, who sees allegory as an antonym of 'symbol' in that allegories are somehow mechanical and symmetrical, whereas symbols are living and supple. Benjamin's treatment bears similarities with this (quite rich) dictionary definition. Two quotes from Benjamin's Baudelaire are quite instructive in this context. First, Benjamin quotes Baudelaire describing the rag picker, the final heroic subject, taken from the refuse of society, who

> has to gather the day's refuse in the capital city. Everything that the big city threw away, everything it lost, everything it despised, everything it crushed underfoot, he catalogues and collects. He collates the annals of intemperance, the capharnaum (stockpile) of waste. He sorts things out and makes a wise choice; he collects, like a miser guarding a treasure, the refuse which will assume the shape of useful or gratifying objects between jaws of the goddess of industry.

The second comes from Baudelaire's observations on antiquity, his views on Rome drawn from Piranesi's etchings, in which the 'non-restored ruins and the new city appear as one'. Baudelaire also appreciated Meryon, an engraver who drew views of Parisian antiquity in his depictions of 'the natural solemnity of the city', of the 'obelisks of industry'. In Meryon,

Benjamin continues, one finds 'an interpenetration of classical antiquity
and modernism, and in him the form of this superimposition, the allegory,
appears unmistakably'.[89]

Allegory here signifies through detail, through complexity. To signify
through complexity is to signify figurally. Discursive signification (or communication) is simple: it takes place through abstract rules which link the
signifying elements to one another. But figural signification takes place not
through rules which regulate the relationships among signifiers, but
through resemblance. Hence there must exist signifiers which correspond
to the infinitude of referents and signifieds existing outside the realm of
signifiers. This sort of signification is of necessity one of far greater complexity. There seem, however, to be two types of allegory. The first of these
is 'referential allegory', in which the painting or story refers to a signified or
referent. In this sense Benjamin's and Baudelaire's antiquity is a referential
allegory for modernity. The second type of allegory is found, for example,
in surrealism. It works through the juxtaposition of widely disparate
images: for example, in Piranesi's etchings and Meryon's drawings, and the
juxtaposition of the antique and the modern in Chirico's paintings.
In Benjamin's rag picker, it draws its signifiers from the world of the
discarded, the lowest of the profane. Here the real acts not as referent but
as signifying elements. This second type of allegory is not referential. If
antiquity is an allegory for modernity to Benjamin, then what indeed are
the figures of modernity an allegory for? The answer may be that they do
not refer to anything at all but communicate through sensation, through
'delirium'. This is what the surrealists called 'profane illumination'. Louis
Sullivan understood the complexity and intricacy of ornamentation in the
orient as conjuring the sublime. Perhaps it is the same for the complexity of
allegory.

Conclusions

This chapter has begun to explore the dimension of the ground in the
second modernity. Our point of departure here in spatial theory was the
notion of the field. The idea of the field is a heuristic that is characteristic
of the other modernity. The logic of the field is opposite to the predicative
logic of high modernity. We opened up the logic of the field not through
phenomenology but through psychology. The phenomenology of the field,
and especially the perceptual field, is a question of philosophy. It deals in
transcendentals.[90] Agency in this phenomenology of perception is centred
of course not in the cerebral ego, but in the body. But the questions asked
are transcendental. The philosopher and phenomenologist asks what is the
condition of the possibility of lived experience, meaning authentic lived

experience. And answers by talking about bodies in perceptual fields. In this chapter we asked not a transcendental but an empirical question, not a philosophical but a psychological question about how empirical bodies experience space. We have at the same time implicitly addressed the sociology of the field, where again not the transcendental but the empirical social experience of space is explored. Now the body or habitus is already social and the question is how different categories of socially constituted bodies experience space. Starting with perception and the spatial field, we want with Jean François Lyotard in *Discours, figure* to understand the field to be not just figural but also discursive, to be the basis of an urban imaginary and an urban symbolic.

Starting with this notion of the field, we asked the question of its production, the question of the production of space. The question of how individual or social bodies in fact produce space. Here we drew on Henri Lefebvre's non-humanist idea of orientation in space, in which the body is understood on the model of the spider. For Lefebvre, like for surrealist-influenced Roger Caillois writing on animal bodies, space is produced through mimesis. The spider spinning her web, orienting herself in space, operating tactilely. Animal bodies extending their bodies through space, establishing symmetries and dissymmetries around their bodies. The spider thus, through mimesis and alterity, feels its way into and produces a space that is more a haptic or tactile field than a visual or figural one. At issue is a semiotics of not symbol or icon, but index, a space that is not symbolic or imaginary, but real. What could be more opposite to the Cartesian space of representations? What could be more opposite than this pre-humanist and haptic real space that is also the predecessor of today's post-humanist fields of parallel space?

What then are the elements of this gothic and grounded space, whose logic is also that of the other modernity? What are the elements of this city as field, as field of neither symbolic nor imaginary, but the real. Insufficiently monumental for the symbolic, yet drenched in myth; too dark for the iconic representation of the imaginary. It operates out of cellars, in the shadow of skyscrapers blocking out the light, and only themselves appearing properly 'by night'. It is a city, a space, through whose paths we still haptically, through touch and smell, find our way about. It is a city which signifies through the real, through the complexity of its towers, alleys and paths, through the gestures of its again dark figures, lepers, prostitutes, rag pickers, encountered along the paths of Paris's twelfth arrondisement, Barrio Xines in Barcelona, beyond the pale of Venice's Ghetto. It is neither word nor image but the real that signifies, as tower, as figure, as event. And the signification is taken in through not the noblest but the basest organs, smells and touches and tastes. This is the real and not realism's real: it evades representation while itself signifying. The city signifies not as representations signify as we sit in the cinema, reading a book, listening to a concert or watching television. The city only signifies as we move through it, along its paths and thoroughfares, it is not a representation but total environment. In the city and the spatial field we are more active than the 'active audience', more interactive than World Wide Web and CD-ROM users. Beyond and more interactive than interactivity is *inhabiting*. And we inhabit or 'live' the fields of urban space. This, beyond representation, or better well prior to representation, is the fundamental significance of what is called the sociology of everyday life.

This lived and tactile space, best evoked by the gothic city, is labyrinthine. It is based on the path. Like the labyrinth its connections are horizontal. This is not the grid and logic of the visitor, who comes from elsewhere, stops for no time at all and goes elsewhere. The visitor wants nodes, vistas, light, a grid to orient himself. The gothic city's labyrinths are home to the homeless, the stranger who comes today and stays tomorrow, the home of both *Obdachlos* and *Heimatlos*. This gothic city signifies to those who travel its labyrinthine paths, its dark and enclosed arcades, connected as if through T-junctions, horizontally. These paths are not circulated through but navigated. These are the paths travelled by the storyteller, operating again horizontally from town to town, before the unification of national cultures through not the *communitas* but the *dominium* of imagined communities. These are communities not of representation but again of the real as storyteller and journeymen move from town to town. Along the paths of this gothic city are the districts in which the various guilds carry on their work, the journeyman dropping off and staying with apprentice in the master's freehold, before carrying on through the winding and festive procession towards cathedral and *Rathaus* on the public square. This is a city defined by its paths, its districts and its edges, the edges dividing and at the same time defining inside from outside of houses, of districts, dividing the city as culture from the surrounding nature, itself defined as a sometimes threatening, sometimes benign subject.

This city of the real is a decidedly non- and pre-humanist city, decidedly gothic and not Renaissance classical, having little to do with modernist humanism. It is a mythic and ultimately tectonic city whose signification is more material than the commodity. But this city of the real and its prehumanist field, grounded in the deepest past, may also provide a future for urban space. This emergent built environment may be at the same time a parallel and hyperspace in which the urban field becomes electromagnetic and digital, in which experience becomes less phenomenological than virtual. The pre-humanist gothic city of the real is also the mould for today's renewed possibility of electronic or virtual communities, not as dominium but horizontally linked again as communitas. As linked horizontally through the connectionism and tactility of microelectronic paths and traces. As linked through the tactile, often sensual nature of virtual relations. As linked through the new journeymen in districts of small producers horizontally multimediated, emerging in digital media districts of today's world cities.

Part II

Society

5

From System to Symbol: Durkheim and French Sociology

Space and Society

This book follows a sort of temporal progression. Part I, on architecture/ urbanism, and part II, on the rise of sociology, which this chapter introduces, have a strong focus on the rise of the first modernity from its humanist predecessor. Parts III and IV, on experience and judgement, address more cultural-theoretical social-philosophical themes. They spend no time on the rise of high modernity from humanism, but begin with the second modernity partly in the context of the first. Parts III and IV begin with the deconstructive moment of the second modernity and then move critically from this to the second modernity's ground, whether the latter be life-world intersubjectivity, the semiotic index, sensation, the real or the pagan. Part V moves further forward and treats the growing dissolution of the second modernity and rise of the global information culture. The global information culture is a turn of the twenty-first century phenomenon.

The historical chronology of parts I to IV belies, however, the analytic reconstruction of these chapters. That is, although parts I and II on urbanism and sociology deal with the rise of the *first* modernity, they deal with a historical time period roughly from 1905 to 1945. The rise of sociology in part II focuses especially on the first decade of the twentieth century and the emergence of sociological positivism, while the pinnacle of the rise of the first modernity in architecture/urbanism would probably be located in the 1920s. Part IV looks at the rise in the *second* modernity in philosophy in Kant's notion of judgement. The chronology here is the onset of the nineteenth century. In philosophy, with the Romantics, and in the arts, in, for example, Wagner and Baudelaire, the second modernity develops from 1800 to 1840, while the first modernity in society and architecture emerges a century later from 1900 to 1940.

A number of analysts, most prominently Daniel Bell and Marshall Berman, have understood the expressive revolution from the late 1960s as 'modernity in the streets'.[1] They mean of course the second modernity, the deconstructive, fragmenting modernity. On this view the second modernity descends, as it were, from the realm of representation – philosophy and the arts – from the realm of reflection into everyday life, into the streets. But what about the first modernity? Is there a first modernity in the streets? What about the first modernity, emerging paradigmatically in the realm of representation as religion (Protestantism) and art (Alberti) in the fifteenth an sixteenth centuries, in philosophy (Descartes, Hobbes) in the seventeenth and as political representation a century later? It is curious that the first modernity seems to descend 'into the streets' in the initial decades of the twentieth century. The rise of sociology and the International Style in architecture are phenomena of the first modernity in the streets.

What happens here is that modernity becomes *technology*. Technology is about the use of knowledge. It is more broadly about the use of representations. It is about when representations, formerly transcendent, become immanent. It is when representations, formerly in another and separate sphere, are all among us, become part of everyday life. It is when culture becomes no more longer primarily interpreted or understood but instead lived and experienced. When representations become technology, become part and parcel of everyday life, they become used. This does not at all necessarily entail use in an instrumental or utilitarian sense. When Marx said use-value was concrete and exchange-value abstract, he understood use-value in a non-utilitarian sense. Indeed, the abstraction of Marxian exchange-value is integral to the utilitarian calculus of pleasure and pain. Use-value in contrast is very much a life-world and immediately experienced phenomenon. In any event, the representations at issue here which become technologies may be on the one hand scientific representations, the representations of science. They can also be representations of art. For example, Le Corbusier often quite consciously worked the representations of cubism into the technology of modern architecture.

Thus philosophy and art, subjects of parts III and IV of this book, are about representation. And architecture and sociology, addressed in parts I and II, are about technology. If science has been understood in terms of a dualism of subjects and objects, then, as Latour notes, technology is much more a question of quasi-subjects and quasi-objects.[2] In technology the transcendental status of subjects and objects is partly lost, is modulated. Ordinary citizens take on more or less the role of subject in relation to transcendental object when they read a book or look at a work of art or listen to a concert. They take on, however, the role of quasi-subjects in regard to quasi-objects as they live the 'technology' of their residences or shopping districts, or go to work in factories or offices. The same is true of thought. Philosophers and artists operate transcendentally, in a sphere of more or less distanciated reflection from the objects of their thought, in a way that sociologists and architects cannot. This is because sociologists, architects and planners deal less with objects than with *technologies* that are not outside of us so much as all around us. Thus in Bourdieu's sense sociologists and urbanists operate in a much closer context to the field of power.[3]

It is no coincidence that the rise of sociology and modernism in architecture coincides with the maturity and pre-eminence of the industrial working class. Sociology arose as a very undistantiated and often practical reflection on the condition – at work and at home – of the industrial working class. And so did modernist architecture and planning. If the first modernity in the streets was integrally connected to the rise of the industrial working class, the second, the expressive revolution of the later twentieth century, had a lot more to do with the working class's decline. In this book, whereas parts III and IV, addressing more philosophical and aesthetic themes, deal largely with modernity as representation and at a reflective distance, parts I and II on space and society largely deal with modernity as technology and in close conjunction with the field of power.

All this said, part II follows largely the same schema as part I. In part I we saw how modernist architecture rose in reaction to beaux-arts humanism. Here we will trace modernity in sociology similarly from its origins in humanism. Whereas postmodernist architecture was a deconstructive move in the realm of space, the more hermeneutic sociology of the late Durkheim and Simmel, which we shall address, constituted a similar movement in sociology. Chapter 4 traced various emergences of the (second modernity's) ground in urban space. In sociology we look at this most closely in the notion of a grounded 'sociality', the life-world intersubjectivity discussed in Alfred Schutz's work in chapter 7.

This chapter will begin to consider modernity in the context of classical sociological theory. In it we will trace not one but two different modernisms. The first is a high modernism, whose tradition emerges from the classical culture of the civilizing process of French court society, yet which is born in a radical break with such classicism. This is the positivist tradition: positivist because of its foregrounding of natural scientific principles, argumentation, its focus on clear and distinct concepts. This is the modernism of abstract system builders. We will discuss them at greatest length under the heading of 'system', focusing on issues of moral regulation and normality versus pathology. The second modernity is born in a rejection of both French classicism and positivism. It is oriented less to civilization than to what the German tradition understood as *Kultur*, and less to system than to symbol. We will discuss this notion of symbol in Durkheim and Mauss's non-positivist, hermeneutic sociology. We will see how primitive, modern and probably postmodern classifications are based in a very strong notion of the symbolic. In chapter 6 we will consider the aesthetic and poetic implications of symbol in the emergence of classical sociological theory, this time in the tracks of the German tradition and the work of Georg Simmel.

System

From Rhetoric to Moral Regulation

In the emergence of French sociology, debate pitted classical humanism and positivism against one another: contested discursive space was between the modern and the pre-modern, with the latter occupying important bastions of institutional power to the present day.[4] The criteria as to where one stood were determined by views on rhetoric, on the relationship of theory to practice and most of all on one's valuation of 'system'. Both in the work of Durheim and in the assumptions of the French state, such a notion of system characterized the modern.

Modernization from the positivist point of view can be read significantly as a process in which rhetoric is progressively stripped away from concepts and propositions, to be replaced by representation possessing clarity and distinctness. The beginnings of the process of inroads into rhetoric – i.e. a sort of proto-modernism – can be seen already in the focus of ancient Roman grammarians on the precision of language, in the clarity of Roman private law in Rome's urban grids. The Italian Renaissance and later French classicism were pre-modern in regard to causation in the sense that the modes from Galilean and Newtonian physics had largely not yet been taken on board. Yet they were already modern as regards description – as rhetoric was stripped away in language, and Albertian perspective and proportion in painting and urban space.

In comparison to the Machiavellian rhetorical and hence pre-modern touchstone, the seventeenth-century advocacy of mathesis in place of classical rhetoric by Descartes and Leibniz's vision of a universal technical language began to give body to a new modernist learning process. The eighteenth century saw decisive defeats for rhetoric. In Britain, Hume and later Bentham had only the most disparaging views of poetry, while English poetry itself took on a mathematical, univocal clarity, and Samuel Johnson demanded a dictionary of clear and precise definitions. In France, Rousseau's dismissal of theatre and the arts was not only for their frivolity, but also for their rhetoric. Condillac urged science to construct a universal language. Condorcet perhaps most influentially introduced the term 'social science', understood as the application of the methods of physical science: as the use of mathematical calculation in the analysis of morals and politics. Over a century later Durkheim himself was to urge social science to avoid common language use. Implicit here was the view that clarity and distinctness would permit the understanding of society as 'a distinct order of phenomena with determinate properties'. Hence the 'social realism' innovated by Durkheim in his doctoral thesis in a productive face-off with Montesquieu.[5]

This development of theory – in the purification of language and concepts from rhetoric – amounted to a view of science – as well as history – as progress. The idea was that the gains of science achieved through the diminution of rhetoric were to be applied so that society itself could move towards greater perfection. For French positivism society became a learning process. Positivism entails a strong articulation of theory and practice. Durkheim's idea of theory and practice was twofold and complex. On the one hand he wanted to apply, like Comte, the advances of social science to bring about positive social change. On the other he wanted broad masses of the population to be educated in the social sciences, partly to recast and rationalize the *conscience collective*. But also partly because Durkheim, no crude believer in social engineering, envisaged large swathes of the population – along the lines of Giddens's 'double hermeneutic' – as themselves bringing about such positive social change.[6] For Durkheim as for Giddens, theory was to articulate *twice* with practice. First, through the expertise of social scientists, and then as the creation of social scientific reflexivity in large portions of the population.[7]

Thus could be understood Durkheim's lectures on the history of education in France. Here he charted a four-phase chronology, beginning from the Carolingian epoch as the age of grammar whose successor was the early pre-absolutist (i.e. mediaeval) University of Paris. This was the scholastic era of logic and dialectic, in which masters grouped in corporations held mysterious sway over the 'secrets of syllogism and disputatio'. If the first, Carolingian age was that of grammatical formalism, and the second scholastic age of dialectical formalism, then the third classical and humanist age was that of literary formalism. This third age is that of the French absolutist state and court nobility. It drew on Renaissance classicism, Catholicized by and proselytized through the Jesuits from the sixteenth century. If the Renaissance also contained a Rabelais-influenced current which in a proto-modern sense encouraged the development of the cognitive faculties and unlimited acquisition of knowledge, dominant was the Erasmus-influenced humanist current in which emphasis instead was on the arts of expression and cultivation of taste.[8]

Durkheim opposed the formalisms and the abstraction from society of all three earlier epochs of French education. He observed – comparisons are appropriate with the modern novel of Balzac or Proust – that seventeenth-century humanist literature dealt with general and impersonal types, abstracted from all definite social context. This was to him part and parcel of an education system which taught that human nature was a 'sort of eternal reality, immutable, invariable independent of time and space'. Durkheim connected this with the abstract individualism of the eighteenth century, to which he opposed a concrete and moral individualism of particular individuals in a given society. He wanted education to be no longer abstract, but to encourage reflection 'on solid, firm, resistant objects'. He deplored the teaching of eternal notions of human nature, for which he substituted the teaching of 'what is irreducibly diverse in humanity'. More than a century earlier Condorcet had already proposed social science teaching in primary education for all, and at the same time advocated the avoidance in secondary education of the classical curriculum and its associated rhetoric. Durkheim himself became an extraordinary pedagogic power in France. At the Sorbonne his course in education was obligatory for all students who later would teach philosophy, history and French literature. He was able to initiate the teaching of sociology to prospective teachers at France's 200 écoles normales.[9]

In Foucault's *The Order of Things* there are effectively two different stages of epistemic modernization. The first, absolutism's 'classical' period, is based in the just mentioned principle of description, when rhetoric is purged so that the sciences can classify through clear and distinct ideas. The second 'modern' period features the principle of causation, based on the Darwinian model of organic systems. In order to sustain this sharp dichotomy, Foucault ignored the more highly codified natural sciences, physics and chemistry, already causal in the classical period. He instead focused on the least codified (and most 'humanist') of sciences – natural history, economics and eighteenth-century linguistics, which followed the principle of (descriptive) classification. Foucault's second modern episteme, however, dealt with the onset of more immanent and systemic thinking in the natural and human sciences.[10] This development of systems thinking, as Paul Rabinow has acutely observed in *French Modern*, was basic to the deepening of Western modernity. This comprised a change from a principle of representation to organicist assumptions. At the very end of the eighteenth century, the generation of thinkers sandwiched between the Lumières and Comtean and St Simonian positivism founded the Society for the Observation of Man. Its members included biologists Cuvier, Lamarck, Jussieu and St Hilaire, the physician Pinel and the philosophical linguist De Tracy. They referred to themselves as 'ideologues' and stated as their goal the unification of the sciences of man based on the rectification of language.[11] Their idea was fully in keeping with the principle of representation of natural history in the classic age: here nature was made up of individuals upon whom classifications were imposed.

Key to the classical model was not just this nominative principle but the assumption – in, for example, classical botany in its notion of 'habitat' – of a pre-existent harmony between species and habitat. The later modernist move to life-systems takes as axiomatic precisely the opposite, i.e. the absence of such pre-existent harmony. In France, encouraged by the experience of the cholera epidemic of 1832, biologists such as Lamarck and Bichat now began to speak not of habitat but of 'milieu', conceived as distinctly exterior to the organism, as a foreign environment which forced the organism to change if it were to adapt and survive. Georges Canguilhem, thus spoke of a theoretical vitalism, in which living beings are condemned to struggle in their milieu.[12] Looking forward to chapter 6, we should note the centrality of vitalism and the notion of life in both positivist (organicist systems theory) and anti-positivist Lebensphilophie. Adaptation and change could only take place in the individual organism – that is in life-systems – and hence Lamarck and Bichat both underscored the functioning of organisms in a physiology of systems. This perspective was quickly transferred over to the budding sociology, in which conservative theorists such as Bonald and Lammenais shifted attention from the individual to the collective. St Simon was one of the first literally to develop the sociological (as Hobbes did the political) metaphor of the body's organs. Taking over uncritically Bichat's model of the three basic organic functional capacities, he placed them as functions in a social order. Corresponding to Bichat's intellectual capacities was St Simon's scientific elite; to Bichat's motor functions his industrial class of engineers and workers; to Bichat's sensory capacities the class of artists, poets and ethical-religious leaders.[13]

Modernist life-systems theory also superseded early modernist mechanism. Early modernism proposed notions of mechanism or 'physicalism' in lieu of the previous metaphysics of religion. Thus classical mechanics presumed a world of isolated objects acting causally on one another. Descartes's cosmology equally assumed the absence of milieu, as action occurs through direct contact between objects. Newton thought ether to be the milieu, which would so to speak carry energy from one object to another. Buffon in biology saw such milieux in terms of climate and place. But this was a very weak notion of milieu compared to the later heuristic of system and environment. The mechanics model was also central in Early Modern political philosophy. Grotius and other Early Modern theorists of absolutist natural law did indeed move towards erasing rhetoric and conceptual clarity, especially in their notions of legitimation, but did not adopt modern mechanistic concepts. For political philosophy to become fully modern was only possible in social contract (or popular) natural law theory, in which civil society came to assume comparable importance with the state. And in which civil society was conceived – as in Hobbes – along the lines of Galilean particles acting causally on one another.[14]

This mechanism of l'âge classique then partly gave way to the later modern vitalist and organicist thinking of systems theory. These two epistemes coexist in contemporary social science explanation. Mechanistic explanation is first of all based on a notion of 'matter', while vitalistic explanation is based on a notion of 'life'. Mechanism is thus materialistic in the strict sense of the word. When Marx and the first generations of Marxists spoke of materialism, mechanics was prominent in their assumptions. Matter, pivotal to mechanics, has 'properties', while life has 'faculties'. 'Matter' consists of isolated entities, and hence notions of totality are weak in mechanical explanation. Vitalism's units of analysis, in contrast, are 'organs', as the faculties of living beings. And this entails strong notions of totality. Matter cannot be spoken of as having 'needs'. Organisms, as Lamarck underscored, must be so understood. What is vital has needs. And needs imply action and the altering of the organism, for purposes of survival, in relation to the environment.[15] All these issues continue to have importance in contemporary debates between 'conventional' and functionalist versions of causation and explanation. Conventional explanation is on the model of mechanics; functional explanation on the heuristic of vitalism. Mechanical explanation in the social sciences treats 'factors' which are properties of social matter and variable as isolated objects with causal powers. Functional explanation assumes totality of the system as living organism. The 'factors' involved in functional explanation are in effect faculties or organs which are explicable only via the totality of the system. The faculties or functions may often coincide with the different needs that the system has for its expanded reproduction. This is an understanding of causation that assumes not only 'feedback loops', but also totality.[16]

The mature Marx as historical materialist, and thus (in the best sense of the word) a positivist, wrote mainly in the paradigm of mechanical explanation. There are points in especially the second and third volumes of *Capital* where he crosses over into organicist explanation in speaking of systems reproduction: for example, in the discussions in volume 2 of the two departments of production. Later twentieth-century Marxism (for example, Althusser or G. A. Cohen) is, like Durkheim and Parsons, organicist, with the focus on system reproduction. In these analyses notions of totality are much more pronounced than in Marx. In much of Weber, especially in the notion of rationalization, there is a certain assumption, not of vitalism, but like in Marx of mechanical causation. Both mechanistic and vitalistic paradigms presuppose metanarratives of progress. But whereas in mechanism progress is – as in Condorcet or Weber – a matter of the application of knowledge, progress for vitalists takes place via a process of structural differentiation, i.e. via the development of ever greater complexity of the organs of systems. Habermas in *The Theory of Communicative Action* gave us a combination of both explanations of progress, arguing that structural differentiation in the realm of culture makes for clarity of thought and argument that then makes social progress through the application of knowledge possible.[17] Not just structural explanation, but theories of action too have mechanistic and vitalistic variants. Rational choice theory is, for example, a mechanistic theory of action, as are other positivistic action theories. If mechanics grew out of (and away from) classicism then vitalism grew from romanticism. Hence Goethe's notion of symbol (see chapters 6 and 9) fits with a vitalistic theory of action. Or more clearly perhaps, the young Marx's notion of human needs and faculties is pre-eminently part of a vitalist action theory.

Norms and Pathologies

Central to vitalism and systems-theoretical positivism are notions of normality and pathology, themselves based on the relationship between system and environment. Canguilhem observes widespread usage of the words 'normal' and 'normalized' from the turn of the nineteenth century. Rabinow observes that the French cholera epidemic of the early 1830s produced both 'classical' and 'modern' reactions. The classical explanation was to label cholera a 'contagious disease', for the *police de santé* to 'establish a grid, systematically inspect its sections, separate islands of unhealth and isolate to avoid contagion'. Moderns would regard it not as a contagious but as an 'infectious' disease, and would investigate how it might be produced by its environment, especially the living conditions of the urban poor who were most susceptible.[18] Modernity, then, saw the birth of public health notions of hygiene, the social question and the collection of social statistics in terms of normality and pathology, system and environment. The social question in England probably more than anywhere else gave birth to particularly British social work oriented sociology and to the garden city idea innovated by British urbanism. It was the social question (no doubt also motivated by the Darwinian heuristic) that fostered organism/milieu thinking in the human sciences. Crucial here was the very weight of the *masses* of individuals. And these were masses, i.e. crushed into big cities, at the same time as individuals, i.e. isolated as individuals when cut off from their rural *gemeinschaftlich* roots. Thus Nietzsche deplored the normative power of mass-ness and average-ness that pervaded modern culture and spatial organization. Norm thus means not just regulation or guidance, but also average.[19]

Normative power and averageness parallel very neatly Durkheim's two definitions of 'social fact'. Both of these definitions of social fact are present in his *Rules of Sociological Method*. The first famous definition is that of social fact as 'institutionalized norms', i.e. as exterior to individuals and as having coercive and imperative power over these individuals. The second is prevalent in Durkheim's *Suicide*, where he refers to social statistics (i.e. varying suicide statistics in different social and geographical groups) themselves as 'social facts'. On this count social facts are aggregate properties of individuals. Social facts can be normal in three ways. First, they can serve as institutionalized norms, as morally regulatory imperatives to social agents. Second, as aggregate properties they tell us about average, about statistical means and standard deviations, about what 'normally' occurs.[20] In this sense too the budding applied science of the massive collection of statistics could give us these sorts of averages. According to Canguilhem and to Rabinow, the social statisticians converged together these two notions of normality. Indeed, for the statisticians the human traits under consideration 'were not normal (i.e. normative) because they were found frequently, but they were found frequently because they were normal, and in that sense normative for a given way of life'.[21] This leads us to the third notion of social facts and normativity: social facts themselves can be normal or pathological to the extent that they help a society adapt to its environment.[22] In this sense Durkheim talks of normal versus pathological divisions of labour. But the Nietszchean could see a dystopia of 'the social' at the end of all this. With the hypostatization of the average, instead of the ideal, to the rank of imperative, social systems would be produced which in the end would *not* thrive in their environment. Such is Michel Foucault's dystopic modern of normalization and individuation all intended to reproduce the social.

The transition from classical to modern is paradigmatically observable in the French institutional locus of world classicism, the Ecole des Beaux-Arts. The Ecole was founded only in 1819 – its predecessor the Academie Royale d'Architecture having been founded in 1671 – and was closed in 1968. It combined craft training through intense, master-supervised design courses with the theoretical training of the lecture hall. Classicism in French architecture had already been given its benchmark formulation in the mid-eighteenth century in the writings of J. F. Blondel, who gave shape to the theory of 'type'. In this 'type' was a question of properly representing the character of different sorts of buildings. To Quatremère de Quincy, 'Secretary in Perpetuity' of the Ecole des Beaux-Arts and author of the canonical *Dictionnaire historique d'architecture*, this meant 'the art of characterising . . . of rendering sensible by material forms the intellectual qualities and moral ideas which can be expressed in buildings'.[23] Thus material signifiers of buildings, or their elements, were to correspond to a meaning or idea of say theatres halls, colleges and arsenals. In classicism elements – walls, columns and the like – had to be a characteristic expression of the orders, which themselves were determined by the idea of the building. These were the eternal principles of classical beauty and beauty was the goal of classical architecture – to be found in mature form above all in Roman architecture and the Renaissance.

The challenge to classicism came first from historicism which argued, *pace* the aesthetics of beauty, for an architecture in which the building suits its environment. Thus Viollet le Duc at the Ecole, maverick partisan of gothic cathedrals, argued that each culture had its own rationality. And Henri Labrouste shocked his judges among Institut de France architects by choosing as the site for his Ecole project an Etruscan bridge which came nowhere near – neither, by the way, did ancient Greek architecture – to the Beaux-Arts ideal of mature classicism. Labrouste was of the controversial (systems/environment) view that architecture should correspond to local conditions. The challenge also came from another kind of functionalism. On this modern model, architectural value depends now on functionality and simplicity. Now type becomes a question of the inner working of a plan. Here elements – e.g. walls, openings, columns in their combination – make up intermediate units – porches, stairs, rooms – in which both elements and units are to be designed according to function and plan.[24]

This second sort of systems based modern architecture had its origins among the engineers trained at the Ecole Polytechnique (founded 1795). Compared to social theory, architecture came late to modernity. Architecture had neither mechanism nor functionalism until recently, from the 1920s and even 1950s and 1960s. But then architecture had both mechanism and organicism all at once. Whereas the human sciences had taken their mechanism from the isolated entities of Newtonian mechanics, mechanism for the architects was already that of the functioning machine. Not theoretical mechanics but *real machines* were their model, as they were for the visual arts – constructionism, futurism, the Bauhaus, De Stijl – more generally. And at this point machines themselves were seen as functioning systems. In this shift from classicism to mechanism/functionalism in architecture and painting came also a transmutation from classical classification or description to modern causal immanence. Instead of architecture or painting being signifiers attempting to represent an idea or a reality, they became self-referential systems themselves, so that each signifier could only be understood in terms of its separate immanent system. This systems heuristic entered sociology, architecture and painting at the time of the rise of the industrial working class. This is significant in the context of the heuristic of speed, indifference and flows – addressed in chapters 11 to 13 – which have risen concurrently with the emergence of today's global information culture.

Symbol: Durkheim and Mauss

Total Social Facts

Milan Kundera in *The Unbearable Lightness of Being* gives us the first beginnings of a theory of symbol. Kundera does this at the start of his novel via a particular reading of Nietszche's eternal return. Kundera holds that only with repetition can life take on meaning. Only with the eternal return of the same can being take on any kind of weight. Without repetition, without ritual, we are instead doomed to the curse of modernity and its fleetingness. We are doomed to the 'unbearable lightness' of being. Kundera's Nietzsche, the Nietzsche of 'weight' and 'meaning', is not the postmodernists' Nietzsche – of, for example, Deleuze, for whom the modernist fleetingness and de-territorialization does not go far enough. It is instead the Nietzsche of what German sociological theorists call the 'second Romantic' (*zweite Romantik*). It is Stefan George's 'metaphysical' Nietzsche. It is the poetic of the Goethe who pitted the weight of Germanic symbol against the already over lightness of French allegory.

To start with Kundera is thus to define symbol and meaning via repetition. In this sense, prior to the transition from nature to culture, events, things, words had no meaning. They were all fleeting events. With the emergence of repetition, with ritual, a sacred realm develops, separating out from the profane. With the development of the sacred, signals can become signifiers and entities, words, events can begin to have meaning. It is also at this point that symbolic structures become possible with the formation of a conscience collective. The conscience collective first enables the ability to distinguish 'in' from 'out' groups, 'them' from 'us'; second, it permits classification, it permits the development of a grid for a particular 'way of seeing'.

But mere repetition is not sufficient. A second condition must be met if symbols, and the symbolic, are to exist. The development of a sacred, the development of a symbolic sphere, is at the same time the birth of the universal. Hence Nietzsche held in *The Birth of Tragedy* that the Dionysian rites – pagan, yet operating out of a sacred and symbolic sphere – were at the origin of the logical categories. But, as Kant himself was well aware, universals may be more or less mediated: that is, universals range themselves along a continuum according to their degree and type of mediation; some are stituated at the universalist pole, others at the particularist extreme of what must still be a (very low) level of generality. Thus the universals involved in Kantian perception are less mediated than those involved in his concepts of understanding. But even the least mediated universals, the most primitive symbolisms or categories, are dependent not just on repetition, not just on ritual – after all an animal can repeat stereotypedly a behaviour without it having *meaning*.

To be symbols repeated activities or objects must be mediated through what Marcel Mauss called a 'total social fact', which itself is present in our experience in every 'fragment of our life'. In other words, no symbols are possible without the existence of a system of symbols. Or a given repeated activity may only enter the sphere of symbol in the presence of a symbol system.[25] Symbols must be mediated first through a system. Symbol is to system what *parole* is to *langue* and action to rules. The difference among the symbols in the system, or the conventions of the system, makes meaning (and thus symbol) possible. This is true with all sorts of semiosis or discursive signification. Allegory, in contradistinction (as we noted in chapter 4), signifies *non*-discursively, and instead figurally, not through semiosis, but through mimesis. Allegory does not depend on, in fact cannot have, system. For Mauss there is also a second mediation normally present where symbols are concerned, and that is the activities of a group of symbol specialists. In tribal societies these are mainly magicians, witch doctors and shamans, occupying marginal positions. Their symbolic lives are quasi-autonomous from the masses in their societies. Theirs is a 'special' as distinct from normal mode of transcription of the total social fact. Their mode of transcription is on the one hand inferior to the normal: witch doctors and shamans are usually recruited from those very low in prestige, from relative outsiders. Yet these same 'outsiders' recruited from 'the disabled, the ecstatic, nervous types' are at the same time more 'sensitive to contradictions and gaps in social structure'. They are the 'abnormals' who, as Lévi-Strauss notes, 'transcribe the state of the group and make one or another of its contents manifest'.[26]

So symbols are doubly mediated, through the total social fact of the symbolic system and through the symbol specialists. But what is the intersection of symbol, as structure – and here structure is conceived more along the lines of *langue* than of social structure – and the social actor. For Mauss this is the 'habitus' and especially the body. Thus Mauss's 'Les techniques du corps', written some thirty years after his collaboration with Durkheim in 1934, deals with how we turn our bodies into products of our techniques and representations. Bodies on this view are not part of the conscious ego or 'discursive consciousness'. The body is instead, as Bourdieu notes, integral to the pre-conscious, to practical consciousness, to the '*sens practique*'.[27] The techniques are learned and in principle available to consciousness, though we are not conscious of them in our practices. For example, the tennis player must not think of her stroke technique if she is to hold service on break-point. The later Mauss, like Lévi-Strauss heavily influenced by psychoanalysis, wanted instead to emphasize unconscious factors, in which processes are in principle unavailable to the conscious mind. On this view the total social fact is expressed in unconscious categories, which then form the interface of subjectivity and collectivity. 'In religion', Mauss wrote, 'as in magic it is the unconscious ideas which are the active ones.' Comparisons with the work of Jung are fully in order here, but Mauss (and by implication Durkheim) did not attribute a Jungian primacy to referents ('artefacts') in the unconscious. Mauss's unconscious gives instead governing semantic powers to the symbol as signifier.[28]

To understand Durkheim and Mauss's *Primitive Classifications* it is helpful to consider Mauss's concurrently written *La Magie* (1902–3). And especially the concept of *mana* which Mauss develops there. This notion of mana explicitly figures less importantly in *Primitive Classifications* but is taken up later with a vengeance by Durkheim in *The Elementary Forms of Religious Life*. Here, as in *Primitive Classifications*, absolutely central is Nietzsche's problematic in *The Birth of Tragedy*: to trace back the fundamental categories of human thought to their earliest and most fundamental progenitors. To trace back the origins of rationality to their earliest basis in irrationality: to find, in other words, the origins of logic in 'sentiments'. This entails a particular notion of cultural modernization: neither a two-stage, tradition to modernity, chronology; nor a 'continuist' model, like notions of rationalization; but instead – as in Weber's methodological writings on religion – a three-stage discontinuist model, whose stages are the primitive, the world religions and the modern. Here the (Aristotelian/Kantian) logical categories of the human mind are seen as having a genealogy traceable from mana through the world religions (religions of China, India, Judaeo-Christianity, Islam). For Mauss mana would be the ultimate source of grounding of Kant's *a priori* synthetic judgements. The fact that these judgements are 'synthetic' entails the existence of things external to the logical mind. It entails that thinking is a relationship between symbols and things. Thus in Mauss's *La magie* thought takes place through the mode in which the mind situates the magical act in the presence of things. The same with mana. Mana 'is the expression of social sentiments which are formed – sometimes inexorably and universally, sometimes fortuitously – with regard to certain things, chosen for the most part in an arbitrary fashion'.[29]

There are three processes at work here then. The first is the relationship of thought to things in mana, in a world with an extraordinary surplus of signifiers over referents (things). This surplus (of mana), according to Lévi-Strauss, is 'shared out' among the things 'in accordance with the laws of symbolic thinking' in a series of 'semantic functions whose role is to enable symbolic thinking'. The second concerns the nature of mana's signifying substrate itself. This is too undifferentiated for logical thinking: it contains antinomies in the same symbol of force and action; noun, adjective and verb all at once.[30] Modernization will bring differentiation and separation of these qualities into the logical categories and into a distinct ordering of utterances and propositions. Mana's symbols are the very most unmediated of universals. Modernization will bring a process of mediation through emptying out. As the symbols are emptied of content they become the 'forms' that Simmel and German Lebensphilosophie so deplored. In this sense the poetic thinking that Goethe and the vitalists of the *zweite Romantik* advocated was akin to the primitive symbolic in its very unmediated, and thus full (and not empty) notion of language. This is discursive signification and takes place via not mimesis but semiosis. Yet it is a semiosis of signifiers of low mediation. The symbolic is less mediated than not only scientific thinking, in which emptied and hence abstract signifiers are able to stand in a position of very good adequation to their referents. It is also less mediated than prosaic language, with the latter's adequation of the signified in a relatively univocal fashion. The very fullness and unmediatedness of poetic language and the *langue* of the primitives' symbolic – with images, with their gods and demons, with adjectives that are at the same time nouns and verbs – blocks adequation of referent and signified.

Les mots (les gens) et les choses

It is to this view of cultural modernization as the emptying out of the symbolic that Durkheim and Mauss's benchmark, yet too often neglected, extended article 'De quelques formes primitives de la classification', subtitled 'contribution à l'étude des représentations collectives', was primarily devoted. In *Primitive Classifications*, although the origins of the modern logical categories are traced, focus is quite distinctly not on 'categories' but on 'classifications'. This is important because classifications are about the relations between representations and things, while logical categories seem rather to be situated in the realm of thought. It makes sense in the context of such classificatory evolution to distinguish between two notions of cultural modernization. One, associated perhaps with Habermas, is a process of differentiation – effectively of signified, signifier and referent, and of poetic language from moral language from descriptive language, so that clear and distinct statements in each of these realms can be made. In the other, often asociated with German *Kulturpessimismus*, modernization proceeds by the emptying out of content of what become cultural forms. The motor of cultural modernization in Durkheim and

Mauss is much closer to this second notion, through emptying out. Modernization in both of these senses is importantly Kantian. The difference here is that whereas in Habermas modernization proceeds by differentiation of the spheres of transcendental thought, in the second model it effectively proceeds via the emptying out of the Kantian categories of intuition – of time and space. Here again Durkheim and Mauss's vision is closer to cultural pessimism than to Habermas.[31] Yet only one dimension of classificatory modernization in Durkheim and Mauss involves changing categories of time and space. It mostly is a question of the emptying out of other entities. And cardinal for them is that what is emptied out is the *social* content of these entities.

Primitive Classifications describes a process in which symbols which serve to classify the world undergo a process of transformation. These symbols undergo a process of de-personification or de-societalization, in a history that spans primitive totems, the Gods of the world religions and the categories of modern logic. The book aims to demonstrate the irrational grounding of the rational: that classifications exist for reasons of 'sentiment' and not because of 'pure ideas'.[32] More precisely, Durkheim and Mauss hold that our 'logical operations' – which enable us 'to define, induct and deduce' – draw on 'a whole set of elements from 'a number of sources' which are 'fully foreign to logic'.[33] This applies, they continue, most fully to the logical function which enables us to classify. This 'classificatory function', Durkheim and Mauss note, harks back to Aristotle's discussion of genus and species. We classify 'in genus and species to subsume some fact under others, to determine their relations of inclusion or exclusion'.[34] Further, every classification, every subsumption – of species under genus – presupposes a hierarchical order.

Durkheim and Mauss disagree with the rejection of classification as pre-scientific by contemporaneous evolutionary theory. They instead see science as today's end of a continuum of development of classificatory systems to deal with an environment (and objects under study) of increasing complexity. The Aristotelian basis of this earlier classificatory tradition, however, foregrounded specific difference and not direct passage from one genre to another. Durkheim and Mauss contest these Aristotelian assumptions and further contend that the 'mere fact of the existence of similarities does not entail the existence of classes'. Their view is far less nominalist than Aristotle's and rooted instead in a deep and fundamental sociology of the symbolic. They argue that for classes (of things and people) to exist there must be a sort of 'reunification in a sort of ideal milieu'.[35] Classification, in other words, is situated in the symbolic realm. 'Consciousness is only a continuous stream of representations which merge with one another: when distinctions begin to appear they are quite fragmentary – past from present, left from right, resemblance.'[36] Only when these representations are symbolically coded does culture fully exist and classification become possible.

'La classification des choses reproduit cette classification des hommes.'[37] Is there a more fecund sentence than this in all of sociology? Durkheim and Mauss's utterance gives shape not only to the entirety of their classic essay, but also to contemporary sociological canon in, say, the work of Pierre Bourdieu. 'The classification of things reproduces this classification of men.' Or 'men classify things because they themselves are divided into classes'.[38] What can this mean, however? In modern societies, as Bourdieu shows, it means that one's social position determines how one will classify and especially it determines what one's hierarchy of classificatory values is. In primitive societies it means so much more. It means first 'that men think under the form of groups'. It means that the classes (that social agents are divided into) themselves recast the symbolic and become the classificatory principles. Thus the subsumption of species under genus is only possible under the condition that at one historical time people thought of 'clan as subsumed under phratry'. Thus 'the first logical categories were social categories; the first classes of things were classes of men into which things were integrated'.[39] In the most primitive Australian tribes, Durkheim and Mauss note, the 'totems symbolise lineages, phratries and clans and all things in the world – including the trees, sky and wind – are divided among the lineages: crocodiles, for example would come under a specific lineage'. The sacred, based on the social division into lineages, becomes the set of classifiers under which all things and events in the world, mutually exclusively and exhaustively, are divided. This also goes, they observe, for causes and effects. In the case of events such as, say, a death, one was directed to look for a mark that led to a lineage or a matrimonial class.[40]

In primitive classifications, and symbolic classifications more generally, relationships between things are prismatically relationships between social agents. 'Things are considered to be an integral part of society and it is their place in society which determines their place in nature.'[41] In other words, things themselves are seen to have social relations. Thus in Marx's commodity fetishism, tribal societies ascribed human and superhuman powers to things, which later, taking the form of exchange-value, took on the same powers for modern societies. Durkheim and Mauss noted that where moderns might metaphorically speak of things as having social or 'moral relations', for primitives these things were seen as literally related. Yet in modernity our 'logical relations' have their grounding in the tribal societies' 'domestic relations', in these archaic 'sentimental relations between things'.[42] Sometimes these take on economic and political form. For example, 'for Zunis, animals which symbolise the fundamental clans' 'are sovereign over their sub-clans and of beings of all kinds attached to the latter', as 'owned objects are seen (almost politically) as inferior to their owner'.[43] Modernization entails an emptying out from things of these social qualities. It entails not a Vergesellschaftung, but an *Ent*gesellschaftung of things. But these de-societalized things still, like Marx's emptied out commodities, maintain even more power than ever over us. The same would be true of that ultimately heterogeneous thing for Simmel, money, which sets the paradigm for the dominance of means over ends in modern society. More recent work in what might be called the sociology of technology or 'social technics' points to the considerable powers of de-societalized things over social agents. For example, Bruno Latour has spoken of the power of things in laboratories; and Luc Boltanski and Laurent Thevenot of the power over us of seemingly ultimately harmless things, like train timetables.[44]

Third, social agents have strong affective investment in both sacralized classifications and the things they classify. Without such original affective investment, i.e. without the original sentimental relation – often in the shape of 'religious emotions' – a category and its successors cannot exist. Each category, each thing, 'has its own affective value'. It is things, then, which are sacred or profane, enemy or friend, pure or impure.[45] This sort of affective investment in the classificatory symbols coupled with their very conception as peopled with social relations makes clear and distinct thought very difficult, if not impossible. Here Weber's plurality of warring gods and demons of the primitive tribal dystopia are cast as logical and moral categories themselves.

In such a context Durkheim and Mauss wrote that the history of ever more scientific classification is that of the 'progressive weakening of social affectivity', 'leaving free place for the reflective thought of individuals'.[46] For reflexive modernization to take place, social affectivity in classificatory symbols must significantly weaken. It must do so through two processes: first, the weakening of affective investment of social agents in the classificatory symbols; second, the de-societalization (Entgesellschaftung) of the symbols themselves. And this is the seeming contradiction and surely the irony of reflexive modernization. In traditional societies there is the coexistence of a highly complex symbolic sphere and a simple social sphere; and in modern societies of a greatly simplified symbolic sphere and a complex social. The precondition of societal modernization, of societal complexification, is symbolic simplification.

If 'the classification of things' does 'reproduce the classification of men', then just what are the most important classes of social agents for Durkheim and Mauss? There is very little talk of wealth, income, labour market, gender and age stratification in *Primitive Classifications*. So surely Durkheim and Mauss are not referring to anything like the Marxo-Weberian class and status stratification which informs Bourdieu's social classifiers in *Distinction*.

What they seem in fact to be referring to is simply the most significantly sensed social cleavages of any given time. Thus, as indicated above, there are often examples given of classification via phratry, clan and lineage. But equally, time and space distinctions are important for Durkheim and Mauss. They offer a four-stage modernization thesis: (a) primitive tribes, the Australian religions; (b) less primitive tribes, the Zuni, the Sioux in North America; (c) Chinese religion (and by implication all the world religions); and (d) modernity.

The second stage of less primitive tribal societies is seen as having classificatory symbols based on the differentiation of space under tribal categories. Though totemism exists, the 'classificatory universe' in these societies takes on a greater systematicity, a more strict coordination and subordination of parts than in the more primitive Australian tribal predecessors.[47] In a further stage of modernization, corresponding to the world religions, totemism disappears and instead in Chinese, Ancient Greek and Egyptian myths the classification of things is taken from religion. Here the process of emptying out, of abstraction, proceeds on several fronts. First there is the abstraction of the sacred, of the symbolic realm, from its immanence in everyday practices and its location as a separate transcendental realm. Second, there is the more precise arrangement and subsumption of classificatory genres under one another. This systematicity is encouraged by divinatory systems, with their temporal concern with afterlives. Third, the classifiers which share out nature and the universe become fewer and more simplified. Fewer in the shift from, say, a clan's totems to the pantheons of Greek gods, and even more simple in, for example, Indian religions' division of all things, including the gods, between the sky, the atmosphere and the earth, and the Chinese division between yin and yang. And more simplified in that in each of these stages the classifiers themselves are emptied out, are 'de-peopled': from totems to Greek gods to yin and yang.[48]

In this, space and time are important classifiers. In Chinese religions space and time figure as classifieds and classifiers. They are classified, i.e. subsumed, under the winds and powers of the 'eight cardinal points'. Yet space and time – not separated in the sense that the 'four regions' are paired with the 'four seasons' – themselves figure as categories under which things and people are classified. Time is especially important. With modernization, as Giddens has also noted, it becomes 'emptied out'. Heterogeneous time becomes homogenized.[49] It becomes progressively less cyclical and more unidirectional. Hence Durkheim and Mauss point to divinatory systems such as the oracles and astrology. Astrological time is heterogeneous and peopled with planets and animals. It is cyclical time: the Chinese horoscope assigns to each year an animal over a period of twelve years, which then repeats itself five times in a sixty-year cycle. Yet this is more simplified and more unidirectional than primitive cyclical time based on seasons and crops. Subsequent notions of historical time based on genealogies of Greek gods lead to further reduced multiplicity and clearer relations of coordination and subordination. And time via the Greek god genealogies is still heterogeneous in comparison with Jewish monotheism: the messianic, metanarrative, time of the latter is even more simplified and unidirectional.[50] It is not far from fully modern notions.

6

Symbol and Allegory: Simmel and German Sociology

Values and Facts

I traced in some detail in part I how urban and spatial modernity developed out of, and against, a classical and humanist tradition. In part II, I am looking at the two modernisms that developed in early sociological theory. Both of these are primarily defined in terms of abstraction and autonomous subjectivity. One is French; the other is German. The French version is positivist. It is based on the model of an abstract 'system' which is then used to understand social relations. The German model is more of an interpretative sociology. It opposed systems and positivism, holding that the latter was corrupting real social relations. To this it counterposed an inner sphere modelled on the lines of a poetics. This inner sphere can be understood under the heading of 'symbol'. But this model – whose precursor of course was Romanticism – is also abstracted from the social, also exemplifies autonomous subjectivity. Hence it is in many respects the other side of high modernity in social theory.

Classics and Moderns

If German thought, a very late developer until the second half of the eighteenth century, continually defined itself in contrast to its French counterpart, then French modernity defined itself largely against what came before in France, i.e. classicism. At issue was an extended war of position of *anciens* and *modernes*. A war of the humanities against the application of natural science principles in the study of philosophy and of man. A war in which among others Descartes and Comte and Durkheim played the leading roles on the side of the moderns. Even during the eighteenth century there was no sharp distinction in France between natural science on the one hand and literature and the humanities on the other. Buffon, for example, who was elected to the Académie française in 1753, was perhaps best known in his famous natural history as a stylist. But later attacks of the classics against the moderns were foreshadowed by humanists such as Pascal, who observed that natural science could be investigated by machines, whereas the 'moral sciences', theology, jurisprudence, history, ethics and politics must always remain human because they require the use of language.[1] It is this sort of thought that still today bears its traces in the low status of the natural sciences and the class background of natural scientists in France, and especially in England, today. Worst, of course, for the *anciens* was when the natural sciences began to make inroads from the Enlightenment into the moral and human disciplines themselves. What did the classicists of the nineteenth century hold against the moderns in the new born sociology? Classicists such as De Bonald disputed the abstraction of Enlightenment thought and held it to blame for the French Revolution.[2] If the anti-communist revolutionaries of 1989 blamed the abstract blue-prints of Marxism for their ills; the anti-democratic counter-revolutionaries blamed the abstract blueprints of Rousseau and others for the excesses of 1789. The *anciens* disputed the belief in progress of the positivists and held instead that the moral sciences should be concerned with old and timeless truths. The classics, further, were in sharp discord with any modernist notions of *reflexivity*. Maurras, a Catholic – through the Jesuits classical humanism had been brought safely under the banner of Catholicism – blamed the Protestants for the continued self-examination which never led to a final and stable verdict. The *ancien* had his classical ideal and had no need for reflexive questioning of the latter. Alternatives, heterodoxy, were ruled out. Literature, the classics held, should be a time defying aid to life. As should be the lessons learned from metaphysics, which stood counterposed to the cold understanding.[3]

Herbert Schnädelbach has observed that from Socratic Greece theoreti-cal discourse has tended to fall into categories of, on the one hand, 'dianoetics', and, on the other, 'noetics'.[4] 'Dianoetics' assumes an activist theoretical investigator armed with concepts and a system which he or she applies to the world. 'Noetics' assumes a much more passive observer who is responsive to the truths of the world. Dianoetics features the investigator as practitioner, while noetics foregrounds a sort of visual or perceptual model of the observer. Kuhn's notion of scientific paradigms as well as Popper's of falsification are eminently dianoetic views of human thought. Classical empiricism, on the other hand, is arguably noetic. The Kantian revolution was dianoetic. It championed the activist categories of the un-derstanding. The two *ancien regimes* against which Kant rebelled – meta-physics and empiricism, for both of which knowledge was acquired via intuition or vision – were in important respects noetic.

In this context the French *anciens* were ultimately a noetic opposition to the dianoetic discourse of the modern positivists. Noetic classicists advocated insight as opposed to argument as the way to truth. Thus Charles Péguy, though a man of the left, mocked the 'argufying' of the positivist Enlightenment, and said that positivists like Durkheim, instead of providing a remedy for the anomie of contemporaneous France, were instead a symptom of such anomie.[5] In the same vein, the classical and noetic mentality opposed the positivist's obsession with 'method'. The mould was set here by the likes of Descartes and Comte, who methodically organized their lives, their thought and their writing style. Comte, himself a great influence on the methodology of John Stuart Mill, in fact emulated the writing style of the natural sciences – of Berthellot and Cuvier.[6] In counterposition to this dianoetic method, the noetic mentality advocated 'spontaneity', not the anything goes, largely activist and anarchist spontaneity of Feyerabend, but instead the cultivated responsiveness and sensibility of classically educated gentlemen.

The classical and noetic mentality pitted the generalist, the educated whole man, against Weber's specialists 'without a heart', and opposed Durkheim's appointment at the New Sorbonne. They rejected the *modernes'* activist notion of a utilitarian, 'work society' – which they associated with the deplorably modern education on offer in German universities – in favour of an education oriented towards the aesthetic and the appreciation of harmonic proportions. In the New Sorbonne, the introduction of modern languages, of the modern PPE degree at Oxford, of analytic philosophy, ran counter to the classic advocates of the Old Sorbonne and of ancient languages and 'Greats' at Oxford. The integration of theory and practice, offered by the modern university, was anathema. Julian Benda reflected the best sense of the classical mentality in his famous references to the *'trahison des clercs'*. Here Benda, himself a Jew and a man of the liberal left, was not attacking socialists who had deserted the cause or become apolitical. The traitors at issue instead were nationalist writers of the extreme right, Maurras and Barrès, and their *trahison* was the abandonment of eternal (humanist) literary values for the practical (fascisant) goals of the moment.[7]

The *anciens* opposed above all the moderns' version of 'system', and the normal versus pathological model of positivism. Positivism's organicist model was based on Spencer's biological heuristic of social differentiation and system reproduction and Comte's ideas of social and cerebral hygiene. This early systems theory seemed to be activist dianoetics at its extreme. To this the noetic counterpart was ideographic instead of nomothetic.[8] Attention was directed away from conceptual systems to Roman law and to Greek classical culture: to society, not as a system of institutions and norms, but instead society as the social life of the French upper classes. Though the classical mentality was attuned to the ideographic rather than the nomothetic, the ideographic was not understood via the particular, say via the daily situation of a peasant or a prostitute of the boulevards; but via the ideal, the best incarnation of humanity. This resonated with the elite mentality of the classics. Thus Tarde's elite-theoretical and classical Institut de l'action française disputed the whole levelling process in which Durkheim's New Sorbonne was engaged. Durkheim's explorations into anthropology were received with a jaundiced eye by classics, appalled by the presumption that French culture could be placed alongside primitive cultures as only one of a number of other cultures; that Catholicism was seen as intrinsically no better than the religions of the primitives.[9]

Paradigmatic for Norbert Elias's *Civilizing Process* was the French court nobility. *Zivilisation* to Germans, and to Elias, produced first French classical culture and then its positivist successor. German letters and thought came to maturity centuries later than their French counterpart, partly because of the characteristic weakness of a German *noblesse de robe*. The common wisdom in the German states at the turn of the nineteenth century was that if German culture was ever to have much of a chance, it must do what it could to model itself – just as the Prussian and later German bureaucracy was modelled on French absolutist rule – after France. In opposition to this common wisdom, and to French classicism as well as to the French Enlightenment, grew German romanticism and *Kultur*.[10]

If there is one central figure in the German notion of *Kultur* it is Goethe's concept of symbol. Here 'symbol' was counterposed to the 'allegory' of not Spanish, but French, classical literature. A number of qualities were implicit if not explicit in the Goethean concept. 'Symbol', for example, was private and interior to subjectivity, while 'allegory' was associated with the publicity of the salons, the manners of court society. Symbol was deep and its signifiers laden with meaning, while allegory was superficial and ornamental, its signifiers empty. Symbol was poetic, allegory prosaic when not essayistic. Allegory pointed to no deep underlying mosaic of meanings and collective representations that made up an organic national culture or the subjectivity of its poets. Instead its signification was more or less mimetic, in which point for point correspondence existed between one narrative and another. Symbol assumed a multitude of possible meanings: of meaning pointing in many directions at once. It assumed a whole lattice of symbols whose deeper structures were to make themselves visible in the *parole* of the poet.[11]

Goethe at the same time turned his guns against French positivism in his novel *Die Wahlverwandschaften*. *Wahlverwandschaften* means elective affinities and has underlain sociological thought from Weber's *Protestant Ethic* to Pierre Bourdieu's notion of 'homology'. But whereas post-war sociologists have often found the concept fuzzy and even romantic, Goethe had quite opposite intentions in mind. Goethe's elective affinities came from contemporaneous chemistry and the mechanical assumptions of affinities between natural scientific elements. Goethe ironically criticized the whole clock-work society which to his mind was operating ever more on the principles of Newtonian mechanics.[12] The origins of a hermeneutically oriented, interpretative sociology and the *Geisteswissenschaften* more generally in Germany were grounded in the same anti-*zivilisatorisch* world-view. After the positivist interregnum following the deaths of Hegel and Goethe in 1832, and lasting through the *Gründerjahre* of the Second Reich, Wilhelmine Germany saw the second coming of anti-positivist and anti-French reaction in the rise of the new *Lebensphilosophie*. This was Germany's *zweite Romantik* whose forefathers were Goethe and Nietzsche. Germany's second roman-tic, out of which interpretative sociology was born,[13] counterposed the isolation of the poet to the positivist conception of science as a profession. Unlike the French literary *hommes de lettres*, the purveyor of German *Kultur* was the poet.

Theoretical figures of the new *Lebensphilosophie* such as Wilhelm Dilthey contrasted life to the life-destroying system proposed by positivists such as Comte, Mill and Spencer: they endorsed the isolated and introspective poetic subjectivity to the instrumental rationality of an increasingly ma-chine-like society. For Dilthey inner experience or *Innerlichkeit* consisted (foreshadowing Bergson) of the very facts of consciousness. This psy-chological life, this subjectivity, corresponded not to Kant's categories of logic but rather to Kantian intuition, and the metaphor of the eye replacing the cold abstraction of the understanding. Thus Spengler understood his-tory not through logic but as physiognomical feeling and illumination and Troeltsch in terms of plastic-sensual perception and sensual thinking. Dilthey rejected the abstraction of the nomothetic and the structural for the ideographic perception of a 'single life', as the key to historical thinking became psychology. Dilthey in his inaugural address in Basel in effect called for a Second Romantic in the cultural sciences, evoking the philo-sophical constellations of Schelling and Hegel as the logical and metaphysi-cal extension of the work of the poets Lessing and Goethe.[14]

If any one German embodied this *zweite Romantik* it was the poet Stephan George, whose inner circle counted Georg Simmel and whose influence extended to Weber and Lukács among many others. The George circle received Nietzsche as a metaphysician and constructed a notion of *Innerlichkeit* along the lines of the above-mentioned Goethean symbolic. George pitted poetic *Innerlichkeit* against a corrupt society which the French *hommes de lettres* merely allegorically mimed. He rejected the sociological notion of society for an 'inward sociability'. His notion of 'life' foreshadow-ing the idea of 'life-world' was at the same time a rejection of what Georg Simmel later was to call *das Soziale*. The Georgean poetic was thoroughly of a piece with Nietzsche's elitist ethos of master moralities. George admired Mallarmé because his language was incomprehensible to the masses and in fact modelled his own circle on the lines of Mallarmé's Parisian circle of symbolist poets. The object of poetry – and by extension the object of the cultural sciences – was for George not a question of progress or social engagement but instead the 'perfection of the poet's own beauty and being'. The goal of education was the man capable of poetic excitation, and the *Geistes-* or *Kulturwissenschaften*, whose practitioners are conceived along the lines of the solitary sage, were to stand in the service of poetry.[15] George, above other contemporaries, served as the model for Weber's concept of charisma, which pitted the inner versus the outer, the prophet versus the dogma of the bureaucratic priest, the genius versus rule and the hero versus convention. In each case the second term – outer, dogma, priest, rule, convention – corresponded to French, first classical and then positivist, *Zivilisation*; the first term to *Lebensphilosophie* and German *Kultur*.

Between Positivism and *Lebensphilosophie*

In between the *lebensphilosophische* charismatic prophet-hero and the positivist dystopia of dogma, priest, rule and convention stood neo-Kantianism and the Weberian ethic of responsibility. This problematique followed the dictates neither of *Lebensphilosophie*'s inner spheres nor of the positivist and instrumentally rational outer spheres of 'system', but responsibly dealt with the conflicting demands of the several spheres in a truly modern decentred subject.[16] Indeed, the first generation of classical sociologists – Simmel, Durkheim, Weber, Tönnies and even Dilthey – operated in this broad neo-Kantian spectrum – with Durkheim and Weber on the positivist end of the spectrum and Dilthey on the vitalist end. Neo-Kantianism occupied the central sections of a continuum which extended from the hard positivism of Comte, Mill and Spencer (in Germany Schäffle, Lilienfeld and Fechner) to the fully blown *Lebensphilosophie* of Nietzsche, Bergson, George and Gundolf.

The major criterion separating individuals into camps of positivists, neo-Kantians and *Lebensphilosophen* was the scope given to science compared to the scope given to philosophy. Positivists would tend to reduce culture rather completely to the scientific; neo-Kantians gave a good deal of scope to science but left a lot of space – as Kant did in his second critique – to philosophy; while *Lebensphilosophen* would give science very little play at all, assimilating very much the whole of human activity and culture to a poetically coloured notion of philosophy. Whereas the positivists, as Parsons described in *The Structure of Social Action*, reduced action to its utilitarian dimension (Parsons indeed argued that the utilitarians, among whom he placed Marx, were 'pre-sociological'), the neo-Kantians left space for *verstehen* as well as *erklären*. The positivist world-view included an image of the unity of all the sciences – Marx dedicated the first volume of *Capital* to Darwin. The neo-Kantians paid a lot more attention to the specific differences of the social sciences.[17]

Positivists, neo-Kantians and *Lebensphilosophen* differed on the relation of fact and value. This is a thorny problem and the cause of a lot of misunderstanding, so considered attention is due here. Now positivists would not want to strictly separate fact and value. For positivists, 'fact' and science would have very strong hegemony over 'value' and philosophy. Indeed, fact determined value and such fact-based values were to play a critical role in deciding in which direction society ought to go. In this sense both Comte and Marx are positivists. Neo-Kantians would be for the separation of fact and value, so that values and facts have a considerable autonomy from one another. On this view values (philosophy) are not determined by facts. And social scientists operating in the realm of fact might be well advised not to concern themselves with the realm of values. For their part, *Lebensphilosophen* would assimilate most of fact to value.[18]

Let us unpack this a bit further. One source of confusion here is that post-war American sociological positivists championed the neo-Kantian and Weberian separation of fact and value. But they misunderstood the positivist tradition *à la* Comte and Durkheim in which there was a very clear and conscious value-engagement, i.e. in which social science was to form at least part of the basis for a civil religion and a moral regulation that would bring about progressive social change. The American positivists, themselves influenced by the American, Deweyan and pragmatist framework, were in fact using facts as value in constituting an 'ought'. Only they were unaware of this as well as unaware of the important differences between positivism and the neo-Kantian tradition. The Marxist articulation of theory and practice is indeed much closer to the positivist tradition than is usually realized. The sociology of knowledge and sociologistic ethics and epistemologies are positivist and not neo-Kantian enterprises. For this Karl Mannheim came under frontal attack as a positivist in the Weimar Republic. His reincarnation as Popperian social engineer in post-war British sociology was fully consistent with his early (positivist) sociology of knowledge. The main difference is that the young Mannheim analysed the factual determination of value while the late Mannheim put facts to work as values in the service of social change.[19]

A number of analysts have said that Durkheim and Weber are neo-Kantians in that both of them have notions of the social constitution of the Kantian categories. In this sense Durkheim's social explanations of ethics in *The Rules of Sociological Method* and of logic in *The Primitive Classifications* are seen as neo-Kantian. The same is true for Weber's types of social action in which *zweckrational* action is modelled on the social construction of Kant's notion of pure reason and *wertrational* action on practical reason. Such an interpretation, however, is false. In these positions Durkheim and this Weber are at their least neo-Kantian and their most positivistic. In these positions the two classical sociologists take philosophical or value notions and reduce them to facts or science. Thus Simmel castigated such positivist thinking as 'sociologistic' and warned sociology against wandering on to territory where it had no rights of access.[20] At their most positivist both Durkheim and Weber take both what is Caeser's and what is God's into the realm of Caeser.

A good deal of the writings of both Durkheim and Weber varies widely from positivism into the space of neo-Kantianism and beyond. We addressed Durkheim in broadly this context in detail above. A brief consideration of Weber at this point is appropriate. The positivist Weber of the action types and of the *Protestant Ethic*'s elective affinities (if one is to take the above discussed Goethean legacy seriously) dominated Weber's reception in the Anglo-Saxon world and in Germany from the end of the Second World War to the late 1970s. The always positivistically inclined US sociology dominated the world's discipline and Germany after the Third Reich could not resurrect anything that deviated even slightly from *Zivilisation* in the direction of *Kultur*. In the positivist Weber, fact determines value (much in the sense that Marx's base determines superstructure), both in the methodological writings on the action types and in the *Protestant Ethic*. The latter, if read outside of the context of the rest of Weber's *Religionssoziologie*, might be interpreted in terms of the explanation of one fact, the spirit of capitalism, by another fact, the Protestant ethic. Here an element quite clearly in the realm of value – religion or Protestantism – is reduced to just another fact or 'factor'. *The Protestant Ethic*, on the other hand, is often understood in terms of the 'elective affinity' of ascetic Protestantism and capitalist rationality. Yet the idea of elective affinity, in the work of Goethe, was integral to the positivist ethos that the poet so roundly condemned.

The reception of a properly neo-Kantian Weber began with the work of Tenbruck in 1975, was continued by Schluchter in the late 1970s and then, following Schluchter, by Habermas in *The Theory of Communicative Action*. Wolfgang Mommsen was maverick in his earlier almost *lebensphilosophische* comparison of Weber and Carl Schmitt, which was precursor to a number of such readings – corresponding with the rise of postmodernism and post-structuralism – in the 1980s.[21] This was the context of an effective 'third Romantic' whose context was the fragmentation of the US–Soviet corporatist and positivist consensus and the rise of pluralism and cultural theory. Key texts for the neo-Kantian Weber are the two essays on methodology in the sociology of religion and the essays 'Science as a vocation' and 'Politics as vocation'. In these Weber traces the differentiation of value

spheres into inner spheres and outer spheres. The inner spheres are 'subjective' and conceived on the notion of the symbolic mentioned above –
they are the religious and the aesthetic and the expressive spheres. The
outer spheres interface with the instrumental rationality of 'system', the
locus of politics and markets and everyday profane action. The outer
spheres correspond to fact and science, the inner to value and to philosophy.[22] That Weber in these writings gave important play to both attested to
his neo-Kantianism.

This doctrine of the spheres in the *Religionssoziologie*'s methodological
writings helps to explain the fact-value doctrine of 'Science as a vocation'
and the ethics of responsibility of 'Politics as a vocation'. In the former
Weber argues against the reduction of value to fact and the use of
social science in the sphere of values. In the latter he argues for the balance
of inner and outer spheres in ethically responsible action: that we must take
cognizance of both facts (Realpolitik) and values in political action.
Exclusive attention to values will mean that the possible consequences of
action are paid insufficient attention. Here Weber constructs an ethics
that runs counter to action determined by an ultimate value. In this he was
taking Marxists – such as the young Lukács – to task, while at the same
time rejecting vitalists such as George who assimilated politics to the
aesthetic value of the poetic. It was very much in this same neo-Kantian
spirit that Friedrich Tönnies gave the opening address at the first national
conference of the German Sociological Association in 1910 on the
separation of fact and value. The positivists were thoroughgoing sys-
tematizers, while their successors in the next, neo-Kantian generation of
sociology shifted their focus to the empirical. Tönnies at the German
Sociological Association characteristically spoke of society's '*unausmeßbar
Mannigfaltigkeit*' (immeasurable diversity). The very institutionalization of
sociology as a separate science, as a specialist field, ran counter to the early
positivist assumptions of the unity of the sciences. Thus specialist sociological journals were founded in France in 1893 and 1896, the *American
Journal of Sociology* in the USA in 1895, and the German *Zeitschrift für
Sozialwissenschaft* in 1898. The first international sociology congress was
held in 1893. And the major national associations were founded between
1900 and 1910.[23]

Central to all of this was the *Abgrenzungsproblem*, i.e. the shifting frontier
between the realm of science and the realm of philosophy. Consider the
philosophy of nature of figures like Goethe and Hegel, in which not just
praxis and sociability but even nature was taken away from science to come
primarily under the aegis of philosophical reflection. This state of affairs
radically changed after their deaths in 1832 – in the German counter-
offensive against Romanticism's resurrection of metaphysics. Now these
spheres of reflection came one after the other to differentiate out from

the domain of philosophy and into the domains of the various sciences. Kant's entire transcendental apparatus was dissolved and transmuted, not just into the domain of sociology – as noted above – but even more self-consciously through psychological and genetic analyses of cognition and perception.

Despite the seemingly impregnable hegemony of such *Gründerjahre* positivism from the 1830s through the 1880s, philosophy began, from the margins, to regroup. This began from the 1850s, led by Helmholtz and the 'back to Kant' movement. Philosophy to be sure was still to be excluded from the majority of spheres of enquiry: instead now the object of philosophy became the sciences themselves via *Erkenntnistheorie*, in which the reliability of our perceptions and the justfiability of our propositions became the prime subject matter. By the end of the nineteenth century such neo-Kantianism was very much in its prime. Now the domain of philosophy was extended to reflect on the principles and categorial basis of other areas of culture (i.e. excluding nature, politics and economics), of law, art, history, ethics and religion. Now the main matter at issue came to be the *limits* of science, and the exclusion of *wertphilosophische Kulturfragen* (cultural questions of value). This current of south-west German neo-Kantianism had great influence on Georg Simmel at the turn of the twentieth century. Philosophy had won ground back from science on a whole range of value and validity questions. And Simmel at the time and other figures such as Windelband and Rickert wanted to develop a value-philosophy (*Wertphilosophie*) of a systematic character. Such a *Wertphilosophie* would seem to inform the notion of *Eigengesetzlichkeit*, or self-legislation, purveyed in Weber's methodological writings on religion, in which each sphere – for example, law, aesthetics, ethics – constructs its own principles of validity. For Simmel, writing at about 1900, each *eigenständig* sphere had its own regulative idea – such as truth, beauty, the good or meaning.[24] Later Simmel shifted from such neo-Kantianism to a position closer to *Lebensphilosophie*, making philosophical and aesthetic questions largely the basis of his interpretative sociology and driving back the frontier of the sciences.

Marx and Marxism of course have also been part and parcel of this. As a young man, writing in the aftermath of the 'first Romantic', Marx was very much the philosopher. Dialectical materialism, i.e. philosophy, not historical materialism, or science, was then centre stage. Marx spoke of human needs: a notion of community and almost a philosophy of nature in terms of the communist paradise was promised. The later Marx's marriage of theory and practice was not dissimilar to the growing positivist currents in Germany and especially France of the later nineteenth century, the first volume of *Capital* appearing in 1867. In the later reception of Marx, Lukács, writing out of the heart of the second Romantic, turned back to the young Marx and pushed back the borders of Marxist science to put forth a *Lebensphilosophie* of the proletariat as the concrete universal. Given the resurgence of positivism in the decades after the Second World War, it is not surprising that pivotal Marxist theorists such as Louis Althusser tied Marxism firmly back to science.[25] Now dialectical materialism made way for historical materialism, and structural determination by a different set of social facts held sway. The subsequent breakdown of the positivist and 'double-corporatist' consensus (of the national corporatism of big trade unions and big employers associations – i.e. the Keynesian welfare state consensus – on the one hand, and of the international corporatism of the two power blocs) has also opened up space for a third Romantic, largely green and postmodernist, including a new metaphysical philosophy of nature. Due to the decline of working class strength and earlier Marxist positivism, this new Romantic has largely rejected Marxism. In retrospect the first appearances of this anti-consensual Romantic – as Alvin Gouldner described it – were in the late 1960s and its early Marxist theory of Marcuse and others was representative of the coming new era.

A further dimension separating positivists, neo-Kantians and Lebensphilosophers was that of order versus contingency. Positivists saw order where the neo-Kantians saw disorder or contingency. Comte, Mill and Marx had a notion of an ordered historical sense with a utopian moment or an 'ought' posited as an ideal future state to which history would reach as progress. Marx's notion of historical change was, to be sure, governed by a series of ruptures, and thus somewhat less continuist than his Whiggish counterparts. In contradistinction neo-Kantians such as Tönnies, Durkheim and Simmel had very discontinuist ideas of history. There was tradition on the one hand, and modernity on the other; mechanical solidarity on the one hand and organic solidarity on the other; *Gemeinschaft* on the one hand and *Gesellschaft* on the other. Weber in his positivist guise – and Weber as rendered in the post-war American dominated reception – proffers a continuist notion of social change via the principle of rationalization. In his neo-Kantian guise – and the *Zwischenbetrachtungen* are the best guide to this – he gives us a discontinuist account, with three main – primitive, religio-metaphysical and modern – stages.[26]

Integral to the neo-Kantian discontinuist view of social change is the notion of contingency. Weber as positivist saw social reality as structured by formal rationalization, but as neo-Kantian saw instead a contingent and disordered world of competing gods and demons. This is consistent with Kant's view of things-in-themselves as not accessible to the understanding, and of our perceptual and cognitive apparatuses as lending order to what would otherwise be contingency. Given this, the question for neo-Kantians was not how is knowledge or how is moral conduct possible, but how is society or how is social order possible? Or, more accurately stated, how is social life in *modernity* possible? For Marx as positivist, society is already ordered through the principle of class struggle. For the neo-Kantians, class struggle was just one of the best indicators of contingency and disorder in modernity.[27] Once the right question is posed, i.e. not how is society possible, but how is modernity possible, then the answer becomes clear, i.e. society. Society, or the structuration of social life by the principles of the new *Gesellschaft*, will make modernity possible. Now the 'ought' becomes not something in the future which will bring about desired social change, but instead the very norms, the forms of moral regulation, which make social life possible in modernity. The operative term here is Georg Simmel's notion of *Vergesellschaftung* (societalization).[28] This means that a given principle, or set of principles, works itself through the whole of a society and imparts to it a certain structuration. Whereas certain principles – perhaps loyalty, sincerity, the principle of the family – had been *vergesellschaftet* to make traditional social formations possible, other principles must be societalized (often as moral regulations) in order for us to have modernity. Paralleling the Kantian activist or dianoetic theory of knowledge, this is a very activist idea of social order. That is, without some kind of dianoetic social activity modernity would bring only chaos, contingency, anomie, the Weberian stew of competing gods and demons. And it is the active *Vergesellschaftung* (societalization) of norms that makes social life in modernity possible.

The question then becomes *what* principle is to be *vergesellschaftet*. In Marx's notion of a more noetic social order, all areas of social life in modernity are already *vergesellschaftet* through principles of work and class struggle. For Durkheim there is the societalization of a sort of moral individualism and for Michel Foucault principles of normalization and individuation. It was indeed such conceptions of individualism that divided positivist from *lebensphilosophisch* wings of turn-of-the-twentieth-century sociology. In 1890, when *Social Differentiation* appeared, Simmel himself was a positivist in the tradition of Darwin and Spencer.[29] Taught by Gustave Theodor Fechner, originator of the theory of 'speculative atomism', Simmel wanted to investigate how social change affected the psychological state of individuals. Later the primarily vitalist Simmel would reject this former belief in 'quantitative individualism' for the 'qualitative individualism' of Stefan George.[30]

The emergence of classical sociological theory sociology – whether positivist, *Lebensphilosophie* or neo-Kantian – took place in the tracks of the first, high modernity. Positivism grew out of and against classical humanism. Romanticism or *Lebensphilosophie* for its part emerged as a movement of deconstruction of positivism. Like modernist architecture, both positivist and romantic sociology – both 'system' and 'symbol' – were a high modernist repudiation of classicism. Both assume a sort of abstraction, an

autonomous subjectivity and a dianoetic methodology that reject classicism. Positivism assumes the abstraction of sociological conceptual frameworks and systems from the concrete practices of everyday life; of
abstraction of the rational ego from inner nature and of instrumental
rationality from outer nature. In doing so the emergence of sociological
theory is part and parcel of the autonomization of culture from concrete
nature: from inner, outer and social nature. This runs parallel to the
autonomization of 'the subject' in Kant's pure practical reason from the
concrete and particular of the everyday.

Positivism's *lebensphilosophisch* counterpart appears to be criticizing just
this sort of abstraction. But instead of recementing relations with the
particular of the *Sittlichkeit* of everyday life, it instead posits itself an abstract
sphere of pure subjectivity or 'life' from which it can criticize or refuse to
join these profane social relations. For such hermeneutic sociology what is
effectively 'the symbolic' is constituted along the principles of *interiority*, an
inward subjectivity separated from mundane forms of social life. Both the
quantitative individualism of the positivists and the qualitative individualism of the romantics involve such high modernist separation from the
fabric of social life. Thus symbol is only one side of the other modernity. It
deconstructs the positivist first modernity, it undercuts the already groundless positivist forst modernity, but does nothing at all to retrieve the ground,
whether that ground is body, sociality or nature.

Both positivists and romantics, both system and symbol, have an activist
or dianoetic view of theory. Reflexivity is a dianoetic principle that presumes an activist subjectivity. Whereas classicism precludes reflexivity in its
already given noetic knowledge of the human ideal, positivism proffers a
reflexivity of the individual (or the system itself) on the system, partly
through the use of reasoned argument. Rejecting both system and reasoned
argument, romantic or hermeneutic sociological theory only substitutes the
self-reflexivity of the expressive and poetic subject. If noetic classicism scoffs
at notions of perfectibility and understands the perfect to be located in the
antique past, positivism offers the vision of societal perfection in the future.
Rejecting this, equally high modernist romanticism still offers a notion of
the future perfection of the individual, of the *Ubermensch*. Finally, whereas
positivism rejects classical intuitionism for an activist interpretation of the
Kantian understanding, romanticism resurrects intuitionism in its rejection
of the cold understanding: this time, however, this is an activist intuitionism, an intuition which does not passively receive ideal essences from the
outer world, but creatively struggles for them in a Nietzschean vein. The
anti-positivist tradition in classical sociological theory, this romantic,
hermeneutic, vitalist deconstruction of positivism, gives just one side, the
groundlessness, of the other modernity.[31] We are still kept in search of the
ground.

From Symbol to Allegory

There is, however, another side to the anti-positivist Simmel, which David Frisby has captured under the heading of 'sociological impressionism'. This Simmel, like the *lebensphilosophisch* Simmel, foregrounds the aesthetic. But instead of a focus on a lasting inner subjectivity, this Simmel is at home in the *fugitif*, the *contingent*, the *transitoire* of Baudelaire.[32] In contradistinction to positivism and *lebensphilosophisch* romanticism, this second 'impressionist' Simmel escapes such abstract subjectivity. This is the Simmel who begins to open up a sociological route to the other modernity addressed in the chapters on space above. This Simmel stands in the 'low modernist' tradition of Baudelaire, where he is joined of course by Walter Benjamin. If the *lebensphilosophische* Simmel is a sociological 'expressionist', then this other Simmel is a sociological 'impressionist'. If the *lebensphilosophisch* Simmel comes straight out of Goethean 'symbol', then this other Simmel has a lot more in common with not classical, but baroque, *allegory*.

Simmel's *Lebensphilosophie* was of a piece with, as Klaus Lichtblau has argued, Nietzsche's 'pathos of distance'. The latter doctrine was very much conceived as anti-positivism and an anti-sociology. Nietzsche in *Twilight of the Idols* attacked Anglo-French sociological positivism for its destruction of 'distance' through the fostering of equality. For Nietzsche this '*Anährlichung*' or proximization (as opposed to distantiation in, for example, Brecht's sense) of sociology was only another 'expression of the theory of equal rights'. Anglo-French sociology, he continued, 'knows from experience (i.e. of their own societies) only those decadence-structures (*Verfalls-Gebilde*) of society', and society in England and France takes its own 'decadence instincts from sociological value-judgements as the norm'.[33] The word norm here, as we will see below, could have and perhaps did have for Nietzsche a double meaning, first as a form of moral regulation, and second – as counterposed to the distinguished – as the average. Together this implies that the average and not the ideal is set up as a form of moral regulation in just those societies where sociology as a 'slave morality' has prospered.

If sociology and mass democracy – and for Nietzsche and Simmel fascism (and communism) would have been only a new form of mass democracy – destroyed 'distance' – for which they substituted proximity – they also destroyed 'pathos'. This was a notion which the young Nietzsche developed in *The Birth of Tragedy*. For 'pathos' positivism substituted 'action' (*Handlung*). 'Action' was a characteristic concept of positivist sociology, assuming the abstracted atomism of the indistinguishable quantitative mass of individuals in society. 'Pathos', to the contrary, according to Simmel, corresponded to a sort of poetics which transcended everyday actions in the social.[34] The 'quantitative individualism' of the positivists called for a sociology of action. The qualitative individualism of the first generation of Nietzschean sociology called instead for 'pathos'. Weber as positivist in the early pages of *Wirtschaft und Gesellschaft* described the outlines of a sociology of action. Weber as neo-Kantian in the 'vocation' and 'religion methodology' papers spoke not so much of action but of 'life-conduct', whose ethic of responsibility presupposed a certain transcendence of the masses. Conduct as pathos deals not in categories of the abstracted isolated social act of the positivists. Talcott Parsons, who in *The Structure of Social Action* bequeathed to us classically non-positivist readings of Weber and Durkheim – of which too close a reading would have seemed dangerous to the post-war consensus – unfortunately subsequently fixed on Weber's action types, from which he built his own positivist theoretical framework.

For Simmel as *Wertphilosoph* (value philosopher), as in Nietzsche's concept of value, no value ethic was possible on the basis of the equal rights – and equal outcomes – assumptions of levelling integral to what Simmel called 'the social' (*das Soziale*). That is, no value ethic is possible without 'distance'. The *Wertphilosophie* which Simmel radicalized in a Nietszchean direction involved the rediscovery of value-problems. Value-philosophy is based on the assumptions that large areas of socio-cultural life cannot be subsumed or understood through facts. That values assume that one entity, one event, one course of conduct is better than another. And that each sphere of socio-cultural life has its own criteria which decide which is the better. Value-philosophy refers in its judgements not just to the practices of specialist areas of high culture such as, say, painting, legal theory, formal ethics and psychological doctrines of sexuality. It refers also to criteria of conduct in everyday life. Hence it colonizes large areas of the study of everyday life that would normally come under the sway of positivism. In the value-philosophical move from neo-Kantianism towards *Lebensphilosophie*, the whole of knowledge becomes ever more subjective: with the discovery of the irrational and emotional in man, the limits of rationality became ever narrower. And the aesthetic-sensual sphere of inward poetic subjectivity comes to assume importance in life-conduct.[35]

Despite hypostatization of subjectivity, value-philosophy persisted in its condemnation of any sort of relativism. The *Wertphilosophen* strove for objective validity. Yet how was one to find a 'transcendental ought', when the foundations of *Wertphilosophie* itself came crucially to be called into question. The answer was an almost Kierkegaardian leap of faith into what Simmel called 'metaphysical conviction' in dealing with the fundamental – meaning and purpose questions of being.[36] Simmel, like Stefan George, read Nietzsche not as a perspectivalist but as a metaphysician of the will to power with a clear foundational set of values. He thus approved of Nietzsche's dictum that 'Das Wertvolle *soll* sein, sein Gegenteil *soll* nicht sein.' In the case of two differently ranking values, then, Simmel observed in 1904, in his series of lectures on Kant at the University of Berlin, that when one chooses a course of action, one must choose the higher ranking value and fulfil its 'immanent *Forderungscharakter* (constellation of demands)'.[37]

Simmelian metaphysics was a step into the Goethean 'symbolic'. If the challenge to positivism via neo-Kantian critique passed in Germany largely via the work of Rickert and Windelband, its more thoroughgoing *lebensphilosophisch* alternative passed through the figure of Stefan George. Whereas George was a strong influence on Weber and Lukács, it was Simmel who at least at first was the very important influence on George. Simmel played the role of Verlaine to George's Rimbaud – which parallel extended to George, like Rimbaud, coming from out of the provinces to the big city and in the end becoming the master of the older man. Like Verlaine *vis-à-vis* Rimbaud, ten years older than the poet, Simmel was the very senior participant in the early days of the looser George circle (publishers of *Blätter für die Kunst*), and met George as early as 1895 when the latter was in his mid-twenties. From 1910, as the circle formalized and published *Jahrbuch für die geistige Bewegung*, Simmel drew away from George, whom he saw as becoming didactic and patronizing, and moved closer to a Bergsonian position.[38]

If anyone were to bring rationality into *Lebensphilosophie* it was Simmel. Where George philosophized in deeds, Simmel used concepts. George himself contrasted Simmel's 'word' with the 'transformative, formative and reconstructive effect on the individual that poetry holds up'. Yet Simmel endorsed George's Goethean metaphysics and symbolic. For the categories of the Kantian understanding, George and Simmel substituted, argues Michael Landmann, a 'Platonist-Goethean' 'hypostatization of the radiance of the eye'. This sort of metaphysics runs at cross-current to Weber's neo-Kantian ethics of responsibility, which must deal foresightfully with the contradictory demands of a whole set of inner and outer life-spheres. Instead of such a decentred Weberian subject, Simmel advocates the '*Einheit der Persönlichkeit*' (unity of the personality), in which, unlike Weberian and neo-Kantian assumptions of contingency, life has a totality of meaning. Here, in 'each of life's details (is found) the totality of its meaning'.[39]

Emerging then in Simmel's metaphysical sociology are the main qualities of Goethe's symbolic. There is the endorsement, for example, of totality versus the fragmentary nature of allegory; of deep meaning versus superficiality; the assumption of a *langue*, a system of symbols accessible probably to the poet and to sociological poetics, in order for each to find their *parole*. Similar to Hans-Georg Gadamer, who in an early article on the baroque advocated Goethean symbol against allegory, Simmel intones against positivism that the sociologist when searching for the significance of an epoch should look not at cause but for 'symbols' which reveal the main 'deep and living opposition of all that is human'. Further, where allegory was connected to the everyday and to '*profane* illumination' in Benjamin, symbol assumes a 'transcendental subjectivity' that only the artist/poet can attain to. Thus the most prominent of the Stefan George circle, Friedrich Gundolf, a right-wing Jewish literary scholar who obtained one of Germany's more prestigious chairs thanks to the politics of the left-liberal Weimar Republic, developed such an idea of symbol in his books on Goethe and Shakespeare. Gundolf exhorted contemporaries to a new methodology of literary analysis; to work back to the '*geistige Gestalt*' behind the work. In similar tones, Simmel spoke of George's work in terms of a 'suprasubjective (*übersubjektiven*)' subject originating from not a 'real individuality', but an 'ideal personality (*Persönlichkeit*)'.[40] Simmel's transcendental subjectivity, in contradistinction to positivism's congnitivist understanding (*Verstand*), involves the aesthetic apprehension or 'intuition' of the 'total meaning' of the world in each of its fragments. Finally, the Simmelian and Goethean symbolic is, unlike allegory, not noetic and passive but dianoetic and activist. It thus, similarly to the *erste Romantik* of the Jena Romantics, follows the '*Tätigkeit*' of Kant's *Erkennende* (knower), but on the model of the artist.[41]

Money

This thematic of the symbolic is played out in Simmel's *Philosophy of Money*. In this the life-world is understood as a sort of symbolic subjectivity which is 'objectified' – into money. To quote Simmel, 'the specific contents of personality are detached and confront the personality as objects with their own independent character and dynamic'. The opposition is between 'subjective culture', conceived as permanent along the lines of the symbolic, and 'objective culture', in which objective culture or 'forms' are detached from the 'content' of subjective life; in which the forms (as money) are detached from and come to dominate the becoming of subjective life. Money emerges from a sort of distantiation, as things only take on value because of the distance of subject from object. But once money is constituted as objective culture, its very contentlessness, its 'pure indifference', is the greatest of levellers. There are three steps to this process. In the first 'our desire (*Begehren*) goes over into the value of the object'; in this 'cultural process' 'the subjective state of the drives and pleasures is transmuted into the valuation (*Wertung*) of the object'. In the second step a large number of individuals similarly invest their desire; the result is a many-sided intensity of desire invested in the object which makes it appear to have objective value. Here the similarities with Marxian exchange-value are patent. The third step takes this objective value to its purest form in money itself, a thing which is characteristically 'full contentless', and pure indifference. Money as objective culture in this context is a matter of full mediation, i.e. pure form, that is the polar opposite of traditional metaphysics' *Gesamtheit des Daseins* (totality of being), or pure content or unmediatedness. In dissolving content, money dissolves 'distance'. It dissolves the irreducible intrinsic value of 'the ideal of Vornehnmheit (distinguishedness)'. Money is *gemein* (common), while 'only the individual is "vornehm"'.[42] This war versus distance is also against the symbolic, itself understood as content rather than form. If for Nietzsche the main principle of life-destroying *Vergesellschaftung* was Christianity and its pale ideological followers, democracy and socialism, for Simmel it is money itself. If the main principle of *Vergesellschaftung* for Nietzsche took place via moralities or ideologies, for Simmel (as for Marx) it takes place via a thing. For Marx this is indeed the abstract thing (capital) which embodies a social relationship. For Simmel it is money.

Alongside money, the main Simmelian enemies of subjective life and the symbolic are positivism and the social. Thus Simmel writes in the *Grundfrage der Soziologie* in 1917 that *Gesellschaft* is a form into which humanity objectifies the content of its life. And more excessively, 'All pure substantial meaningfulness, in which our spirit [*Seele*] somehow take part – logical knowledge, metaphysical fantasies of things; the beauty of existence [*Daseins*] and its image in its self-overcoming in art, the realm of religion and nature . . . [are] subjective [*innerlich*] in their essence and have nothing at all to do with society [*Gesellschaft*]'. Nietzsche's idea that the 'spiritual potential of modern life' is transmuted into the masses, for Simmel becomes a transmutation 'into the form of things'. Thus Simmel's social, unlike Nietszche's, 'is not the insurrection of the masses, but that of the things'.[43] But money (as abstract thing) carries on a war in Simmel on another front. It carries on a war not just versus symbol or subjectivity but also versus allegory. That is, money 'translates the many-sided diversity [*Mannigfaltigkeit*] of things . . . [as] homogenous [*gleichmäßig*]'. Money is at the same time an essential 'colourlessness' which empties out 'the core [*Kern*] of things, their singularity, their specific value, their incomparability'.[44] We are in the realm here of Benjaminian allegory, in the realm of his *Sprache der Dinge* (talking things). If in symbol the content of the subject is objectified into abstract things, in allegory the contentlessness of money empties out the particularities of things. And money as system, as the embodiment of positivism, carries out simultaneously a war on symbol and allegory.

But, not fully dissimilar to Adorno's assessment of markets in liberal capitalism, Simmel sees another, positive side to money. And this is again on the model of allegory. That is, for Simmel, money may empty out the particularity of things but at the same time it provides the motor for the very colour, the fleetingness, the contingency of the other modernity. Simmel was impressed by all the commodities and commercial colourfulness of the 1896 Berlin Trade Exhibition, and spoke famously of the 'neurasthenic', bombarded on all sides by the 'phantasmagoria of commodities and impressions'. The neurasthenic, paradigmatic for Simmel of modernity's emptied-out subjectivity, thus 'inwardly lacking in independence' and presenting a 'blasé', false individualism, needed all this excitement for stimulation.[45] But if the neurasthenic was a negative case of the sort of empty subjectivity associated with a monetized modernity, Simmel himself was impressed by the commercial splendour of the market place. Money, according to Simmel, though it might destroy the heterogeneity of the thing, at the same time turned the thing into an interaction. That is, 'exchange raises the specific object and its significance for the individual . . . into that lively interaction which is the substance of economic value'. 'Exchange creates an inner bond between people – a society in place of a mere collection of individuals . . . exchange is a form of *Vergesellschaftung*.'[46]

Simmel's *Soziologie*, in both its 1894 and 1908 editions, foregrounded relations in space. But a less known article by him penned in 1897 on money and time bears out this positively valued reading of money as a sort of modern allegory. Simmel contends in this article that the issue is not whether modern life goes faster or slower than previously, but the representational contents of a given unit of time. That is, the number, the variability and the intensity of representations in a temporal unit. Thus, as the mass of money increases in a society, representations become more concentrated, intense and varied. New social classes appear on the scene engaged in struggles for distinction with the old classes by means of the more intense and variable representations themselves. Further, the spatial concentration of money-mediated interactions between previously isolated individuals – and Simmel's favourite example was the action on the stock exchange – increases the 'colourfulness and richness of life'. Finally, money itself comes to be a symbol for absolute movement, for the increase in speed of interactions: money becomes a 'carrier of movement, in which all that is not movement is fully obliterated' (*ausgelöscht*).[47]

Life and Allegory

In Simmel there are two theories of agency and structure. In each case he begins from agency and derives structure. In the first, described above, in the Simmel of *Lebensphilosophie* and 'symbol', it is *innerlich* poetic subjectivity which is objectified as structure, form or objective culture, as in money or in the social. The second way in which agency creates so to speak structure is along the model of allegory. Here Simmel begins not from subjectivity but from *inter*subjectivity or interactions (*Wechselwirkungen*). Here it is interactions that lead to forms. But interactions create forms not through objectification, but through *Vergesellschaftung*.[48] This said, Simmel's interactions are not always fleeting: only in modernity do they take on this character. In traditional societies interactions are rare, lasting and diffuse, in modernity, frequent, fleeting and intensive. Interactions are *vergesellschaftet* into forms. In *Grundfrage de Soziologie* he writes: 'there is a persistent knitting together, a dissolution, and again knitting together of the Vergesellschaftung between people, an eternal fleetingness and pulsating that individuals knit together'.[49] 'Love' here, for example, is a type of interaction that may be *vergesellschaftet* into 'fidelity', which is a form. Once a form is created it takes on it own logic, its own proper self-reproducing dynamic. Forms, once created, are spatio-temporally ordered dynamic structures.

This logic of creation does not, however, exhaust the relationship between agency and form or structure. Simmel directs our attention in the study of social forms not to the structures but to their 'relational' characteristics. These relational characteristics – i.e. Objectification and *Vergesellschaftung* – are those between agency and forms. In modernity the forms are relatively stable. It is the interactions and agency more generally that are fleeting, pulsing, unstable. Once the forms are created they provide a context in which the interactions proceed. Once love is *vergesellschaftet* into fidelity, fidelity provides a context in which love relations are then enacted. And once a form is created, the relational characteristics between them and interactions are not exhausted. Simmel thus writes in *Soziologie*, whose subtitle is *Untersuchung über die Formen der Vergesellschaftung*, about the continued investment of 'social energy' of interactions in forms and that 'organs in intimate reciprocal exchange invest their energies in the latter as if in some sort of external being'.[50] Here not just complementary interaction such as love produced forms: so did conflictual interactions in which 'opponents have something in common around which they struggle'. Finally, *principles* can be *vergesellschaftet* so that they come largely to characterize whole societies. Thus Eder speaks about the *Vergesellschaftung* of nature in the context of romanticism, ecology movements and tribal societies. Here nature is differently *vergesellschaftet* in different sorts of societies.[51] A Marxist would insist upon the *Vergesellschaftung* of work relations. For Simmel money is the most important principle of *Vergesellshaftung* in modernity. And as such it is, as noted above, responsible for both stifling, positivist instrumentality and the colourful, though commercialized, fleeting allegory of interactions in modern life.

The notion of '*life*' takes on a different colouring in this context. In *Soziologie* he spoke of the 'opposition between the fleetingness, the essential propulsion [*Bewegtheit*] of subjective life [*Seelenlebens*] and the capabilities of the forms'.[52] Similarly, he wrote towards the end of his life of inner life in terms not of stability but of flux: 'The essence of modernity as such is psychologism, the experiencing and interpretation of the world in terms of the reactions of our inner life and indeed as an inner world, the dissolution of fixed contents in the fluid element of the soul.' Brigitta Nedelmann, in writing about the contradiction between 'life' and forms, observes that in the late Simmel forms are generally stable, whereas life connotes '*Unruhe, Entwicklung, Weiterströmen*', a 'naked unmediatedness'.[53] She includes under the heading of life both poetic subjectivity and interacting intersubjectivity. This is largely an aesthetic intersubjectivity counterposed to the formalisms of 'system'. Simmel then gives us two theories, two notions of life: one grounded in symbol, the other in allegory; one expressionist and the other 'sociological impressionism'.

Conclusions

Let us recapitulate a bit. We have distinguished – in this chapter and the last – between two types of modernism in social theory. On the one hand positivism and on the other *Lebensphilosophie*. Positivism we understood as structured along a principle of 'system', and *Lebensphilosophie* along a principle of 'symbol'. The forerunner of positivism, whose paradigmatic system-building figures run from Rousseau/Condorcet, through Comte, the late Marx, Le Corbusier and, I think, Habermas's later work, is French humanist classicism. As Norbert Elias has stressed, both classicism and its Enlightenment and positivist successors are paradigms grounded in 'civilization', whose breeding ground was most importantly French absolutist court society. In opposition to the principle of *Zivilisation* is of course that of *Kultur*, the world of the first, second and third Romantics, of *Lebensphilosophie*, of the eternal return of metaphysics, of 'symbol'. We have traced in these chapters central dimensions of both 'system' and 'symbol' in Durkheim and Weber. Simmel, for his part, as we just saw, worked much more in the idiom of symbol than system.

But in his 'sociological impressionism', Simmel also began to work in a different register, the register of *allegory*. The idea of allegory is central to the whole of this book. Simmel's idea of allegory was essentially a deepening and development of Goethe's concept. Goethe's notion of symbol was developed in contrast to French classical allegory. But let us shift attention from the classical to the baroque: from French court society to Spanish absolutism and thus to *baroque* allegory. We discussed neo-Kantianism above. Baroque allegory is in a completely different register from the original juxtaposition of symbol and allegory: it has to do with neither *Zivilisation* nor *Kultur*.

Whereas classical allegory proffers a point for point homology between two narratives, the baroque version posits a significant absence, or with Benjamin a 'hole' (*Loch*) in the underlying narrative. In Benjamin's *Origins of German Tragic Drama*, the real-life story to which the German baroque narratives referred was the Thirty Years War.[54] But something about the real story just wasn't right, just didn't make sense, was impossible to pin down for Benjamin. Once the original narrative itself becomes elusive, impossible to pin down, impossible to categorize, then the notion of allegory undergoes mutation. If the original, 'true' story somehow is not quite right, then the point for point homology between the second narrative and the first is no longer possible. At issue is neither the form of classicism nor the substance of *Kultur*, but an orthogonal, ornamental and metonymic idiom of signification. The same is true of baroque organization of space. Baroque space opens up huge boulevards with straight lines on the model of Cartesian rationalization, but then ends up spatially symbolizing the irrational principle of the arbitrary will of the absolutist monarchy. The seemingly harmonic lines of the baroque church leave no coherent vantage point on which to balance sight lines.[55] Baroque allegorists such as Nietzsche, Simmel, Benjamin, Adorno and Karl Krauss write in the form of the essay. Where does this stand in relation to positivist science and *Lebenphilosphie*'s poetic? The essay might well look *wissenschaftlich*, but emerges in an aesthetic mode: serious and at the same time superficial, light, ornamental. There is indeed a tradition of the ornamental in baroque allegory, traversing absolutist Spain through to Viennese turn-of-the-twentieth-century Jugendstil art nouveau, art deco and the literature of Jean Cocteau.

Baroque allegory is opposite to Marxist or 'deep realist' explanation. In the latter the complexity of the everyday hides the simplicity of real ordering mechanisms. In baroque allegory apparent simplicity is just a guise for underlying webs and networks of complexity. Classical allegory will allow the possibility of description of the thing itself. Baroque allegory only allows us to listen mimetically to the *Sprache der Dinge* which we must inaccurately record in another register. Unlike both system and symbol – unlike high modernist dianoetics – baroque allegory is noetic. But it is not noetic in any sort of classical or platonic sense in terms of being able to perceive ideal essences.[56] It is also not noetic in the sense that theoretical realism is, i.e. where one can uncover the underlying mechanisms that make society tick. Or even as empirical realism, in which real objects make themselves known and knowable through the mind. Allegory proposes instead a sort of 'brute realism' in which real objects take on a life and language of their own. Its practitioners live this sort of reality. But they know they can never fully transcribe it. They can only listen to it and respond to it with their own mimetic narratives. That is, in allegory's 'brute realism' there is a strong affinity and valuation of things: there is an imitation of things which can never quite match the things themselves.

The practitioners of allegory give their practice off as 'light' and ornamental in comparison to the 'heaviness' of symbol and system. Yet there is something quite permanent and lasting or even messianic about it. Thus Baudelaire left a space for moments of antique permanence in the heart of his ever shifting modern. Simmel as allegorist is no different. His sociological impressionism left open a space for permanence: he wrote of Rodin that his is 'the impressionism of the supra-temporal, the timeless impression'. Other regions of life had this sort of atemporality for Simmel, especially moments and figures in which life is conceived as 'adventure'. Thus the sexual adventurer and the 'philosophical adventurer' have a timeless quality. Perhaps paradigmatic of the atemporality of Simmel's adventurer were gamblers, who 'cut out a piece from the endless, continuous series of perceptions or experiences . . . and give it an autonomous, determinate and cohesive form as if from an inner core'.[57]

The allegorist, thus, while looking ornamental, is simultaneously dead serious. As mime, the allegorist listens to and permits the anarchy of things themselves. The allegorist himself or herself is also anarchist, and more importantly outsider. Unlike the system builders who have also systematically built their own followings, and unlike symbolist Goethe and school builders and later *hommes politiques* like Stefan George, the allegorist builds no school, founds no party, holds no ministerial office. The allegorist leaves nothing behind. He, like Rimbaud, stops writing at the age of twenty-six and goes off to live a life of physical adventure in Africa. And he never stops to argue why. The allegorist is outsider. He is father of the illegitimate child of modernity's other. He is substance abuser. He is more than likely a member of one or the other of Proust's two famous confraternities of outsiders. He is the Jew. He is the homosexual.

The idea of allegory, as mentioned, is central to this book. We broached it in the discussion of Benjamin and urban space, beginning to talk of an allegorical spatiality in chapter 4. Here we have through Simmel spoken of allegory in terms of sociality, of sociation, of modes of social life which go on outside of the normativity of the institutions. Of allegorical modes of sociality which are also external and unavailable to the knowing subject, and of which only glimpses, only impressions, are accessible. In part III we speak – especially in discussion of Jacques Derrida – of an indexical register of experience, of indexical signification, as we look at allegory in the dimension of the sign. In part IV we return again to the juxtaposition of symbol and allegory and consider allegorical modes of judgement. But allegory is perhaps most important with the erosion of the first *and* second modernities in the explosion of *indifference* of the global information culture. If Simmel's allegory is a question of fleeting moments of intersubjectivity, then in the emergent posthumanism of the information order, allegory becomes increasingly a matter of inter*objecti*vity. Hence the relevance of Walter Benjamin's world of talking, gazing and judging objects. We will discuss allegory in Benjamin's tragic drama at length in part V. Allegory is largely a question of the language of things, a language perhaps more accessible to the eye and to touch than to the categories of logic. The question of allegory is more than ever relevant when the world of things and the production of things becomes increasingly pervaded by symbolic and informational objects.

Part III

Experience

7

The Natural Attitude and the Reflexive Attitude

Parts I and II of this book, on space and society, have begun with the first or high modernity, not as representation in, say, the arts, science or philosophy, but as pervading into everyday life. Parts III and IV, which address experience and judgement, begin with the second or other modernity. But they deal with the realm of representation, the realm of thought. Parts III and IV treat the deconstructive moment of the second modernity. Then they shift to a critique of such pure deconstruction from the standpoint of the ground. As in parts I and II, the ground appears variously as memory, tradition, situated intersubjectivity, sociality, bodily perception, the index and sensation.

These explorations in parts III and IV will also be explorations in *reflexivity*. In the idea of 'reflexive modernization', reflexivity involves the ordering through reflection of social processes, and on the other hand those same social processes slipping out of control and escaping the logic of such an ordering. It consists of a moment of self-ordering and a moment of 'ambivalence' or 'contingency'. In the book *Reflexive Modernization*, I criticized Ulrich Beck and Anthony Giddens for overly stressing the determinate, subsumptive, ordering moment of reflexivity.[1] This has not turned out to be at all the dominant reading of reflexivity, which has focused on the moment of contingency, the moment of loss of control, on the new modernity as 'experiment', its violation of metanarratives, its aspect of '*riskante Freiheit*'. That is, predominant has been its deconstructive moment. The subsumptive, 'determinate' moment of reflexivity was dominant, as we saw in the sociological positivism of the young Durkheim discussed in chapter 5. This presumed the reflective power of sociology in the engineering of improvement, in a process that was effectively a 'metanarrative'. But it is not the positivist moment of reflexivity that is predominant in the idea of reflexive modernization but the moment of contingency, of ambivalence, of out of control-ness. The theory of reflexive modernization – in contrast to positivist and high modernist ideas of social engineering – asks what sort of self, what sort of institutions are possible in an age of *chronic* contingency, of chronic ambivalence.

Parts III and IV consist of social-philosophical interrogations of both the determinate and indeterminate moments of reflexivity. Both the social-philosophy of experience and the theory of judgement use the notion 'reflective'. The former, i.e. phenomenology, talks of the 'reflective attitude', the latter of 'reflective judgement'. There are strong connections with the idea of reflexive modernization, though in the latter reflexivity descends as it were from the realm of thought into the activities of everyday life. I will understand the term 'reflec*t*ive' in the pages that follow as 'reflex*i*ve'. When phenomenologists or theorists of judgement use 'reflective' I will often use 'reflexive'. In doing so I am bringing these more philosophical considerations intentionally into contemporary debates, and equating them intentionally. The important point here is that the philosophers, like the sociologists, use reflective (reflexive) as a move outside of positivist determination.

If the sociological theory of reflexivity is primarily about the moment of contingency, of experimentation, then there is little to separate it from contemporary ideas of deconstruction and difference. But if we take the notion of difference seriously, as explicated in Jacques Derrida, then a major cleavage arises. For Derrida, to move outside of positivities, to deconstruct, is always at the same time to enter into an engagement with the meaning of being. Difference is always at the same time *ontological* difference. Similarly, to be reflective in phenomenology or the theory of judgement, unlike for the sociologists, is also to engage with ontology. In both cases it is to engage with ontology through encountering a thing, a particular. The sociological theory of reflexive modernization has had considerable political implications and political influence at the turn of the twenty-first century. But these politics will be necessarily restricted and dissatisfyingly superficial in the absence of such an ontological dimension.

Thus part III addresses experience. Experience is a mode of thought characteristic of the second modernity. It is a mode of thought that breaks radically with the older subject–object thinking of the first modernity. If in the first modernity thought is based in *cognition* and is *epistemological*, in the second modernity thought shifts into the dimension of *experience* and becomes *ontological*. The epistemological, subject–object thinking of the first modernity presumed the subsumption of a particular by a universal. The second modernity's subject of experience becomes no longer universal but *singular*. Indeed, in Hegel's *Phenomenology of Mind* subjectivity already was conceived not as the universal (*das Allgemein*), but as the 'singular' (*das Einzelne*). Whereas the universal subject of the first modernity 'subsumes' the particular, singular subjectivity *encounters* or *experiences* the particular. As subjectivity becomes at once singular and experiencing, there is entailed a shift from epistemology to ontology.[2] The epistemological subject knows things according to the categories of classical logic, while the experiencing subject knows things in terms of the ontological structures proper to things themselves.[3] Finally, temporality is vastly different in the shift from the subject–object mode of first modernity epistemology. The epistemological subject is outside of time and space. This subject interfaces with an object that is subject to the temporality of cause and effect in homogeneous Newtonian time. The subject of experience for its part operates itself in the flux of time. The hypostatized 'being' of the epistemological subject is displaced by the unstable and fleeting 'becoming' of the subject of experience.

Part III, on experience, deals mainly, however, with the critique of phenomenology, and then mainly from the position of the ground. Chapter 7 consists of considerations of the 'life-world' phenomenology of Alfred Schutz and Paul Ricoeur, in which the reflexive attitude of transcendental phenomenology is relocated in the *natural* attitude. Here we begin with Schutz's account of the 'traverse intentionality' of the reflective gaze amidst the flux of experience, and the creation of meaning through the reduction of Husserl's transcendental phenomenology.[4] Schutz is predominantly concerned with the dimension of temporality in Husserl's 'internal time consciousness' and the time-framework of social action. Here he deserts Husserl's reflective attitude for the natural attitude. Schutz, we will see, disputes the notion of memory which fixes meaning for Husserl. Schutz understands memory as not transcendental but as situated in the life-world and based on experience, on a 'stock of knowledge'. Moreover, unlike in the reflexive attitude, his socially embedded subjects can attach phenomenological meaning not only to things but also to intersubjective understanding. Schutz's historically grounded intersubjectivity is radically different than Habermas's transcendental intersubjectivity based on discursively redeemable validity claims. Schutz's ground is a strong basis for a situated notion of community, an important corrective to the very individualistic assumptions of the sociological theory of reflexivity.

Paul Ricoeur adds a strong ontological dimension to life-world phenomenology. In comparison to Schutz, Ricoeur proffers a 'depth hermeneutics'. Ricoeur's move towards the ground, towards the natural attitude, starts, we shall see, not with intersubjectivity *per se* but with *perception*, which he contrasts to the 'signification' of the reflective attitude. Through perception we open out on to the world. Perception involves 'the mediations of the body on to the world'. If meaning through signification, via the universal subject, yields 'certainty', then meaning via perception and singular subjectivity gives us 'truth'. Meaning through signification takes place through the 'sign', through perception via the 'symbol'. Such symbols create a matrix for revaluation of the past understood by Ricoeur as a 'long intersubjectivity'. The symbols of perceptual meaning are also for Ricoeur the materials of the dialogic relation of psychoanalysis, through which they open out on to 'desire's archaic heritage' of being. We will thus explore Ricoeur's bodily and ontological understandings of the second modernity's ground.

Alfred Schutz: from Meaning to Understanding

Social theory today has now begun to use the notion of 'reflexivity' in a way similar to classical sociology's usage of rationality. We will see in this chapter that the second modernity entails a displacement of reflexivity. The origins of the emergence of the notion of reflexivity in this context would seem to be some sixty-five years ago in the work of Alfred Schutz. And Schutz introduced the notion precisely through a reworking of class-ical sociological theory's notion of rationality. Schutz's *Phenomenology of the Social World*, the *Sinnhafte Aufbau der sozialen Welt*, is subtitled *eine Einleitung in die verstehende Soziologie*.[5] It is an attempt to rework Weber's theory of meaningful social action. Here Weber proposed four types of social action: traditional, affective, instrumentally rational (*zweckrational*) and value-rational action. The point is that arguably for Weber – and this is surely Schutz's reading of Weber – only the latter two action types pre-sumed *meaningful* action. That is, for Weber action is meaningful through its being rational. For phenomenology, action is meaningful insofar as it is reflexive.

Schutz starts not from the assumptions of rational, scientific observer: he begins not from mediated knowledge, but from immediate experience. For him meaningful human activities have little do to with reasoned means–ends chains of unit acts. They involve instead reflexivity: that is, phenom-enology's transcendental reduction of the flux of immediate experience. What does this mean? Schutz assumes with Bergson that the human condition is one of an ego caught up in the stream of consciousness, the flux of immediate lived experience.[6] This is what is known as the 'natural attitude' (*natürliche Einstellung*). In the natural attitude, objects and experi-ences are encountered as a flux of indistinct and vague shadows. These are meaningless, or their meaning is 'trivial'. It is only as we move into the reflective attitude that things are endowed with meaning. The reflective attitude involves a measure of transcendental reduction, a reduction of the chaos, flux and confusing complexity of immediate experience, a certain fixing of discrete units of experience so that meaning is possible.

This juxtaposition of natural and reflective attitude is much the same as Bergson and *Lebensphilosophie*'s counterposition of 'life' and 'thought'. But whereas Bergson (and Simmel, as we saw in chapter 6) largely sides with life against thought, Schutz argues that meaning is only possible through thought, through reflection. Here thought or reflection is not understood as in the positivist tradition. Rationality is thus not *erklären*, not the positivism of cause and effect. Instead of positivism's and the epistemological tradition's focus on the 'why' and causality, Schutz subscribes to Husserl's focus on the 'what'. Instead of positivism's and epistemology's presumption of the problematic relation between the categories of the subject and the thing itself, Schutz's assumptions are consistent with Husserl's dictum that we can know things themselves. Thus, instead of a search for causes and effects of things that are themselves empty variables or black boxes for explanation, phenomenology prefers explication, or *Auslegung*, the descriptive 'laying out' of the character, 'the what', of things themselves.[7]

Schutz's idea of the reflexive construction of meaning on to experience involves a creative banalization of the work of Husserl. Schutz's often implicit use of the transcendental reduction partakes of little of the rigour of Husserl's method in his (non-positivistic) 'science' of phenomenology. Husserl's reduction too starts with the flux of experiences, with the encountering of an object in at first a succession of primal impressions, a set of perceptions. What phenomenological science is to do, then, is to 'fulfil' the object; the task set for phenomenological inquiry is to construct polythetically a unity out of the many aspects, the many sides, of the object.[8] This involves, first, the 'transcendental reduction', i.e. the removal of the ego from the stream of experience in order that it can take a reflective attitude towards the latter. It involves, second, the 'eidetic reduction'. In this the unity and the meaning of the object results from the 'intuition of essences' of the object. This essence must include any aspects of the object without which the object could no longer be the same object. In this sense phenomenological psychologists have inquired not causally, but into the description, 'the what' of the nature of such phenomena as 'guilt', 'laughter' and 'shame'.

Schutz, however, uses a much looser notion of the reduction. One that is not so much a scientific and philosophical method, but a method of meaning construction through complexity reduction in everyday human activities. Let us specify first what Schutz means by the *natural* (as distinct from reflective or attentive) attitude. In this context we must note that the natural attitude is not any sort of Buddhist or 'easternized' lostness in the flow or stream of impressions. It is also not being caught in the flow of life of *Lebensphilosophie*. The natural attitude, i.e. in immediate lived experience, does presume a very strong 'egology', a very strong notion of the ego. Here the ego is understood as analytically separate from its experience. The ego is 'intentional', already constituting its experience. The idea of intentionality is one aspect of Husserl's departure from the Enlightenment's idea of an infinite subject of knowledge. In intentionality no subject is conceivable that is not already intentionally related to an object.[9] Even in the *pre-reflective* natural attitude the ego constitutes the objects of experience. The ego constructs these objects only as 'outlines', as empty, as impressions, as 'data'. The objects of consciousness the ego constitutes in the natural attitude are not 'fulfilled', but empty, and not discrete, but vague and elusive. Even in the natural attitude the ego is a discrete entity, so that pre-reflective experience has already a mine-ness to it. That is that each experience is personal to a self or ego that already is endowed as a more or less coherent totality with both memory and a sense of 'protention' or anticipation into the future. The ego is already an 'I' with a discrete spatiality and a discrete temporality.[10]

What then does the reflective attitude add to this? Only in the reflective attitude do objects and experiences become meaningful. Things are constituted as objects in the natural attitude, but they only take on meaning in the reflective attitude. Experience in the natural attitude is 'pre-phenomenal', while phenomena are only constituted in the reflective attitude. Objects constituted in the natural attitude are 'pre-predicative', while predication (hence meaning) is only possible in the reflective attitude. The semiotics of phenomenology, unlike those of structuralism and post-structuralism, do not take the 'signifier' or even the sign as the point of departure. For Schutz, following Husserl, the sign is only introduced in the context of inter-subjectivity. Phenomenology starts instead from the thing as constituted by the ego through experience as object. And in this sense meaning is predicated not of the sign or signifier but of the thing. In the reflective attitude the ego's intentional object is (a) discrete and (b) fulfilled. Only with the 'reflective glance', Schutz writes, is 'experience engendered as a discrete entity'.[11] The act of reflection lifts the experience out from the flow and 'fixes' it. An experience is fulfilled once the original outlines and primal impressions are, through a sequence of experiences, shown in their many aspects and a single fulfilled entity is constructed 'polysynthetically' out of these experiences. The ego does not leave immediate experience to take up the reflective attitude. The act which casts the 'light' of the reflective glance is part and parcel of the flux of experience. 'The actual here and now (*Jetzt and So*) of the living ego is the very source of [the] light', i.e. 'the beam [itself] is a phase of experience' . The 'attending ray', as Husserl termed it, of the reflective glance 'is and remains personal'. Through it the here and now becomes the 'here, now and thus'.[12] Through reflection the here and now is explicated.

The terms generically used for this constitution of meaningful experience by Schutz, following Husserl, are 'reflection' (*Reflektion*) and 'attention' (*Aufmerksamkeit*). The visual metaphor is consistently used: Schutz speaks most often of a 'reflective glance' (*Blick*), of a 'ray', or 'ego-ray' or 'cone of light' that endows the multitude of experience with discreteness and fulfilment. Experience is often in various shades of grey between reflexive and natural attitudes, various shadings of 'attentional modification' betwixt and between, from actually comprehending, to fixing attention on, to hardly noticing. Schutz quotes Husserl to distinguish between different types of reflective attitude, best grasped through phenomenology's distinction between the 'noetic' and the 'noematic' sides of experience. Experience on the *noetic* side has to do with the kind of attention 'that the ego gives to lived experience', with 'attentional modification' and the different kinds of reflective intentional experience. The different kind of reflective attitudes are such as memory, judgement, will, belief, presumption, valuation, pleasure and perception. Through them the ego is involved in a process of 'noesis' with regard to immediate experience and to things. Phenomenological inquiry into these modes of attentional modification of the ego is 'noetic inquiry', in which intentional experience itself becomes the object of reflection according to its essence.[13]

The *noematic* side of experience addresses the objects of experience, the things of the external world that have a 'noematic content' which itself is made visible through intentional experience. These 'noema' for Husserl become fully accessible in 'pure intuition'. Noetic and noematic sides of experience are integrally interdependent. Corresponding, for example, to noetic attitudes such as judging and pleasure are noematic contents such as 'the judged as such' and the 'pleasing as such'. Meaning, for its part, is constituted at the interface of the noetic and noematic sides of experience, at the interface and through the tension between, as Schutz put it, 'life and thought'. Thus perceptual meaning is constituted at the interface of perception, as noesis and the noematic content, the perceived as such. The sociological point is, and here is the 'realist' kernel showing through Schutz's seemingly radical constructionism, that whether a given socially located ego will assume either natural or reflective attitude, and what type of reflective attention the ego will pay to experience, are 'pragmatically' determined. That is, there is a social contextualization of where the reflective glance will fall (and consider problematic) and where 'something will be taken for granted'.[14]

Temporality and Action

If for the first, high modernity, humankind's *differentia specifica* is the ability to reason, then for the second, the other modernity, it is *experience*. And if the *a priori*, the transcendental *a priori* of rationality, is the logical category, then the constitution of possibility of experience is *temporality*. Heidegger was quite explicit about this in *Being and Time*. Here 'understanding' as the mode of access to the truth of being (which is only revealed through the meaning of beings) is experiential. It is also thoroughly temporal. Understanding for Heidegger is a mode of 'being-in'. Modes of being-in for Heidegger fill out an adverbial space proper to the 'is' and to becoming, thus displacing the forms of knowledge based in the substantive and adjectival predication of a more logocentric tradition.[15] Temporality as experience is also central, of course, to the novel of Proust and Joyce and the philosophy of James and Bergson. Schutz like Heidegger literally presumed a temporal *a priori*. For him reflexive meaning, action and the transcendental reduction are temporally constituted. Schutz contrasted Bergson's *durée* (duration) with the fixed, static time of 'conscious states'. For Bergson the artificiality of homogeneous everyday time was counterposed with the pure *durée* of the heterogeneous, irreversible flux of conscious experience. *Durée* was the time experience of inner life, a constant transition from a 'now thus' (*jetzt und so*) to a new 'now thus'. If this inner time represented 'life' for Bergson,[16] then the homogeneous time of 'thought' was in fact only 'spatialized' time; spatialized in its assumption of events as divisible and in principle repeatable in homogeneous space, and in its Newtonian understanding of motion as traversed space.

The meaningfulness of experience in phenomenology, for its part, is constituted as discrete through the operation of the reflective glance. Here in the 'act' of 'attention', 'shafts of light' make the 'phases' of the stream 'sharply defined and hence meaningful' as 'marked off'.[17] In the 'longitudinal' and irreversible intentionality – the *durée* of the stream of consciousness – experiences are only indistinct 'phases'. But in the 'traverse intentionality' of the reflective gaze, 'experiences' are 'lifted out' of the irreversible stream of duration and 'awareness is modified'.[18] For Husserl this stream of consciousness is not only pre-phenomenal but 'pre-empirical': only with reflection is there 'differentiation' of the stream into discrete units. Only the 'directed glance of attention' constitutes the distinction of the object of the glance from the glance itself. Only such differentiated experiences can have 'identity' in that they no longer irretrievably fade in and out of the flux. Meaning can only be 'predicated', Schutz concludes, to such discrete experiences because predication of meaning to the indistinct flux must be 'necessarily trivial'.[19] For objects to have meaning they must have identity, and must in principle be *repeatable*.

Husserl and Schutz speak of objects as having an 'immanent' and a 'transcendental' temporality. Their immanent temporality is their location in objective time; their 'constancy' in space-time is also an aspect of their identity and discreteness. Objects are transcendentally temporal insofar as they are located outside of internal time consciousness while at the same time experienced through this internal *durée*. Fulfilment of objects has also to do with their constancy and identity. Objects cannot attain identity and constancy in objective time unless they are 'built up' in internal time. Pre-phenomenal objects are experienced as an 'outline' or an 'impression', as we see only fleeting aspects of them. The 'temporal object', argues Husserl, must be 'built up' through many 'presentifications', 'so that we perceive it, but only seemingly, as if'. Once objects are 'built up' through acts of attention, they become 'full-blown experiences' or 'fulfilled'.[20]

But the reflective gaze can never be fully transverse and must itself be longitudinal and successive because it too is only a moment, a phase of experience, a new, specific sort of 'now here'. What looks like transverse-ness is never simultaneity and can only take place in the past, through *remembering*. In the natural attitude there is only 'primary remembrance' or 'retention', which Husserl stresses is 'not an act of looking back'.[21] Indeed, it is something that takes place not at all via a metaphoric visualization – whether distinct or blurred – of the past. It is simple 'retention' in that it conforms directly to the primal impression. The intentionality of this pri-mal impression is also retained. In primary remembrance what is remem-bered is not a fulfilled or discrete object but an elusive primal impression. Secondary remembrance, in contradistinction to primary remembrance, takes place through looking back. In fact reflexivity as understood in phenomenology is first and foremost secondary remembrance. Secondary remembrance is in its simplest form 'recollection' or 'reproduction'. Here in looking back, i.e. in recollecting, the glance lifts out and modifies aware-ness. Recollection stands in contrast to retention. We *retain* water which has no substantial identity, we don't recollect it or reproduce it. The closer an experience is to the intimate core of a person, the less accessible it is to articulation, to 'rationalizability', to recollection or reproduction. Recollec-tion and reproduction are only possible, Husserl stresses, with discrete objects.[22]

For Schutz 'acts' (*Akten*) or 'behaviour' (*Verhalten*) are a particular genre of activities. Only those activities which are reflexive are acts. When Schutz speaks of acts (*Akten*) he means not unit acts so much as acts of attention. These are always of attention on a past lapsed experience, an attitude taken towards 'primordial experience'. These are the most elementary acts of attention. They are reflective perception as a *spontaneous* activity, in which for the first time there arises the distinction between the constituting act and constituted objectivity. Acts differ from 'action' (*Handeln*) in that the former presume only recollection, while action also presumes 'protention'. Acts or behaviour differ from action in three ways. First, an act is not a process, while an action is. Second, acts (behaviour) are always reflexive. Action, on the other hand, is not necessarily reflexive. It can also take place in the natural attitude. Action does entail looking to the past and to the future. But this looking into the future can be as either 'natural protention' or 'reflective protention'. In the natural attitude protention, like retention, is not of discrete units of future experience but is instead a blurred and empty extending forwards. Reflective protention does involve a certain discreteness about future experience or objects in the future. Reflective protention is mistranslated in the English version of *Der sinnhafte Aufbau* as 'anticipation'. The German '*Vorerinnerung*' could be better translated literally as 'fore-remembering'. In this the reflective glance lights on a single future phase as the goal of the action and thus, through transverse intentionality, 'intercepts' future experience.[23] Reflective protention involves two types of fulfilment: first of the action itself and second of the projected goal of the action. The latter takes the shape of a fulfilled picture built up from many primary impressions. But *Vorerinnerung* is literally fore-remembering in that it is looking into the future for the past as the pictured 'planned act or goal' has the temporal character (to the reflective glance) of pastness.

The temporal character of meaningful experience for Schutz seems to suggest that he may have more in common with Heidegger than Husserl. Indeed, for Heidegger, Dasein gains access to the truth of being through modes of 'being-in'. These modes of being-in are *Befindlichkeit*, *Verstehen* and *Rede*. *Befindlichkeit*, which is literally translatable as 'finding oneself positioned' or 'finding oneself located', points to a pastness into which one is thrown simultaneously into 'the there' of (albeit angst ridden) forms of life.[24] Thus, finding ourselves in a past, Dasein understands (*Verstehen*) through projection of an outline (*Entwurf*) into the future. There are two major differences between Heidegger's and Schutz's temporality of understanding. Both involve Dasein's being somehow in 'the there' in a sense that Schutz's ego is not. First, Heidegger's temporal *a priori* is transcendental only in that it is a condition of possibility of understanding; while for Schutz transcendentality entails an abstract distance from 'the there'. Second, Heidegger's temporality is adverbial, a spatio-temporal clearing in 'the there' in which Dasein has access to the disclosing of being through beings. While Schutz's temporality is not adverbial but a string of more or less fulfilled (or predicated) substantives.

Experience: *Erlebnis* and *Erfahrung*

Erlebnis and *Erfahrung* are both translatable as experience. Up to now we have spoken of experience in the sense of immediate lived experience. This is *Erlebnis*. *Erfahrung* is on the other hand mediated experience. *Erlebnis* is inner experience. Gerhard Schulze's *Erlebnisgesellschaft*, now translated for English speaking readers as *The Experience Society*, for example, charters the expressive individualism of the 'me society'.[25] The traditionalist critique of this presumes the standpoint of *Erfahrung*. The *Erlebnisgesellschaft* is criticized, on the one hand, for its valuation, not of being experienc*ed* (*erfahren*) but of immediate experience (*Erlebnis*); and, on the other, for its valuation of inner life and its concomitant isolation of the individual from public life. Thus Erlebnis is immediate and private, while Erfahrung is mediated through past traditions and knowledge and is public. Gadamer, in part I of *Truth and Method*, understands art in terms of *Erlebnis* and *Erfahrung*. For him *Erlebnis* is instantiated in, for example, the immediate, inner and Faustian nature of Goethe's poetry and of romanticism and modernism in the arts. Erfahrung for its part is found in the learned and traditional mediatedness and publicity of classical Greek allegory.[26] The notion of 'life' to which *Lebensphilosophie* gives primacy is at the root of *erleben*, and Bergson's stream of consciousness is of course a stream of *Erlebnisse*. *Erfahren* on the other hand is a modification of *fahren*, to drive, to travel, to journey. In German a experienced craftsman, a travelled journeyman is an *erfahrende Geselle*. Walter Benjamin contrasts the *Erfahrung* of the storyteller to the *Erlebnis* of the novel (see chapter 13).

Schutz uses the notion of *Erlebnis* in many juxtapositions: as *sinnhaftes Erleben* (meaningful experience); in terms of a noetic-noematic *Struktur des Erlebens*; of intentional *Erleben* and even of *erfahrende Erlebnisse*. The point for Schutz, however – and here he must depart from Husserl (who consistently and systematically speaks of the phenomenoogical reduction in terms of *Erlebnis*[27]) – is that no sort of transcendental reduction, no reflective glance, no meaning and no understanding is possible without *Erfahrung*. The ego alone cannot construct meaning from *Erlebnisse* without a structure of *Erfahrung*. Schutz's ego consists of a 'double directionality' when it operates reflectively, with attention on the one hand to the immediate *Erlebnis* and on the other to the structure of *Erfahrung*.[28] From immediate *Erlebnis*, the reflective glance builds up out of 'polythetic' impressions an object of 'monothetic' attention. With this synthesis is born, says Schutz, a 'meaning-context' (*Sinnzusammenhang*). In the course of many and various actions there takes place a synthesis of many meaning-contexts, that leads to the constitution of *Erfahrungsgegenstände*, or Erfahrungsobjects.[29] These Erfahrungsobjects as second-order objects are different from the first-order objects (or effectively Erlebnisobjects) just described. The reflective glance constitutes meanings as fulfilled and discrete Erlebnisobjects. A number of various syntheses of such Erlebnisobjects leads to the constitution of Erfahrungsobjects. Erfahrungsobjects, sometimes called 'stock of knowl-edge' by Schutz, resemble Durkheim and Mauss's classifications and Bourdieu's habitus. These are 'ideal objects' such as judgements or catego-ries. They are called objects because of the phenomenological way in which they are 'built up'. Even these second-order objects of *Erfahrung* (stock of knowledge) are produced through 'polysynthetic intentional acts'. Now a number of these second-order Erfahrungsobjects themselves make up the 'context of *Erfahrung*' (*Erfahrungszusammenhang*), a set of the latter comprising the total context of *Erfahrung*. And a good deal of this total context of *Erfahrung* is in fact a 'reserve stock of knowledge' (*Wissensvorrat*) or a stock of knowledge at hand'.[30]

Schutz in his move from *Erlebnis* to *Erfahrung* has, I think, already laid the ground for the shift from the phenomenology of the ego to the sociology of practice. He has already made the move that will make a theory of intersubjectivity possible. Now no longer will primacy be given to the ego, which through its actions constitutes (social) phenomena from pre-phenomenal immediate experience. Instead the starting point is a situation in which two *Erfahrungs* confront each other with the possibility of intersubjective understanding. *Erlebnis* is and *Erfahrung* accumulates experience. For Schutz, socially acquired accumulated experience will condition what and how the ego will select from immediate experience for reflection and constitution as phenomena.

Schutz refers to Erfahrungscontexts as 'schemes of experience' (*Schemata unserer Erfahrung*). Through these schemes of *Erfahrung* the ego provides the explication (*Auslegung*) of objects and immediate experience. Meaning endowment in which the ego reflexively fulfils objects is also a process of explication, which is at the same time self-explication. This is not explanation, but is polar opposite to it. Explaining (*erklären*) is concerned with 'the why', while explicating (*auslegen*) is concerned with the 'what'. It is concerned with the (non-positivistic) description of the what. Auslegung or explication provides the template for Schutz's reworking of *verstehen*, which he addresses in the context of intersubjectivity. Explication takes place through a 'synthesis of recognition', in which an *Erlebnis* is 'subsumed' under second-order 'objectification' of the schemes. An experience (*Erlebnis*) is, continues Schutz, 'referred back' to the 'schemes at hand'; this referring back takes place through identifying a specific *Erlebnis* with a specific scheme. The schemes, then, are involved in the (already transcendental) ego's eidetic reduction of the *Erlebnis*, a 'synthesis' that 'fixes' the 'specific essence' of the *Erlebnis*. But unlike in, say, Bourdieu, in which the ego and the schemes of experience are merged in the habitus, Schutz sees the ego as mediating between the schemes and immediate experience.[31] Here the schemes are so to speak analogous to means of production and the data of lived experience to raw materials. The ego, for its part, through this synthesis explicates the experience and creates a 'product' which is meaning.

In this context Schutz also suggests a sociology of structural location. This is introduced in his distinction between Husserl's notions of 'formal' and 'transcendental logic'. In the formal logic the schemes of experience are already constituted 'logical objectifications', the formal logic comprising 'ideal objects'. It is in the 'transcendental logic' that the sociology comes in. If the formal logic addresses 'modes of awareness' of being and thought, then the transcendental logic addresses modes of awareness of not being but becoming, and not thought but life. In the transcendental logic different schemes in the stock of knowledge are selected for ordering and interpretation of immediate experience. Schutz notes, though, that the essence of a lived experience (*Erlebnis*) is its 'noematic nucleus', that 'any *Erlebnis* is open to numerous noeses, or interpretations'. Such interpretation takes place 'through the referral of an unknown to a known'.[32] Scheme selection and the schemes to which referral will be made are 'dependent on a particular here and now'. Husserl's formal logic is philosophical, remaining within the sphere of thought: transcendental in Schutz's logic is sociological in that the social and institutional location of any given ego will determine which scheme is selected and which meanings are synthesized. The social is the transcendental instance in Schutz's transcendental logic. Schutz's phenomenology is then hermeneutic in the ego's contextualization in *Erfahrung* (stock of knowledge) and structural in that schema selection for meaning constitution depends on social location.

Intersubjectivity: Understanding Alterity

In much phenomenologically influenced thought – in, for example, Ricoeur, Levinas, Derrida and Heidegger – meaning refers to the significance that the ego attaches to things. Phenomenology is much less equipped to deal with the relation of the ego to other human beings. Husserl had no satisfactory way of moving from the transcendental reduction of objects by the ego to the understanding of the 'alter ego' or 'other'.[33] This shift in focus from the thing to the other is a shift from subject–object relations to intersubjectivity. It is most importantly a shift from the problem of meaning to the problem of *understanding*. Let us repeat: if the problem of '*meaning*' lies in how the ego grasps the object or the thing, then the problem of '*understanding*' is a question of intersubjectivity. For Schutz understanding is not primarily of the locutions, the 'writing' or the background assumptions of the alter ego, but instead the content of the alter ego's experience; it involves not the reflective but the natural attitude. It necessarily comprises a very strong mediation of signs.

Schutz is well aware that the ego cannot understand the alter ego's experience through the reduction and reflective attitude. He takes instead Dilthey's classical hermeneutic idea and attempts to rework it through phenomenological concepts. Schutz agrees with Husserl that we cannot explicate 'the Thou's' experience but can only approach the 'concept of the other person's meaning' as a 'limiting concept'. In *Ideen*, Husserl made the

distinction between self-interpretation (*Selbstauslegung*) and the interpretation of another's experience. The former, Husserl wrote, proceeds via 'acts'
that are 'immanently related', while interpretation of another is carried out
via acts that are 'transcendentally directed' to 'experience streams' of other
egos'. Schutz was influenced by Scheler's assumption of an originary and
transcendental intersubjectivity, grounded in the nature of experience.
Thus, for Scheler and Schutz there is no originary transcendental 'I'.
Instead 'Thou-spheres' and 'We-spheres' exist as a condition of the reality
of the 'I'.[34]

For Schutz following Husserl, while I can only observe my own
lived experience in the past, I can observe yours in the present. I do this
from my immediate stream of lived experience. This simultaneous temporality is intersubjective understanding in its simplest form. Meaning
construction here – and understanding is always a particular type of
meaning construction – again involves a synthesis through the 'double
directionality' of the ego, though this time fully in the natural attitude.
Schutz follows Bergson's presumption that 'I see my own stream of
consciousness and yours in an observational experience that embraces
them both.' Schutz claims that in the natural attitude I can grasp 'phen-
omenally' aspects of your lived experience which are 'pre-phenomenal
and undifferentiated' for you. I, for example, am pre-reflectively aware of
your voice as you are not. Simultaneity and the natural attitude would
hold also for the understanding (n.b. not *meaning*) of texts from a more
or less distant past. In this double directionality, ego points to my immediate experience, whose 'phases' are grasped in simultaneity with
phases of 'signitively grasped' 'cultural artefacts' through a 'synthesis of
identification'.[35]

But Schutz is not speaking of immediate experience (*Erlebnis*) here. Even
the natural attitude is not primordial. It is preceded by the 'We' of background knowledge and the stock of experience (*Erfahrung*).[36] My stock of
experience is an interpretative and 'signitive code' that directs my (pre-
phenomenal) intentional acts to your lived experience, without judgement
or inference in the normal sense. This is a step beyond the double
directionality of intersubjectivity in which the ego synthesizes my lived
experience with your lived experience. It is not a matching of streams of
experience; it is instead a matching of the background knowledges, the
stocks and 'contexts' of experience. In this the more closely contexts of
experience match, the more possible it is to achieve simultaneous flow of
experience. This is what Schutz refers to as 'genuine understanding'. The
less that the other is part of this 'We', the greater the extent to which I see
his or her acts as 'external facts' in the mode of *erklären*. The more, on the
other hand, I can enter into a We relationship with you and come to grasp
your project, your 'in-order-to motives, the more genuine understanding,

i.e. *verstehen*, is at issue. And for Schutz, as in Gadamer, this requires an awareness of one's own horizon as well as the other's.

Signs play no role at all in Schutz's discussion of meaning and the solitary ego. It is only in understanding, or intersubjectivity, that the sign is introduced. In intersubjectivity, my immediate experience is not matched by my ego directly with your immediate experience. Instead it is matched with the other's lived experience as represented in *the sign*. Husserl says in the *Cartesian Meditations* that we can know the 'psychic side' of the alter ego only through the 'physical side' which is an 'index' of it.[37] He notes further that my experience of your experience appears within mine as 'appresentation'. The connection between my experience and yours is made through a synthesis that 'identifies the primordially given body of the other with his body as appresented under another mode of appearance'. Schutz elaborates: we do not perceive others' experience as a thing or event but only others' 'bodily movements, speech and cultural artefacts': we only perceive their experience as 'signitive (symbolic)'. Despite apparent similarities, this is not post-structuralism's 'materiality of the signifier'. Schutz insists that though I 'apprehend [others'] experience (*Erlebnis*) only through their signitive-symbolic representation', I do not perceive this representation as a 'physical event'; instead 'my intentional gaze is directed right through [the representations] to his lived experience signified by them'.[38]

Schutz makes the distinction between signals (*Anzeichen*) and signs (*Zeichnen*). Whereas signals (or indicators) point to things, they do not represent things. Whereas signals function also for non-human species, signs (and symbols) can only represent things for humans. But how do we confront the sign? To begin with, we synthesize meanings of signs through special kinds of interpretive schemes. These are different from other schemes because they are 'not adequate' to the sign as 'external object' but instead are 'adequate to what they [the signs] signify'. These special schemes, like other schemes, are constituted polythetically through experiences. But these experiences are not of the sign but of the object that is signified. More specifically, we use two sorts of interpretive schemes in the encounter with a sign: one for the 'sign-object' and one for the signified object. Meaning is created through the interface of the two by means of yet a further set of interpretive schemes, which Schutz and Husserl call 'sign systems'.[39]

This said, there are two 'functions' of any given sign: first the 'significative function' and second 'the expressive function'. The significative function serves in syntheses of *objective meaning*, and the expressive function in those of *subjective meaning*. The same sign comprises subjective meaning as a sort of 'aura', Schutz insists, which 'surrounds the nucleus' of objective meaning. 'Objective meaning' does not in principle entail intersubjectivity and is much like the solitary ego's constitution of meaningful lived experience. 'Subjective meaning', which refers to 'events in the mind of the sign-user', is more of a piece with intersubjective understanding. Let us first address objective meaning. In the case of the solitary ego, meaning becomes predicated to objects of lived experience, as the objects become 'discrete' and 'fulfilled'. There is, however, a third property to meaningful objects as constituted by the solitary ego. They are also *repeatable*. This third characteristic of phenomena, i.e. repeatability, is constituted by the reflective gaze through the operation of secondary remembrance. There is an indispensable reference in objective meaning to signs of previous experience. In particular my unique experience when I first learnt to use a sign stays in my memory. At the point, however, Schutz insists, when the meaning synthesis takes place, objective meaning is repeatable.[40]

In contrast, subjective meaning is not repeatable, but 'occasional'. Subjective meaning does not refer to my 'inner self', but to my grasp of the experience of the other. I constitute this meaning of the other's experience through polysynthetic acts linking my and your experience. These meanings, once constructed, are both fulfilled and discrete. They are, however, not repeatable. Only objects in the case of the solitary ego are repeatable. But in intersubjectivity what is involved is not the eidetic reduction of objects, but instead experience which is unique and not repeatable. Objective meaning is of a piece with *erklären*, positivism and the natural sciences in its very realism. Here objective meaning can only be predicated of the product as such, as effectively abstracted from the experience of the producer. In subjective meaning, the interpreter (the listener, the 'I') needs to grasp 'the polysynthetic in the experience of the producer (speaker) which, made up as a unity the subjective meaning of the product'. Objective meaning is then 'abstracted', and entails the 'anonymization' of the producer as 'the one' (*Das man*).[41] The assumption is 'repeatability', 'and so forth', of, for example, unit acts in the market place. In economics, Schutz notes, action is totally abstracted and anonymized as objective meaning. The state, art, law and language, on the other hand, can be studied in terms of either objective or subjective meaning. Objective meaning has the characteristic temporality of the ego in its encounter with the thing. It is constructed, built up in step by step polysynthetic acts of the reflective gaze on the ego's past experience. Subjective meaning for its part is grasped in a mode of simultaneity or quasi-simultaneity. But such simultaneity is contextualized in a complex set of *a priori* temporal structures for both listener and speaker. The speaker, Schutz notes, is concerned about whether her project will be fulfilled by the listener's future interpretation of her words. The 'listener', for his part, will grasp subjective meaning in attempting to 'uncover the speaker's project' (which itself, we will recall, is pluperfect) on 'the basis of something past'.[42] The project of the speaker (whether it is an action, a book, an oeuvre, a historical epoch), unlike in the repeatable synchronicity of objective meaning, is fundamentally diachronic. It can be a whole lifetime or history of subjective meaning, Schutz notes, such as the 'demonic' for Goethe or 'civilization' in French thought, which 'crystallizes' the 'development of mental life'.[43]

What connects phenomenology and the problem of structure or order? According to Ilya Srubar in *Kosmion*, it is due to Schutz's connection with *philosophical anthropology*. 'Philosophical anthropology' was a very prominent current in German thought from 1920 through the 1940s. The tradition, whose illustrious figures include Max Scheler and Arnold Gehlen, has been above all concerned with 'man' (*der Mensch*) and man's place in the world.[44] At issue is 'man's invariant structures', necessary for species survival, accounting, on the one hand, for humanity's characteristic creativity and openness, and, on the other, for the possibility of order among humankind for the regulation of the characteristically human war of all against all. Philosophical anthropology's concern for order was crystallized in Gehlen's claims that 'man', unique among animals, is characterized by an *Instinktarmut*, a poverty of instincts that does not regulate our drives. Lacking instincts to regulate their drives, human beings must devise and then depend on institutions. In this sense Peter Berger has understood religion's 'sacred canopy' as the institution which would supplement man's insufficient instincts and create order. For his part, Schutz, as a student in Austria, had come under the influence of the celebrated jurist Hans Kelsen, whose 'legal positivism' also primarily addressed the problem of order. Kelsen, like Max Weber, was pre-eminently concerned not with 'natural rights', but with how the 'positive law' of the state helped to ensure social order. Comparison with Niklas Luhmann is instructive here. Luhmann, educated by the previous generation of philosophical anthropologists in Germany, was like them both strongly influenced by Husserl and concerned with the problem of order. Thus for Luhmann 'observers' located in systems carry out a sort of complexity reduction on the system's environment. In this they semantically attach meaning to this environment in communications with others. The kind of complexity reduction which will take place depends on where the observer is located in the system.[45] The semantics constructed from such complexity reduction themselves then define the shape of Luhmann's systems and provide order in the face of environmental contingency.

Schutz was introduced to philosophical anthropology through Scheler and his notion of 'sociality' (*Sozialität*). *Sociality* was an invariant human structure, was an eidetic foundation, argued Scheler. Scheler arrived at this conclusion using phenomenological method in the description of sociality as an *a priori* essential structure (*a priori Wesenstruktur*). Though constructed though a sort of reflexive and phenomenological reduction, sociality itself is pre-reflexive. Scheler's sociality is quite similar to Schutz's 'We', which, as noted above, is the condition and basis for the reflexive 'I'. For Scheler, sociality opened up the possibility of uniquely human creativity in the construction of our world. At the same time it provides the order which counteracts all too human angst, which itself is the 'motive' for the construction of social order. Thus the social world, later the 'life-world', for Schutz has its basis in Scheler's transcendental intersubjectivity. Scheler's transcendental intersubjectivity shows a tension in phenomenology whose logic leads to its very undoing. If phenomenology broke with 'the why' of positivist *erklären* for the phenomenological description of 'the what', it might not have gone far enough. Thus Schutz, as we just saw, discovered that phenomenological reduction of intersubjective experience led to its one-sided positivistic interpretation as 'objective meaning'. Subjective meaning and understanding must break with such phenomenological description for a focus on forms of life, which is a question never of 'the what' but of 'the how', never of semantics but of pragmatics. Knowledge here is not a question of knowing that, i.e. being able to define or give an account of something. Knowledge instead involves 'knowing how': knowing 'how to go on' in the presence of a word, or act or object.[46]

Thus phenomenology's inadequacies in dealing with intersubjectivity lead to abandoning its constructionism of 'the what' and instead to a focus on 'the how', to forms of life, to ordinary language philosophy, to a sociology of practice. In short, to a set of questions more properly part of the domain of not phenomenology but hermeneutics. But hermeneutics is at the same time far more than this. Hermeneutics opens up another dimension broached by philosophical anthropology yet ignored by both phenomenology and the Wittgensteinian assumptions of theorists of 'practice' such as Bourdieu and Garfinkel.[47] Philosophical anthropology broaches this question in its conception of the body, of man's 'unfinished body'.[48] Animal bodies, on this account, with their sufficiency of instincts are 'finished products', while human bodies are not. Human bodies, unable to survive as just nature by adaptation to the environment, must change the environment via culture. Thus via culture, institutions, language, we transform the natural environment. But our bodies are unfinished in another sense, in the sense that they are open to the ravages of the environment. They create 'worlds' to fill this unfinishedness, yet (not finished by instincts) they are vulnerable and suffer pain through these very worlds.

Culture and language enable human subjects to attach meaning to objects and thus transform the natural environment. Culture and language make possible not just such 'objective meaning', but a second type of meaning: subjective meaning or understanding. They make possible understanding between subjects, and thus begin to solve the problem of order in the social environment. But there is a third type of meaning that is neither the objective meaning of phenomenological constitution of objects nor the subjective meaning of practical forms of life. And human bodies are opened to this third type of meaning through their very vulnerability and unfinishedness, yet always, at the same time, through language and the world. This third type of meaning cannot be reduced to the mundanity even of intersubjective understanding. It is, to be sure, only accessible through everyday life, but its implications are far vaster. This third type of meaning is in Joyce's sense 'epiphanic', and sometimes found in poetry, politics or religion. This third type of meaning is not merely a sort of 'regulative concept' whereby there must, in order for us to go on, be something else. It is that there *is* something else. This something else can be experienced by human bodies in virtue of the two sides – vulnerability and culture – of their unfinishedness. It is this third type of meaning that is the issue in hermeneutics.

Signification and Existence

Hermeneutics is always and irreducibly two-sided. It involves, on the one hand, a break with the 'infinity' of the reflective for the 'finitude' of the natural attitude. And it always involves through this very situatedness in the natural attitude some sort of access to the *meaning of being*. In terms of this book's thesis of the two modernities, the break with the reflective for the natural attitude is just as important as the issue of access to the meaning of being. We just mentioned Schutz's break with the infinity of Husserl's transcendental ego for the finitude of intersubjectivity. Husserl himself in his late work – in the *Cartesian Meditations* and *Die Krisis der europäischen Wissenschaften* – changed registers from the transcendental ego in favour of the natural attitude – in perception and intersubjectivity. His counterpart in effecting a similar shift was of course Wittgenstein. Wittgenstein broke with the transcendental and formal, the 'well formed' language of the *Tractatus Logico-Philosophicus*, for the natural attitude and natural language of *Philosophical Investigations*. Here Wittgenstein's influence on theory in the second or 'low' modernity has nearly matched Husserl's.

Wittgenstein and Husserl had a common source, in their earlier 'transcendental' phase, in Gottlob Frege. Frege, for all the purity of his logic, was already involved in a departure from the Cartesian high modern, and epistemology-centred, philosophy of the subject.[49] Here epistemology had been understood as providing the groundwork for ethics, aesthetics, the philosophy of history and the like. Epistemology was literally a philosophy of consciousness, based on a notion of meaning, in which – in empiricism and rationalism – the meaning of an expression was ideas, the mental images, the mental processes aroused in the hearer of those words. Frege criticized this notion of meaning as 'psychologistic'. He argued for the displacement of epistemology by *logic*, a logic removed from the uneasy relationship with empirical consciousness of the logical categories of Kant's transcendental analytic. For Frege meaning was taken out of consciousness: a statement was meaningful when it met certain truth conditions.[50] Meaning is taken out of consciousness and comes closer to practice and natural language in the sense that meaning now is a mechanism or rule determining the use of an expression. There is of course a major gulf between this and natural language. Logic entails a formal language of properly formed sentences. Further, for Frege the unit of meaning is the word, which is not the case in natural language. For speech act theory, closer to natural language, the sentence is a linguistic act, i.e. it is the linguistic act in a properly constructed language that confers meaning. Here too the linguistic act is abstracted from, it is lifted out of, ongoing activities, ongoing and situated practices, and still vastly different from natural attitude and natural language.

Frege's assumptions form part of the context of both the first generation of analytic philosophy – the early Wittgenstein and logical positivism – and Husserl's transcendental phenomenology. For both meaning is linguistic meaning. For logical positivists language is a set of formal structures which stand above the world. Husserl's transcendental ego similarly is no natural ego, but a formal and *a priori* condition of possibility of objective meaning. For logical positivism, with Russell, the crucial linguistic acts are propositions, which are 'complex symbols'. What is analytic in analytic philosophy is the analyses of such 'sentences into their constituent propositions'. From this comes the idea of the 'elementary proposition', itself a 'determinate configuration of simple symbols'. The simple symbols are 'names'. What they stand for is objects, and the object is the meaning of the name.[51] Compare the Husserlian transcendental ego's constitution of phenomena via the eidetic reduction. Phenomena are constituted by this ego through acts, which are signifying acts, i.e. through linguistic acts. Phenomena are predicative or meaningful objects. The transcendental ego is a logical condition for the possibility of meaning, of true linguistic acts. The notion of truth involved is one of certainty, as it is in logical positivism, where the 'determinacy' of meaning is achieved, the certitude of knowledge is guaranteed.

Philosophy became irredeemably linguistic with Frege's paradigmatic departure from what Habermas and contemporary critical theory have called the the 'philosophy of consciousness'. This shift is, as I said above, to what Habermas calls the philosophic discourse of modernity. It involves truth being no longer grounded in the subject but in propositions, in linguistic acts of logic. It involves extra-subjective conditions of validity. These extra-subjective conditions of validity can be logical and transcendental – as in Frege, Husserl, the early Wittgenstein and logical positivism.

Or they can be intersubjective. In Habermas himself and speech-act theory, these conditions of truth are intersubjective yet transcendental, in the very lifting-out of speech actions from ongoing activities. In the late Wittgenstein and Heidegger in *Being and Time* they are intersubjective and immanent. They are in the natural attitude. Speech act theory effects a major departure within linguistic philosophy from the topical and formalist assumptions of Frege and Russell. Now an utterance is no longer primarily a proposition but an expression with an aim to do something. An expression in speech act theory is not a signification but an action. It is not to be understood via the meaning of the object it signifies, but, like all other actions, via the rule it is following.[52] Thus statements concerning ethics and values which would be meaningless in terms of the truth conditions of logic have a meaning like any other actions that follow rules.

Both the break with the philosophy of consciousness for intersubjectivity and the new salience of the natural attitude are above all captured in Wittgenstein's 'forms of life'. Language here is natural language – no longer logical and formed structures standing above the world, but a practical medium through which individuals participate in the world.[53] Meaning is no longer a question of either 'sense' or 'reference' in Frege's terms. Meaning is not 'sense' in that it does not lie in predication meeting local truth conditions. Meaning is not 'reference' in that it is no longer the object denoted by the work. Meaning is thus no longer subjective (as in Descartes or Kant) or objective (as in its logic-based successor), but *intersubjective*. As intersubjective it lies in the rules governing natural language use. These rules define how expressions are used. These rules are the 'constitutive conventions' of language games. Intersubjective meaning lies in my recognition of the rule you are using. This depends on a virtuous sort of hermeneutic circle in which knowing the rules is necessary for understanding the language game or form of life, while I must understand the form of life in order to grasp the rule. To understand the rule is not 'knowing that', it is 'knowing how'. It is not the ability analytically to describe the rules.[54] It is the ability of a winger to take the ball past a fullback; it is an experienced centre-back's knowing how and where to position himself for a corner kick.

Wittgenstein and, in sociology, ethnomethodology radically rethink what *verstehen* or understanding is. In this context Hans-Georg Gadamer and Schutz – armed with Husserl and Heidegger – have reworked the notion of understanding, unhinging it from the old philosophy of consciousness. Gadamer thus rejects Dilthey's 'empathic excavation', in favour of a genuine intersubjectivity of two finite subjects in dialogue. Schutz's implicit project, as we saw, was to criticize assumptions from the philosophy of consciousness in Weber's theory of action. He rejects the mentalism in Weberian *verstehen* and his means–ends chains of action for a notion of understanding grounded in the intersubjective, natural attitude and life-world. Wittgenstein and ethnomethodology are perhaps the least mentalist of all. They see understanding not as grasping the *mentalité* of an experiencing subject (like Schutz does), but the rule which is being followed by that subject. Gadamer's 'merger of horizons' and Schutz's 'stock of knowledge' are also mentalist and somehow inside the subject, while Wittgenstein's rules are external to the subject and graspable through finding their function in a form of life. But all these writers still give priority to one form or another of cognition. All these thinkers more or less ignore the *bodily*. This is not the case for Paul Ricoeur.

Signification and Perception: Ricoeur

For Paul Ricoeur human beings irredeemably are transcendentally reducing animals. The transcendental (thus anti-natural) attitude which eidetically reduces things to their logic-bound meanings is part and parcel of human nature. Our relationship to things comprises both (transcendental) 'infinitude' and (natural) 'finitude'. Humans are creatures indeed suspended between poles of finitude and infinitude. Ricoeur's considerations of finitude are not concerned primarily with intersubjectivity. His focus is on our specific and bodily mode of being in the world. Here the bodily at the pole of finitude is involved in 'perception', while the transcendental at the pole of infinitiude is involved in 'signification'. In activities of perception we are open to the world, while in activities of signification we are closed to the world. The body is thus understood in the natural attitude, in which immediate experience becomes the flux and succession of perceptions. Ricoeur's theory of finitude is a theory of *existence*. Ricoeur reworked Sartre's notion of existence. In an encounter with Husserl, existence becomes for Ricoeur the natural attitude: existence becomes 'life'; on the side of *mythos* in contrast to the *logos* of phenomenological signification. Existence is being-in-the-world. More than just the forms of life of Wittgenstein's surface hermeneutics, Ricoeur want a depth heremeneutics, one which addresses the meaning of being.

Ricoeur's phenomenology foregrounds signification. To signify, to constitute meaning, it is necessary to 'negate' the 'life' of the natural attitude, it is necessary to negate one's own 'seeing' in order to signify. This destruction of content creates a certain 'void of signification'. Yet this abstraction and negativity is necessary in order to have access to things themselves, for it is in the thing that I perceive this negative of which my transcendence consists.[55] This is integral to the very nature of intentionality.[56] Husserl's early work, developing Brentano's concept of intentionality, aimed to reduce the status of the subject in order to find meaning in the object. The early Husserl, before he developed the notion of the reduction, assumed that the subject, the ego, always acted intentionally, always acted in an intentional relation with an object. Gottlob Frege criticized these notions as psychologistic, and Husserl in response drew on the assumptions of logic to develop his transcendental ego. Signification in Ricoeur is based in such a strong and transcendental intentionality. When I intend something, when I signify, Ricoeur notes, 'I intend the thing in its meaning beyond all point of view'.[57] Signification for Husserl and Ricoeur takes place in acts. The constitution of phenomena and the conferral of meaning take place through signifying acts. Knowing things involves descriptive utterances, which can be valid only when the utterance is differentiated from the thing intended by the utterance. The utterance must be in a position of infinitude in regard to the thing. The linguistic sign can 'only stand for something if it is not that thing', i.e. there must be some 'empty space' between the sign and the thing. In order for us to enter 'this symbolic universe' of signs, there must be something akin to the phenomenological *epoché*; there must be a distanciating act that creates this space. Everyday life thus involves infinite acts of signification.[58]

To grasp ourselves as beings, we must adopt a position of infinitude. Unless we have an Archimedean point to look at ourselves in relation to others, we cannot conceive of ourselves as finite beings. Hence in intending the meaning of the thing beyond all point of view I am aware of my finitude, 'aware that the thing is given to me from a point of view'. I know I must 'deploy the flux of silhouettes in which the thing presents itself in succession from this angle and then from that angle'. I am also aware of the inadequacy of finite perception 'as always being in progress'. Thus I must move from the intentionality of perception to a 'signifying intentionality' and 'judge of the thing itself by transgressing the face of the thing onto the thing itself'.[59] Though hermeneutics is a doctrine of finitude, there thus must be a moment of infinitude for hermeneutics to be possible.

For Ricoeur man is infinite and finite, signifying and experiencing. Yet our infinitude, our signifying nature, is fully derivable from our finitude and pre-predicative intentionality. Thus Ricoeur understands Husserl's *Kehre* as a shift from phenomenological signification to hermeneutic 'explication'. This entails in *Ideen I* a shift from the 'linguistic plane' and its 'functions of denomination, predication and syntactic liaison' to the perceptual plane. In the linguistic plane phenomenological analysis involves the description of predicated objects, while the perceptual plane looks at ego intentionality towards pre-predicative objects. Predication involves the attachment of a universal to a particular, while perceptual investigations look at the noema as a particular 'intentional modification' of the monadic life of the ego.[60] Husserl had always, even in *Logical Investigations*, understood an object's meaning to include both the general and logical level of predication and the particular and psychological level of singularity. Beginning with the *Ideen* came a focus on perception: a notion of apperception which involved meaning as not only the understanding of an expression or logical representation (*Vorstellung*) but also as explication or interpretation of intuitive presentation (*Darstellung*).

This introduces temporality into the question of meaning. Phenomenological meaning in which one segment of experience reflects on a past segment entails the suspension of time. It presumes meaning to be constituted in a moment of the glance of the attentive ray. Husserl thus holds in *Logical Investigations* that opening up temporality also opens up the flux and succession of perceptual images, interfering with meaningful predication. Meaningful predication must abstract from the flow of temporality. It must hold time still in expressions that have an 'act' character, so that meaning is fixed and repeatable. Husserl's later work on perception opens the temporality of the noema's objects, opens the presence and memory of these pre-predicative objects.[61] This is integral to Heidegger's shift from a logical *a priori* of eidetic reduction to a temporal *a priori* in which meaning comes not through abstraction from experience but in the temporality of experience itself. The *Cartesian Meditations* is further confirmation of this shift towards the perceptual plane. Husserl begins to speak of phenomenology less as the account of the 'well formed' expression and more in terms of the meaning of experience. Now objects are no longer only in general but are 'for me', and derive their meaning and 'validity of being from me'. Meaning and truth lose their act character. If signification is an act, explication is an activity.[62] If signification entails the atemporality of both speech act and its object, explication is a temporal process with temporal objects. Phenomenology, once a science of ego description or self-reflection, becomes a science of self-explication, of the self's 'open and indefinite horizon'; a meditation, not with the character of an act, but instead infinitely pursued uncovering layer upon layer of the surplus of potential meanings in the *Lebenswelt*. Phenomenological description, the 'clarification of horizons', becomes 'ontological explication'.[63]

Body Ontology: Ricoeur

Signification and perception are 'mediations of the body on to the world'. In these mediations bodies 'produce' through signification and receive through perception. Here reception exposes the body to suffering and pain. Producing, the body is open, 'displaying the inside upon the outside as a sign for others'. Receiving, the body begins to close. Threatened, as an 'oriented fragility', it cannot be fully open, cannot be 'pure mediation', but needs to engage in 'affective closing' to be 'immediate for itself'. Producing, speaking the body, unthreatened because transcendent, is pure mediation.

The body offers to my will a set of powers. Signification is meaning intending, and transgresses perspective. Perception is fully perspectival. Ricoeur's body in reception/perception is a mode of being-in, of *Befindlichkeit*. *Befindlichkeit* is finding oneself thrown into the brutality of the world; it is finding oneself threatened. It is mood, affectivity but in particular mood as angst. We are, through our bodies, 'a two-fold intentionality': at the same time a 'will to do' and a finite 'will to live'. We are on the one hand the 'power of speaking', of 'signifying in the absence of this here', and on the other the power of seeing in the 'presence' of the particular. Hegel noted 'the richest of certainties is the poorest of truths'. In signification meaning is certainty, in perception it is truth. Certainty as 'non-vision of the thing' cancels its truth just as universality of the 'I' is also 'the negation of the not him'.[64]

Ricoeur's pre-predicative flux of perception is an experiential stream of unconsciousness. Meaning is initiated by means of a 'semantics of desire', accessible through not linguistic 'signs' but instead 'symbols'.[65] These symbols signify figurally, not logically or through *logos* but analogically through '*bios*'. Psychoanalysis here is a hermeneutic enterprise of explication through dialogue of analyst and analysand of these pre-predicative symbolic objects, thus enabling the analysand to recover finitude through the 'restoration' of desire's 'archaic heritage'. In this sense Ricoeur is advocate of an 'hermeneutics of suspicion' where – like in the three 'masters of suspicion', Marx, Freud and Nietzsche – immediate experience is a distortion of truth. But his is primarily a 'hermeneutics of retrieval', restoring respect for the object as a revelation of the sacred. His analytics of desire, whose symbolic exchange retrieves both our finitude and archaic heritage, opens out on to the domain of the menacing and mysterious power of the sacred. Authentic symbols straddle language and being and include a past (*arché*) and the future (*telos*). The retrieval of this past is also the recovery of finitude as archaic fallibility. In his *Symbolique du mal*, Ricoeur's analysis of pre-philosophic myths reveals 'man's pre-comprehension of himself' as evil, as a flawed and miserable creature. Unlike the emptiness of the sign, the symbols of this 'primitive language of avowal' are endowed with a fullness, a fulfilment. They are universal, yet fulfilled.[66]

The bodily dimension of Ricoeur's hermeneutics is of a piece with Heideggerian 'existence' and his *Existentialen*, the existential structures being-in (*In-Sein*) of *Befindlichkeit*, *Verstehen* and *Rede*: the structures of the existential constitution of 'the there'. Here *Befindlichkeit* is mood, the angst with which Dasein confronts the thrownness of its finitude. In *Verstehen* Dasein is always ahead of itself, projecting its ownmost possibilities on to the future. And *Rede* or talk is just that: it is not signification (*Aussage*). *Rede* is presentation (*Darstellung*) and not representation (*Vorstellung*), which is derivative of it. Thus Gadamer features play and art as forms of *Rede* (presentation) as primordial activities in *Truth and Method*.[67] These are the existential structures of 'the there' which each Dasein must face as its own. These – and the concern with which Dasein encounters ready to hand beings in the world – comprise the structure of 'care' which constitutes the being of Dasein.

This temporal *a priori* of pre-predicative meaning is the basis of hermeneutic intersubjectivity. In Husserl the possibility of meaning required a 'properly constructed' constituting subjectivity, a presuppositionless subjectivity abstracted from the suppositions of any given object. In hermeneutics the condition of understanding is intersubjecivity, including the presuppositions or prejudices inherent in this empirical intersubjectivity. Ricoeur draws on Gadamer to distinguish between 'short' and 'long' intersubjectivity. Short intersubjectivity in immediate dialogue follows the rules of Fregean 'sense', in which meaning is determined through the rules of forms of life. Short intersubjectivity also involves reference, but only the 'first-order reference' of the world.[68] Long intersubjectivity is found in cultural artefacts, in texts – in poetic, literary or historic texts, in monuments and narratives. Long intersubjectivity is interested in not sense but only reference, and in not first- but second-order reference. Second-order reference is existence as being-in-the-world itself. Long intersubjectivity achieves 'distanciation' through its extended temporality, which outflanks the world of manipulable objects and immediate understanding of the everyday.[69] Text or history as long intersubjectivity explicates the horizon of my own life and project.

Thompson has insightfully captured this as a 'semantics', not of *langue*, but 'of discourse'. Ricoeur's hermeneutics is a critique of both Husserl's egology and structural linguistics. Here Chomsky would be rejected for mentalism and French structuralism for its exclusion of meaning through pre-phenomenal intentionality, its privileging of sense (the signified) over reference and its very formalism. For Husserl, following Frege, the ego constituted meaning in light of the truth conditions of a predicated object. Here the singularity of the object was emptied out; its significance for any given subject negated. Similarly, Saussure's signifier is an emptied-out symbol, a symbol lacking any affective weight, abstracted from the experience, and bodily mediations, of any given subject. Ricoeur also disputes the semantics of *langue* for its predicative logic in which the meaning of a sentence is the conjunction of 'singular identification' and 'universal predication'.[70] Here Bertrand Russell's sentence as a complex symbol would again be an empty symbol. Ricoeur's semantics of discourse comprises not speech acts of immediate intersubjectivity, but instead texts comprising a threefold distanciation, in which second-order texts (distanciated from the speaker) address second-order interlocutors about second-order referents. Here the 'false infinity' of the author is challenged in the same way that symbolic texts of unconscious desire challenge the false infinity (infallibility) of the 'narcissistic ego'. Ricoeur's texts are thus also 'post-predicative' in their very excess over the author: their symbolic power infuses the otherwise empty language of the everyday world with the fulfilment and value constitutive of existence.

Ricoeur's understanding of existence and being is illuminated in his critique of Sartre's *Being and Nothingness*. If transcendence of finitude in Husserl's signification is a matter of negation, argues Ricouer, then Sartrean existentialism is a negation of this negation. Key here is the notion of value. Value expresses absence, what is lacking in things, constituted as phenomena in eidetic reduction. Empty value is the project of such negation. In terms of transcendence as negation, 'I suffer' yet at the 'same time judge this suffering on a scale of values more precious than my body'.[71] To judge, then, is to valuate and to judge generally is to valuate in abstraction. Thus, for Marx value is abstract homogeneous human labour, different from any particular and concrete working human being, which becomes a property of products. And exchange value or price is an abstraction assuming an aggregation of preference schedules, negating the use any particular human being will have from a good. For contemporary sociological positivism values are what individuals 'score' on variables. These values are already a reduction, an abstraction from this individual's activities, the variables taken across a sample and reduced to the contours of a normal curve.

Similarly, Husserl's reduction and the Cartesian ego negate (full) value to constitute empty value. For Descartes, Ricoeur notes, the idea of the infinite is identical with being, and the finite is grasped as at 'fault' in regard to being. Here being is understood as *a* being, i.e. *Sein* is understood as a *Seienden*, as infinite substance. For Descartes, Ricoeur notes, there is more reality in infinite substance than in finite substance: I have in me the notions of the infinite (God) before that of the finite me.[72] Sartre, Ricoeur argues, reverses this in his negation of the Cartesian primary negation. Sartre's nothingness is the negation of this. Sartre does support 'fact' (Heidegger's 'facticity') or finitude against abstract value. Yet he understands finitude as nothingness, as 'fault'. This 'nihilating act of nothingness' becomes Sartre's realm of freedom. His negation is the affirmation of brute fact against not just abstract value but all value.

These notions of fault, finitude and nothingness are Kierkegaardian. Yet Kierkegaard's angst is not grounded in notions of God as supreme being *per se*. For Kierkegaard, as in Judaism, God is not knowable, not a being and not categorizable in any great chain of beings. Sartre does understand God as infinite substance, as a supreme being. Thus Sartre misdefines being as what exists (not as what Levinas calls '*existence*' but '*existents*'). Being is understood by Sartre in terms of physical causality, as the 'in-itself', as a thing. Freedom in contrast is 'no-thing'.[73] Defined in contradistinction to being as being*s*, Sartre is condemned to an impoverished notion of existence. Sartrean existence understands the past as a nothingness: his future is not a horizon for one's ownmost possibilities, but instead nihilating freedom. Sartrean authenticity is not affirmation of the finitude of one's thrownness, one's projects, one's concern in the totality of the world, one's finitude in face of death. Instead all authentically human acts are 'nihilating withdrawals' from being and the world. Despite his writings, Ricoeur observes, Sartre's own nihilating acts are 'primary affirmation' of being, are 'projects' in which full value 'surges forth into the world'. The slave who rises forth against his master is 'testimonial' of an 'I am' beyond factual being; equivalent to 'I have worth', to 'existence-value' or dignity.[74]

'To think', Ricoeur quotes Anaximander, 'is to think being'; to think a source of things which has no source; a source of intelligibility to physics, ethics, politics and other domains and activities. Being is the source of existence-value to this plurality of domains and practices: it is at once fact and value. 'The first', proclaimed Anaximander, is 'not this', 'not that', indeed not a being at all; the first is 'not even infinity'. It is neither this, that nor infinity 'precisely because it is purely and simply'.[75] Human beings are those beings whose being is such that we think, meditate and affirm being through endless interrogation. To avoid this is our complacency. To accept this brings vertigo and angst. For Kant, as for Ricoeur, God is value. All thought is thus thought of the unconditioned. Human beings blessed only with the understanding cannot think God and the realm of reason. The origin, the primary affirmation, is primordially lost. The body opens us up to the world and to being. In the face of death my body forces me to define myself as Dasein, as finite being, as my being-in-the-world. But my 'finitude is suffered like a wound'; as a closure inherent in my openness to the world', which at the same time necessarily 'dissimulates from me the thought of the origin'.[76]

Ricoeur is invoking primordial myth and Christian mystery of the body as incarnate subject, entailing a transition from the language of the symbolic to the signification of the *logos*; from archaic assumptions of finitude and guilt to 'logical' assumptions of infinitude and 'fault'. For Gabriel Marcel existence consisted of an eidetic dimension of human brokenness (finitude) and a noetic dimension of a longing for the beyond. For Marcel and Ricoeur the eidetic dimension of infinitude and fault is derivative of the dimension of empirical brokenness of finitude and guilt. Through hermeneutic interrogation of the eidetic dimension we can recover its archaic foundations. Heideggerian thrownness here becomes fallenness, and angst becomes anxiety in the face of guilt and fallibility. We need to avow and participate in this brokenness of what Marcel saw as ' the mystery of the body as incarnate subject'. We need to participate in it actively in order to pass from 'objectivity' to existence. As we let the primary affirmation pervade our bodies, we exist in the transcending of our embodiment.[77] For Ricoeur, then, primary affirmation as 'Christian hope' is 'a directive principle of reflection'. This 'regulative feeling', this 'eschatological hope', is incurably mythical. It is inaccessible to the *logos*; it postpones syntheses, limits my reflection and keeps it finite.[78] When 'I reflect on my finitude; on the vital anguish of contingency and death', primary affirmation surges up in me as 'a vehemence to exist'. Not accessible to *logos* but only to the 'trust' I put in its 'hidden meaning', primary affirmation, despite my archaic brokenness and contingency, surges up in me in the 'act by which I wish to live'.[79]

8

Difference and Infinity: Derrida

Like Schutz and Ricoeur, Jacques Derrida proffers a critique of the transcendental reduction in terms of a notion of the ground. Schutz, we saw in
chapter 7, achieves this through an idea of a situated intersubjectivity, an
in-the-world intersubjectivity. Yet Schutz's work is only in the very weakest
sense 'ontological'. Derrida like Ricoeur is strongly ontological. Further,
like Ricoeur his critique of the reduction takes place not through
intersubjectivity. It is instead semiotic and involves a dimension of perception. Like Ricoeur, Derrida opposes the closedness of Husserl's
'productionism' with a focus on reception and opening. At issue is the
idea of the *trace*, the idea of the 'index', which is sensate, radically material
and receptive. This chapter will address Derrida's critique of phenomenology via this notion of trace (index), and draw on it to develop
the notion of the ground in the second modernity. But unlike in Schutz
and Ricoeur, we shall see, Derrida's critique via the trace moves not to
the more finite level of the natural attitude or life-world. Derrida, unlike
Schutz and Ricoeur, does not dispute Husserl's reduction for being
insufficiently finite, for being insufficiently grounded. Instead he finds the
reduction to be too finite, and Husserl's project to comprise a 'finite
totality'. Schutz and Ricoeur find the route to being via the finitude of the
ground, a level a lot more finite than the reduction. Derrida finds the route
to being through the trace: the trace that opens out from the finite totality
of the reduction to the *infinity* of being. The trace, however, is neither the
'same' of the finite totality, nor the other of being's infinity. The trace
occupies instead the third space of différance, which is semiotic difference,
that Derrida develops through critical analysis of Husserl's theory of the
sign. As important, however, it is ontological difference, and as such it
constitutes the limit between, and the condition of possibility of, both finite
totality and being (infinity).[1]

Kant, Husserl, Derrida

We saw in part II of this book how theory in an earlier modernity – the modernity of the turn-of-the-twentieth-century emergence of sociology – could only be thought through seriously in terms of Kant, in terms of Kantian pure and practical reason. Now we have discussed phenomenology – and its successor in hermeneutics – sufficiently to begin to put another argument. It is that theory at the point of the turn of the twenty-*first* century, concomitant with the rise of *cultural* theory, and the study of culture in its broadest sense can only be thought seriously with regard to Husserl. Perhaps against Husserl, perhaps with Husserl but surely not in ignorance of Husserl. And this is not only because of the whole litany of thinkers – from Heidegger, Levinas and Derrida to Gadamer, Merleau Ponty and Ricoeur to Gehlen and Luhmann, Schutz and Garfinkel – who studied profoundly and were profoundly influenced by Husserl.

Compare the earlier Kantian and later Husserlian turns – the latter in which rationality is thought literally as post-Husserlian reflexivity. In the first modernity of social theory the Enlightenment tradition thinks itself through as rationality and positivism. In the second modernity the Enlightenment tradition thinks itself through as reflexivity, as phenomenology's 'reflexive attitude'. This may well be a continuation of metaphysical tradition, but it is at the same time fully opposed to positivism. For the classical sociological theorists – Durkheim, Weber and Simmel – central was the Kantian cleavage of pure and practical reason.[2] That is, Kant's division of rationality into a realm of the understanding (*Verstand*) on the one hand and a realm of reason (*Vernunft*) on the other.[3] Here cognition or knowledge *per se* was confined to the realm of the understanding. What were involved in reason, what Kant called the ideas of reason, were freedom, God, ethics (the categorical imperative), infinity and noumena or things-in-themselves. These ideas of reason were inaccessible to the understanding, to knowledge and cognition. That is why Kant's first critique is called the *Critique of Pure Reason*. Pure reason or what Kant called metaphysics presumed that the Ideas of reason – especially ethics and the ontological proofs of the existence of God – were also accessible via cognition, were also questions of knowledge.

Thus for Kant – and for post-Kantian and classical sociological theory – Durkheim, Weber, Simmel and Marx too, there would be a realm of the understanding, of knowledge, i.e. a realm of *fact*, and a realm of reason, not cognition, a realm of *value*. Where one stood as a theorist depended on where one drew the line between these realms. If you drew the line so that the proper study of mankind was the inquiry into value, then you were a Lebensphilosopher along with Simmel and Dilthey's

Geisteswissenschaften. Before the neo-Kantian movement proper, the neo-romanticism of the young Hegelians and young Marx of alienation would also draw the line between fact and value, so that what was primarily studied was value, which is also of course the realm of praxis. If you drew the line so far over to the 'right', or should it be to the 'left', that values were only effects of facts or caused by social facts, as the superstructures of values and ethics are caused by the facts of the economy (Marx, Gramsci) or in Durkheim's sociologistic ethics and epistemologies, then you were a positivist. Not just Durkheim, but the mature Marx wrote in the atmosphere of neo-Kantian (and neo-utilitarian) positivism. If you left space for a realm of fact *and* a realm of values as did Weber, the early Wittgenstein (and logical positivism), Rickert and arguably Gramsci, then you were a neo-Kantian, staking out a position between, or if you like embracing, positivism and hermeneutics, embracing, or perhaps living with and accepting, the central aporia of sociology itself.

What is crucial to grasp here is that Kant's notion of knowledge, of cognition *per se* was positivistic. It was not subjectivist, but positivistic and in important ways objectivist. He spoke of objective knowledge. The critical philosophy signalled Kant's departure from metaphysics. Thus he spoke of a finite realm of the understanding and an infinite realm of reason. Inside the realm of the understanding, in which knowledge was at issue, Kantian theory is positivistic. Positivistic, in the sense of scientistic, does not of course entail empiricism. Kant's epistemology was indeed a critique of empiricism. Yet Kantian knowledge acquisition via the activist construction of a subjectivity endowed with the categories of Aristotelian logic is *not* a movement from empiricism's objectivity to a subjectivist notion of knowledge. What concerned Kant was not the objectivism but instead the scepticism, the relativism that empiricism allowed. This scepticism was drawn out explicitly by Hume but was of course already implicit in the Lockean doctrine of knowledge through association of sense impressions. Kant would not accept this scepticism, this psychologistic notion of knowledge dependent on the sense impressions of an empirical subject. He criticized empiricism as subjectivist. Kant's reference to a non-empirical – and hence transcendental – subject of knowledge is intended to combat subjectivism and save a place for *objective* knowledge.[4]

Kant's 'subject of knowledge' is no empirical, no existing subject. Kantian knowledge is not empirical in the sense of being psychological or socially determined. Kant's subject of knowledge is a general subject. It is a transcendental subject of knowledge: thus Kant views the understanding as comprised of a 'transcendental logic' and 'transcendental aesthetic'.[5] The transcendental subject is not any empirical subject. The knowledge involved is valid for any subject – not just to your or my particular psychology, or to working class, middle class, British or Asian, male or female, 'epistemologies'. It is fully objective knowledge. The knowledge is surely not (as phenomenological knowledge is) of a transcendental or infinite realm. Knowledge is only of our finite world. But a general (thus transcendent to any empirical subject) subject is necessary for there to be objective knowledge. This entails an activist yet not subjectivist notion of knowledge: at issue are the categorial conditions of possibility of objective knowledge.

This objective and anti-empiricist knowledge is positivistic, in the mode of mathematics and the natural sciences. Kant says you cannot know noumena or things in themselves, you can only know phenomena or appearances. To know a thing-in-itself is not like knowing some everyday thing like a fly or a desk, it is to know the particular ontological structures of significant entities, like humankind, or the good, or the political. It is to have an intuition into the ontological structure of such things-themselves, into the idea that animates such things. This sort of infinite intuition is for Kant only possible for God. Things themselves or noumena are not only not knowable 'objectively', but are unknowable *tout court* for human and finite subjects. All we can know are phenomena or appearances. But here what Kant means by knowledge of appearances is equally not knowledge of the surface appearance of, say, a fly, but a knowledge of its empirical structure (for example, its cellular structure) on the model of the natural sciences. The categories of logic – of cause, effect, identity, difference, syllogism and the like – are conditions of how we will know appearances or phenomena. This is a thoroughgoing positivism, i.e. a knowledge not of things themselves via their ontological structure, but of phenomena or appearances via their naturalistic (in the sense of the categories of natural science) structure. Thus Kantian knowledge is both objectivist and positivistic. And social theorists such as the early Durkheim, the mature Marx and much of Weber are positivistic (though not empiricist) and objectivist. The first modernity in social theory, to the extent that it subscribed to this sort of Kantian epistemology, was positivist.

Now the *second* modernity, perhaps more in cultural theory than in social theory, has a similar connection to Husserl. It is always post-Husserlian. For it rationality must be understood as reflexivity. Reflexivity is the basis for the 'different rationality' of the 'other modernity' as it is conceived in this book. For Husserl it was possible to know things in themselves. Here the language is a bit confusing in comparison to Kant. First, what Husserl called phenomena have more in common with Kantian noumena than with Kantian phenomena. So for Husserl, the things-in-themselves that are possible to know, of which it is possible to intuit the essence, are called phenomena. Phenomena are appearances for Kant; they are – in an important sense – essences for Husserl.[6] Husserl many times commented that he was extending cognition into the realm of

Kantian Ideas. In this sense he was treading on the realm of the sacred. Now Husserlian knowledge of things in themselves, of phenomena, is also objective knowledge. Unlike Kantian knowledge through the logical categories, this phenomenological knowledge is not positivistic. Husserl, like Kant, is opposed to empiricism. Husserl's knowing subject, the ego, is, like Kant's, no existing empirical ego. Knowledge based on an empirical ego was dismissed by Husserl as psychologistic and entailed a scepticism that he combated his whole life long: a scepticism in which knowledge is based on association of ideas or sense impressions, that empirically are found together with some kind of regularity. This could not yield objective or apodictic knowledge And it was apodictic knowledge that Husserl was after. Knowledge of things themselves is, further, not knowledge through naturalistic (positivist) categories. It is instead knowledge of the particular ontological structure of different 'ontological regions' of objects.[7] Thus, although phenomenological knowledge is via the intuition of essences, this is no simple essentialism. If, say, orthodox Marxism and economic reductionism is naive essentialism, and positivism in which things are known according to naturalistic categories is less naive essentialism, then Husserlian intuition of vastly differing essences is, at worst, a most sophisticated essentialism indeed.

Whereas Kant's subject of knowledge is transcendental and finite, Husserl's (and he was well aware of this) is transcendental and *infinite*. This is crucial, because it is the notion of infinity in Husserl, the extent to which Husserl transgresses finite totalities, that is, it seems to me, the basis of deconstruction in both Emmanuel Levinas and Derrida. Thus both Kant and Husserl have two main notions of the transcendental. For Kant most important is the sense in which the ideas of reason (including the noumena, i.e. the ontological structure of significant things) are transcendental to the understanding. The second sense is the way that the general subject of knowledge, i.e. the categories of the under-standing, transcends individual and empirical psychology. The transcendence of the ideas of reason is infinite, while the transcendence of the understanding, in Kant's 'transcendental unity of apperception', is finite. Both are universal, both are general, but only one is infinite. In Husserl this unity of apperception becomes the ego, and it is infinite in both of these senses.

For present purposes we have schematically understood the 'transcendental reduction' as that which through bracketing the world establishes the non-empirical ego transcendental to the world. We have understood the 'eidetic reduction' as the subsequent intuition of essences of objects (of things themselves) in the world.[8] The second and eidetic reduction makes possible knowledge of the Kantian realm of noumena. The first, transcendental reduction makes possible the eidetic reduction. The transcendental reduction also partakes of the infinite. It is the 'eruption', as Derrida calls it, of infinity, of reason, of the *logos*, of Ideas into what was previously the finite subject itself. It is this eruption of infinity, of God – because for Kant only God could intuit essences – that makes the intuition of essences possible. This absolute and transgressive intuition is further developed by Husserl in that notion of 'absolute'or primordial 'intuition' which is possible in the absence of the world. It is this absolute intuition, meaning or sense without a world, this god-likeness even in the absence of the noumena, this infinity which Derrida calls self-presence or '*voice*'. It is this absolute intuition – which Derrida finds all along the history of metaphysics (in which he includes both Husserl and Kant) – that through its deconstruction is the basis of the theory of *difference*.

How then does Derrida relate to the phenomenological reduction? How does deconstruction relate to Husserl's reflexive attitude? Surely not in anything resembling a 'postmodern' fashion. Deconstruction does not adopt the natural attitude of hermeneutics – does not counterpose forms of life to the reduction's reflexivity, does not counterpose natural language to phenomenology's logical language. But how then *does* deconstruction relate to the reduction? It is faithful to Husserl and the reduction to a surprising extent. It stays with Husserl and the reduction a lot longer than do Schutz or Ricoeur, or for that matter Heidegger and Gadamer. Deconstruction stays much more faithful to Husserl's reduction than any of these moves into the life-world and the natural attitude. Deconstruction does not say the reduction or reflexive attitude is impossible, but instead that after the reduction there is still left an irreducible 'supplement', an irreducible excess that itself is the condition of possibility of both reduction and the reflexive attitude. Though Derrida does have a very strong notion of ontology, even 'deep' ontology, central for him is not Heidegger's world, or the life-world, or the ground and grain of forms of life, but instead the *supplementary excess*, which makes knowledge through the transcendental ego possible, though never again apodictic. Reflexivity, infinity and the reduction are taken very seriously and investigated at great length indeed in Derrida. Husserl rejects Kant aggressively, and insists that even the Kantian ideas and sphere of reason are fair game for knowledge. Derrida is the more consistent Kantian, preserving from the powers of the knowing ego the sacredness of the supplement, trace and excess.

Derrida is the consistent advocate of an opening to such an infinity in order to escape the structures of finite totality. His earlier work first champions the infinity of Husserl's reduction against the finite totality of both Kant and various varieties of structuralism. It then begins to perceive Husserl's assumptions themselves in terms of a new finite totality – this time not that of structuralist positivism but instead of a more general and extensive domination of the *logos*. Deconstruction describes the escape into infinity from this totality and leaves us with the notion of difference as that excess which escapes the reduction and *logos*. Derrida's very recent work, this time not on reduction but on 'donation', on symbolic exchange and the gift, follows a similar trajectory. Here his first move, like Mauss's, is that from the finite totality of the market economy out into the gift economy of symbolic exchange. But this gift economy is only one more finite totality for Derrida, which must again be deconstructed for the difference and excess of Heidegger's 'es gibt'.[9]

But let us look at all this in far greater depth in detailed consideration of Derrida's early work, which forms a basis for the theory of difference. Here we will see the considerable extent of Derrida's fidelity to Husserl, albeit, with Heidegger, a strongly ontological reading of Husserl. Then we shall address how différance is also the deconstruction of Husserl. Derrida's critique shows that Husserl's temporal and spatial presence of objects before consciousness is identical to the interiority and self-presence of consciousness within itself. His position hinges on the demonstration that 'presence' is the same as self-presence. His larger argument is that the philosophical tradition is grounded in a 'metaphysics of presence' which is always also a metaphysics of *self*-presence; that is, a 'philosophy of consciousness' in the strictest sense. He rejects the metaphysics of presence and philosophy of consciousness because they entail such self-presence and self-consciousness. In his foundational work, *Speech and Phenomenon*, and other early essays Derrida makes his case through investigations of temporality and the notion of the sign. In this discussion 'presence' is understood in terms of the presence of phenomenology's ideal objects before consciousness. Derrida demonstrates that this presumes an original 'pre-expressive' meaning or sense internal to consciousness; that is, independent of the existence of the objects. Thus Husserl cannot go, Derrida shows, beyond the finite totality of consciousness to know things-in-themselves, i.e. to carry out his epistemics of infinity. Derrida introduces différance not in order to reject Husserl but in order to pursue the possibilities of the task that Husserl set for himself. In a very important sense Derrida's work is dedicated to the escape from the new finite totality of phenomenological consciousness to know the forbidden fruit of the Kantian noumenon. At times – for example, in the discussion of the gift – this excess emerges as a diabolical knowledge,[10] a knowledge in which the noumenon appears rather as the *part maudite*. Derrida attempts to realize Husserl's task through an epistemics of transgression. But let us focus our critical energies in this chapter on Derrida's early work and the laying down of the elements of the theory of différance. Let us focus on the necessary limits of this theory of différance.

Escape from Totality

What was the attraction of phenomenology? For Derrida as for Heidegger and life-world phenomenology, of central importance was Husserl's break with epistemology. Husserl's transgression of what Kant reserved for God and infinity was not just a question of consciousness constituting meaning. In the phenomenological reduction meaning would also be revealed by the ideal object. Consciousness would be receptive as much as productive. Meaning is constituted through the *encounter* of transcendental conscious-ness and ideal object. Such constitution of sense Husserl often refers to in terms of 'animation' (*beleben*) or 'lighting up' (*beleuchten*). When an object is phenomenologically 'fulfilled', when a thing in itself is known, this happens through an animation, a lighting up, that is two-sided. The light on the one hand is being thrown (*projeter*), as Derrida notes, by consciousness. On the other it is being thrown (*jeter*) by the object. Animation is meaning, endow-ing and fulfilment that is at the same time *projeter* and *objeter*.[11] In this sense, even though there can be no ideal objects without acts of intending, Derrida notes, transcendental experience is simultaneously 'active and passive', 'producing and revelatory'.[12]

Also important was a dimension that phenomenology shared with *Lebensphilosophie*. This was that phenomenology 'reduces naive ontology and returns to the active constitution of sense and value, to the activity of a life, which produces truth and value in general through its signs'. Like *Lebensphilosophie*, phenomenology breaks with any notions of staticness or stasis. It is 'a philosophy of experience, of becoming, of the temporal flux of what is lived'.[13] Thus not just the 'natural attitude', but also the reflective attitude, partakes of the vital, of life. And the natural versus transcendental attitude is not the counterposition of life versus reason. Both transcendental and natural attitude are understood instead as life, the first as the transcen-dental life of a concrete yet general (meaning constituting) ego. The second is 'empirical experience' (*Erlebnis*), or empirical life (*Leben*), understood in a sense that is not dissimilar to Bergson's *durée*. Here both transcendental and empirical life refer to mental life. Transcendental life is the bracketing of the empirical life of the psychological ego. It is transcendental in the sense of being the condition of the possibility of meaning. But sense or meaning is not determined, as in logic, by the truth conditions of statements, but by transcendental life, in that 'sense is determined by an act of living'.[14] Meaning is a question of the animation (*beleben*) of objects. Only life can lend such life to objects.

The extent of agreement with Husserl is perhaps most apparent in Derrida's article originally presented in 1959, eight years before the publi-cation of his major works, entitled ' "Genesis and structure" and phenom-enology'. This is largely a critique of structuralism using Husserl. For an example of structuralism Derrida uses Husserl's critique of Dilthey's notion of *Weltanschauung*, of his structural typology of *Weltanschauungen*. Husserl, Derrida notes, applauded Dilthey for breaking with naturalism, first in his conception of social life not in terms of causation, but like Husserl himself in terms of 'acts of understanding'. Husserl also saw positively a second convergence of Dilthey with his own work, namely the distinction of 'physical structures', whose 'principle' is 'external causality', from 'mental structures' in relations of 'motivation'.[15] Derrida's reproach to structuralism would then not be for naturalism or positivism. It is instead for the idea of structure as a finite totality. Husserl in this context accuses Dilthey of relativism and scepticism. Dilthey's *Weltanschauung* philosophy, like structuralism, must be a 'science of fact' and not a 'science of reason'. Dilthey's project must necessarily be sceptical in its 'historicism', in which 'norm' and 'validity' are reduced to 'historical factuality'. This entails a set of confusions, Husserl remarks, in which, for example, art as a historical and empirical form of culture is confused with valid art and historical and factual law is confused with valid law,[16] in which factual objects more generally are confused with ideal objects such as norms and values. Husserl is bothered by the empiricism of it all, that structures like *Weltanschauungen* connote 'factual totalities'. Derrida for his part is much more worried by their finitude. Structure, he writes, is 'closed by definition'. It leaves no transcendental opening to truth.

Derrida calls for phenomenological clarification before engaging in such structuralist analysis. Thus outside of finite (hence subjective) structural configurations of say law, one must circumscribe the domains of objectivity, and the meaning of the categorial structure of various phenomenological regions, of things-in-themselves. One must know, for example, he notes, 'What is the historical thing?' 'What is the psychological thing?' Derrida compares the factual, empirical and finite structures of structuralism to the eidetic-transcendental structure of a very special type of being, to the 'primordial structures of transcendental consciousness'. This is comprised, he notes, of two structures and four 'poles'. There is first a structure of meaning-giving, of intentionality, of the production of meaning, made up of noetic and noematic poles. In this the noetic is the subjective moment and the noematic the objective moment. The noema is the ideal objectivity, though not 'the determined thing-itself', but the appearing for consciousness of the latter. The second structure, still within the transcendental ego, is a structure of meaning-taking, or effectively reception, of the 'opening to the light of phenomenality'. This is composed also of two poles, 'hyle' and 'morphe'. *Morphe* is the intentional element of the experienced in consciousness, i.e. the animation from the phenomenality of the object. Morphe is form, in contrast to *hyle*, which is matter.[17]

Up to this point Derrida has agreed with Husserl's opening up on to infinity in critique of structuralism's finite totality. But now Derrida begins to part ways with Husserl. The constitution of meaning of transcendental things-in-themselves for Husserl is primarily dependent on the activity of consciousness: on noesis and the noema. For Derrida, however, the opening to infinity is through hyle. Hyle, as just noted, is the 'reception side' of the transcendental ego, but it is not reception as form or ideal object but 'the sensate material of affect before any animation by intentional form'.[18] Derrida thus wants an opening to infinity and an opening from the empirical to the transcendental that – given the confines of phenomenology, though perhaps already in a break with phenomenology – is radically *material*.

Derrida's position here already has in germ the theory of différance. Derrida is arguing for a notion of knowledge and experience that through its very materiality transcends finite subject positions. This is a notion of difference vastly variant from that common in the cultural studies literature. The notion of difference in the cultural studies literature agrees with Foucault that truth is necessarily linked with power, and hence is sceptical about notions of the true. Derrida, on the other hand, with Husserl, wants to sever the linkage of power and knowledge and move towards a notion of truth that will not speak its name. Derrida is fully in agreement with Husserl's project of a knowledge that breaks through the finitude of subject positions. The only problem is that he thinks that Husserl goes about it the wrong way. That Husserl's preference for the hegemony of the productionist and formalist components of transcendental consciousness leads to an epistemics, a metaphysics of self-presence in which nothing can be known outside of the finite totality of pre-representational meaning. Derrida says that the way out of this, the way towards exteriority from the finite totality towards truth, is not through productionist intentional moments of consciousness (or speech, voice) but through the receptive, the sensate and material moment, which provides the opening; that is, through *hyle*, which itself provides a basis for Derrida's notion of 'writing'.[19]

With the opening out to the world exterior to consciousness, exterior to a metaphysics of presence, the sort of truth which will be reached is not a knowledge of things in themselves or 'ideal objectivities'. It is also not apodictic or certain. It is instead a knowledge of the material side of objects. Of things not as they are in themselves, but none the less of things as they are. Things as they are, for Husserl, before their animation by intentional form as things-in-themselves, are a mere succession of '*Abschattungen*', of shadows, or *traces*.[20] It is the knowledge of such traces – by means, of course, of signifying material – which points to a certain 'brute realism' in Derrida. Knowledge of such things as they are, knowledge of traces, is just as likely through narrative, poetically or pictorially, or even through touching, as through the formal discourses of the natural and human sciences. If knowledge is no longer to be of Husserl's ideal objectivities, then the 'clear evidence' of a fulfilled intuition is to be lacking for Derrida. Without such evidence, apodictic or certain knowledge is impossible. Thus Derrida's idea of truth, though in principle universalistic, must always be a question of knowing things as they are, knowing traces, but uncertainly.

Derrida's subsequent and sustained deconstruction of the metaphysics of presence always takes Husserl's notion of consciousness as a model for the metaphysics of presence. Derrida's subsequent deconstructions, not just of structuralism – of Lacan and Lévi-Strauss, of Heidegger, all the way to the recent work on Mauss's gift economy – consistently takes the metaphysics of presence to be a finite totality, understood on the model of Husserl's transcendental consciousness. Thus Dilthey's structured *Weltanschauung* is itself a sort of *conscience collective*, ruled over by a transcendental signified. And the deconstruction of the gift economy is at the same time a deconstruction of the finite *consciences collectives* described in Durkheim's more explicitly structuralist *Formes élémentaires de la vie réligeuse*. Again there is a *Weltanschauung* or master structure operating as a transcendental signified, ruling over the elements of the finite totality and prohibiting exit from this claustrophobic finitude on to the infinity of the world and knowledge. Thus, too, the Lacanian unconscious symbolic is understood as a system of signifieds ruled over by the phallus (and the Oedipus) as transcendental signifieds precluding any connection on to outside materiality.[21]

Derrida has no quarrels with simple presence. For Husserl, presence involves knowledge of external objects, unproblematically present to consciousness as things-in-themselves. Derrida applauds this Husserlian knowledge of things external to consciousness. The problem for Derrida is that presence always must lead to self-presence, to a form of knowledge in which meaning or sense is 'pre-expressive'. This is why he always argues against not a transcendental signifier but a transcendental signif*ied*. The signifier is material, hence mundane and worldly. It already has a foot out on to the external world. But the signif*ied* is ideal.[22] It represents immediately without any mediating material. It keeps thought locked up in the finite totality of meanings, of certain determination of meaning of elements. Without any signifying material, linguistic 'expressions' that hook on to the external world are impossible. With the transcendental signified,[23] knowledge and meaning are 'pre-expressive': knowledge is already produced before any reference whatsoever to objects in the external world.

Whereas Husserl is upset by the scepticism and empiricism entailed in finite totalities, Derrida is more concerned with their totalitarian implications, with the sort of 'locked-in-ness' they entail. The main point, however, is that Derrida has the same objectives as Husserl, i.e. the possibility of knowledge of things outside of finite or the finitude of consciousness. Husserl thinks that he has accomplished this through the reduction. Derrida must argue that he has not done. He must argue that all the reduction can yield is self-presence, and that différance is the only way out. Note finally that Derrida, though opposed to transcendental siginifieds like the phallus or the *Weltanschauung*, is *not* arguing against the transcendental. For him it is the materiality of the trace, of différance, that is the transcendental: the condition of possibility of experience, knowledge and meaning.[24]

Time and Self-presence

The first thing we learn about deconstruction is that 'différance' is not just an absence of identity in the order of signification. It is also a matter of deferral, the verb différer having not one but two entries in the *Petit Robert*, the first entry focusing on to differ and the second on to defer. To differ is a difference whose opposite is identity. But the opposite of to defer is not identity. The opposite is to do something or for something to take place in 'the now'. What unifies the two types of differer is a certain opposition not so much to identity as to *presence*. To 'spatial' and temporal presence. I put spatial in quotes here, because both presence and difference in the sense of deferral are types of temporality, whereas in the order of signification difference is spatial. In the order of signification, presence, which is at the same time self-presence, partakes of no spatial extension outside of consciousness. Let us first consider Derrida's preliminary treatments of temporal difference.

In '"Genesis and structure" and phenomenology', Derrida first addresses structure in Husserl. He notes that Husserl's classic works, *Idéen* and *Logische Untersuchungen*, are about structure and not genesis. He says that only in the later work, *The Phenomenology of Internal Time Consciousness*, *The Cartesian Meditations* and *The Crisis of the European Sciences*, does Husserl address genesis. Derrida contrasts the sort of temporality found in Husserl's later works with those of classical phenomenology. In classical phenomenology there is no genesis, temporality is formal and organized by a present point in time of 'the now'. In the later works, when Husserl begins to break with the pure reduction, and begin to address intersubjectivity, the life world and the 'horizon', temporality takes on a sort of grain, a certain spatiality. Instead of a self-generating and unmotivated transcendental ego and a self-generated temporality, it becomes possible to speak of genesis, and 'the emergence of theoretical and practical predication on the basis of

untamed pre-cultural life'.[25] Derrida looks approvingly at this shift, and
notes that hyle, the opening of presence on to the materiality of the world,
is itself primarily temporal, while calling for a 'new transcendental aesthetic', consisting of a time of alterity that puts the presence of the thing-
itself into question.

The essay based on the celebrated 1968 lecture 'Différance' focuses in
the first instance on difference in temporality, upon which the difference in
signification is apparently derivative. In this essay Derrida addresses temporal différance in three ways – as detour, as genesis and as primordial.
Here signs and time are initially introduced at the same time. Thus
différance is a 'detour' that 'suspends the fulfilment of a "will"', or suspends
the fulfilment of the phenomenological reduction. The detour here is
always via a sign. Via some thing that stands in the place of the thing to be
fulfilled, that stands in the absence of the thing to be phenomenologically
reduced. The sign is thus a 'delayed presence', delayed until the time that
the thing-itself is there.[26] Derrida mentions in the context of psychoanalysis
that the reality principle is thus a detour by which the pleasure principle
fulfils itself. He does argue here that the detour itself and not the self-
identical 'I' is the origin, is primordial. But detour here is a matter of
'temporalization', of delay, of taking more time. Of something that mediates or comes between the ego and something else.

The second sense of temporal différance in the essay is when the opacity
of the signifier or the trace comes not between ego and object, or mo-
mentarily in the place of the object for the ego. But instead the sign or
the trace comes *before* or in the 'past' of both ego and object, in the sense
of not so much priority but historically before, in the sense of trace as
history with a small 'h', or as tradition. This is the sense of genesis mentioned above. Here différance is a 'network' or 'assemblage' of traces, a
moving assemblage of traces by which 'language or any code becomes
constituted historically as a fabric of differences'. Traces are like the empirical side of Husserl's objects: they are shadows, appearances, the aspects
of ideal objects out of which the latter are 'polythetically' constituted. The
trace, Derrida writes, constitutes the present in 'relation to what is not'.
Thus the trace 'is not' in two senses. First, in terms of the predicative logic
of 'S is P' that phenomenology subscribes to, it is the ideal objectivity to
which the copula 'is' refers, and not mere appearances, mere traces. Here
traces have spatial extension, but do not have ideal essences. Second, the
trace 'is' not in the sense that it never *is* but always *was*. In psychoanalysis
the unconscious thus is a question of différance as a 'network of traces' with
'delayed effects'. Here the incursion of a 'dangerous investment' is 'deferred' by 'constituting a reserve'. In psychoanalysis the detour of the trace
is original. The unconscious trace is thus 'a past which has never been
present'.[27]

The third type of temporal différance in the essay is pastness, not in the factical sense of tradition but in the sense of constitutive, primordial, original, a sort of source point before, and in place of, the source point of the now of Husserl's ego. Here, similarly to in the seminal essay 'Violence and metaphysics', Derrida follows Levinas in taking his distances from Heidegger. Here the trace, like Levinas's ethical relation of 'I' and 'Thou', is 'more ancient than Being'. It comes perhaps as a revelation that cannot be known, before the epoch of Being, which indeed the trace sets into play.[28] If beings in their ideal objectivities have phenomenological sense or meaning, Heidegger's Being through the existential reduction and only accessible via beings still has, though never determinable, a sense or meaning. Derrida's trace, like Levinas's other, takes on meaning, takes on *sens* or *Sinn*, very much as does Being in fundamental ontology. One can speak of the 'Being of beings' as Heidegger does in his existential analytic of Dasein from one end to the other of *Sein und Zeit*. But one cannot speak of the trace of beings in anything like the same way. Like Kierkegaard's God of revelation without law or history, the trace makes 'ontological beings tremble'.[29] If at Heidegger's 'dawn' the Being of beings was already forgotten, it is only later in metaphysics and the age of technology that the ontological difference, the 'matinal trace of difference' also effaces itself.[30] Derrida thus sees the task of deconstruction to be to find the trace that the forgetting of this '*frühe Spur*' has left.

Thus presence in the order of signification depends on presence in the temporal order. If there is no temporal detour via re-presentation, then instead all that exists is the translucence of the sign without the opacity of the signifier. There is no representation but instead direct presentation in the order of signification. Thus it may make sense to speak in phenomenology of a third 'temporal reduction' that takes place immanent to consciousness and with which the ego reflexively brackets immediate experience. Direct presentation is signification without a signifier, i.e. it is signification via only a signified. And since the sign's only mundane element is the signifier, a signifier-less sign must always be a 'transcendental' signified. Philosophy, Derrida understands, is always about the transcendental. What he rejects, however, is the sort of transcendental found in the philosophy of consciousness.[31] The philosophy of consciousness – only repeated in Lacan's 'philosophy of unconsciousness' – lacks any materiality outside of the ideal object. Derrida proffers this external materiality in the trace.

Phenomenological temporality enters only with the reduction, freezing the flux into discrete repeatable elements of experience, reducing matter to form. The organizing principle of time for Husserl is the 'self-identity' of this 'now' as a 'source point'. A source point of self presence in comparison, for example, to the self-différance of the trace in psychoanalysis. This

source point is primordial in both the order of signification and the order
of temporality, not in being more ancient, but in being unmotivated by
material beings, in being the source of animation and meaning for objects
and beings. It is primordial in the sense of being foundational and universal, and finally it is primordial in its persistence as a form that persists
through various changes of matter.[32]

It is difficult to see how Husserl can speak of the reduction as an
instantaneity of the now, because as we saw in the discussion of Schutz,
a moment of experience can only reflect on a moment of past experience. And much of Husserl's discussion in *The Phenomenology of Internal Time
Consciousness* seems to assume precisely this. Husserl gets round this irreducible pastness by bringing in the distinction – as we noted – between
retention and recollection. When you retain something it is still present,
while you recollect what is past. Husserl distinguishes between the 'absolute
certainty' of retention and the 'relative certainty' of recollection.[33] He needs
the notion of retention for the phenomenological reduction, for the possibility of certainty, repeatability, identity and presentation. Because of the
principle that two moments in experience cannot occur simultaneously,
Husserl must create a moment of the past (retention) that is nevertheless
in the present. Derrida's view is that there can be no such radical distinction between retention (primary memory) and recollection (secondary
memory), but that all memory must be in the past and not available for
immediate presentation, but must be approached through the detour (and
opacity) of representation.

The function of Husserl's temporality is to make the eidetic reduction,
the intuition of ideal objectivity, possible. These objects are on the one
hand ideal, but on the other they must also be in the external world. Now
if retention can be present not to representation but immediately to perception (of transcendental consciousness) then it cannot itself have spatial
extension or partake of matter. It must be an ideality, a pure form, and thus
be interior to the self-presence of consciousness. Hence phenomenology
and the temporality of the metaphysical tradition entail self-presence. The
classical notion of substance is a question of presence, of temporality self-
presence. Truths in the history of metaphysics from Plato through Husserl
are expressed in statements of presence, propositions of the form 'S is P'.
Indeed, for Heidegger the ontological tradition's posing of the question of
Being only as a question of beings is also the reduction of the verb to be to
the third person singular predicative proposition, in which the meaning of
Being is reduced to the mere copula of the 'is' in 'S is P'. This is indeed the
statement of presence, of meaning in the phenomenological reduction. But
self-presence is not expressed in the 'S is P', and that is because the 'S is P'
involves an extension into the materiality of the external world. Neither
self-presence nor its temporality, Derrida notes, ever involves a real predi-

cate of being. Predicative logic of the 'S is P' presumes that 'S' is not a
pronoun (hence not indexical or an indication) but a *nom*, i.e. a noun and
a name. If this is so, as it is in classical and phenomenological time, then the
movement of Husserl's temporalization can give no name to the 'S is P'.[34]
Hence such temporality involves not the presence of the 'S is P', but instead
the *self*-presence of the 'I am I' or the 'I = I'.

Derrida's claim is that neither Newtonian time, i.e. everyday clock time,
nor phenomenological time sees time as having substance, matter or spatial
extension. Both would be pure form. Both are horizons against which we
understand the meaning of beings, horizons against which we make the
statements of predicative logic, of the 'S is P' variety. In this sense both
phenomenological and Newtonian time are 'source points'. Clock time is
not, however, the same as phenomenological time. Newtonian time is the
temporality of only one region of beings, whose truth can be understood according to the laws – cause, effect etc. – of the natural sciences.
Phenomenological time, though assuming pure form and the now as
absolute source point, is a horizon against which other regions can be
understood in non-naturalistic senses. Phenomenological time like clock
time receives nothing – is unmotivated – from the world, it is thus a 'pure
production', in which 'the absolute novelty of each now', 'is engendered by
nothing', but instead 'engenders itself'.[35] Without the now as absolute
source point beings cannot have meaning, or the meanings that they
have are only 'occasional', or 'trivial'. What Husserl saw as empirical
temporality, from the natural attitude is a lot closer to Bergsonian *durée*,
Heidegger's time and Gadamer's tradition. It is an opacity of temporalization, a material coarseness and mundanity of duration and irr-
egularity, that forms the horizon for the (non-predicative) meaning this
time not of beings, but of being.

Derrida's time of the trace, of différance, partakes of this sort of spatially
extended temporality of life-world phenomenology. The truths and meanings it makes possible are not predicative, but may be poetic or pictorial.
Yet unlike life-world phenomenology, deconstruction does not operate
from the natural attitude. Its reduction, like Husserl's, is much more
extra-worldly, temporal différance being often only a detour on the way to
fulfilment of an intuition that can never quite be fulfilled. It is Derrida here,
and not the life-world phenomenologists (Heidegger, Schutz, Ricoeur,
Gadamer), who is more the hostage of the philosophy of consciousness.

Three Modes of Signification

Derrida's strategy is consistent. It is to show that presence entails self-
presence. It is always to show that the 'S is P' in its *'telos'* must be the 'I =

I'. It is thus to show that the metaphysical tradition to which he now assimilates Husserl cannot yield knowledge of things but only a solipsism of the I = I. It is to show in the end that knowledge and truth cannot be based in the everyday and social scientific assumptions of predicative logic, that truths about things as they are are not propositional truths. His main way of doing this is not through analyses of temporality, but, especially in *Speech and Phenomenon* and *Grammatology*, through examinations of the structure of the sign. Hence his critique of 'voice' is not primarily an argument in linguistics but instead an argument that knowledge in the metaphysics of presence entails self-presence.

Voice is one of three modes of signification that Derrida finds in Husserl. The other two, already addressed in our discussion of Schutz, are indication and expression. Thus in Husserl there are three types of signs: (a) *indicative* signs; (b) *expressive* signs; and (c) signs associated with voice or speech, which Derrida calls '*phonic*' signs. Here *indicative signs* (*Anzeichen*) in Husserl are traces and presume the dominance of the signifier,[36] if not the purity of the signifying element of the sign. Indication presumes spatial extension without any sort of ideal content. Indicative truths are truths that are not pronounceable in predicative logic. Expressive (*Ausdruck*) signs presume the signification of presence. These signs are comprised more equally of signifying and signified elements, they are ideal and material at the same time. The metaphysics of presence expresses truths in the expressions of expressive signs They partake of the predicative logic 'S is P'. 'Phonic signs' (voice, speech) are the signification of *self*-presence. They comprise only signifieds without signifying elements. They are only ideal, without material extension. What Derrida calls the 'pre-expressive' truths of self-presence are uttered in phonic signs. They partake of propositions of the sort 'I am I', in which the 'I' is no empirical pronoun, but the 'fulfilled "I"' of the transcendental ego. It is Derrida's project to show that that expressive signs are 'in their *telos*' necessarily phonic signs. And this is the major task of the book *Speech and Phenomenon*. If the book *Writing and Difference* addresses the connection between indicative signs (writing) and difference, then *Speech and Phenomenon* is in fact a sustained argument that the simple presence of the phenomenon entails the solipsistic self-presence of speech, of voice or phonic signs.

Thus we have three modes of signification, each of which is comprised of three elements: subject, object and sign. Note that there is only one subject, and no intersubjectivity here. Derrida (like the philosophy of consciousness) has very little time for intersubjectivity and communication.[37] And to the extent that one leaves the logocentrism and formalism of self-consciousness for the opacity and materiality of forms of life, it is necessary to think of signification in terms of some sort of communication (no matter how situated). To understand deconstruction's ideal types of indication, expression and voice we should consider first the elements of each mode and then the relationship between elements. Each element, subject, object and sign has two sides, or is two-dimensional. Each element has a material, extensive, spatial side and an ideal side with no spatial extension. In this sense indication is a pure type of material signification in which the empirical or material side of subject, object and sign appear. In fact Derrida uses the term 'trace' to refer to the material sides of all three. In terms of the subject, he speaks as we saw of the hyle as the opening on to the world in terms of trace. He also speaks of the shadows, the aspects, the appearances of the Husserlian object as traces. Finally, he speaks of the signifier, the material side of the sign, as a trace. It is this third sort of trace, the trace of the sign, which is the driving force in perhaps the whole of Derrida's work. In 'voice' the ideal side of subject, object and sign is featured, while in 'expression' there are two sides, material and ideal, to subject, sign and object.

The subject in the mode of signification can be individual or collective. It can be empirical or transcendental. In 'expression' it is two-sided: empirical and transcendental. In 'indication' it is only empirical. In a mode of signification there are two types of relationships between elements: motivation and animation. If semiotic force has its source on the empirical or material side then it is possible to speak of 'motivation'. If semiotic force is exercised from the transcendental or ideal side then we speak of 'animation'. Husserl understands indication (*Anzeichen*) in terms of subjects being motivated to believe in the existence of objects by other objects which are signs that stand for the former objects.[38] Linguistic anthropologists make a similar distinction between the less motivated 'semiosis' and more motivated 'mimesis', or between symbol, icon and index in a diminishing scale of motivation. Thus Husserl's highly motivated indicator, Peirce's index and ethnomethodological 'indexicality' are similar in nature. Here the object motivates not the subject but the sign. It is thus that I have understood 'figural signification' (chapter 4) and figural communication in Walter Benjamin's idea of urban space. Thus cinematic images are more motivated by the object than is writing in phonetic alphabets, and graphic alphabets are somewhere in between. In indicative signification (i.e. difference), the subject is motivated by object and especially by the sign, and the sign is motivated by the object. Hence we have a fully empirical and 'caused' subject. The notion of difference in Saussure gives priority to motivation rather than animation, in that the difference between signifiers in a *langue* gives rise to meaning. In voice or self-presence the subject as transcendental ego 'animates' the object by fulfilling it as a phenomenon. The subject is the unmotivated animator, possessed with primordial and absolute intuition. This is the self-identical subject of self-presence. Similarly, the sign is animated from the transcendental ego. In expression or simple presence subject and object animate/motivate each other

reciprocally and the sign is at the same time animated by the ego and
motivated by the object.

For Derrida the sign is irreducibly two-sided, with both functions of
expression and indication. It is not only empirically two-sided, but still
two-sided when it is reduced. Derrida disagrees with Husserl's reduction of
the sign to its pure expressive essence. If it is so reduced, he maintains, there
can be no empirical externality of the object. Husserl confirms this in his
privileging of solitary mental life over empirical communication between
subjects as the mode in which reduction and constitution of meaning
take place. Thus Husserl can comment that the reduction can take
place without the existence of any empirical objects. The critique of this
solitary mental life is the basis for Derrida's understanding and rejection of
voice.

We should note that Derrida does not so much disagree with the reduction or even 'essentialism' or the intuition of essences, but claims instead
that in its essence the sign is irreducibly expression and indication. We
should note the convergence with Heidegger's existential reduction of the
sign in section 17 of *Sein und Zeit*, in which the being of the sign is similarly
two-sided. Neither Derrida nor Heidegger counterposes contingency or
ambivalence or *durée* or desire to reason or the *logos*. Both valuate knowing
as irreducible, though complex, processes of expression and indication.
Derrida's limit condition, his third space of difference as the margin between spaces of absence and presence, is also the limit that lies between the
irreducibility of indication and expression. Moreover, in *Sein und Zeit*'s
introductory exposition of the task of the preliminary analysis of Dasein,
Heidegger explicitly constructs the inquiry into the existential analytic, the
categorial structure of Dasein in contradistinction from both philosophic
anthropology and any sort of natural attitude (*'natürlichen Weltbegriff'*).[39] The
analytic of Dasein, while still in the world, is none the less transcendental –
in the sense of the condition of possibility of authentic experience, and in no
way empirical as is the natural attitude. Finally, Derrida's argument from
presence to self-presence – or from an ontology of beings to a philosophy
of consciousness, is implicit in Heideggerian 'onto-theology'. Here Derrida
contrasts the sign as irreducible joinedness of expression and indication
with perception or the word: i.e. the tendency of isolated expression (without indication) to slide into voice. In this sense the transcendental ego and
the history of the philosophy of consciousness is a continuation of theology,
in that the ego is a being whose self-presence, whose transparent 'voice', in
no empirical language constitutes meanings and 'creates' ideal objectivities.
This being is of course God.

Expression is at the same time logical expression, the predicative logic
of 'S is P'. A proposition of the form 'S is P' is for Husserl 'the primordial
and apophantic operation from which every logical proposition may be

derived'.[40] Here the S must be not a pronoun and thus only an index or indicator; that is, only having sense in regard to another empirical being – a he, she or it – which is its antecedent. The S must instead be a noun or name of an object. The point here is that Husserl consistently subordinates linguistic meaning to logical meaning. He subordinates natural language grammars to logical grammar,[41] governed by the relation of signs and objects. His notion of expression has the 'logical character of a signifier that is animated in view of the ideal presence of a Bedeutung related to an object'.[42] His determination of language in general, Derrida observes, is on the basis of 'theorein'. If the pronominal unfulfilled and empirical 'I' of indication is to be replaced by the noun (the name) of logical expression, then the telos of expression is the fulfilled I = I of the philosophy of consciousness. This is mostly because of the very repeatability of what must be ideal objectivities in expression. The P of the 'S is P' as the meaning of S must be repeatable. Because no empirical object is repeatable, because nothing with spatial extension is repeatable, then purely ideal objectivity cannot by definition be of the world, but can be constituted as pre-expressive sense by pure consciousness. The repeatability of the (ideal) object for Derrida must at the same time be the 'reactivation of origins', the reactivation of spatio-temporal self-presence.[43] Heidegger, Derrida notes, saw similar connections between propositional truths of S is P and the determination of being as beings. The ontological tradition, which determines being as beings, reduces the whole of being to the simple 'is' of the copula S is P, reduces the whole of Sein or to be to the third person present indicative of the verb.

Pointing, Seeing, Hearing

Derrida finally develops his argument for a material critique of the phenomenological notion of the sign in his notion of 'Zeigen'. Zeigen means to show, and in German is etymologically related to *Zeichnen* or sign. In section 17 of *Sein und Zeit*, on the sign, Heidegger works from this connection. Introducing Zeigen in the famous paragraph on the turn-signal (indicator) of an automobile, he looks at this type of sign as a 'Zeigzeug' (indicating tool).[44] But whereas Heidegger states that Zeigen is not the ontological structure of the sign, but only addresses the being of the sign insofar as the sign is a tool or Zeug, Derrida has a much broader notion of Zeigen. For Derrida it is an 'essence' which cannot be an essence as the irreducible combination of indication and expression.[45] Zeigen or showing in everyday language, notes Derrida, has two meanings: on the one hand to point to something, and on the other hand to demonstrate something. To the extent that a sign is involved in showing, to the extent that the sign shows, it both points to and demonstrates. Zeigen is at the same time the pointing (touching, tactile) finger and the demonstration, the gesture of demonstration of the eye. Showing or Zeigen is always 'an intending that predetermines the unity of indication and expression'. 'Phenomenality', Derrida notes, should then be the 'state of encounter' in which something is 'ob-jected' (*objeter*) and something is pro-jected, signification the unity of the 'pointing finger' and 'the eye of gesture and perception'.[46] What is being thrown in this *objeter* and *projeter* is the meaning of phenomena, the meaning of objects. Derrida contrasts the combination of reception through pointing, touching (*objeter*) and production through seeing in the sign, in showing, with the ear and the voice of phonic signification. Phonic signification has no Zeigen, no showing, because it operates through not the sign, but 'the word'. If the sign is the unity of indication and expression, of touching/pointing and seeing, then the word is instead the unity of phone and sense. The phoneme 'designates nothing', Derrida intones, 'because it is encountered nowhere'. 'Its irreducibility is that of . . . the unity of thought and voice in Logos'. It is the 'pre expressive stratum of sense'. It constitutes meaning without objects, prior to worlds.

Husserl wants phenomenological meaning, constituted through the sign as expression and the expression of the statement 'S is P', to be this sort of combination of production and reception. The problem is, notes Derrida, that he wants it both ways. On the one hand, phenomenological meaning does involve 'animation', does involve the 'light' of 'animation' coming from subject *and* object so that the independence of the object (from consciousness) can be 'protected'. That is, expression must protect the sense of the object before us, or protect the 'pure noema'.[47] But at the same time the sign as expression in phenomenological meaning must 'protect presence as proximity to the self in interiority'. The problem is that expression cannot do both of these at the same time. The light, the animation, here cannot come from the empirical object in the real vulgar material world. Such objects can only 'motivate' as in indication. For Husserl they must have nothing to do with meaning, but only with trivial associations or occasional meanings. The question is where does this animation, this light, this *beleuchten* and *beleben*, come from? It can come only from the ideal object and only as constituted by the self-present transcendental ego. It is the pre-expressive stratum of sense that passes into the ideality of the object. Thus there is no reception side, there is no possible opening for Husserl's ego. Phenomenology in this sense is pure productionism.

And 'productionism' has always been paradigmatic for the second modernity's reflexive critique of high modernity. Thus Adorno and Horkheimer rejected the identity thinking, in which subject dominates and extinguishes any supplement of the object, that is transferred into the real economy of production itself, not just as commodification but as the domination in production of man over nature and man over man. Thus Levinas criticized Husserl's reduction as the reduction of the other, a reduction continued in the 'ontological tradition', in which a certain productionism also pervades everyday life, in the economy and notions of property, destroying the possibility of any opening to the other and the ethical. Heidegger renders productionism as technology as Gestell or the frame. Gestell entails production, sharing roots with *vorstellen*, *darstellen*, *bestellen* and *herstellen*, in which objects are framed and put from one place to another. The verb *stellen* means 'to put'. In each case the object or the alterity of the object is nullified by this putting. The logic of Gestell is involved in *vorstellen* as representation. Here consciousness represents the object, man takes the object and re-presents it otherwise, instead of somehow listening receptively to the object's being. *Vorstellen* leads to *bestellen* or ordering, as when one orders some good for a factory as a raw or intermediate material. *Herstellen* means literally to manufacture. Hence the logic of the standing reserve in Heidegger's idea of technology is of alterity of the object being reduced to a reserve for consciousness for productionist framing.[48]

Heidegger and Derrida oppose the productionism of phenomenology. Thus Derrida castigates voice in Husserl as a pure signified, abstracted from any empirical signifier. Phonē here is a sign animated from consciousness alone as a *Bedeutungsintention*. Voice is the place of pure proximity to consciousness, the only and absolute source point, of pre-expressive sense reducing the signifier to transparency.[49] Yet for Derrida Heidegger's Being is also a 'transcendental signified'. Heidegger's and Derrida's non-productionist, receiving subjectivities differ importantly. Heidegger's Dasein knows objects through reception, through Dasein's opening to the light of Being. In Heidegger's existential reduction, Dasein as being-in-the-world is open to the world, is open to ready-to-hand beings in the world, is receptive to the being of those beings through the light, the animation, by the sending of Being. In the generosity and plenitude of the 'es gibt', Being fills up objects or things with its light in its sending to Dasein. Dasein must stand in the light of this opening to receive this light.

The operative metaphor here is light. Here Being itself is an (unread-able) signified uncorrupted by the paucity of signifying matter: it is an absolute source point. In contrast, Derrida's trace, itself primordial, doesn't have a light, it is the brute appearance of the empirical aspects of the object, which itself takes the place of the transcendental, but the transcendental as brute externality. Being is somehow underneath, sending and illuminating through the being of objects, while the trace is not underneath but in-between. In-between as a detour, as the mediating being between subjects and objects. In-between as the limit, the 'invaginated' limit separating the signifier's externality from the interiority of the signified, and the condition of possibility of both.

And Derrida means, *pace* Baudrillard, a primacy not of the object, but instead of the *sign*. If Heidegger takes the 'is', the copula mediating the subject, with the rest of a predicative judgement and opens it up into a fundamental ontology, then Derrida takes the sign mediating between subject and object and opens it up into the destruction of the metaphysical tradition. Derrida does this via the empirical, yet parts with empiricism. In every case in which he dismantles Husserl, Derrida resurrects what Husserl sees as the empirical against the transcendental. This is what life-world phenomenologists like Schutz, Ricoeur and at points Gadamer do, though Derrida is more empiricist than they in that his objects have no essence. But Derrida, unlike the empiricists, does not see truth as a matter of the association of ideas as sense impressions. He differs from the empiricists' ideas of propositional truth, and truth as certainty or the probability of certainty anyway. His focus would not be on the empirical or material side of ideas in any event but on the trace on the empirical or material side of the sign. Most of all, in any event, Derrida, as we saw above, seizes on the empirical and renders it as transcendental. He takes the most vulgar bit of matter, the trace, and makes it the condition of possibility of meaning, experience and knowledge.

Thus Saussure and linguistics take on a featured role in the lecture introducing the concept of 'différance'. Saussure, Derrida notes, a linguist and not a philosopher, breaks with the classical notion of the sign as unity of name and object. For Saussure instead it is the unity of signifier and concept or signified, and it signifies to us through its 'relative position' in a 'chain of differences'. These, Saussure emphasizes, are not – like in classical metaphysics – differences between 'positive terms', i.e. between types of objects or things, but between signs themselves.[50] Here neither subject nor object is animating, but the sign itself is primordial and a condition of both subject and object. The sign is the origin, though 'a non-simple, non-fulfilled origin'.[51] To open this middle term of the sign, Derrida is opening the mediating space of the limit. He is operating in neither reflexive nor natural attitude, but in a third in-between space of the sign, of the trace, the complex origin of both forms of life and the reflexive subject. Thus this origin of difference entails neither the passivity of the natural attitude nor the activity of the reflexive attitude, but something wholly other, a middle voice.

Conclusions: Experience and the Second Modernity

We have seen in this chapter that Derrida's idea of différance is first and foremost a contestation and transgression of totality, of finite totality. Hence his notion of the sign opens up the closedness of Husserl's transcendental ego. It opens up a reception side to this ego, exterior to the finite totality of structure and the phenomenological reduction, on to the irreducible materiality of the trace, of difference. We have seen that this material trace has a grain, a texture to it closer to the tactility, the haptic nature of the 'index' than it is to either 'symbol' or 'icon'. Yet it seems to me there may be some problems with the theory of difference. The first is that as philosophy it understands the trace and difference as transcendental. As a sociologist I attempt to read philosophy against its grain, as not transcendental but a particularly acute formulation of spatio-temporally specific *Weltanschauungen*. What Derrida takes as transcendental, the sociological will take as paradigmatic of the other modernity. For the sociologist difference is a condition of *late modern* experience, subjectivity and meaning.

Second, and perhaps consequently, there is an insufficient notion of groundedness in the idea of difference. Thus I argued above that in a very important sense it is more transcendental than the transcendental reduction. Derrida is always on the lookout for a way out, a way out is always somehow 'above', where the theory of the ground is always looking for a way *under*. The theory of difference is a theory of dissolving all that is solid, whereas the notion of the ground presumes that even the first modernity had done a lot of this dissolving, and instead searches somehow to retrieve this ground. The dimension of the ground is perhaps largely forgotten, yet crucial to our other modernity. The other modernity both undercuts and overcuts, at the same time grounds and dissolves its Enlightenment predecessor. Life-world phenomenology – the early Heidegger, Gadamer, Ricoeur, Merleau Ponty, Schutz – developed such a notion of a ground. Life-world phenomenology is thus involved in a necessary hermeneutics of retrieval. Deconstruction for its part, which finds no ever already existing ground, is engaged like its predecessors Nietzsche, Freud and Marx in a hermeneutics of suspicion.[52]

The third limit of difference looks forward to part V of this book. In part IV we will see that the notion of aporia, of undecidability in Kantian reflective judgement, is the progenitor of ideas of both difference and reflexive modernity. This space of difference and reflexive subjectivity, caught up in the tensions of undecidability, in the aporias of ambivalence, describes the very ethos of late modern sensibility. But what happens when the shift to the global information economy, the eclipse of national borders, the emergence on an expanded scale of things that think, explodes this space of difference? What happens when the risk society turns into the catastrophe society, when the classic narratives and their deconstruction both retreat to the margins? What happens when the space of difference is exploded into a general and molecular ether of indifference, a molecular revolution of contemporary economies of signs and space? What happens when communities formed with non-humans are as important as those formed with humans? What happens when Dasein and the subjectivity of difference are no longer beings of quite so different a status from other beings? This too is a very important limit of the theory of difference.

Thus far we have explored the ground of the other modernity, first in the arena of space, in terms of the production or rather weaving through mimesis of a gothic, labyrinthine space. Then we turned our attention to 'society'. Here we saw that in opposition to an abstract notion of the 'social', the other modernity emerged as a grounded *sociality*: a sociality understood in the classical sociological theory of Durkheim and Simmel in terms of 'symbol' and the symbolic. Both Durkheim and Simmel were concerned with the problem of 'life', in Foucault's sense in *Les mots et les choses*, in which the earlier modern episteme dealing in subject–object dualisms and categorial knowledge is displaced by a later modern episteme which foregrounds life, in almost Darwinian, physiological terms. The earlier modern, for us 'high modern', episteme was concerned with mapping '*les mots*' on to '*les choses*', whereas the later, low or other modernity went directly to '*les choses*' themselves and looked at their life, at *their* physiology. Durkheim addressed life in his discussion of the normal and the pathological. Simmel looked less at society than at subjectivity, problematizing the subject not *vis-à-vis* knowledge but, like *Lebensphilosphie* and Nietzsche, in terms of life.

It is a short move here from life to life-world, to forms of life. Here in philosophy, Heidegger's rooting of Nietzsche's life in the life-world is re-peated in sociology through Alfred Schutz's effective transformation of Simmel. With life-world we are already in the realm of experience. The other modernity's ground in the life-world or forms of life takes place in the realm of experience. Now the shift is rather total from high modernity's *epistemology* to low modernity's *experience*. We are now dealing not with a knowing but with an experiencing subject. The place to look for this, of course, is phenomenology. Husserl was already dealing with an experienc-ing ego in his transcendental phenomenology. None the less, in terms of the reduction by a transcendental ego, Husserl seemed to be reverting back to the first, high modernity. The shift to life-world, from Husserl's reflexive attitude to the natural attitude or life-world of Schutz, Heidegger, Ricoeur, Gadamer and Merleau-Ponty, gave us a subjectivity that was not abstract as in Husserl, nor '*innerlich*' as in most of Nietzsche and Simmel, but whose experience was thoroughly grounded. And here is where, as we saw, Derrida departed from life-world phenomenology. Whereas life-world phenomenology saw Husserl's egology as too infinite and undercut it through the finitude of the ground, Derrida, for his part, saw it in terms of a finite totality and 'overcut' it into a further realm of infinity. Derrida started by approving of Husserl in comparison to the finite totality of structuralism. His solution, however, was to move even further into the realm of the infinite than Husserl.

The break with transcendental phenomenology is already implicit in the temporality of the reduction. It is implicit in the temporality entailed in classical phenomenology's notions of sign, signification and meaning. This temporality does fix and cross-cut the flux of experience into discrete, repeatable units. But the only place where the reduction can be performed is also from the flux of experience. This, Alfred Schutz underscored, is dependent on memory, dependent on a previous segment of memory. Hence the transcendence of the transcendental ego must always be in the past. Once the reduction becomes dependent on memory, on 'recollection' from the reflexive attitude and retention from the natural attitude, the reduction itself becomes situated in the temporality of the life-world. Derrida develops Schutz's position in a more complex argument. Derrida too rejects the temporal assumptions of Husserl's sign, for the materiality, the opening on to the world of the trace. Derrida's temporality in this sense is also the temporality of the ground.

Once the constitution of meaning that we attach to objects or experiences is grounded in memory, another step is necessary. Memory must have a content. And that content must be social, must be drawn from some equivalent of the Durkheimian symbolic, from the elementary forms of modernity's 'religious' lives. What this presumes is that experience becomes no longer just immediate experience or *Erlebnis*, but must also be contextualized by the past long-term memory of *Erfahrung*. This is what Gadamer addresses as tradition and Paul Ricoeur as 'long intersubjectivity'. Here past experience is necessary for us to attach meanings to things. It also connects us to intersubjectivity proper, to Schutz's notion of understanding. If our *Erfahrung* is what makes it possible to constitute meaning for things, it allows us to connect to other subjects via *understanding*. Here the distinction between meaning and understanding is crucial. We constitute meaning in the reflexive attitude, whereas understanding takes place in the natural attitude. Understanding of other human beings is not 'constituted', it is not activist, it is not constructed. In the natural attitude, in the ground of the life-world, we are more receptive than productive in understanding, we must be open to the reflexive and natural attitudes of other egos, of other subjects. Understanding has more to do with mimesis than high modernist praxis. It is not activist.

So far we have talked of the grounding of experience in the other modernity in regard to subjectivity, time and intersubjectivity. The sign is also grounded here. Hence Derrida's sign is material, more indexical than semiotic or iconic. This trace is open to the world. Ricoeur captures this in his distinction between signification and perception. Signification is activist and transcendental, but it is through perception that we relate to signs in the life world, whether towards other human beings or artefacts. Ricoeur takes us into a problematics of the body, the perceiving body in the natural attitude. This problematics is of a piece with Lefebvre's anti-productionist production of space that we discussed in chapter 4. Lefebvre's anti-productionist production is mimetic, as the body extends itself like the weaving of a spider's web, mimetically through its own symmetries and dissymmetries into space. Ricoeur's bodily perception is dependent on notions of memory not just as long and social (historical) intersubjectivity, but also as bodily and unconscious memory. Experience is grounded not just in Durkheim's collective symbolic, but also in Lacan's unconscious symbolic. Thus our sign-mediated understanding of the world is doubly bodily through the materiality, the index-likeness of the trace, and through this somatic memory.

This primordial openness to the world leads us in the direction of neither sociology nor philosophy, but instead philosophical anthropology. Philosophical anthropology asks neither philosophy's question of the transcendental, nor sociology's question of change, but starts from assumptions of 'man's' fundamental nature. Here Schutz and Ricoeur, but also Gadamer and perhaps Lacan, take on assumptions of philosophical anthropology, in which man is the incomplete animal who must supplement his fundamental woundedness and openness to the world by culture, by institutions. Rooted in philosophical anthropology, Ricouer and Gadamer (but not Schutz) can also ask questions about fundamental ontology. They can through tradition, the monument, myth, open up experience to ontology, to the meaning of being.

And the other modernity must necessarily ask the question of ontology, must explore ontology. If high modernity consistently problematized epistemology, low modernity's turn to experience must also necessarily problematize ontology. By ontology I have meant not theory of reality, but a notion of being, in the sense of 'fundamental ontology'. In this sense social structures, as distinct from ontological structures, have to do with epistemology. Wittgenstein and Schutz make the break with epistemology's reflexive attitude for the natural attitude and experience. But they do not take the extra step to engage with ontology. They do not take the step from surface to depth hermeneutics. Ontology was already pregnant in Husserl's notion of experience. For him the experiencing ego grasped the meaning of beings, of things or objects, or experiences themselves, via the ontological structures of the things or beings themselves. Kant and neo-Kantian sociology, with their separation of fact and value, cannot have this. To know things-in-themselves, i.e. to make the phenomenological reduction, is to know value. Kant and neo-Kantianism said we cannot know value but only fact. To know things in themselves is to put value at the heart of fact, to know the 'value-structure of fact'. Husserl would not of course have called this fundamental ontology, but his followers, from Scheler to Ricoeur, from Heidegger, through Gadamer and Levinas to Derrida, knew it was.

Sociology, insofar as it separates fact and value, is rooted in epistemology and the first modernity. The second modernity entails explorations of fundamental ontology. Simmel and Nietzsche and *Lebensphilosophie* take the side of life against social forms, of value against fact, but they will not ask the question of the 'value-structure of fact', the question of the being of beings. Hegel may have addressed this question through his notions of love and ethical life.[53] Heidegger surely asks this question. And so does Derrida. For Heidegger, of course, we cannot directly know the meaning of being, but only under the right conditions have access to the meaning of being through the being of beings, and especially of that being which is subjectivity. Derrida also promotes ontology. He says we can have access to the being of beings. But we cannot *know* them. We can only *experience* the being of beings through their trace.

Part IV

Judgement

9

Reflexive Judgement and Aesthetic Subjectivity

In the first modernity the subject is in principle epistemic, in the second and reflexive modernity there is a shift to an experiencing and judging subjectivity. Part IV of this book deals with judgement. Like experience, judgement is integral to the break with the epistemic subject's universality for instead the *singular* subjectivity of the new modernity. Like experience, judgement necessarily reaches out to ontology. Like experience, judgement reaches out necessarily to a ground.

In some ways, however, judgement takes us only halfway towards the more full blown reflexivity of experience. The subject of judgement is in important dimensions half way between high modernity's epistemic subject and the second modernity's experiencing subject. Unlike the experiencing subject, the judging subject, we will see, does not operate fully in the flux of time. The judging subject is in this sense suspended as it were between the transcendence of epistemology and the full groundedness of 'life'. Experience takes place in the flux of life. Judgement has not yet fully 'descended' into life. The judging subject is already ontological. But where the experiencing subject can come to glimpse ontology through knowledge and understanding, the judging subject can only do so ethically or aesthetically. The experiencing subject so to speak teases an essence from the flux of experience. The judging subject, for its part, attempts to subsume a particular under a rule and at the same time attempts to bring the rest of its faculties – its moral, epistemic and aesthetic faculties – into juxtaposition.

The first half of this chapter deals with the deconstructive, the antifoundational moment of the second modernity. It works from the distinction of the first epistemic modernity from the second one. We explore this through the distinction of what Immanuel Kant called 'determinate judgement', on the one hand, and 'reflective judgement' on the other. We will see how judgement takes place when subjectivity encounters an event or an object that it cannot subsume under a rule of the epistemic categories of the understanding. Judgement is the faculty that then goes in search of a rule for the event or object. It is at the same time the faculty that, in the face of the event (or object) encountered, attempts to mediate and regulate between the other faculties – the imagination, the understanding and reason. These attempts, these operations of the faculty (or power) of judgement, then lead to the making of judgements.

These judgements are not statements like legal judgements, or moral judgements. They most of all lie in subjective *feelings*. When the imagination can subsume and synthesize the event or object encountered and there is a harmonic juxtaposition of the faculties, then the feelings are mainly of pleasure in what are aesthetic judgements of 'beauty'. When the imagination cannot subsume the event or object and no such harmony is achieved there are aesthetic judgements of the 'sublime'. The operative term here is *feeling*. The epistemic categories of the universal subject do not feel. It is only the singular subject, no longer transcendent – whose attitude is not objective but subjective, who works through feelings and what Kant calls 'taste'. The first half of this chapter will explicate the nature of judgement and the singularity of the subject of judgement.

The second half of the chapter shifts from subjectivity to ground. And it is the thesis of this book that sociological and cultural theory – theories of 'reflexivity' and of 'difference' – have focused far too much on the subjective, anti-foundational moment of the other modernity. Some understand this anti-foundational and subjective moment as experimentation, '*riskante Freiheit*'; others as an identity politics of difference or performativity. Both social and cultural theory have paid insufficient attention to the moment of the ground. In the second half of this chapter we trace the moment of ground in Kantian judgement. We explore Kant's dictum of the work of art or the object as a 'finality without end'. Here the object cannot be an instrument towards an end but must instead be itself a finality. As a finality it is a ground and medium which does not refer outside of itself but instead carries existential meaning in itself. The object as finality carries Reason or being within it. Thus the moment of the ground in the theory of judgement is also necessarily that of *ontology*. It is now that we can finally square the circle of the second modernity. Now we see how the moment of reflexivity (or difference) in the second modernity *necessarily* entails both ontology and ground. We see how full reflexivity is impossible without ontology and ground. Having shown that reflexivity is a question of singular subjectivity in the fist half of the chapter, we see how the indeterminate nature of the singular subject necessitates a ground or middle that is not instrumental but a finality, and hence ontological. The first or epistemic modernity, we shall see, is determinate, and its ground (its middle) takes the shape of instrument or means. In this sense the first modernity is indeed not fully modern. The second and reflexive modernity is fully modern. But this entails both ground and ontology.

The first, epistemic modernity with its universal subject and instrumental object is inscribed in a logic of *theorein*. The second modernity, with singular subject and 'final' object, is inscribed in logics of *poesis* and *praxis*. All the various manifestations of the ground in this book involve either poesis or praxis. 'Poesis' comprises relations of subjectivity to the object, to the object of work, aesthetics, consumption, dwelling and the like, in which the subject is in an 'I–it' relation. We discuss the ground as poesis and the 'I–it' relation in this chapter with special reference to the work of Tzvetan Todorov on the symbol. 'Praxis' is for its part the 'I–thou' relation, the intersubjectivity of ethics, of memory, of tradition, community, history, sociality and forms of life. We inquire into the ground as praxis that also opens out on to ontology through Hans-Georg Gadamer's idea of permanence. Permanence for Gadamer is not absolute, but only relative to fleetingness. Permanence is 'retaining what threatens to pass away'. For Gadamer the phylogeny of permanence emerges with the rules of children's games in their self-sameness, repetition and independence from instrumentality. It develops in the intergenerational duration of works of art and poetry, whose particulars in their very non-instrumentality open up on to the universal. It is epitomized in memory: in the long-term historical memory and tradition of communities. This intergenerational duration of the ground reveals subjectivity in the second modernity, in not just its singularity, but also its finitude.

Transcendence and Undecidability

In his famous very late essay 'What is Enlightenment?' Michel Foucault pointed to a lineage of philosophers from Kant to Nietzsche to Artaud and Bataille.[1] The presence of Kant in this litany might be a bit puzzling to some. But what Foucault was referring to was the idea of *reflective judgement* developed in *The Critique of Judgement*. Now 'reflective judgement' is defined by Kant in contradistinction to *determinate judgement*. 'Determinate judgement' is the subsumption of a phenomenon under a concept, under a rule. Reflective or 'reflexive' judgement happens when an event, a phenomenon or an object comes along which cannot be subsumed under a concept or a predetermined rule. It is when an object, an event, a phenomenon exceeds the categories of theoretical knowledge. In reflective judgement a rule must be found to deal with the phenomenon. It is reflective, and not determinate, judgement that is involved in the 'aesthetic judgement of taste'.

Reflective judgement can at the same time be understood as *in*determinate judgement. Determinate judgement, we will see in this chapter and the next, brings under its heading the 'identity-thinking', the 'technology', the instrumental rationality, the abstract Cartesio-Newtonian spatio-temporality of the first or high modernity. Reflective judgement for its part is the emblem of socio-cultural theory in the second modernity. Its trace informs what Adorno understood as 'mimesis' and Derrida as difference, what Heidegger meant by poesis, what Max Weber understood under the 'ethics of responsibility' and the temporality recorded by Bergson and Gadamer. Determinate judgement evokes humankind aping the infinite in the pursuit of survival and security. Reflexive judgement is at the same time beyond and 'beneath' the conceptual categories of determinate judgement. In its breaking through the limits of knowledge, to point towards an excess of indeterminacy, reflexive judgement is an attack on the ground, the foundations of the first modernity. But in its own insertion in a set of very basic and material practices, its own concern for the warp, woof and grain of events, of experience, reflective judgement is also very much itself a ground. Reflexive judgement is, then, very much the groundless ground of the second and other modernity.

The 'third' and 'aesthetic' critique was intended by Kant largely as an attempt to bridge or mediate the seemingly unbridgeable gap between theoretical and practical reason of the first and second critiques.[2] That is, if theoretical judgements are determinate, and if moral judgements are quite fully indeterminate (in the sense of comprising the space of the 'realm of freedom'), then reflexive judgement is partially determinate. Put another way, the theoretical judgements of the *Critique of Pure Reason* presume the graspability of phenomena under concepts or rules of the 'understanding': hence full determination and objectivity. *The Critique of Practical Reason* and the categorical imperative concern the judgement of *acts*. At issue are judgements of whether acts are moral or not. These acts cannot be referred at all to the logical categories of the understanding and instead are judged according to the just mentioned radically indeterminate and disem-bodied 'ideas' of the sphere not of the understanding but of 'reason', which cannot be formulated in terms of the truth conditions of statements of propositional logic.[3] These ideas are fully indeterminate. These indeter-minate ideas address not logical meaning, but the meaning-matrices of existence. Now 'reflective judgement', the subject of *The Critique of Judgement*, is *partially* determinate in that it concerns not logical meaning of theoretical statements, but the same sort of existence-meaning as does practical judgement. Only now such meaning is not indeterminate as in the realm of reason's ungraspable Ideas, but *partially* determined in an aesthetic object, in a cultural artefact. Such meaning is not graspable directly via these objects or events, but only as if through a glass darkly. Further, to the extent that such existential meaning is embodied in these aesthetic objects, it is so in a way that is not graspable by concepts, but only via feeling, only via the imagination.

This said, reflexive, or more precisely indeterminate, judgement is the cornerstone of the Critical Philosophy *tout entière* and was already a major presence in *The Critique of Pure Reason*. The Critical Philosophy was of course aimed at opponents on two sides: on the one side 'dogmatics' such as Leibniz and Wolff, who wanted to extend the realm of determinate judgement to include the subsumption under concepts of virtually the whole universe of objects, experience and action; and on the other side 'sceptics' such as Hume, who claimed that determinate judgements, or descriptive truth statements, were applicable to no objects or events whatsoever.[4] We encountered a similar opposition between 'sceptics' and 'dogmatics' in chapters 5 and 6 in discussing the emergence of classical sociological theory. Here positivists such as the late Marx and early Durkheim, like Kant's 'dogmatic' rationalists, saw the whole of social life as subsumable under determinate concepts, under 'social facts' of one kind or another. Lebensphilosophers like the late Simmel, like Kant's sceptical opponents, would hold that nothing in social life was explicable in terms of 'fact' or determinate judgement. Neo-Kantians like Weber have more in common with the Critical Philosophy and would understand some forms of social life as subsumable in the realm of fact, while other regions of sociality could only be addressed in terms of value. This opposition once again returns much more recently, this time counterposing some critical theorists such as Habermas on the side of the rationalists and 'dogmatics' and other critical theorists such as Adorno and Benjamin on the side of the sceptics and Lebensphilosophers, where they would be joined by post-structuralism. Almost no one anymore today seems to stand in the tradition of the Critical Philosophy.

So against both extreme determinists and extreme 'indeterminists', Kant wants to establish that there is a sphere of valid knowledge – a sphere of 'what we may know' – but that there are very strict limits to this sphere. For Kant, such valid knowledge is stated in 'synthetic *a priori* judgements'. Here 'synthetic' judgements are counterposed to 'analytic' judgements. Analytic judgements are 'tautological' and produce no new knowledge. Synthetic judgements for their part do produce new knowledge. Synthetic judgements do not necessarily have to be applied to phenomena in the world. They can comprise the application of the rules of the understanding to other rules, as in mathematics or formal logic. They can also, and Kant's example is always physics, be applied to empirical phenomena in the world. For our purposes crucial is not so much the synthetic but the *a priori* nature of such judgements. Some synthetic judgements are not *a priori*; that is, they are not universal but only trivial. They do produce new knowledge, but this is the trivial and meaningless sort of knowledge or cognition of everyday life. By *a priori* is meant such judgements are based on principles that are necessary and universal. Universal statements or judgements are true *ceteris paribus* at any point in time and space. By universal is mainly meant that *a priori* judgements are not just 'empirical', 'psychological', true for some people and not others, and hence trivial, but universally true. Kant insists that only in a very few spheres of life can we make such universal statements.[5]

It is of critical importance to make the distinction between the judgements (statements or propositions) on the one hand, and the *faculty* of judgement on the other. All three critiques address judgements in the former sense, but only the third, aesthetic critique – and I will argue below that the third critique is indeed an aesthetic critique – addresses the faculty or power of judgement. It is for Kant faculties (or powers) (*Kräfte*) which produce or 'synthesize' the statements (judgements). Kant's faculties are: (a) the 'imagination', which is the faculty of 'intuition', i.e. the imagination has *powers* of intuition; (b) the understanding (*Verstand*); and (c) reason (*Vernunft*). In the *Critique of Judgement* (*Kritik der Urteilskraft*) Kant adds a faculty of judgement.

The various faculties 'synthesize' different sorts of judgement. The faculty of the understanding synthesizes cognitive or theoretical judgements; it is with regard to the faculty of reason or at least the 'ideas' of reason that we synthesize moral or ethical judgements; and it is in regard to the faculty of judgement (or through reflexive judgement) that we synthesize what Kant calls 'aesthetic judgements of taste'. The faculty of the imagination (*Einbildungskraft*) synthesizes not judgements, but 'presentations' (*Darstellungen*) or 'representations' (*Vorstellungen*).[6] In each case what produces these *a priori* statements is a power which is itself *a priori* or 'transcendental'. Each faculty is a power which has its own rules of synthesis. The faculties of understanding and imagination, for example, acting together, work through their own principles: such effectively 'meta'-principles make the sort of rule or principle making we do in physics and mathematics possible.

Each of the faculties is transcendental. Here transcendental means not empirical, not psychological. These faculties are not necessarily located in the psyches of specific individuals. For any empirical individual, however, to have valid knowledge, to make valid cognitive judgements, the existence of such rule-bound faculties is necessary. Thus Kant introduces the 'transcendental aesthetic', the 'transcendental logic', the 'transcendental analytic' and the 'transcendental dialectic' in *The Critique of Pure Reason*. Kant also insists and insists repeatedly that no matter how transcendental these faculties of the imagination and understanding are, they are, at the same time, eminently *finite*. There are two sorts of Kantian faculty of cognition: finite cognition, characterizing the human intellect and capable of knowing only 'phenomena' or appearances; and infinite cognition, possessed by the divine intellect, which can know 'noumena' or 'things-in-themselves'.[7]

Kant observed that rationalist 'dogmatics' such as Leibniz and Wolff presumed access by finite cognition to what for him was only knowable by divine intellect.

Kant begins the first critique with the transcendental aesthetic and intuition, in which phenomena or appearances are synthesized from the outer world through the pure *a priori* forms of time and space to make presentations. Here Kant distinguishes the 'empirical content' or 'sensation' that is filtered out by the transcendental forms of perception. Kant thus contrasts empirical and transcendental perception, the latter effectuated through the 'pure productive syntheses' of the imagination.[8] Kant's empirical perception and sensation sets the paradigm for Maurice Merleau Ponty's bodily and 'pure perception', as well as for the 'logic of sensation' that Deleuze will address in his homage to Francis Bacon's painting. His transcendental perception through the imagination's syntheses will set the paradigm for the 'schematisms', for the primitive classifications of Pierre Bourdieu's habitus, in which perception or 'taste' is refined and 'transcendental' – albeit through social categories – to produce distinctions.[9]

After the transcendental aesthetic, Kant works towards the deduction of the concepts of the understanding, or the 'categories', in the transcendental analytic of the understanding. The 'concepts of the understanding' must be distinguished from the 'concepts of reason', presented in *The Critique of Practical Reason*. The concepts of the understanding, which are principles of logic, Kant calls 'categories'.[10] The concepts of reason – which embrace infinity, God, freedom, the noumena and the moral imperative – Kant calls 'ideas'.[11] In *The Critique of Pure Reason* the reader is not presented with, so to speak, lists and explications of the individual categories (e.g. identity, difference, substance, syllogism) whose origin is Aristotelian logic. Instead the categories are only deduced as part of the overarching project of explicating the *unifying and legislating force* of the understanding. Thus the subsumption of appearances synthesized through intuition under a concept is not so much a matter of applying an individual principle or rule to the presentation of a phenomenon, but of applying the understanding as a 'legislative unity'. This originary unifying synthesis is called by Kant the 'necessary' or 'transcendental unity of apperception'.[12]

Mimesis and Practice

A number of analysts have seen in Kant the 'Copernican Revolution' in the human sciences; the inauguration of the principle of modernity. Most influentially, Blumenberg in his *Legitimation of the Modern Age* identifies the modern in terms of a fundamental break with the Judaeo-Christian teleologies of salvation and redemption. Similarly, Wolfgang Schluchter and Jürgen Habermas in their discussions of Max Weber understand the modernity that Weber sociologically inaugurated as succeeding the pre-modern 'religio-metaphysical age'.[13] As 'religio-metaphysical' would be classified not only the world religions, but also Enlightenment, Marxist, positivist and Whig teleologies. Modernity on this account truly heralds the emergence of an order-giving subjectivity as all other heteronomous orders have withered, as all that is solid has melted into air. Here pre-moderns would foreground 'speculation' or theoretical knowledge, while moderns give priority to practical knowledge. The principle of 'reconciliation' on this view is importantly characteristically pre-modern – from salvation to utopianism to Hegel's dialectic to Marx's reconciliation in communism – while a preoccupation with the impossibility of reconciliation, and instead the presumption of an unbridgeable 'lack', or 'aporia', is characteristically modern. If Kant made the Copernican Revolution in philosophy, he may have done so less via the *Critique of Pure Reason*, than via the aesthetic critique, *The Critique of Judgement*. In such a context, full-blown modernity would be aesthetic modernity.

Let us begin by addressing more specifically what constitutes judging. Judging may be understood as an operation of measuring, estimating, determining or especially of proportioning. Howard Caygill in his seminal *Art of Judgement* draws systematic contrasts between ancient and modern modes of judging. For ancients such as Aquinas, judging or measuring is effectuated not by human but by divine intellect.[14] In this the natural order of objective proportion is judged and measured out by God. In Kant's modernity it is the knowing subject that creates the order according to proportions decided and measured by the subject. In contrast to the old metaphysics and Thomist natural order, the modern order is 'jurispruden-tial' and it is not God but man or reason that determines and then judges from its 'critical tribunal'.[15] Instead of God doing the proportioning and the judging, it is reason which measures out phenomena according to its categories. It is reason which determines phenomena and then assesses or judges the 'conditions under which its determinations are valid'. Reason is a legitimate judge because only it 'can see into what it produces through its own proportion'.[16]

Ancient and divine knowledge was primarily speculative and theoretical knowledge. God's creation of the world was not practical, but speculative and carried out through divine intellect's knowing of proportion. Aquinas divided the divine intellect into 'categorial' and 'transcendental' knowl-edge. Here through categorial knowledge the divine intellect established a set of 'determinations', a set of 'measures in Being'. Here each of the logical categories 'adds something essential to the essence of being'. Transcenden-tal knowledge is supra-categorial, and establishes the conditions – being, unity, goodness, truth, beauty – of categorial determination. Thomist and

ancient categorial knowledge corresponds of course to Kant's categories
of the understanding, while the ancient transcendental knowledge corresponds roughly to Kant's ideas of reason. There are two main differences
here. The first is that for the ancient there is no aporia: there is no clash of
the faculties, no conflict between categorial and transcendental knowledge. The second is the very small role assigned to practice. According to
Thomist doctrine the practical, as distinct from the speculative or the
theoretical, entailed the production of actions and things. The practical as
distinct from the speculative can be understood as comprising 'poesis' on
the one hand, and 'praxis' on the other. On this view, in 'poesis', actions
'caused' things as if in some inorganic mechanism. Further, actions caused
things out of matter 'irradiated with divine proportion'. God was responsible for the creation of universals out of which, through poesis, man could
give only particular form, as 'artefacts'. Regarding praxis, for Thomist
natural law, virtue is 'the habitus' that realizes an objective proportion
through action; virtue is an 'ordered disposition of the soul'.[17] Hence the
divine is seen in terms of the speculative, and the human in terms of the
practical.

To judge is to estimate, in German *schätzen*; in French to guess is *diviner*,
and indeed human practice takes over from God's intellect as we are cast
as 'divining animals', called upon to carry out the activities of judgement.
This divides into three stages. First, human activity constitutes proportion:
from the Renaissance the old objective proportion of divine speculation is
already translated into 'subjective proportion created by human activity'.
Second, human artifice then measures its own artefacts, in terms of their
truth, rightness or aesthetic value. Finally, we are called upon to legislate
the limits of our own legislating power: we must judge the limits of judgement. Indeed, the 'paralogies' and 'antinomies' in the first critique address
just these limits of reason, while *The Critique of Practical Reason* is about the
transcendence of these limits, about the beyond of the understanding. The
second critique addresses the sphere not of necessity but of freedom, in
which reason is not determined, but may directly constitute the world.
Only we must do this in a 'hypothetical', an 'as-if' mode. The ideas of
reason cannot subsume or be applied to such world-constituting experience. Instead, moral judgement must 'hypothetically identify noumenal
and phenomenal realms'.[18] Looking forward, we will recognize again the
sociological positivism foreshadowed by the first critique in contrast to the
hermeneutics and constructivism foreshadowed by Kantian practical reason and indeterminate judgement.

But in Kant there is neither the rejection of such positivism for
hermeneutics nor their Hegelian reconciliation, but instead their persisting
antinomial existence in a series of aporias. There are instead successions of
perplexities, of clashes of the faculties, themselves recognizable as mould

setters for contemporary cultural theory's core notions of 'lack' and
'différance'. Kant traces these aporias in the first critique in his paralogies
– in, for example, the rule of causal succession, which leads to an infinite
regress that can only find its origin in an unconditioned. And the unconditioned must be not a category but an idea – not applicable to sensible
intuitions and lying outside of the sphere of the understanding. Hence
the non-graspable ideas of reason are the grounds of (cognitive) reason's
own legislation. Reason must strive to know these grounds but never can.
Reason can subsume under a rule, and recognize whether a phenomenon
stands under a rule. But it cannot give itself a rule for subsuming under a
rule.[19] Thus the main aporia, the pivotal clash of faculties, is between the
understanding and reason.

Thus when subjectivity must take itself and its being as its own creations,
the upshot is not ancient order but modern lack. The upshot is what
Benjamin called a *Lücke*, an unbridgeable gap, between intuition and
intellect, and most of all between the intellect's sphere of determination
and reason's sphere of freedom. The self-identity of the intellect, of the
subsuming intellect of cognitive knowledge, is threatened from
'below' – from intuition and imagination – and from 'above' – from
freedom. Modernity on this view is not about self-identity but instead
'self-difference'. It is also radically about responsibility. With the Enlightenment and Marxist metanarratives there was still an external order on
which to off-lay responsibility. In modernity's risk culture no such off-laying
is possible. The buck stops here. We are radically responsible for the
consequences of our own judging, for our own divining and proportioning activity. We are also responsible in Weber's sense for continually
attempting to reconcile the irreconcilable. We are, with Ricouer, condemned at the same time to finitude and to strive unsuccessfully for infinity.
We are condemned not to know but to strive to know the ideas of reason.
We are condemned to be determined and simultaneously to strive to be
free.[20]

Taste, Beauty, Sublimity

Thus the critical philosophy establishes its 'island of truth' in the 'sea of
freedom'. Thus the critical philosophy's 'what can I know?' is situated in
the middle of – and as part and parcel of – the 'what should I do?' But the
'what should I do?' is uttered in such utter darkness, in the presence of such
inaudible voices of infinity, freedom, God, the moral imperative and the
ghostly noumenon, that subjectivity seems indeed to be lost. It is in this
context – given the limits of cognitive reason and the dark indeterminacy
of moral reason, the very hypothetical nature of whose imperative seems to

stamp out any glimmer of hope – that a few signposts for practice are sought. Subjectivity that dares to utter the 'what can I hope?' will look for these signposts in aesthetic judgement. But what is aesthetic judgement? And more generally what is judgement? At issue in *The Critique of Judgement* is not judgements as statements but the faculty or power of judgement. This faculty unlike the understanding does not subsume under concepts. Unlike the imagination it does not synthesize representations of appearances from outside events and objects. Instead the faculty or power of judgement mediates in the finding of rules for particulars presented in syntheses of the imagination. If the imagination, through its forms, apprehends objects; if the understanding (via its transcendental unity of apperception) subsumes objects; and if reason via its ideas and maxims (always in a hypothetical mode) directs subjects; then judgement *searches* for rules.

The faculty of judgement or *Urteilskraft* does this in two possible ways: either via 'determinate judgement', in which it relies on the faculty of the understanding to provide a principle for, and subsume, a particular instance; or through 'reflective judgement'. In the latter a general rule for a particular case is not already given and must be sought. It must be sought either in concepts of the understanding or in those, we shall see, of reason. If determinate judgement is positioned in a logical idiom of subsumption, then reflective judgement follows the much less bounded idiom of *analogy* in its search, in its proportioning of a phenomenon to a rule or concept. The *Critique of Judgement* is mainly concerned with this second type of judgement. Reflective judgements come in two categories. The first of these are 'teleological judgements', in which the rule is sought in 'objective ends', which themselves are categories of the understanding.[21] Teleological judgements are uninteresting in terms of the 'what can I hope', because the possibility of hope entails that we must be presented with cultural artefacts or events that allude to the meanings of the ideas of reason. And cultural objects can only do so when they are not a means to any other end but, we shall see, 'finalities' in themselves. Thus the whole of our interest turns towards the majority of the third critique devoted to the second type of reflective judgement. This second type of reflective judgements Kant calls 'aesthetic judgements of taste'. We note a slippage here from judgement as power to judgements as types of statements (or feelings or experiences), and indeed *The Critique of Judgement* is as much about judgements – as statements, or experiences, or feelings – as it is about the faculty or power of judgement. This said, Kant's explorations into the faculty of judgement amount to an inquiry into the transcendental conditions of aesthetic judgements of taste.

But why this curious phrase: 'aesthetic judgements of taste'? Here again Kant establishes his critical island of, this time, artistic truth in an *Auseinandersetzung* with, one the one hand, German rationalists and, on the other, British empiricists. By *aesthetic* Kant means the formal aesthetics theory of such rationalists as Baumgarten and Mendelssohn. By *taste* he refers to the 'philosophy of taste' of such British Isles 'moral sense' theorists as Hutcheson and Burke. Now unlike cognitive judgements, aesthetic judgements of taste are not objective but subjective. Like cognitive judgements they must be universally valid. Thus Kant (against the rationalist aestheticians) and in line with the philosophers of taste – already discussed among moral sense theorists such as Shaftesbury in *The Critique of Practical Reason* – agrees that evaluations of art and cultural artefacts must subjective. Like, however, the rationalist aesthetic philosophers he holds that they must be universally valid.[22] The pivotal question then becomes *how does the subjective aesthetic experience of a singular individual become universally valid?* We shall devote space to this below. For the moment let us note that Kant takes the singular notion of subjectivity of the taste theorists (as opposed to the assumptions of objectivity of the 'aesthetes'),[23] but disagrees with the taste theorists in regard to elements of scepticism and external ends or 'interests' in their theories.

Aesthetic judgements of taste can be understood in terms of a seven-step process:

1 An instance – which can be an object or event, natural or created – is encountered by the imagination's power of intuition through the forms of time and space.
2 The imagination may or may not be able to synthesize a representation from this encounter, but either way it is not immediately subsumed under a rule of the understanding and the faculty of judgement goes in search of such a rule.
3 Because of this absence of subsumption, the judgements that the faculty of judgement produces are subjective, not objective.
4 This active search of *Urteilskraft* as a mediating power among the other faculties brings the imagination, the understanding and reason into either harmonious or clashing juxtapositions.[24]
5 These harmonies or clashes result in feelings of pleasure and/or pain. It is these *feelings* (rather than predicative propositions) that are the judgements. Thus judgement (as power) produces judgements as feelings.
6 Despite the fact that they are subjective, these evaluations are universally valid: they 'command universal agreement'.
7 They command such universal agreement, not due to objective validity or rational argument but (a) via an idealized horizon or a *sensus communis* and (b) because the objects of such aesthetic judgements of taste are motivated by universal ideas of reason.[25]

We will come back to each of these points in some detail below. For the moment it is important to note that all aesthetic judgements of taste are failed-in-advance attempts to bridge aporetic realms. They first attempt to bridge the realms of the sensible and intelligible. Second, and far more important, is their attempt to bridge the realm of 'nature', finitude and necessity (which embraces both the sensible and intelligible), on the one hand, and the realm of reason, infinity and freedom on the other. We should note here that the rule-finding activity of judgement is subordinate to its activities that bring into juxtaposition the faculties of 'nature' with the Ideas of reason. More accurately, it is because an object cannot be subsumed under a concept and hence made intelligible that judgement can bring nature in juxtaposition with reason, that it can bring necessity (as determined and determining) in conjunction with freedom.[26] In all aesthetic judgements of taste this is done through (in the very broadest sense) symbols. In moral reason and the second critique there is only a hypothetical identification of nature and freedom, while in judgement there is a 'symbolic identification' of the two realms.[27] Thus the fully indeterminate 'what should I do?', becomes the partially determinate 'what may I hope?' This said, such identification is always failed in advance. We are forever condemned not to being but to becoming: this is the aporia, the lack, at the heart of the *condition moderne*.

This also is the context for the two main types of aesthetic judgements of taste: 'judgements of the beautiful' and 'judgements of the sublime'. In judgements of *beauty*, intuited phenomena come under the power of the imagination, which carries out free syntheses of intuitions through its schemata. These syntheses present representations to the understanding which has no pre-ordained rule to subsume them. Judgement then goes in search of a rule. Judgement, then, in a sense short-circuits the understanding by bringing the imagination and Reason together via symbols.[28] That is, in aesthetic judgements of beauty the highest goals of Reason are symbolized in the imagination in aesthetic ideas. None the less, judgements of beauty bring the imagination and the understanding and the ideas of reason into a possible harmony, they reverberate, as it were, together and not in contraposition, and from this we derive a feeling of pleasure. The imagination and Reason are identified via symbols which underlie and constitute the *sensus communis* and through universal communicability command universal assent.

In judgements of the *sublime* the schemata of the imagination are overwhelmed by the objects or events it encounters. War, natural disasters and soaring mountain ranges are the sort of example Kant gives of objects and events which thus overwhelm the imagination. Thus the powers of the imagination are not able to synthesize presentations or representations of these phenomena. They are unable to convert sensation into form. Thus Lyotard has influentially always spoken of the sublime in terms of the 'unpresentable'.[29] But although the imagination is not able to make a representation there is still a symbolic identification of the imagination and Reason through that very unpresentability, through that very lack. If experience of the beautiful symbolically gives access to Reason as the plenitude, the giving, Heidegger's *es gibt* of Being, then experience of the sublime in events, objects, works of art and cultural artefacts opens out on to the emptiness, the void, on to lack, on to the aporia itself. Aesthetic judgements of the sublime, which are not logical statements but instead felt experiences, then symbolically invoke the fear and trembling, the darkness of what Levinas has called the *il y a*.[30] Needless to say, the sort of feeling we get from this is in the register of a clash and discord of the faculties, a reverberation at clashing rhythms, and feelings of discomfit, and even pain, though often, as Kant says, a certain admixture of pleasure and pain. Here there is an absence of the 'full' symbols of the *sensus communis*, whose own disorientation and discomfit itself bears witness to the universality of the experience. This sort of universality was notably absent in Edmund Burke's notion of the sublime. For Burke the beautiful and the sublime derived from 'passions' of sociality and individuality.[31] Kant's aesthetic judgement, which is transcendental and not empirical, deals not with Burke's sensations, but with representations which the imagination's schemata abstract through the forms of time and space from sensations. Burke's passions were for Kant an 'empirical interest' and reflective judgements of taste can claim validity only to the extent that they are free from empirical or psychological interests.[32]

Reflective or reflexive judgement – and Kant's book of this title lays the groundwork for not only the advent of aesthetic modernity but also more generally a full and *reflexive* modernity – breaks with the notion of universalist individualism for an idea of freedom based on *singular* individuality. Here the universalist individual is, like cognitive judgement, determinate: the universalist individual is determin*ed* as well as determin*ing*. The 'singular' individual is indeterminate and reflexive: no longer determined – and hence autonomous – and at the same time not really determin*ing* but engaged in activities of more a bricolaging nature, whether in the fashioning of the self or the making of things.[33] The point is that the last vestiges of heteronomy, of being determined, are in cognitive judgement itself. The last vestiges of determined determining are in the transcendental unity of apperception, the Cartesian 'I think'. Here the 'I' is the 'determined determiner', determined by the universalism of the logical categories and determiner through its processes of subsumptive syntheses. As such we cannot be singular but are heteronomous vassals of the universal and abstract logical categories as we go about estimating and making things. The third critique thus ushers in full and reflexive modernity, in which subjectivity is constituted not as knowing, but as judging. In knowing we place a particular under an already legislated universal. As judging, we encounter the particular reflexively, looking for the rule and self-legislating. In this context Kant's first critique is not, as Walsh had it, *Kant's Critique of Metaphysics*, but is instead in some ways more of a piece with Leibniz, Wolff and Baumgarten, as well as Descartes, as the last book in metaphysics.[34]

To what extent can the same thing be said of *The Critique of Practical Reason?* To what extent are the ideas of reason and in particular the moral imperative also part of this pre-modern world view? To what extent do they also presuppose a universal individualism rather than a singular individuality? Clearly, the ideas of reason do not subsume and synthesize in the same way as the categories of the understanding. Subjectivity stands in an as-if relationship with the latter. Yet Kant does refer to the understanding and Reason as two higher faculties of knowledge.[35] In *The Critique of Practical Reason* he repeatedly insists on the contradistinction of autonomous versus heteronomous legislation. The moral imperative does legislate to the self here, but as self-legislation.[36] This said, such self-legislating subjectivity does not look for its own rule. It follows instead the dictates or maxims of the imperative. Does this mean that there is also a certain heteronomy in practical reason, and that it too is importantly metaphysical and pre-modern? I think so. The comparison again with Weber is instructive. For Weber neither *Zweckrationalität* (i.e. instrumental or formal rationality) nor *wertrational* (or value-rational or substantive rational) action is autonomous. In the former, like in Kantian cognitive reason, we are legislated to by the determinate calculation of the market place; in the second we are legislated to by substantial and ultimate values like Marxism, art for art's sake or the categorical imperative. It is only in Weber's ethics of responsibility, where we choose among competing rules and competing claims, that we find a rule for our action for our decisions; it is only here that judgement and singularity, and full modernity, emerge.[37]

The putatively autonomous legislation of the categorical imperative is also chimerical in its extraordinary indeterminacy. Hegel never tired of saying this, especially in *The Philosophy of Right*. His point was that the very indeterminacy of the imperative made it impossible to apply it to concrete forms of life. His solution is to synthesize the universal, what he calls *Moralität*, with *Sittlichkeit* or ethical life, with ethical forms of everyday life. But the notion of a singular subjectivity tended to disappear progressively in the late Hegel in favour of the universal. In the *Phenomenology of Mind*, however, consciousness was conceived not as the universal (*das Allgemein*) but as the singular (*das Einzelne*).[38] This singular could not be legislated to by an abstract imperative. It had instead to be concretized in something more *grounded*, more *material*. Thus singular subjectivity in the 'what can I hope?' of fully modern reflexivity – in the absence of legislation from God, concept or moral law – needs help not from above, but from, as it were, 'below'. Singular subjectivity needs guidance from a *ground*, in which to be sure the more truly universal ideas of reason, or meaning of Being, do from time to time find their epiphany. This ground can be the ethical life (and the traditions) of the community. But it can also be the materiality of the object and the thing, as it is in Theodor Adorno's *Negative Dialectics*.[39] In Kant such finality is found in the aesthetic object; in the object of aesthetic judgement. Thus singular subjectivity, or fully modern freedom or reflexivity, is impossible in the absence of the finality of the object: the object which can stand as a signpost to the self. This is the great achievement of Kant's aesthetic critique. Let us return a bit more closely to it.

Finality of the Object, Singularity of the Subject

The thrust of Kant's challenge to both English philosophers of taste and German aestheticians was that neither located finality in the aesthetic object. The pivotal criterion for the validity of a judgement of taste is that it must be 'disinterested'. Disinterested judgements, Kant defines, are judgements having no end outside the object. They are judgements which must be given no rule outside of reflexively judging subjectivity. The philosophers of taste Kant criticized were empiricists in their capacity as moral sense theorists. Kant argued that empiricism of sense or sensation must be abstracted from through the imagination's faculty of intuition. Only then could objects be experienced as symbols in order for there to be the possibility of universally valid aesthetic judgements. Taste philosophers such as Hutcheson spoke literally of a new sense, an inner and moral sense. This was operative in both the ethical and aesthetic experience, in that moral action and the decisions as to the beauty of an object depended on this moral sense. Thus the idea of a beautiful object or moral action results in a feeling of pleasure to this pre-formed moral sense. Hutcheson maintained that the idea striking the moral sense was disinterested, because it was separate from and antecedent to any utility, advantage or interest. But Kant defines interest to be much more than utilitarian advantage. For him an interest can comprise any end outside of the object. Any such outside end would concomitantly entail a heteronomous legislating source to subjectivity. For Kant the very passivity involved in a moral sense being 'struck' by an idea cuts against autonomous and active subjectivity. Further, Hutcheson's idea of beauty, defined in terms of a rational principle of 'uniformity amidst variety', contradicts autonomy. This is because this idea had pre-modern sources in notions of 'providential' proportionality, i.e. through forms in which Providence realizes its rational designs.[40]

The same can be said for Burke, also a moral sense theorist. Burke broke with Humean scepticism – where taste was a mere 'accident of sentiment' – again for a providential argument. Taste for Burke in his *Philosophical Inquiry into Our Ideas of the Sublime and the Beautiful* depends on the human 'passions'. These passions – whose blueprint is inaccessible to man – are designed by God. They then operate for the greater good through a sort of 'primeval oath' or 'contract', itself constituting in effect a great chain of being. On this view 'pleasure', deriving from the (primary) passion for 'sociability', through which God binds society via a sort of empirical *sensus communis*, gives rise to judgements of beauty. The other primary passion is an asocial passion for 'individuality', which Burke understands in a Hobbesian vein as self-preservation. This passion, when confronted with an object, gives rise to feelings of pain and fear of danger: in short, to feelings of the *sublime* that are 'aroused when the individual is faced with the unknown, with the infinite extent and power that threatens the individual's existence'.[41] Crucial here in regard to interest and external ends is how subjectivity's estimation of the object comes about. If our estimation –as either producers or receivers – of the object comes about through some other end than that finality which is integral to the object, then we cannot speak of aesthetic judgement. In fact we cannot speak of the faculty of judgement at all, and something else is at work. And the statements rising from it would not be universally valid. Burke would be faulted in this on three counts. First, the determining God-designed passions are not part of the 'finality of the object'. Second, given Providential design, the subject is legislated to heteronomously. This (empiricist) subject is not so much singular as 'particular'. Third, the passions aroused and the 'sensory delight' involved are for Kant empirical and not transcendental.

Thus beauty is the form of a finality in an object apart from representations of an end: what Kant famously called *Zweckmäßigkeit ohne Zweck*. Aesthetic judgement presumes on the one hand the disinterestedness of the judging subject and, on the other, the finality of the judged object. On the side of subjectivity, where there is a passive disposition to judge due to the powers of a source of legislation that is given, then there is an interest.[42] To be disinterested is to be a rule finding subject. It is to be a subject free not just from heteronomous legislation, but also from the *self*-legislation of both possessive individualism and categorical imperative. Subjectivity is always oriented, whether consciously, pre-consciously or unconsciously, to, on the one hand, other subjects, and, on the other, material or non-material objects. To the extent that we are always oriented to objects, we cannot be autonomous or 'rule-finding' when our orientation to such objects is not aimed at them in terms of their own, internal finalities. That is, our autonomy necessitates that we treat objects or practices as 'internal goods'. In, for example, Marx's notion of use-value, and especially its equivalents in Marx's early work, there is no external end to the object produced. Subjectivity here – whether of the maker or the user of the goods – is not 'interested'. In exchange-value, the good or object is not a finality. Its end is external, and producer and consumer are interested. Alistair MacIntyre's discussion of the virtues hinges on the finality in the object of a given practice. Subjectivity in these practices is not regulated by external goods – not by wealth, power or prestige – but by properties internal to the given good or practice.[43]

The other modernity, as ungrounded ground, must centrally address the question of how we can have community while at the same time leaving space for difference. Perhaps we can open up this problem in this context. The notion of difference is crucially based on the idea of not a universal, but a *singular*, subjectivity. We are singular only to the extent that we are not subsumed under the identitarian logic of 'the concept'. We are singular only to the extent that we do not subsume ourselves in self-identity. We are singular only in our difference and self-difference. I believe, with MacIntyre, that communities must be communities of practice with an internalist orientation towards the practices and the goods they involve. I disagree with MacIntyre in that he does not leave sufficient scope for difference and the singularity of the subject. The idea of reflexive judgement in which the singularity of the subject is dependent on the internality of goods thus at least begins to open up possibilities – and perhaps the key is in Marxian use-value itself – of how communities-in-difference may be possible.[44]

Rationalist theories of aesthetics as well as the philosophy of taste presume such externalities. Such formalist rules for the rationalists are a determinant of subjectivity which does not then reflexively search for the rule. In rationalist aesthetics, once again determinate judgement – and hence metaphysics in Kant's sense of the word – is brought in through the back door. Against the rule-bound determination and classification of the formalist aestheticians Lessing, Baumgarten and Mendelssohn, Kant insists on the 'singularity of the judgement'. For him the singularity of judgement depends on a cultivation (and his *sensus communis* is premised on such cultivation) of subjectivity. This goes well beyond the level of cultivation necessary in cognitive reason (and, it would seem, the moral subject). Indeed, the idea of rule finding – and the notion of 'rule' altogether – is just a first approximation to what reflexive judgement involves. Reflexive judgement, Caygill notes, is a 'formative activity'. It is a 'technics of judgement'. It involves not so much a judgement of art but an 'art of judgement', in which subjectivity has one eye turned outward towards the proportionality of objects and the other turned inward on the proportional harmony of the faculties.[45] Given this sort of model, it is easier to see how determinate judgement – or our decision to choose the rules of logic from the logical categories of the understanding – would be only one species of reflective judgement. This technics of judgement – a set of primitive classifications regulating the natural attitude – is at the same time an 'orientational activity', not unifying but 'configuring' the manifold and 'creating horizons of discrimination'. It is not a logical but an analogic activity: not in which phenomena are brought under rules, but in which objects in the world are set in proportion to one another. Here logic would be just one from of 'analogics', one in which one object was taken as rule and another object or 'configuration' as the phenomenon.

Through reflective judgement as a formative activity we synthesize or make other objects. Through the objects and configurations in the world, subjectivity creates judgements or estimations and creates other objects or configurations according to these estimations. This said, how is it decided which objects and configurations become the 'classifiers' (or configurations through which judging takes place) and which become the 'classified'? Kant's allusions to contingent laws,[46] on the model almost of the English Common Law, in *The Critique of Judgement* are instructive in this context: that is, that entities become classifiers through precedent, through ex-perience. But experience and mere repetition of trivial events and objects is not enough. What would become the classifiers are those objects which are finalities. Objects which are not ends in themselves would be the classified. And which objects, which configurations, become classifiers is dependent on reflective judgement itself, which itself posits finality in (certain) particulars.[47]

Poesis and Symbol

This problem of the finality of the object leads to the issue of poesis. In his book *Theories of the Symbol*, Todorov's central claim hinges on such a juxtaposition of 'mimesis' and heteronomy of the ancients and the 'poesis' of again the finality of the object in a fully fledged modernity. *Poesis* has, of course, already implicitly been centrally at issue in this chapter. Indeed, what has been at issue along much of the length of the present book is a sort of theory of poesis. I have tried to develop a theory of practice – as distinct from a theory of action – in this book that foregrounds not praxis in the classical sense but poesis. That is, my focus has been less on the relationship between subjects than on the relationships between subjects and objects. Even the notions of intersubjectivity I tried to develop in the chapters addressing phenomenology are in the context of the natural attitude: itself established by the *poetike episteme*. This entails not the *theoria* of Kant's first critique featuring the theoretical attitude towards the object, nor the intersubjectivity of the second and *practical* critique, but instead the aesthetic attitude of the third critique.

In *Theory and Practice* Habermas drew on the young Hegel to effectively suggest a modern reworking of the Aristotelian distinction between the theoretical, practical and poetic epistemes. Here Habermas agrees with Hegel's critique of the Kantian notion of the 'I'. He supports Hegel's criticism of the Kantian abstract and universal 'I' for a 'fundamental experience of the "I" that is at the same time universal and singular'. Instead of understanding the 'I' as an 'original and transcendental unity', Habermas draws on Hegel to understand the 'self-formative process' of 'the human species' in terms of 'three heterogenous patterns of self-formation': a 'dialectic of labour, a dialectic of representation and the struggle for recognition'. Here he made it clear that his own contribution was placed in the tracks of recognition, as distinct from representation and labour.[48] The thematic of the theoretical, practical and poetic seems to reappear in *The Theory of Communicative Action*, though this time the aesthetic-expressive sphere took the place originally assigned to 'work' in Habermas's more Marxist days. In both cases Habermas gave the least primacy to poesis. In the communicative action theory all three sorts of utterance are brought back under the theoretical episteme, given the importance to him of utterances as propositions, validity claims and discursive argumentation. In contrast, however, to the transcendental intersubjectivity of *practice* that unites such strange bedfellows as Habermas, on the one hand, and Levinas, on the other, I would want to suggest a theory of sociological *poesis*.

Here, with the early Marx and the early Heidegger, poesis would be understood in counterposition to instrumental rationality. It is only when poesis at work or in art comes under the subsumption of theoria or the theoretical attitude that instrumental rationality arises: that *Zuhandenheit* becomes *Vorhandenheit*, that use-value becomes exchange-value. Important to this is a notion of the means, the *Mittel*, the middle, the material in, again, the context of the Kantian finality of the object. Adam Smith, in his discussion of pleasure, spoke of perceiving a fitness or proportion of a means to an end without any consideration of an end.[49] Here the object which is itself a finality is understood as a means. It is understood crucially as a means apart from any end. Too much of contemporary cultural theory has dispensed with this notion of means, ground, *Mittel* – linking it straight away with instrumental rationality and dismissing it. Thus Gillian Rose has critically characterized theories of difference in terms of 'the broken middle', in her book of the same title.[50] This picture changes, however, when the means is thought from the viewpoint of poesis. When Hegel in *The Phenomenology* spoke of the necessity of grounding consciousness, of grounding singular subjectivity, he spoke of such grounding in a means. In the same vein, Adorno's negative dialectics places its moment of negation in the aesthetic material, itself a means, a *Mittel*. Adorno's material (and through poesis) critique of identity-thinking is, as Adorno says, through the moment of the object, a material moment, never to be finally sublated by the universal. Here again Adorno's aesthetic 'object' as a *Mittel*, again a means, is a finality without external end.[51] Finally, Marx's means of production, as a use-value in the labour process, provides a notion of work as poesis and the means of production as the ground for realization of singular subjectivity. Once the means of production, however, come under the sign of determinate judgement, come under the *theoria* of the production process, they become simply productive capital.

Let us return to Todorov and the contrast of pre-modern mimesis versus modern poesis in the conception of the symbol. In modern poesis, the artist does not imitate nature (as in 'ancient' mimesis) but takes on nature's productive principle.[52] The artist, as Nietzsche indicated in *Uber Lüge und Wahrheit*, indeed is nature.[53] The shift from mimesis to poesis thus entails a modal change in emphasis from the product to the production process; from being to becoming; from an artist who sees in harmony with the world to one who listens to an inner voice that clashes with the world. For the ancient and mimesis, beauty is form. For the modern and poesis, it is pure activity, pure becoming: hence the currency of the dialogue and the fragment. In mimesis signs were significant for their 'said'; in poesis, of course, for their 'saying'. For mimesis and pre-moderns, following Augustine, only God, the One, was an end in himself. For moderns and poesis we all are singular; we are all finalities. Thus the Cartesian 'I think' is not fully modern, because the 'I' is less than an end in itself. The Cartesian 'I' is instead heteronomously legislated to by determinate thought, by the 'I think' or the transcendental unity of apperception. Indeed, the 'I am' itself entails a subsumption by the principle of identity or self-identity, while the principle of modernity's and poesis's becoming lies in self-difference. In other words, singularity is self-difference: we are singular to the extent that we are not subsumed through self-identity. Finally, mimesis and antiquity's symbol entail reconciliation and are 'syncretic', while poesis and the modern symbol is aporetic and 'synthetic'.[54]

Central here to modern poesis is the finality of the cultural object. This is the context of the aesthetic thinking of Goethe, Novalis and Schelling. For the last the sign as finality must always be 'motivated' by meaning. The sign (work of art or cultural object) here is motivated not by determinate meaning but by indeterminate or infinite meaning. In terms of Frege's contrast of *Sinn* or 'signification' and *Bedeutung* or 'designation', the cultural object as finality can only be signified, but can find no adequate designation. This entails a sort of 'intransitive signification'. The Romantics joined Kant in criticism of the old rationalist aesthetics. They took to task, for example, Mendelssohn's notion of 'the perfect'.[55] The perfect, as distinct from the beautiful – very much like agreeableness, catharsis and utilitarianism – was again a matter of an external end. Worse, it was bringing determinate judgement into the sphere of reflexive judgement.

For Novalis and Schelling, poesis's work of art as finality without end is similar to an autopoetic system.[56] This would be an organic, not a cybernetic, system. It would be characterized by internal cohesiveness: indeed it is a closed totality, an organic unity with characteristic organizational rules. The work of art as a finality is like a natural being comprising dispositions and elements juxtaposed in relations with one another. Only it is more tightly organized than an empirical and everyday organic being; more tightly bound up in itself. It needs to be so in order that the aesthetic material can allow the revelation of the ideas of reason, the meaning of existence.[57] Kant counterposed such an organic work of art to applied art, to *Kunstgewerbe* or 'artefacts'. Applied art, unlike the organic work of art, is not intransitive, but transitive in signification. It is adapted to a goal, to producing an effect such as sales on the market. Applied art is not organic but 'artificial' or 'mechanical'. In this sense, in mimesis art or the artefact is mechanical; it is 'unmotivated' by substance or content. It is hence 'arbitrary'. In mimesis, with the domination of 'the referent', art *imitates* the *referent*. In modern poesis, art *'expresses* the *signified.*[58]

Thus Goethe understands *allegory* as unmotivated, as arbitrary and trivial like normal speech. In contrast, *symbol*, like poetic speech, is motivated. Goethe wrote of the development of a mechanical 'clockwork' society, in which relationships, previously organic and integral, were becoming more and more arbitrary like the mechanical and external 'elective affinities' of atoms in chemistry. The mechanical nature of 'allegory' in its externality was also like elective affinities. Goethe's model for allegory was the court comedy and drama of modern superficial and ornamental French theatre. Emblematic for Goethe of 'symbol' were the organic connections of the work of Shakespeare. The latter was celebrated by Kant, in comparison with the mechanical nature of French theatre (and its rule-bound similarities to determinate judgement), as the model for his discussion of 'genius' in the *Aesthetics of the Sublime*. Benjamin too was to write first on elective affinities and later on allegory, with a rather different meaning. For Benjamin, illustrations for allegory were taken from baroque drama rather than classical theatre. Here the paradigm shared with determinate judgement does not hold because of the constitutive *Lücke* (gap, breach or lack) in allegories of German Tragic Drama. In Goethe's allegory, meaning is transmitted and learnt, whereas symbol gives us a different kind of meaning through the effect it produces. Whereas allegory is artificial, transitive and only designates, signs which are symbols are natural, intransitive: they simultaneously represent *and* designate. Allegory is expansive, while symbol is 'laconic', dense.[59] In allegory access to the general is given via the particular, while in symbol we immediately see the general *in* the particular. Allegorical signification is rational and mediated, in contrast to the immediate evocation of the general by the particular of symbol. Allegory is effective via 'the concept', and its finite and dead meanings. Symbol does its work by 'the idea's' infinite and live meanings.[60] Schelling praised myth for being not allegorical but 'tautegorical'. He distinguished between: the 'schematic', in which the particular was apprehended through the general; the 'allegorical', in which it is the particular that signifies the general; and the symbolic, in which general and particular are one, and do not *signify* each other at all. In the schematic and the allegorical, the general is at the same time finite and can be adequately designated in words. But in symbol the general is the infinite, the particular becomes singular: no adequate designation is possible and indirect evocation is necessary. In symbol the finite does not signify the infinite; it *is* the infinite.[61]

Reflexive Modernity: Ontology and Ground

In this shift in Kantian reflective judgement from the singular subject to the finality of the object,[62] we are now in a position to show the connection from groundlessness to ground in the second modernity. Up to now we have spoken of the ground as the second dimension of the other modernity. The first dimension here we have understood in terms of reflexivity or difference, in terms of the experimental freedom, the invention associated with the idea of modernity in terms of 'all that is solid melts into air'. Up to now I have spoken of the ground as a much neglected, sometimes forgotten dimension of the second modernity, that is prima facie polar opposite to its first deconstructive moment. Now we are in a position to see how the deconstructive moment and the grounded moment logically entail one another. I want to show that no reflexivity is possible without ground. That reflexivity (or difference) and the freedom and invention that is associated with it *necessitates* the ground. Here we will see the completion of the logic of the second modernity.

The germ of the argument for this is implicit just above: now I must make it explicit. The argument consists of several steps:

1 Reflexivity is only possible when the universal subject is displaced by the singular subject.
2 This singular subject logically entails the finality of the object. The object when it is a finality is also a ground. When it is not a finality it is a means to another end, or *de facto* an instrument.
3 To the extent that the object for us is an instrument, we are the universal subjects of the first modernity, operating in an analytic of 'epistemology'.

Only when the object is a ground (medium, middle) are we singular subjects. Only then do we address the realm of ontology. Thus reflexivity necessitates ontology. Reflexivity is not complete, is only partial, without ontology.

4 Full modernity is reflexive modernity.

Let us return to the classical triptych of theorein, praxis and poesis used by, for example, the early Habermas, Todorov and so many others. Reading Habermas's *Theory and Practice* as well as his later works, it becomes quite clear that theorein or epistemology logically entails instrumental reason. This is a particularly difficult point to grasp for the theorist whose *raison d'être* is so centrally the avoidance of the commodity and instrumental rationality. But it is already clear in Kant's *Critique of Practical Reason*, which works from the juxtaposition of instrumental or 'empirical reason' and 'pure practical reason'.[63] Here empirical or instrumental reason is the use of the scientific (in maths and physics) rationality of 'pure reason', of the cognitive reason, the epistemology of the first critique. The question is: why does theorein entail instrumental rationality? Theorein is the understanding of the natural sciences and positivism. And in the natural sciences and positivism things and social things are reduced to what are more or less 'variables' of Newtonian time-space. They are reduced to being functions of a theory, equations etc. When this sort of theory descends into the realm of the practical it is but a step to instrumental rationality: to means–ends type thinking and action. Further, subjects of theorein are *caused*. They are not free. They are determined in this sense and not reflexive. They are determined in thinking as theorein and in treating things instrumentally. In treating the object not as a finality, but as a means to an ends, as an instrumentality. To the extent that we are not determined, either by social structures or by theorein, we are reflexive. Indeed, the theory of reflexivity has been widespread in sociology – in ethnomethodology, in the sociology of science, in the conflict theory of Bourdieu and Gouldner and in Beck's and Giddens's theory of reflexive modernization. In each case reflexivity is the critique of determinate reason: as much in the sense of experimentation as in terms of freedom from social structures.

The logic of theorein for Kant and Critical Theory (Horkheimer, Adorno, Habermas) is that we also treat human beings as instruments, as means to ends in a sort of 'strategic rationality'. For humans primarily to use determinate reason is for us as universal subjects to be determined. On this model God is the only singularity, we are the determined universals. Even as God recedes in the background, determinate reason still operates as such. Hence Kant spoke of human beings operating through theorein, through pure reason as the 'heteronomous will', in comparison to the 'pure practical will' of praxis and the categorical imperative.

The only way out of theorein, the only way out of the of the first modernity epistemology, whose logic determines us as positivists and utilitarians with regard to things and people, is through the ground. It is through praxis and poesis. Through intersubjectivity and the object. Indeed, every form of the ground I have or will use in this book is a variant of either praxis or poesis. Kant gets half way towards the second modernity in the second critique, in his outline of a sphere of indeterminacy, of undecidability, but goes the whole way – with the development of a notion of ground – in the third. In the second we see praxis as treating other people as ends, not means to combat theorein in the practical realm. This gets us half way to full reflexivity. Reflexivity and this freedom are meaningless, however, in the absence of sociality of community, of a situated intersubjectivity. It was just such an abstract morality that Hegel so rightly criticized in *The Philosophy of Right*. Indeed, the notion of *Sittlichkeit* in the *Philosophy of Right* not only makes it possible to situate the imperative of the *Critique of Practical Reason*,[64] it also opens up on to ontology or Reason (*Vernunft*). For Hegel, singular subjectivity could not aspire to freedom or Reason in the absence of the ground of forms of ethical life. What Hegel, drawing clearly on the third critique, does in the realm of praxis, of the 'I–thou' relation, Kant in *The Critique of Judgement* did with the finality of the object (nature, art) and the grounding of the I–it relationship of poesis.

The point is that no ontology is possible without a ground; without the ground of praxis that is some sort of situated intersubjectivity. Or the ground of poesis in which the freedom of subjectivity is grounded in the thing. Thus the possibility of the meaning of being, on the one hand, through praxis or, on the other, through the thing and poesis. Through the 'I–thou' or through the thing and the 'I–it'. Kant achieves this in the *Critique of Judgement*, perhaps the site for the emergence of both modern ontology and reflexivity. The third critique's singular subject is no longer caused. It is set free. But as the object also escapes the clutches of instrumental reason, the subject must invest itself in the object – as work, as language, as art – in order to realize that freedom. As such the object, the 'it', opens out on to ontology, on to existential meaning. This is what Gillian Rose meant by the 'broken middle'. That is, what we have been calling the ground in this book is clearly the 'middle'.[65] The middle is between subjectivity and freedom, subjectivity and being. The middle here is never a means (or an instrumentality), always a finality. When the middle is broken, we, as subjects, relate to freedom in a meaningless and ungrounded – Weber would say irresponsible – way. The broken middle conditions instead perhaps a Faustian individualism. When the middle, the ground, disappears only meaningless abstraction and instrumentality are possible. For full reflexivity and full modernity there must be such a middle.

For us in this book in terms of poesis and the singular subject encountering the 'it' we consider the work of art (this chapter), language (chapters 7, 8 and especially 13), the psychoanalytic symbol (chapter 7), 'place' in the built environment (chapters 4 and 12). This could be extended to nature, work relations, artefacts of everyday life (chapters 4, 11 and 13) and the urban fabric. Without these as medium, as ground, as middle, no freedom, no reflexivity, no existential meaning is possible. When the ground becomes a means, a utilitarian or instrumental means, as in, say, language when language refers outside itself to a signified, then the middle is converted to a means, and we are back in theorein. When language becomes a finality and carries its meaning within it rather than through referring to an externality, then it itself is the ground, the middle, and reflexivity is possible.

So the 'it' or the thing or the object in its various guises can be the middle or the ground in poesis. In *praxis* it is always some form of situated intersubjectivity. The transcendental intersubjectivity of Kant's third critique, of Habermas's discursive will formation, of Levinas's or Buber's 'I–thou', are emphatically not such a middle.[66] In grounded praxis, singular subjectivity does not relate to a thou, but to what is already an 'I–thou', to what is already a situated and in principle historical intersubjectivity. This 'I–thou' is ground, a middle for the reflexive subject of praxis. We have seen this in chapters 5 and 6 in Durkheim's collective representations and Simmelian sociality; in chapter 7 as the 'We' of Schutz's stock of knowledge. It is there in Gadamer's idea of memory and the monument in the present chapter, in Ricoeur's 'long intersubjectivity' (chapter 7) of memory and tradition. It is found in urban community (chapter 4) in the East and the West.

Gillian Rose finds the ground of praxis in law, more as an expression of community than as abstract law. She finds it in love, in Christian *agape*, in the fecundity of the generations, in the intersubjectivity of sexual love.[67] The theory of reflexive modernization, for its part, in Beck but also in Giddens, comprises a risk thesis and an individualization thesis. In terms of the risk thesis no reflexivity in the risk society is possible without nature as not instrument but ground, as middle opening out on to the possibility of ontology. No convincing individualization is possible without some sort of community as ground and middle. The second, reflexive modernity is not only the era of the groundless ground: but no groundlessness is possible, no escape from determinacy likely without the ground.

Permanence and Finitude

There are, then, two sides to the ground in the second and reflexive modernity. One resides in the finality of the object in the 'I–it' relation (poesis). This we have just discussed in terms of Kant's object and Todorov's symbol. The other resides in the 'I–thou' relation of intersubjectivity and praxis. We will now explore this in Gadamer's idea of memory. Kant's idea of the *sensus communis* lies, as Lyotard notes, in a '*promise*' of community,[68] which is ultimately a variant of a transcendental intersubjectivity. Gadamer relocates the *sensus communis* in grounded and *real* communities of tradition.

In this chapter we have described, drawing on Kant and very much on Howard Caygill, a notion of reflexive judgement in which subjectivity is engaged in a set of proportioning activities. This proportioning is carried out through the estimating, or judging, of some configurations by means of other configurations. This 'figuring' activity, which circumscribes aesthetic production and consumption (though we need to break with these 'determinate' terms for present purposes), results in aesthetic judgements, themselves subjective feelings with universal validity. What we haven't sufficiently inquired into yet is how it is that certain of these configurations come to be classifiers and others count among the classified. So far we have no even vaguely adequate answers to this. The place to begin, it would seem, is *memory*. It is perhaps pre-eminently through memory that a set of classifying configurations is built. For Hans-Georg Gadamer such memory is first and foremost *collective* memory. Gadamer, however, poses threats to our emergent model of modernity and poesis. He undermines the assumptions of an activist and productivist (even in the most 'reflexive' and non-determinate understanding of productivism) subject in the Kantian (and Goethean) ideas of poesis. He does this through a sort of life-world phenomenology that leads us to rethink reflexive judgement in terms of a phenomenological but effectively 'aesthetic reduction'.

Gadamer's aim in the *Relevance of the Beautiful*, and implicitly in section I of *Truth and Method*, is to relegitimate art. His method is what amounts to an attack on both determinate judgement and the Faustian reflexive judgement of modernity's poesis. The legitimacy of art has, according to Gadamer, always been due to our recognition of ourselves as not just singular but *finite* through art. Art is legitimate because of the dimension of permanence in art and in history, through which we recognize our impermanence and finitude. Art thus has its legitimacy in that through it we 'recognise ourselves in our own worlds'.[69] As Robert Bernasconi notes, aesthetic judgement does not concern the logical status of speech acts about art, but instead is a question of *experience*.[70] This was already true, as we saw above, for Kant, for whom such judgements had primarily the status of feelings. But Gadamer has a vastly different view of experience from Kant. For Kant, as for Goethe, aesthetic experience is a matter of *Erlebnis*, whereas for Gadamer it is along the lines of *Erfahrung*. Whereas *Erlebnis* takes aesthetic experience to be an interlude, to be *an* experience, *Erfahrung* features continuity and permanence. It is true that for Kant the *sensus communis* takes an enormous amount of cultivating, an enormous effort of the *aesthetische Erziehung*, before it becomes capable of reflexive judgement. But once aesthetically educated, individual judgements and feelings are *Erlebnisse*. The same would seem to be true of Kant's notion of genius. Surely the genius for Kant, as well as for Goethe and Schiller, must be comprehensively *erfahrend* (or experienced), but the production of the work of art for this genius is much more a question of Faustian *Erlebnis*. Gadamer like Heidegger, in reducing man from his Faustian (and arguably Nietzschean) heights to a finite being in the world, cannot assent to the separation of *Erlebnis* and *Erfahrung*. For both of them it is *Erfahrung* which must be primordial and whose ontological structure can also account for *Erlebnis* in the modern age. Further, for them aesthetic objects – including architecture – are things you live with and 'tarry' by: they are never separable as *Erlebnisse*.

For Gadamer this sort of aesthetics of *Erlebnis* is largely responsible for the *de*-legitimation of art in modernity. Such de-legitimation, claims Gadamer, comes not only from such Faustian *Erlebnis*-based notions of reflexive judgement. It also comes from determinate judgement. Thus Gadamer criticizes Hegel's pronouncements on the end of art: that art in its best days of classical antiquity had been snuffed out by Christianity's determinate representation of the divine in an unproblematic and self-evident way.[71] This sort of threat is reproduced in modern times through the 'perfection' of industrial (re)production that destroys the mimetic impulse and brings art under the concept. Gadamer agrees that art by definition must involve the finality of the object. But, he notes, today's objects of art no longer provide a common language for our self-understanding. The autonomization of art would instead appear to be based on the alienation of this self-understanding. In its age of legitimacy, art effected the integration between community, church and other institutions, on the one hand, and the self-understanding of the creative artist, on the other. Now the self-understanding of the artist is defined against the community. The artist lives outside the community. His or her 'message is the one true message': no communicability, no *sensus communis*, is possible.[72] Gadamer argues for a revaluation of art, no longer only as poesis, but as mimesis. He observes that in the eighteenth century there was no single word for art, but instead the division between the fine arts and mechanical arts. Both of these, Gadamer observes, come under the heading of Aristotle's *poetike episteme*. In this the mechanical arts presume production for use: here Plato's example was the shipmaster who (externally to the object) will determine what the shipbuilder will build. Fine art in contrast has no real use but 'finds fulfilment when our gaze dwells upon the appearance itself'.[73] Art is less intentional than work: here makers of the human spirit are part and parcel of '*physis*', nature's formative activity. Art, for Gadamer, like history is a mimetic, is not a useful or productive, but instead an imitative, practice. But whereas history's mimesis is only of particulars, art teaches us to recognize universals in particulars.

Unlike Todorov, Gadamer does not understand mimesis in terms of externality, or the externality of the end. Gadamer differs from Kant in that for him the ideas of reason, or Being, are understood not as indeterminacy but as inseparable from permanence and constancy. For Kant both reason and the aesthetic practices that reveal the ideas of reason are indeterminate. For Gadamer what counts is permanence, which is neither determinate nor indeterminate. Such permanence is comprised in both aesthetic objects (for him objects are more important than practices) and the sort of meaning that the objects reveal. Thus Being for Kant in the second critique, in its indeterminacy, its contingency, partakes of the 'Judaic', while Gadamer's notion of Being is similar to the plenitude of Heidegger's *es gibt*, is its 'Greek' counterpart. Only Gadamer's *es gibt* – in contrast to Heidegger's becoming – is conceived in terms of tradition and as *permanence*. Thus it is the Greek model, the idea of the beautiful, of vision, permanence and plenitude that he turns to. Gadamer thus invokes Pythagoras's contrast of the heavenly order of the regular movement of the cosmos as the true vision of beauty, in contrast to the instability and ambiguity of human affairs.[74] He points to Plato's Phaedrus, where the human charioteers following the Olympian Gods at the vault of the heavens see the true world – of 'true constants and unchanging patterns of being'. When they subsequently plunge back to earth, they have only the vaguest remembrance of his, and can only recall it – through a glass darkly – in the earthly experience of the beautiful.[75] Gadamer hails the original permanence of rhetoric, for the Greeks 'the universal form of communication' without which human understanding and the ever changing face of science is impossible. For Gadamer being reveals itself in the work of art and in tradition, which he undertands as the merger of horizons, much the same as Ricoeur's 'long intersubjectivity'.[76] But unlike Heidegger, Gadamer speaks little of being *per se*. And that is because Gadamer is even more ontological than Heidegger. He cannot conceive of being apart from its internality to art and tradition. He cannot even remotely, cannot even analytically, separate value from fact.

If we follow the argument in 'The relevance of the beautiful', we can see how Gadamer derives this aesthetic – a properly hermeneutic aesthetic of both symbol and mimesis. The title in German of this seminal essay is 'Die Aktualität der Schönen', and the English 'relevance' misses the full meaning of 'Aktualität'. The latter does indicate relevance, but it is also semantically charged with connotations of urgency, immediacy, possessing the characteristics of a sort of life-force. This essay, written in 1980, and part I of *Wahrheit und Methode* are sustained reflections on art as the basis of understanding, as the condition of possibility for the exchange of speech acts and for coming to an understanding. *Wahrheit und Methode*, part II, on historical hermeneutics, addressing Schleiermacher, Dilthey and others, is not fundamental but derivative. Thus part I is entitled the 'Freilegung der Wahrheitsfrage an der Erfahrung der Kunst', and part II is only the 'Ausweitung der Wahrheitsfrage auf das Verstehen in den Geisteswissenschaften'. Thus part I, on the experience of art, 'lays open' (*Freilegung*) the truth question, and part II, on understanding in the human sciences, is only a 'development' (*Ausweitung*) of the truth question already laid open. Thus both the critique of method in the human sciences, and understanding in the exchange of expressions of everyday life, as well as historical understanding and 'the merger of horizons', are contingent on a set of preconditions that Gadamer sees as properly aesthetic. And 'understanding' (not *Verstand* but *Verstehen*), i.e. statements in the human sciences as well as everyday communications, is conditioned on background assumptions, which are aesthetic.

Gadamer begins to address art through a treatment of 'play'. He shows how what is at stake in art can be found in more basic form in play. The basis for this lies in philosophical anthropology, particularly the work of Arnold Gehlen, and its assumption that unlike those of animals, human instincts are 'underdetermined'. For philosophical anthropology it is indeed this indeterminacy of our instincts that forces human beings to be free. The attendant danger of such freedom is that human finitude is – in certain important senses – far more 'exposed' than animal life. In *The Will to Power*, Nietzsche intoned that we compensate for such a lack, this gap in our instincts, through the development of the categories of determinate judgement, through using our subsumptive and logical powers to survive and thrive. Gehlen, and following him sociological theorists such as Peter Berger, argue that *institutions* are necessary to 'compensate for this underdetermination: that we fill this lack or gap in our instincts through institutions. Gadamer's view is somewhat more complex. For him we compensate for our "Instinktarmut" through *retaining what threatens to pass away*'.[77] And it is especially art that 'endows the ephemeral with [such] permanence'. Gadamer conceives this in terms of 'transcendence', going beyond the finitude of our individual (through the tools of logic) and collective (through institutions) survival. At issue also is our 'pole of infinity', our striving beyond the finite, beyond logic and calculation. The way we 'retain what threatens to pass away' is what later becomes consolidated as 'tradition' in Gadamer.

In this sense of retaining the transient, play sets the paradigm for art, and art for understanding. We first retain permanence in play. Games that are played entail repetition, a self-sameness of activity.[78] A game played necessarily involves the idea of identity once we can identify a pattern of play. So play entails the retaining of permanence in (a) its rules, (b) the identity of a pattern, (c) the fact that others must play along with, which means that this identity, this permanence, is not just for me over time, but also for others, who occupy different spaces from me. Now not just play, but work too, entails rules, identity and extending these to others. Play, however, entails another crucial element that work does not. And that is that play is '*in excess of purpose*'. It is in excess of 'pragmatic purpose'. Moreover, and this is the linchpin of modern hermeneutics, '*representation*' is only possible through activities that go beyond pragmatic purpose. Whereas work mainly involves determinate judgement, play, which frees us from particular ends, mainly involves indeterminate, self-rule-giving activity.[79] It is here that we as 'permanence-retaining animals' transcend the pragmatic purposes of survival we share with other species. Our permanence-retaining capacities allow us, on the one hand, to survive in immanence, through our empirical wills using the logical categories; and, on the other, to do a lot more than survive through representation, which, in excess of determinate judgement, allows us some measure of transcendence.

The move from just play to art carries with it a substantial reinforcement and supplement to this permanence. In, for example, early archaic burial art, this excess of pragmatic purpose revealed in play comes to be more explicitly and concretely embodied in representations. Such permanence, far more enduring than the also reflexively chosen rules of games, at the same time reveals our finitude. That is, our transcendence through the creation of permanence in art reveals our finitude. Or, in short, our transcendence reveals our finitude. We are, then, animals characterized by 'transcendence in finitude'. We are beings who are able to *recognize* our finitude only through this transcendence. As merely permanence-retaining animals, occupied in pragmatic purpose and work activities, our Faustian, striving nature is uncontrolled. We see ourselves instead as infinite. Only through the excess of purpose involved in the representations of art are we able to recognize our finitude. But we cannot recognize this finitude until we transcend.

This sort of notion of collective memory as an excess permanence-retaining capacity must supplement any adequate notion of reflexive judgement. Without it there is a deficit of reflexivity; without it we are unaware of our finitude. Starting from play, Gadamer sees a progression to ritual dance and then to ritual observance. With ritual observance, the excess already emergent in play takes for the first time the form of re-presentation. Finally, there is the 'liberation of representation' in theatre, poetry and the visual arts. Gadamer's understanding of 'symbol' differs from Lessing's, Kant's and Goethe's classical notion in its absence of a notion of genius and the creative artist, but sees the latter too in terms of finitude. Shakespeare's genius is thus not a question of Promethean or Zarathustrean creative activity as listening to 'the voice of nature'. In contrast to Kant and Goethe, Gadamer's artist heeds the 'flow of speech rushing past us and coming to stand within a poem'. Symbol, on this view, allows meaning to present itself. Aesthetic experience concerns not primarily the innovation of the particular, but 'the totality of the . . . experienceable world, and man's ontological place in it'. Gadamer's individual is not so much singular as finite. For him the work of art as well, again as opposed to Kantian poesis, is not primarily singular. It is devalued as a particular and gains value only where the 'particular represents itself as a fragment of being that promises to make whole' our world. Symbol then results in 'an increase in being'.[80] It is a 'facticity', in Rilke's sense of 'such a thing stood among men'. This mimesis is imitation not of the familar, but of the ungraspable that is 'represented in such a way that it is actually present in sensuous abundance', in 'its ontological plenitude'. This plenitude calls on the *sensus communis* 'to dwell upon it and give our assent in an act of recognition'.

Having added the dimension of permanence, and implicitly of collective memory, to reflexive judgement, Gadamer now gives it a phenomenological twist. Aesthetic experience, he observes, as opposed to the 'full understanding' of determinate judgement, always involves an indeterminate 'anticipation'.[81] Here, on the one hand, 'the particular represents itself as a fragment of being that promises to make itself whole'. As indeterminate meaning, on the other, it can never make itself whole. This describes the arc of a hermeneutic circle, in which we experience by 'performing a constant hermeneutic movement guided by anticipation of the whole'. The anticipated and unrealized whole in this is the 'horizon', the life-world instantiation of the phenomenological noema. If the whole were fulfilled, if the hermeneutic circle – the '*Zirkel des Verstehens*' – became too virtuous, and did become whole, it would self-destruct. It would dissolve into determinate judgement and hermeneutic experience could continue no longer. The point here is not that the hermeneutic circle and hermeneutic method is unworkable because you can never even approach a full picture of the whole. The point is that it is only operable when you cannot. If the whole ever became a clearly perceivable structure of social and cultural elements, then hermeneutic truths would become impossible. In their place instead would be determinate judgement and pure method.

This movement between particular and the horizon, this anticipation of the unrealizable whole, is of a piece with the Kantian relation between object and indeterminate rule. Gadamer sees this parallel, yet criticizes

Kant for his Platonic division between aesthesis and noesis, between perception and intellect. He instead looks to Aristotle, for whom *nous* has no
separate ontological status and the *logos* is the linguistic medium of our
being in the world. Perception, Gadamer argues, should not be radically
separated from intellection. We perceive, for example, 'man' and not
'white', as intuition is already possessed with formative (and intellectual)
powers of distinction.[82] Gadamer thus wants to speak of an 'inner intuition',
effectively performing the phenomenological reduction. The temporality of
this reduction is not Husserl's momentary 'now', but instead, like in festivals, a 'full' and indivisible time. In festivals time is arrested, one 'tarries':
time is not 'spent' but 'experienced', like the time of childhood or mourning. Gadamer's 'inner intuition' performs its 'aesthetic reduction', not
transcendentally and through a moment, but as immanent in the world,
and through 'tarrying', letting the 'temporal succession of aspects (of an
object) build up', so as to obtain something which 'stands' and has a sort of
permanence. On this view the original reduction was aesthetic. Kantian
'intuition' is the English translation of the German *Anschauen*, which also
means insightful: *anschaulich* poetry lets us, through tarrying before the
temporal succession of aspects, build up something that stands, a noema or
a schema – but one which is prior to concepts. Gadamer cites Kant on
genius, which 'seizes the quickly passing play of the imagination and unifies
it in a concept (which is even on that account original and at the same time
discloses a new rule . . .) that can be communicated without any constraint
of rules'.[83]

Gadamer's life-world phenomenology thus gives reflexive judgement a
hermeneutic ground. Kant already gave us the prototype for the aesthetic
reduction through indeterminate rules. The problem is – and here is where
the theory of difference must be grounded and finds its grounding in
life-world phenomenology – *where* subjectivity can find these rules. In the
Kant–Goethe *problematique* subjectivity is more or less free to find such rules.
For Gadamer subjectivity finds the rules, already there in the horizon, in
the 'world', in the given social and cultural formation where subjectivity
finds itself. Subjectivity in the other modernity has, as we have continued to
note, two sides – one of ungrounded difference and the other grounded in
the life-world, in tradition, in indexical signification. Chapters 7 and 8 were
a critique of such ungrounded difference: first, through Derrida himself
and the importance of the index in his critique of Husserl's notion of the
sign; second, via the very situatedness, the very 'worldedness', of the 'We'
relation, of intersubjectivity in Schutz's life-world phenomenology. This
chapter has been devoted to Kantian reflexive judgement as a challenge to
high modern determinate judgement. This has been criticized and supplemented with a ground by Gadamer's notion of finitude in permanence.

Gadamer has thus provided the ostensibly 'Greek' counterpart to the iconoclastic 'Judaism' of the Kantian sublime. This juxtaposition of Jews and Greeks, Greeks and Jews, into which now and then the materiality, the indexicality, of the heathen pokes his head, is the subject to which we now turn.

10

Discourse, Figure . . . Sensation

We have seen in chapter 9 how our species-specific incompleteness, our constitutive lack, suspending humankind in the world, between ground and groundlessness, forces us to be subjectivities; forces us to be subjectivities that are continually and chronically engaged in processes of judgement. This instinctual underdetermination, this constitutive *Instinktarmut*, condemns us to judge. Condemns us to be judging animals. Thus placed, subjectivity seems to stand under an equal but different sentence to strive for infinity, to strive to be God. This divine striving takes place first through determinate judgement, through attempting to attain omniscience. Necessary for our physical survival, our logical categories – effecting a sort of closure, papering over the opening of the lack – constitute us as closed systems. We survive in this vein through the making of tools, through work and production, through calculation in the market place. In this man wants to be God as omniscient, as the all-seeing, the all-knowing champion of speculative reason, the master of the great Panopticon, seeing into both past and future. This is the techno-scientific god of informational capitalism: the god of perfect memory. We try thus to be God through expanding our powers of determinate judgement.

But subjectivity also strives for infinity in another way. This time it has nothing to do with closing of his lack, her wound. Here subjectivity does not so much want to be God, as to undermine, even to kill, God. Here Doktor Faustus will do a deal with the devil, and in return be granted *übermenschlich* aesthetic powers. Here Icarus and Daedalus will fly. Here the French or Spanish syndicalist at the turn of the last century will intone 'ni dieu, ni maitre, ni patrie'. But here too God is viewed differently. He is not so much that omniscient king, reigning over beauty, the suzerain of the Great Chain of Beings. This God is a punishing God, the God of Job, the voice in the darkness, an arbitrary will, out there in the realm of fear and trembling. God is invisible and temporal, so Faustian man, raw wounds open and bleeding, is not so much striving to fly high, because spatiality has disappeared, but somehow to defeat time. If omniscient man tries to be

God through that extreme type of judgement which is determinate judgement, Faustian man tries to kill God through that other extreme form of
judgement, i.e. fully *in*determinate judgement.

Cultural theory has tended to think in terms of this sort of binary
opposition: between the attempts of closed and open subjects at infinity;
between cognitive and aesthetic individualism. Perhaps to avoid Hegelian
trinities, this irresolvable binary opposition has appeared and again appeared as nature and culture, capitalism and schizophrenia, identity and
difference. It has with renewed force appeared now in ethics and aesthetics.
Thus Levinas contrasts a totality, a finite totality of cognitive reason,
beyond which and opposed to which there is the infinity, the contingent
ungroundedness of ethics.[1] For other writers, there is the finite totality of
the beautiful, beyond which there is the excess, the infinity of the sublime.
Here the finite and 'visual' totalities of cognitive reason and the beautiful
are understood in terms of *the Greek* or *the Hellenic*, while the beyond of these
totalities in ethics or the sublime is understood as *Judaic* or *the Hebraic*. Thus,
as Derrida concludes his seminal 'Violence and metaphysics', we are all
now 'JewGreeks'; we are 'all GreekJews'.[2] When Lyotard's equally influential 'Qu'est-ce que le postmoderne?' contrasts the totality of the beautiful
with the unpresentability of the sublime, we know that the Judaic iconoclasm of 'the word' is not far behind.

What I want to argue in this chapter is that there is a third party or a
third space involved. A party or space that is other than determinate
judging Greek and indeterminate judging Jew. This third space comprises
neither the hybridity nor the performativity of the JewGreek, or indeed of
anyone else. It is also not a fold, not a limit condition of the JewGreek
within which we must all work. It is finally not any sort of sublation or
reconciliation of totality and infinity, of beautiful and sublime. The third
space is a ground, an underneath, a base in the sense of basis. Human
beings, we have been arguing, are neither determinate nor indeterminate,
but reflexively judging animals. And the condition of possibility of reflexive
judgement is the existence of such a ground. This ground is in perception
and in community, This ground brings subjectivity down (or now and here)
from its omniscient and deathbound while death-defying Faustian flights.
Subjectivity is forced to judge through the materiality of this ground. It is
in regard to this ground that subjectivity is made to be aware of its own
finitude.

This ground is in something that does not lie between the finite logical
categories and infinite ideas of reason, does not lie in the space of difference, in the limit condition between the Greek and Jewish realms. The
ground lies *beneath* both reason and the understanding, beneath both being
and logic, beneath both ethics and cognition. The ground finds its home in
the imagination, its girding in sensation. In short, the foregrounding of this

ground is perception. Thus aesthetic judgements of the beautiful capture the imagination and circumvent the understanding to compel the ideas of reason. With regard to being, with regard to the collective memory that makes such judgements possible, we are mercilessly finite. Thus aesthetic judgements of the sublime circumvent both the imagination and understanding, direct from the sphere of sensation as phenomena enter subjectivity from outside.[3] Here subjectivity is living in the raw media of *sensation*, the raw materiality of (not realism) but the real. Here subjectivity stands in awe of the vengeful and violent God and His infinity. Here we discover our finitude through not memory, but forgetting. This chapter returns to aesthetic judgements of the sublime, not through an interest in the infinity to which it opens us, but because of the means, the material, the order of 'sensation' we must go through as ground in order to get there. This chapter, beyond the discourse of reason and the figure of the imagination, wants to ask if there is indeed a third logic, if there is such a logic of sensation.

The Body with Organs

The Logic of Sensation

In the *Auseinandersetzung* of Jews and Greeks, of iconoclasts and iconologues, Edmund Burke is quite clearly on the side of the former. His *Philosophical Inquiry into Our Ideas of the Sublime and the Beautiful*, written in 1757, thus agrees with Lessing's pre-critical aesthetics in their distancing from the rationalist beautiful. In his *Laocoon: an Essay on the Limits of Poetry and Painting*, Lessing at the same time valorized poetry over painting and the aural over the visual. Thus Lessing as much as Kant instantiates that shift from the speculative to the practical, from the fixity of space to the becoming of time, which characterized the change from pre-modern to modern notions of the sign. Understanding the sublime and the aural as masculine and painting and the beautiful in terms of woman, Lessing pre-figures early and late twentieth-century psychoanalysis.[4]

For his part, Burke enthused over the admirable sublime of Virgil's poetry, with its overload of confused images, its blind experience overwhelmed by voice. This he contrasts to the mere clarity, distinction and beauty of painting.[5] Today we tend to equate the becoming and constant change of the sublime with radicalism and the fixity of beauty with conservatism. How, one wonders, can Burke be an advocate of both iconoclasm and conservatism? In chapter 9 we discussed Gadamer's conservatism and traditionalism, but here it was the aesthetics of beauty, i.e.

not iconoclasm but iconology, which was integral to tradition. Without this plenitude of the *es gibt*, how can Burke too be a conservative? The answer is that he is dependent on a particular ground, a very special tradition, itself as condition of possibility of the sublime. Burke invokes this tradition, this ground, in championing the darkness and overload of similitudes of Eastern religion versus the light of the West. Burke points to the virtues of primitive and Oriental languages, with their excess of resemblances, in contrast to the clarity and judgement of ('Western') vision.[6] At issue here is not just something ungraspable and infinite like the voice, but something very fully material. Something 'lower down' and more basic than even the 'half way up' of the understanding and determinate judgement; something even lower than the figural and the imagination. At issue is *sensation* as the route to the sublime. As the pathway to Being. At issue is the very materiality of *sensation*.

Here we can learn from consulting Burke's *Reflections on the French Revolution*, written over thirty years later than the *Inquiry*. Like Lessing and Kant, Burke took on the opposition of the English versus the French to revisit the sublime and the beautiful. Thus the English and sublime is the 'obscurity' of the English Revolution and Milton's 'ruins of a monarch'. It is 'a tower, an archangel rising through the mist', as opposed to the 'cold beauty' of French neo-classical verse. It is the English ear versus the French eye, English 'passion' versus French reason, English 'experience' versus French system: the humble practices of day-to-day life of the English as opposed to the abstract speculation of the ideas of the French Revolution. What we have here as 'the English' is not just experience, not just the sensation of radical empiricism.[7] What we have is sensation and experience as integrated with 'custom, tradition and habit', in much the same way that Kant saw aesthetic judgement by way of analogy to the tradition and experience of English Common Law. On this view the ideas of both reason and sensation are 'English', and aesthetic judgements of the sublime bridge (the as it were 'pre-figural') sensation and the ideas of reason. That is, the sublime is not the ideas of reason, but sublime are *judgements* which *connect* sensation to the ideas of reason.

Aesthetic judgements of the sublime or the beautiful do not bridge the first and second critiques in the sense that they bridge the understanding and the ideas of reason. They do so only in the sense that they connect the whole sphere of 'nature' or necessity – including sensation, the imagination and the understanding – on the one hand, with the sphere of freedom on the other. And they do so each time by short-circuiting the understanding: they work either through the imagination or directly through sensation. The 'French', for its part, comprises not only the determinate judgement of the understanding (clear and distinct ideas) but also the neo-classical order of the aesthetics of beauty. This is the hegemony not of sensation, but of the figural order of the imagination. Burke is critical of a certain presence of both the determinate judgements of the understanding and reflexive judgements of beauty, i.e. judgements passing through the imagination. Judgements of the sublime presume a much more radical experience of finitude than those of beauty. Indeed, the idea of finitude in Gadamer's aesthetics of beauty, as we saw in chapter 9, is already presence, already transcendence, already an absence of openness and woundedness, already a denial of lack. It is most fundamentally through the logic of sensation – which encompasses the inhuman (though not the inorganic) as well as the human – that we deal with our finitude. And we deal with it on the level of other organic beings. We always were finite, but only become aware of it through the significations of the unpresentable, i.e. through aesthetic judgements of the sublime. This is the finitude of genius[8] in which experience is overwhelmed by this logic of sensation, which is perceptual and universal at the same time.

What we are getting at here is not just a matter of philosophical speculation as to the meaning of Being. What we are getting at is some very human-scientific notions of transcendental or existential meanings. Existential meaning is quite simply different from and transcendental to determinate meaning. These are meanings more important and less determinate than logical and market place calculation. We cannot understand the deaths of those close to us, births, long striven for life goals, falling in love, our children's joys and crises through the determinate meaning of logical statements. At issue instead is transcendental or existential meaning. What reflective judgement presupposes is simply that the path to these meanings is through the particular, through the eminently trivial, through everyday cultural artefacts and habitual forms of life. The trouble in our age of 'technology', however, is that the world of objects and death itself come increasingly under the sway of determinate judgements and logical meaning. Hence both our finitude and transcendence are lost. Worse, we come increasingly to encounter the particular, the cultural artefacts of sensation and experience themselves as already instrumentalized, as already under the spell of determinate judgement.

The aurality of the sublime on the one hand and the visuality of cognition and the beautiful on the other are bound up with two very different notions of the sacred. There is the Protestant, 'Northern' God, like in Judaism, singular, arbitrary, unknowable. And there is the French, Mediterranean (light) God as not singular but universal, a supreme Being manifest through not its arbitrary will but its bequeathal of order. God as singular is addressed via the verbal sublime, via the indexical and 'metonymy', the bluntness and habitualness of customary linkages.[9] The universalist God of plenitude and order, for his part, is addressed through the rational and specular construction of 'metaphor'. There is, however, a possible contradiction at the very heart of the beautiful. Like the sun, the abstract speculation in beautiful images can proliferate endlessly. Like the sun, the cold radiation of revolution in its unintended consequences can blind, can 'denucleate', can result in *in*visiblity and overwhelmingness of the *specular sublime*.[10]

The specular sublime is evident in the 1789 Revolutionaries' attempt to imitate God in their expansion of the sphere of determinate judgement. It emerges with Plato's charioteers, who fall to earth after trailing the gods, and then experience the heavenly through the forms of the beautiful on earth. We cannot experience the infinite directly. There is no immediate access to existential or transcendental meanings. Such access comes through our experience of indeterminate temporalities and spatialities. When such experience is mediated by forms, by the imagination, by the imaginary, we are talking about judgements of the beautiful; when they are mediated by sensation outside of forms, these are judgements of the sublime. The sublime is, on the one hand 'verbal', on the other 'specular'. The verbal sublime has to do with the beyond. It is felt as overwhelming, but as darkness, as cold, as contingency, as the voice.[11] Although Kant addresses this in terms of aesthetics, there is something very *ethical* about the verbal sublime. The specular sublime is much more of a piece with Joyce's artist and Nietzsche's Zarathustra. If it has to do with revolutions, it is not with the emancipation of determinate judgement, but with the revolutionary terror of Marat or Babeuf. Here we leave the idiom of the ethical more or less altogether. Here we find existential meaning not through ethics but through, for example, murder. Existential meaning is found through an aesthetic that is in no way ethical.

The 'specular sublime' is conceived by Georges Bataille in an almost dialectical nature: its emergence through sailing too close to the sun, 'annihilating' determinate judgement's logic of identity.[12] This logic of identity Bataille understands in terms of a rampaging and violent determinate judgement, one which is not so much omniscient as 'omnivorous', as 'omniphagic'. Here *self*-identity is less self-monitoring but 'autophagous'. Out of control and carnivorous, identity and self-identity are conceived first on the model of the Understanding's 'I', but also on the metaphor of the imaginary's, the figural's *eye*. Thus the 'eye's' aesthetic judgements of beauty are just as destructive and just as violently colonizing as cognitive judgements of the 'I'. The way out from what is 'identity-feeling' even more than Adornonian identity-thinking, the way out of this logic of identity of the imaginary as well as the understanding, is with surrealism through the auto-mutilation of the eye. Instead of the eye's autophagous self-identity of imagining the self, substitute the eye's self-mutilation in a tactile version of *écriture automatique*. The eye on this account is tactile. It is more an organ for cutting or slicing than an organ for seeing. Instead of mediating the closed subjectivity of the imaginary, the eye is opened. The eye is mutilated into a wound; cut open in order to expose the lack, the wound that opens us up to not figuration but sensation.

This is instructive in rethinking the idea of community. In Jean Luc Nancy's *Communauté désouvré*, communities form between individuals to the extent that they are *not* self-identical. To the extent that we are self-subsuming, that we monitor ourselves through determinate judgements or market calculations or discursively redeemed validity clams, to this extent we cannot form communities. Community is only possible through those regions of ourselves that are 'singular', that do not come under the universalism of identity or self-identity. It is in our moments of self-difference that we form communities. Now there may be two main types of community that form from such self-difference. We recall from chapter 9 Gadamer's notion of community forged in self-difference, escaping the logic and technology of the understanding. This was grounded in the beautiful, in the forms, the intuitedness through time and space of the forms of the beautiful. But cannot community also come together as self-difference, not via the forms of the figural, of the imagination, but instead the realm of sensation, via judgements of the sublime? Levinas gives us such a notion of community as a sort of being-in-common bearing witness to the sublime.

Bataille also implicitly gives us a community of the sublime. Unlike Levinas, however, this is not of a verbal and ethical sublime but of the thoroughly unethical dimension of the specular sublime. Bataille's communities of self-difference forge, for example, literally in the specular sublime's blinding light of shells in the trenches of the First World War. They bond here through degradation, through pollution. Community comes not through social or even aesthetic order, but through disorder, through sensation. Community is never stronger than where perspicuity fails.[13] Community, on this view, is welded together, not by forms of the understanding or the imaginary, but through the *informe*, the *part maudite*, through excess. 'The gift' is important here. But the gift must be understood not as Maussian reciprocity, or Baudrillard's *Gemeinschaft* bonding reversibility. It is also not a matter of the plenitude of Derrida's *es gibt*. Community comes through the potlatch ceremonies, through bearing another kind of witness to the flames consuming the wealth.[14] Community begins thus in waste, in *dépense*. Bataille's general economy is in excess not only of the restricted economy of determinate judgement and the commodity. It is also in excess of the *Gemeinschaft* of symbolic exhange. Further and, for our purposes, primarily, it is in excess of the figural economy, of the libidinal economy. This general economy is inscribed in a logic of sensation through which transcendental meanings now and then for various durations flicker.

These communities and aesthetics of sensation must be understood in a radically anti-productionist sense. In the previous chapter we noted how Kantian judgement like *Lebensphilosophie* could be understood as a configuring process, an analogic and figural process. Here not only the understanding, but also the imagination, proceeds via subsumption and syntheses, i.e. both operate through production: they *produce* presentations or representations. Presentations are *Darstellungen* and representations *Vorstellungen*. These share roots and sense with *Herstellung* (production) and Heidegger's *Gestell*, which is the 'frame' necessary for representation and production.[15] Once so framed in our age of 'technology', beings are stock-piled as frames in a sort of 'standing reserve'. The only way out of this incessant productionism, this fully modern productionism of reflexive judgement, is to break with the imagination and the figure for a 'reception-ist' aesthetics of sensation in which subjectivity is open to the grain of the world's materiality. Bataille rails against the visuality, the 'eye', the productionist imagination of legible space and visual order of 'architec-ture'. Pitting the labyrinth against the pyramid, '*l'informe*' against form, he evokes instead a subterranean disorder of underground tombs.[16] Thus – and Lyotard is right – the reflexive judgements of beauty are representative of a full and aesthetic modernity. But here we are talking not of all reflexive judgements, but only those of beauty, those of form. Reflective judgements of the sublime give us another kind of subjectivity altogether: a wounded subjectivity open to the logic, the materiality, of sensation. Thus the way, the path to transcendental, to existential, to indeterminate meaning, is not through the figure but through the ground. The way to groundlessness is through the ground of sensation.

But what about this framing the productionist and constructionist imagi-nation carries out? What about this *Gestell*, this form of the *Vorstellung*, the *Darstellung*, the *Herstellung*. The frame, as Derrida maintains, is also that which keeps any externalities from disturbing the finality of the Kantian object. If the work of art is the *ergon*, then its frame is the *parergon*, *protecting* the work of art from the trivialities of such externalities. But the parergon is also the 'limit' which separates Jew from Greek: the Jewish and contingent outside, from the Greek inside; that separates the voice of Being, on the one hand, from the understanding and the figures of the imagination on the other. The frame itself – as neither infinite nor part of the finite totality of cognition and imagination – does constitute a third space. This space is in no way 'hybrid'. It is instead material. It is somehow like the index, haptic, tactile. This limit, this frame, is also for Derrida an organ. It is material, a Marxian use-value at the same time as a bodily organ. This frame or limit as organ constitutively folds back on itself in 'invagination'.[17] This frame, bearing material traces, is the condition of sense of both inside and outside. It is the ground of Hellenic and Hebraic groundlessness. This ground, this material, is Adorno's aesthetic material, the mediations, the *Mittel* of his aesthetics of redemption, which starts also in the '*informe*', not in form but in the aesthetic material. It is never subsumed by the speculative reason of the universal, the categories. This aesthetic material, in its negative dialectic, never subsumes but works through sensation in anti-productionist judgements of the sublime. It opens us – it opens our ears, our wounds to the possibility of redemption and the voice of Being.

Blindness as Lack: the Verbal Sublime

The theme of reflective judgement would seem to repeat itself in psychoanalysis, at least to the extent that psychoanalysis is not dominated by ego theory. That is to the extent that psychoanalysis is not devoted only to strengthening the ego, and making us into determinate-judging animals. Psychoanalysis, like Kantian reflective judgement, starts from perception – whether in the sphere of sensation or the imagination. And it does so to undermine the 'present-at-hand' assumptions of the ego and 'technology' to make some connections between perception and existential meaning. Let us continue to speak of three types of meaning: trivial or banal meaning, determinate meaning and existential meaning. Like reflective judgement, psychoanalysis connects banal meaning (of instinct or the body), short-circuiting determinate or logical meaning, to get at existential meaning.

Thus Freud in *Civilization and Its Discontents* charted a civilizing process in which man evolves from a hominid, on the ground, 'sniffing at nether regions', to the elevation of sight. *Homo sapiens* here on the one side is horizontality and the sensibility of the nose, and, on the other, the verticality of the eye and the I. In this the basis of course is the shame of exposed genitalia on which ego development is based. Freud constantly contested determinate judgement: he was more concerned with subjectivity as a whole than with merely the ego. This anti-positivism informed, for example, his early disagreements with Charcot's use of clinical observation of hysterics' symptoms in the latter's clinic at Salpêtrière. For the later Freud the desire to know stemmed from the desire to see, from infantile scopophilia.[18] This overdetermined and archaic desire to know emerges once again in Lacan's mirror phase. To this Freud counterposed the 'talking cure' – substituting the 'voice' of existential meaning for the eye of determinate meaning.

The talking cure – Habermas was right in *Knowledge and the Human Interests* – is thus more fundamentally hermeneutic than positivistic. It is hermeneutic in opposition to final subsumption and prescription of open endedness. It is hermeneutic in its concern with existential meanings. It links sensation and sexuality with existential meaning in the 'private sphere', again short-circuiting the public sense of determinate judgement and the hypertrophied ego. In its very focus on the unconscious mind it encourages the cathecting of primary process and a certain de-cathecting and disinvestment of libido from the conscious and pre-conscious ego. Moreover, psychoanalysis does presuppose a type of intersubjecivity, and even arguably a dialogic intersubjectivity.[19] Yet this intersubjectivity, unlike communicative rationality, is asymmetrical. Psychoanalysis as process has been described as not Greek but fundamentally Judaic, in its focus on the voice and asymmetric intersubjectivity. In Judaism God does the talking, God issues the commands and the 'chosen people' do the listening. This is turned upside down though when analysand does the talking and the analyst – *loco parentis* or *loco deus* – does the listening. But Yahweh hardly engages in the chattering of *das man*. What He utters are laws, they are 'universals'. Similarly, the analysand is mired in the banal, the particular. And it is the analyst who must do – in silence and more or less analogically – the reflexive judging.

Thus the talking cure focuses on the unconscious, on this 'mystic writing pad', which erases yet keeps traces of what disappears. And the analyst is a 'blank pad', on which traces are salvaged and reworked during the transference. Again the Kantian model is instructive. The 'trace' itself is neither visual nor aural, neither iconic nor symbolic, but surely tactile, surely of a kind with Heidegger's *Holzwege*, surely indexical in the sense of an imprint, like footprints. The trace belongs not to Kant's imagination but instead to the sphere of sensation. The trace opens up the possibility, when linked to existential meaning, of the sublime. The unconscious as a mystic writing pad erases yet keeps traces. Thus traces are not accessible to reflection, but only as in reflective judgement, through a glass darkly via the particulars, the cultural artefacts, the banal statements and meanings of the analytic situation, the meanings of profane dreams and everyday life. The traces are of course always *memory* traces: they are highly cathected events or objects, but cathected only at first in the sphere of sensation.[20] That is, they become traces and are as such cathected after sense data has entered the 'perceptual-consciousness system', but before it has been subsumed either by the ego or the unconscious mind, i.e. by the imaginary or symbolic of the unconscious.

When sense data enters the perceptual-consciousness system, it initially remains as 'raw' sensation, though already invested with considerable psychic energy. This pre-digested sphere of sensation, which is not necessarily more unconscious than conscious, can be cathected.[21] Sensation can be the locus of massive investment of libido as well as the imaginary, the symbolic and the ego. Such patterns of cathexis of traces in the realm of sensation, through indexical signification constitute what Deleuze called a *logique de la sensation*. The tactile traces, whose origin is in sensation, then enter the figural logic of the imaginary to the extent that trace-matrices structure the mystic writing pad as a field. Now the traces themselves have come under the logic of the imaginary, have been reworked in a figural vein. The traces are reworked into the unconscious and the figural, the iconic and visual field of dreams, of the unconscious, with their logic not of subsumption but of displacement and condensation. The analyst then encourages the subject somehow to rearticulate this visuality in words, in discourse. Through this the analyst becomes the blank writing pad for transference. She gains access to the traces and their reworking on her own writing pad, again using words of rearticulation through the counter-transference. We will see below in our discussion of Lyotard how the ego is discursive and inscribes a *langue*, while the imaginary is figural and inscribes a field. If this is so, then the logic of sensation inscribes the tissue of an organ or a body without organs. In this sense, as Deleuze noted, it partakes of neither the symbolic nor the imaginary, but the real.[22]

If Freud's point of departure is effectively the verbal sublime, Lacan, with his notion of lack, takes us even further away from ego theory's iconicity, all the way to the specular sublime. Lacan can helpfully be understood in the context of philosophical anthropology, in his own very early conception of instinctual underdetermination in his work of the 1930s. Drawing on contemporaneous biology, Lacan noted that whereas the animal sense of self is based on organic sufficiency, human beings are born prematurely. We are born as underdetermined organically and instinctually and hence undergo 'postnatal fetalization'.[23] Where animal selves are thus coherent and complete, human selves are constitutionally less coherent and incomplete. They have a constitutive lack. Not unlike Gadamer, Lacan understands human beings as compensating for this lack through their presentations and representations. Through the latter the lack is fulfilled, and coherence and stability and a sort of permanence are established. Human beings tend to do this through visual presentations. We 'paper over' our lack visually. That is, whereas animals are complete already in 'the real', we can only be complete through presentations, in the imaginary (Lacan) or in the imagination (Gadamer).

We do this initially – both Gadamer and Lacan suggest – in play. Play involves compensating for lack through presentations. Thus Lacan noted that animals, unlike children, do not take their mirror reflections for them-selves. Children play the game of Fort! Da!, in which there they are and there they are no longer as the mirror is first put in front of them and then taken away. Here the image in the mirror is taken not so much for the self as for the existence of *coherent* self (an ideal ego). Thus after birth original incompleteness is compensated by a overdependence, indeed a sort of fusion with the mother. This is prior to the separation of the real and the imaginary and the conscious mind and the unconscious. With separation, when the mother's breast becomes no longer part of 'the real', but integral to a separate silhouette, a figure of the mother, we have compensation for lack not through fusion but through the visual and the imaginary.[24] Here retention and permanence, as in Gadamer, are also preserved through a sort of secular memory as the compensation via the visual. Thus fusion with the mother is possible in her absence, via wish fulfilment in the imaginary.

From the start, then, Lacan understood this identity-thinking, this unconscious denial of lack through visual compensation. Here the shift from self-identity to self-difference and the affirmation of lack is only possible through the recognition of the other. This was the master–slave dimension of Lacan's thought that Franz Fanon – who attended Lacan's lectures as a young man – would seize on. The argument is, given that we are born with *Instinktarmut* and constitutive lack, once we are in the 'world' of interactive situations the only way to affirm this lack is to affirm the other. Thus, in the mirror-stage, wish-fulfilment entails the visual completion of the self with the mother. In Hegel's *Herrschaft und Knechtschaft*, the master or subjectivity reduces the other to the image of the self, to the self's specular double.[25] Infantile psychosexual development foregrounds introjection and hence negation of the other as an imaginary compensation for lack as a visual completion of the self. This is illusory and based on false faith in a mirror image or the figural field constituted by traces of the mother. It is further like the master's denial of the slave's existence and reduction of the slave to the abstract other of the master. It is above all denial of lack. The introjection of the mother, the imaginary having of the mother, involves release of psychic energy. This energy is constituted along with our constitutive lack. The differential space between irreconcilable poles is the aporia that constitutes these quanta of energy.[26] In infantile and primary identification, though introjection, what we internalize is not the mother with her constitutive lack, but only the compensatory functions of the mother's *gaze*. We internalize not the mother but the visual. And the self denies the mother her otherness through such specular projection.

It is later through secondary identification – with the entry into language – that the symbolic is created. Now in place of the dyadic specularity of primary identification in the imaginary with the mother, there is the triadic interaction of the Oedipus drama. With the introjection of the figure of the Oedipus triangle there is the introjection of lack itself. Of lack as law, as prohibition, as law against incest with the mother. Of lack as the impossibility of fusion with and completion (by introjection) by the mother. This entails an acknowledgement of ineradicable otherness. It entails the recognition of the other as ineradicably not a part of the self. It entails living with lack, self-difference and aporetic subjectivity.[27]

It is significant, Martin Jay notes, that Lacan introduced the notion of the mirror stage in 1936, in the context of a 1933 investigation into paranoid psychosis, a clinical study of two sisters who committed murder while plucking out the eyes of their victims. Lacan's argument was that the enucleating murderesses were fixated at the stage of primary identification, a narcissistic identification through the projection of their gaze on to an idealized other. This is an idealized ego, an ego without lack; that is, an ego whose completion is guaranteed by possession of the phallus. In the case of the sisters, when the person who embodied this idealized other lost her ideal status,[28] the false unity of the sisters' own selves was threatened and the former ideal ego became seen as a persecuting other. This other had to be physically negated, murdered and symbolically castrated through enucleation. The sisters' gaze, formerly that of specular projection, became the 'gaze of Medusa' which literally castrates, literally enucleates.

With Lacan we leave Freud's verbal sublime for the specular sublime's fatal dialectic of nihilism. In knowing, introjecting, subsuming the mother, subjectivity's will to knowledge, like in *Jurassic Park*, is flying too high. Subjectivity is trying to be the father, trying to be God in his will to knowledge. He is flying too close indeed to the sun. The result is the secular sublime of enucleation, of castration. We cannot be God or the gods and fly too close to the sun. We cannot be complete as is God. We cannot be the father. In trying to be so, like Oedipus, we are blinded. In the story of our eye, our oeil, our testicles, or worse like Lacan's Medusae, we blind, we negate and castrate others. To accept the aporetic unbridgeability and otherness of the mother, the impossibility of having the mother is to accept not just the law but also symbolic castration, symbolic enucleation. Enucleated, the eye is no longer for seeing, but for cutting with a razor blade. It is open as a wound in the tactility of the sphere of sensation.[29] The gaping wound of symbolic castration leaves subjectivity open to the haptic realm of raw, unpresentable fullness prior to the organization of drives. It leaves us open to cathect, by means of the *informe* – which is neither form nor matter – to cathect to displace one's libidinal economy into the fullness of sensation.

This sort of drama of the specular and verbal sublime is played out in the Regeneration Trilogy, the First World War novels of the British writer Pat Barker. These 'faction' novels, *Regeneration, The Eye in the Door* and *The Ghost Road*, feature three protagonists: William Rivers, an Oxford anthropologist and psychoanalyst who during the war must cure war shocked officers so they can be sent back to France and face almost certain death; and two war traumatized officers that he treats. The officers in these 'faction' novels are Siegfried Sassoon, the sometimes pacifist war hero and war poet, and a young officer from a Manchester (Salford) working-class background called Billy Prior. The novels thematize both the 'eye' and the voice. Prior encounters the enucleated eye of a fallen and dead comrade, which resembles a bit of penny candy he would eat as a kid, a 'gobstopper'. It is this traumatic event that caused him to lose his voice and important bits of medium-term memory. Shipped back to Britain, he enters a special clinic in Scotland for war traumatized officers and therapy with Rivers. Rivers for his part, like Freud has very minimal cathexes of the imaginary. He is deficient in the visual sense full stop, and does not, for example, dream in pictures. With such libidinal underinvestment in the figural, he is a man of more or less pure discourse. The therapy – a very democratic and symmetrical one – restores voice and memory to Prior, and partly cures Rivers of his visual deficit.

The candy ball gobstoppers were purchased as a child by Prior from the neighbour woman, Beattie, who ran the local corner shop, herself a pacifist and serving time in prison, accused of attempting to poison the Prime Minister. Painted on the door of her cell, as Prior visits her, is an eye ('the eye in the door'), an eye of surveillance. Nothing, however, could be further away from surveillance than the psychotherapeutic situation between Rivers and Prior, given its democracy and fluidity of counter-transferences and healing as much of the therapist as the patient. Prior also deals with the indelible trace of the eye in his own *Unbewußt*, through his self-sacrificing relationship with Beattie. Cured, Prior's voice and memory are restored so that he can go back to the front and die, while at the same time Rivers pays symbolically for sending the much younger man back to the front by his growing physical illness and frailty. The desire of all these young men to go to their deaths is seen by Pat Barker not in an individualistic Heideggerian sense of Dasein facing death, nor as the over the top straining for the Faustian rawness of Bataille's and futurism's specular sublime. It is for her instead the stuff of myth and institutions. Rivers's narrative of reminiscence as a young anthropologist, in which the Melanesians he studied satisfied a grieving widow by bringing back a shrunken head from another tribe, looks mild in comparison with the 'mythic head hunting' of the First World War.

But key was the formation of communities of intimacy between men on the front. These were real communities of the sublime. Not 'imagined communities', because of the face-to-face of the trenches. Also not really 'reflexive communities' in the sense that freely chosen subcultures of, say, heroin users or environmental activists are reflexive; they had none of the voluntarism of the sect. But communities of the sublime. Unchosen and not of original blood. Forged in the white heat of battle. Forged in the greatest intensity of existential meaning. Facing death. Ready to die not so much for one's country, but for one another's singularity. But also in the greatest banality of intimacy. Of the surprise of the sound of gas expelling when stepping on a friend's dead body. Of the greatest homosocial and some-times homosexual intimacy.[30]

The relationality of the trenches in Pat Barker's novels evokes the relationality recorded in Jean Luc Nancy's *The Inoperative Community*. The French title of this book is *La communauté désouvré*, meaning literally the unworked community. Here *ouvré* or work is understood first in terms of Marxism. In Marxism, Nancy argues, 'man' constructs his human essence as work or as labour, and this essence is understood as community.[31] Here man is 'infinite' both spatially and temporally. Man is spatially out of the world in which he constructs his own timeless essence. This infinity is most closely seen in the context of death. In communion man reworks the body and blood of Christ as infinite substance. Communism and communion are in this sense 'worked' communities in which the relationality of finite beings is worked or fashioned or processed into an infinite substance, be this humanity, or the body and blood of Christ, or the proletariat. Death itself is the extreme limit condition in which we come to terms with ourselves as finite and relational beings. It too is worked or fashioned into infinite substance, in Christian salvation or the future of the proletariat, or of mankind. This is most apparent in nationalism, in which we die not as finite relational beings but for an infinite national substance, a thousand year Reich.

This quality of 'workedness' is what makes any sort of meaningful community impossible or makes community inoperative in the English sense of the word. If finite beings are seen as just little atoms of infinite substance, then like atoms they are immanent; that is, closed in on them-selves and closed off from one another. Relationality is thus impossible. For community to be possible we need to incline, to decline, to inflect in a sort of linguistic sense outside of and exterior to this immanence. We need to inflect to the exterior of our universality and into a singularity.[32] We need to exist no longer as universal in the sense of being infinite and present for all time and outside of space, but instead singularly open and finite. Here we are relational and we can form community. This is much more easily done in the Orient than the Occident. Oriental languages, for example, are much more relational, much more place and position inflected than are Occidental languages. Women, to the extent that Carol Gilligan is right, are often better at it than men. And that indeed is Pat Barker's point. Her communities of the trenches are Nancy's *communautés désouvrés*; that is, communities of the antithesis of work. The *désouvré* is a bit like the *informe*. Such communities are not active and combative but passive. They wait in trenches for death: for their friends' deaths. These are communities of *dépense*, formed in the greatest waste. They are literally familial in this sense, almost feminine. The two younger men in Barker's trilogy, brave in war, were bisexual. And Rivers never married. This relationality is very much of the private sphere. And existential meaning does come almost always through the private sphere. Through the sphere of intimacy. The institutions and bureaucracies, including the military ones, embody determinate meaning. Not so the trenches.

Greeks and Jews

Juridical Revelation, Aporetic Redemption

To talk about the sublime and the beautiful is to address the Judaic and the Hellenic. The Judaic versus the Hellenic in the first instance means the counterposition of ethics versus cognition, the good versus the true. Thus the focus on the law, on Levinas's elevation of Plato and the principle of the good above knowledge, is paradigmatically Hebraic, as among others Nietzsche was well aware. While the departure from a two-world Platonism to Aristotelian nominalism and the valuation of the senses is characteristically Greek. In this sense too must be understood the Greek valuation of the male body in contrast to the Judaic obsession with hats and layers and layers of clothing. The point here is that ethics but not knowledge is possible without some valuation of the senses. Thus even positivistic knowledge – the abstract realism of mirror of nature epistemologies – is Greek. As are Renaissance aesthetics grounded in the geometry of the rays emerging from the eye and grasping the work of art. The Hebraic, for its part, devalues the profane world to the extent that it is not even worth knowing. Instead of observing the world, one instead observes the law.[33] The God of Judaism is *so* transcendental that even a two-world notion does not do Him justice: even a two-world cosmology positing holy beings in a sacred world apart from the profane world does not capture the spirit of Judaism. Yahweh is a being apart from and without any world. In this vein Kant was wrong in his assertion that the sublime was essentially Judaic. The sublime – in which aesthetic judgements form the bridge connecting sensation (before perceptual presentation) with existential meaning – is well too sensual to be Hebraic. Instead the Hebraic is a lot closer to the categorical imperative itself: to the *second* critique. Phenomena of the beautiful and sublime, of *Zweckmäeigkeit ohne Zweck* as bridges to the Ideas of Reason, to God etc., would be merely icons to be destroyed in the violence of Judaism's iconoclasm. There is something of not just the Antichrist but the anti-*aesthetic*, though not, we will see below, the anti-Oedipe, in Judaism.

    The contrasting primacies of cognitive versus ethical are seen in what Buber saw as the Greco-Christian priority of the 'I–it' relationship as opposed to the Jewish 'I–thou'. This is of course the contrast between Greco-Christian 'disclosure' and Jewish 'revelation'. *Disclosure* presumes a plenitude of world that is disclosed to the 'knowing ' subject.[34] *Revelation*, in contradistinction, is a question of 'the saying', of the 'discursive practice' by which God addresses the singular Jewish subjectivity. This bequeaths two opposing temporalities: a Greek and Christian temporality structured around the couple disclosure/salvation, and a Judaic temporality formed around the couple revelation/redemption. For Christians time starts with disclosure, the disclosure of the divinity of Christ, the Son of Man in this world. For the Jews time begins with revelation, the revelation of the law of the Torah. For Christians time ends with salvation, for Jews with redemption. There is thus in Christian temporality an implicit individualization, a primacy of personal narrative and personal memory. Jewish temporality and redemption, for its part, partakes of the *longue durée*, it is much less immediate, hence less 'in-the-world'. It is also collective: what counts is not personal, but historical narrative and collective memory. Redemption is the fate of the chosen people. Greco-Christian temporality is based on the contrast between the finitude of the individual soul and the much more eternal, yet still also worldly, time of the Church, of architecture, of institutions. Jewish temporality devalues the individual soul to the extent that his death matters, in the scheme of things, less. His salvation does not count. There is no Jewish church. Just a text.[35] Only the law. There are no Jewish institutions. In this sense Judaism is indeed a religion of the sublime. Dead Christians are subsumed into the beautiful imaginary of the heavens, where they join the (only partially) transcendent world of the sacred. Dead Jews exist only in sensation, a material body to decompose in the earth, or are literally sublimated in the ever more common practice of cremation. Secular and modern dying is increasingly 'Judaic'.

Greco-Christian temporality is fundamentally spatial, disclosure being mediated by the mother, the Virgin Mary in real space of this world. Even the salvation of the soul is inscribed in a certain spatiality of the sacred world. Jewish temporality is eternal. It is anti-spatial: it is not at all of this world. Even the Jewish cosmos is much more transcendent, much less spatial. Jewish redemption is not pictured, is not imaged, is not thought spatially in the sense of Christian salvation, or even the Second Coming. The Jew is always left in doubt if it will ever happen. He cannot imagine it. Even if this is to be, the Jew must live in Job's aporetic tension[36] that this unimaginable may well never be.

In a very important sense, then, it is possible to speak of Greco-Christian dialectics versus Jewish aporetics. Even in Greek tragedy, in the Oedipus trilogy, there is reconciliation, where even horror is at Colonus recuperated in a theatrical economy of the same. In Christianity time is structured in metanarratives of dialectical disclosure, whereas in Judaism time is structured via a succession of revelatory events. Indeed, the New Testament is based on narrative structures while the Old Testament is not so much narrative as discursive, especially in its foregrounding of law. To the extent that the New Testament is narrative it narrates the individual life story of Jesus. To the extent that the Old Testament is narrative it is the collective narrative of God's chosen people. For Christians there is reconciliation in the word made flesh, in corporeal incarnation in human form. This for the Jew smacks of course of idolatry. Judaism's prohibition of graven images, the Mosaic taboo on graven images, means that there can be no Jewish iconology.[37] Christ, who is also the Son of Man, in his incorporation spirit is in Christian cosmology significant. Moses, in contrast, is insignificant in Judaic cosmology. He wonders why he was even chosen by God. He is a man slow of tongue, a stutterer. When God addresses Moses, God considers the earthly world to be so insignificant that He need not even be responsible for who is blind, and who speaks well. He chooses an insignificant man who stutters – who is little given to discoursing and dialectics – who will be involved in the ultimate asymmetrical speech situation. Who speaks so badly that his brother Aaron will have to address the Jewish people.

Christian reconciliation means that the Word must be realized, must be reconciled with the worldly in the institutions of the nation state. The abstract Word must be realized in the institution of the church, where priests engaged in religious competitions for believers among the illiterate masses, the latter to be attracted by the sheer mass and permanence of the churchly architecture, and the visual power, the figural semantics of church frescoes and stained glass. Judaic aporetics have never reconciled God's word with the nation-state – hence the eternally wandering Jew – or with the body or with the institutional apparatus of the church. Judaism is a religion less of priests (though the Pharisees and Saducees, the 'money changers', were priests) than of prophets and rabbis. The prophet again does not partake of the sacred as does the priest, but is a vessel, a *Trager*, as Weber noted of not ecstatic so much as epiphanic moments of revelation.[38] The rabbi cannot dispense grace like the institutional priest. The rabbi is much less significant. He is teacher. He imparts the text, the law. Talmudic interpreters may interpret, but within very strict limits. What counts is the word of God. The priest is the father, the rabbi is not. The priest, in the grandeur of his robes, incorporates the law, the rabbi, impoverished, dressed in threadbare black, incorporates nothing. Plato's Christian great chain of being means that a little less 'sacredness' is possessed as we move down the links of the chain from God to Christ to Pope, priests, man, animals and nature.

The notion of 'the great chain of being' is helpful in thinking through the Jews versus Greeks polarity. The great chain of being is here clearly on the

Greek side of the ledger. Beginning with Plato's *Timaeus*, the chain of being was understood in terms of plenitude, meaning not just fullness and plenty but mainly variety and differentiation. The conception was that the Demiurge, being good, wanted the world to lack nothing. The creative and hence aesthetic power of the Demiurge, later Augustine's Christian God, would be realized through the creation of the greatest variety and multiplicity of differentiation of beings on the earth.

The great chain of being is thus based on an aesthetic notion of God as creator. God is at the same time seen as the Good, and lesser beings as being apportioned lesser measures of the good. Even evil, then, can be seen as that which bears very small measures of the good. This connects directly with the issue of 'theodicy', a governing concept in Weber's sociology of religion and arguably in his sociology tout court. Augustine's theodicy account for evil in terms of good: in terms of God originally fashioning man as perfect, and of man's own willed fall. This cosmology of misery and the contingency of life as accounted for in terms of God and the world of good and plenitude was in the early modern period worked through in Leibniz's monadology in his *Théodicée*. Voltaire's *Candide* was a savage satirical critique of Leibniz's theodicy. Weber's writings revive the issue as a sociological problem. His point was that every society must culturally deal with the problem of evil in the misery and contingency of everyday life. This would extend to interpreting symbolically with the fact of death, inasmuch as the most extreme misery, the most extreme contingent and evil fact of everyday life, is the death of parents, children, partners and selves. With the death of God in later modernity, theodicy is displaced by 'sociodicy' or 'logodicy', in which the concept explains misery and death in terms of the greater good of a functioning social totality.[39] But once the concept and sociological positivism are challenged, then what is left? Either the plenitude of Being and *es gibt* of the Greek or the dark contingency of the ultimate iconoclasm which smashes idols, the concept, Being and theodicy itself: that is, Levinas's postmodern Hebraic of the *il y a*.

This much said, in Judaic aporetics, without the possibility of reconciliation, there is sacredness in just one place. Prophets and rabbis have none. Neither surely does man partake of the sacred, though men are allowed in the temple to listen to the law and become literate. The Christian priest, partaking of limited amounts of divine intuition, is involved in surveillance of the communicant. The communicant operates *vis-à-vis* the priest in confession, in the register of shame. The rabbi for his part is not given the sacred power of surveillance.[40] The Jew is responsible in front of the Lord, and not through the outer eye of shame but the inner eye of *guilt*. Christianity is a church. Judaism is neither church nor voluntaristic sect, but a community. A wandering and diasporic community. Unlike with sects, membership is not voluntary, and is not developed in the context of chosen

Table 10.1 Discourse, figure and sensation

Discourse	Figure	Sensation
Hebraic	Hellenic	pagan
groundless	foundational	ground
formless	form	material
symbol	icon	index
symbolic	imaginary	real
aural	visual	haptic
sublime	beautiful	
reflective judgement	determinate judgement	
existential meaning	logical meaning	banal meaning
singular	universal	particular
the desert	the city	village
metropolis	architecture	path
towers	catacombs	
distant	mediated	immediate
time	space	place
	exchange-value	use-value
individuality	individualism	community
aporetics	dialectics	non-diremption
praxis	theorein	poesis
	technology	poesis
charisma	legal-rationality	tradition
prophets	priests	magicians

common practices, as in some sect-like bodies like the environmental movement or in revolutionary syndicalism. Jews do not comprise an institutional community of blood and body communicants. The Jewish community has more in common with communities of the sublime, formed in the face of the aura of a raging God and external persecutors. Like in the community of the trenches, the Jews are passive, familial. They are an already blind community of the word.

Words and Things

Lyotard devotes considerable attention to Jew and Greek, working through a psychoanalytic prism in his seminal, yet often neglected, essay 'Figure foreclosed'.[41] We will study this in some detail. 'Figure foreclosed', an essay effectively addressing subjectivity in the age of reflexive modernity, considerably extends Lyotard's theory of the discursive and the figural.[42] He draws on Freud's notion of 'foreclosure' to underscore the fundamentally anti-figural nature of both the Jewish experience and, by extension, late modern subjectivity. His argument is that late modern subjectivity in its foreclosure of the figure is so dependent on the voice as to be fundamentally schizophrenic. This was already foreshadowed in Lyotard's earlier 'Jewish Oedipus'.[43] In this the classical or Greek Oedipus, in the wake of symbolic castration, portrays a myth of reconciliation. The modern and Jewish Oedipus is instantiated for Lyotard in the figure of Hamlet. We recall here Kant's recourse to Shakespeare in the *Critique of Judgement*'s analytic of the sublime. Hamlet as Jewish Oedipus is addressed by not earthly oracle but invisible ghosts. He is addressed by the – unpresentable and hence sublime – invisible ghost of the father. Further, unlike his Greek counterpart, the Jewish Oedipus never is reconciled, as *Hamlet* ends in an aporetic of multiple deaths. Classical Oedipus, the figure of symbolically castrated reconciliation, is Greek. Modernity asks the question: what happens when reconciliation is impossible? What happens when we stop papering over the cracks, stop covering up the lack? What happens when we stop lamenting a lost totality that perhaps never was? Reflexive modernity, similarly aporetic, always denies the possibility of identity, of self-identity. The modern Oedipus, indeed Freud's Oedipus, is *l'oedipe juif.*

Lyotard's 'Figure foreclosed' features not just the party of two of Jews and Greeks, but the triptych of Jews, Greeks and *pagans.* Here the Jews are the discursive, the Greeks a combination of discursive and figural, while the peasant, the primitive, enacts a pure ideal-typical logic of the figural. The point in the essay's title is that the Jew, the Judaic, forecloses the figure. What can this mean? When objects or sense data filter through the perceptual-consciousness system, what takes place is not 'mere' perception but normally two types of presentation of the object: on the one hand, 'thing-presentations', and, on the other, 'word-presentations'. Here on a Fregean model word-presentations correspond roughly to '*Sinn*' or signification and thing-presentations to '*Bedeutung*' or designation. Similarly, with regard to Kant, word-presentations correspond to subsumption by the concepts of the understanding and thing-presentations to subsumption and presentation through the imagination. For Freud word-presentations are made of objects, of sense data in the pre-conscious ego and thing-presentations in the unconscious. Word-presentations are thus discursive and thing-presentations figural. Lyotard's point is that the Jewish prohibition of graven images entails the de-cathexis of image-presentations and sensory perception altogether. This is a de-cathexis of the unconscious as a whole and a surplus-cathexis of the word-presentations of the conscious mind.[44] This cathexis of the word and conscious mind and disinvestment of the unconscious is so pronounced in the Hebraic experience that the figure is foreclosed altogether.

What are the implications of this? The Greek, Lyotard notes, occupies the pivotal position between discursive Jew and the figural pagan: la *pensée grecque* midway between *pensée juive* and *pensée sauvage*. The Hellenic entails both thing- and word-presentations and *pensée sauvage* only thing-presentations. On this view the Jewish and Greek West entails an escape from myth. Both Judaism and Christianity as transcendental and world religions renounce the myth of the immanentist *religions sauvages*, with their chthonian divinities, their mother earth goddesses. This said, Greco-Christians retain a measure of myth, in their combination of thing- and word-presentation, in, for example, the virgin mother, in the ritual of communion, in a certain valuation of nature. To be fully iconoclastic is to be fully without ritual, without myth. The Jews have no place for the mother. No place for the earth. No place for Mary or Hera. The Jews, people of the word, are also the mythless people , the ritual-less people. Jews – and modern Jews tack on their holidays to match the rituals of Christian holidays – are instead the people of the text.

At issue are three types of wish fulfilment. For the pagan (*paienne*, *paysan*), wish-fulfilment takes place in the unconscious via the pleasure principle and primary process. Psychic energy is released through thing-presentations, through libidinal investment in the silhouette of the mother, papering over and closing the lack in the unconscious and releasing psychic energy. Greek wish-fulfilment operates via the reality principle. This entails a strong cathexis both of the ego and word-presentation and of the unconscious and thing-presentation. Subjectivity cannot test reality without it filtering through thing-presentations. Psychic energy, accumulating with the lack and the diremption between poles, is discharged with the reality principle's operation on the environment. Again the lack is closed and energy released. For the Jew whose intellectuality precludes investment in the unconscious and so diminishes thing-presentation, it is impossible to act via the reality principle. Reality testing becomes insignificant. The result, however, is the permanence, the chronicity of lack. The impossibility, the eternal deferral of wish fulfilment. The Jew is anxious. He is neurasthenic.

Collective Oedipus

These semiotic *differentiae specificae* have substantive implications. To start, Lyotard notes, the Greek and not the Jew is the scientist. For science to be possible a double subsumption is necessary. First, in the realm of thing-presentation, sense data must be presented in 'observational constructs' which then come under the subsumption of designation, of word-presentations of theoretical constructs. The Greek is thus the creature of determinate judgement, of determinate meaning. For the Jew, devaluing observational constructs, de-cathecting subsumption through the imaginary's thing-presentations, appropriating the ideology whereby mere things are not of sufficient value to be *worth* presenting, all we have is the word-presentation. All we have – even though attribution is to Yahweh as heteronomous legislator – is indeterminate or transcendental meaning. All we have are the ought-statements of normative, of moral-practical, utterances. If the Jew thus gives us law and the Greek science, then the pagan gives us myth. The pagan de-cathects word presentation and its operation by means of logic, reflection and inference. He de-cathects the transcendental unity of apperception. Cathected instead is thing-presentation, hence the omnipresence of myth and ritual as modes of wish fulfilment. The gap, the lack, to which sensation is opened up to the world is closed and psychic energy released through the imaginary's narratives.

The pagan is inscribed in a non-determinate order of meaning. Phenomenologists might describe this order of meaning as trivial in the sense that the meaning of the aspect of a phenomenon is trivial. They would be wrong though, because considerable quanta of libido are invested in the traces, in the totems and symbols and other memory traces that structure the field of mythic meaning. These traces set up a certain sort of analogical classificatory matrix, which itself attributes meaning to other sense data entering the perceptual-consciousness system. Myth always bespeaks the logic of origins, the logic of a birth-giving earth, not only spatially with its particularistic locatedness, but also temporally in the genealogies of gods whose origin is earth mothers. The earth and nature are pagan space; origins are pagan time. Where temporality is constituted through the reproduction of earth and mother, time and space are as yet not fully differentiated, not fully experienced as diremption. Temporality is experienced as generations, in terms of origins and ancestors, of giants on whose shoulders we who are not worthy now stand. Temporality is thus pervaded with heavily cathected symbols structuring the pagan everyday sense of reality. This is neither as Jewish and transcendental nor as Greek and logical meaning: it is the immanent and mythic meaning of pagan experience, of aboriginal philosophy.

This said, what sort of politics, what ethics, is at stake for Jew, Greek and pagan? For the transcendent and irreconcilable diremption of the Judaic (their constitutive aporetics means that the Jews must remain the 'alien nation'); for the mediation and reconciled alienation of the Hellenic; and for the never diremptive immanence of the pagan? Politics entails place, presupposes institutions, involves positive law. Jewish natural and canon law does not suffice. Politics is in need of mediation: in need of a measure of reconciliation between transcendental and immanent moments, between 'ought' and 'is'. The mediation of the polis, Lyotard argues,[45] is necessary for Greek democracy – the polis as a 'circle in whose centre man is placed by statutory right'. The isonomia of the polis is also necessary in the scientific circle of interlocutors, in which each must be listened to. In which each speech act and its legitimations is judged by the 'many' of equally *berechtigt* subjects. This isonomia is absent in the Judaic, in which the other and the transcendent is regulated by a fully alternative set of norms to everyday subjectivity. In which the transcendent is *so* transcendent as to have His speech acts regulated by no set of norms at all. And in which the particular is so insignificant that it really doesn't matter what sort of norms regulate profane existence. Particular subjectivities here surely have no chance of answering back or asking for legitimation, beyond the 'I am the Lord thy God' of the transcendental, of the 'absent and absolute other who speaks and doesn't listen'.[46] The Jew, living in the ether of the pure ought, cannot experience this: he has no politics, cannot do science. Pagan ethics for their part depend on the absence of diremption between ought and is; are based in the ground of the earth, of the goddesses, of the generations, of the Great Chain of Being in which we are all to find our place. If Greek ethics are the ethics, the isonomic intersubjectivity, of the Many, of democracy; and Jewish ethics are a matter of the antinomia of the One; then the pagan's are the ethics of immediacy, the grounded ethos of the Few, of neither democracy nor monarchy but aristocracy, of family and the generations. Pagan legitimacy depends not on argument, but on origins, on ancestors.

Politics, Lyotard is aware, needs a social contract. The social contract of the polis is that of the *cité*, the contract first of the tribes and then of the subjects. It is a contract voluntarily entered into by the parties, in which the parties are isonomic of equal rights, and only the state itself, created by the contract, is a higher instance. The contract is dependent on place, the place of the city, but also on this universal instance, the state and its abstract law, a universal instance that transcends the particulars. The social contract is irreducibly Greek: emerges only from cultures of mediation, of dialectic conciliation of universal and particular. Cultures of immediacy, of immanence like pagan cultures, tend to keep to themselves. When they encounter the stranger, or the collective stranger, the first instinct is to kill him. The gift, in this context, is the original social contract. Here, instead of killing the stranger, the pagan tribe, the *religion sauvage*, gives. It gives not in expectation of any even *gemeinschaftlich* expectations of reciprocity. But the tribal chief gives all he has. He gives in excess. He gives the surplus. The other tribal leaders also give in excess, in gift giving competitions, gift burnings, total *dépense*. And the savage mind ingests, he introjects. He smokes, and inhales, he eats, he partakes of the ethical substance, of the ether and the ethos of the other culture, of the other culture of immediacy.[47] This is hybridity with a vengeance. This is grounded hybridity, a heterophagous hybridity in which each culture ingests the other. How close is this to the exchange of wives? The 'here you may have our women', of Lévi-Strauss's *Tristes Tropiques?* This is also, as Nietzsche and Weber knew, the basis of the original peace. Of the original transcendent instance. The gift is not so much the original social contract, presuming isonomia and consent, as the aesthetic-expressive basis of the original contract. The pagan gift constructs the contract, which is itself the destruction of pagan and immediate culture and the beginning of the *cité*.[48]

There is, however, another and parallel transition from the pagan to the Greek: from an ontology of origins to a political ontology. This concerns a mode of politics closer to Carl Schmitt's or Clausewitz's ideas. Here the original pagan village, the ancestral village, constitutes a space into which collectivities of young men are forbidden to enter during initiation rites. During such 'liminal time' they are forbidden to enter the real and symbolic space of the village. Let us shift our attention to Sparta, in which circular configurations of warriors, as Lyotard notes, collectively give rise to the archaic city.[49] These warriors, grouped outside of the village in their camps, come back to dominate the village and make helots out of the villagers. They descend to constitute a heteroglot city and subordinate ancestral law to written law. Now ancestral place is subordinated to movement, and origins to politics. Whereas previously liminality was on the margins, as young men left structured space for initiation rites, now liminality is permanent, transition is absolute, chronic. The city is transition, it is movement.

The Jew is involved in a very special kind of social contract. The Jew's is the original covenant. The Jewish covenant is not a social contract entered into voluntarily. The Jews didn't choose God. They were chosen by Him. Original gift giving also had little to do with it. Pagans give gifts. We are told to beware of Greeks bringing gifts. Jews don't bring gifts. They do not enact the social peace with the other. The Covenant is God doing the choosing. It is also the act by which the Israelites accept the Torah, the Pentateuch, the Five Books of Moses that start with the Beginning and ends with the death of Moses just before the conquest of Canaan. The Covenant is the act by which the Israelites accept the fundamental law, regulating moral and physical conduct, which set the paradigm for the remainder of the Old Testament and the Talmud.[50] These laws are not negotiated or agreed to. The Covenant came from the violence of the Revelation. The Covenant came from an infinitesimal collective finitude before the power and awesomeness of the sublime. The unpresentable, the unsayable. The Jews have not all that much choice as to whether they accept the law or not. The Jews as thus chosen are constituted as a people, a chosen people, who are the vessels of God's law. There is no agreement on the law, no constitutional congress, no necessity of legitimation. In short there is no politics.

The Jews are also forbidden the other sot of politics: the politics of war. The Jews are to be but the vessels of God's law, but are not to fulfil God's will on earth. This would be already too mediate for this constitutively transcendent culture.

Greco-Christian cultures of mediation can reconcile by fulfilling the transcendent God's will in the profane of this world. As for not transcendent nor mediate but immediate pagan culture, it is, as Weber wrote, a matter of our gods versus your gods. You win and we accept your gods. Jewish and transcendental culture considers real property and terrain too insignificant to conquer. But if conquered, one never accepts the opposition's Gods. The Jews with Job only reckon that they have done something to displease the Lord and struggle only to figure out what it is. The Jew is without origins, without politics, without place. If the pagan had the ancestral village and the Greek and Augustine the City, the Jew has no place, no place at all. Like late modern subjectivity he is condemned to be nomadic: his place is the no place of the featureless desert, governed by neither the figure nor logic. The featureless desert is not even analogical.

What sort of narrative can be held responsible for this Jewish 'collective Oedipus', which is for Lyotard the Oedipus drama of modern subjectivity? First let us rehearse our understanding of libidinal economy. Here the discursive economy of the conscious mind is based on 'word presentations' and the reality principle; while the figural economy of the unconscious is based on 'thing-presentations' and the release of psychic energy by reconciliation in the unconscious and the pleasure principle. For Lyotard both the symbolic and the imaginary in the unconscious are not like a language but figural. The difference is that the imaginary is constituted through primary identification and the introjection of the mother. In this the mother is so heavily cathected that her silhouette becomes the field for the entire figural economy of the unconscious, both imaginary and symbolic. The symbolic, for its part, emerges with the introjection of the Oedipus drama. This (for Lyotard as for Lacan) can involve either more or less reconciliation, more or less 'lack'. The point, however, is that all of this still plays itself out on the figural field that is the introjected mother. In cases of regression, the imaginary captures almost all of the energy. Otherwise, much of this figural drama plays itself out in the symbolic. Thus dreams involve the displacement of energy from the verbal trace-matrices of the preconscious ego to the field of the unconscious. And condensation remaps the energy on to the 'transposed figures' of the symbolic. Such symbols Ricoeur understood as 'fantasies that have been denied and overcome'.[51] Involved in both economies are memory traces. Traces that filter through the perceptual-consciousness system as already highly cathected wind up in either the discursive or the figural economy, depending largely on the extent to which each of these latter is invested with libido. Both conscious and unconscious minds, then, are regulated by trace clusters, or trace-matrices.

Discursive and figural memory traces, however, operate differently. The discursive trace matrix of the ego operates via memory, inference and reflection, the figural trace matrix in the unconscious operates in the secondary process largely of displacement and condensation. The discursive trace matrix thus operates logically and the figural matrix analogically. The figural matrix forms a field like a phenomenological field. In this there is a mobility of cathexis and a continuity of the field. The discursive trace matrix is structured not as a field, but as a *langue*. This is a 'discrete' and not fluid space, 'determined by the intervals of langue'.[52] There is no mobility of cathexis here. It is instead a tightly organized and discontinuous, 'diacritical', space. This discursive space thus involves negations to make distinctions, whereas there are no negations in the figural field, in which distinctions are just one type of 'indistinction'. In the discursive space of verbal traces 'energy is saved and bound' and has a 'spacing governed by the laws of structure'. Energy is comparatively unbound in the figural space. The traces themselves, originally material in the sphere of raw sensation, just as they enter the perceptual-consciousness system become verbal in discursive space, while they take the form of images of things, are thing-presentations in the figural space. At stake are two modes of meaning, though the figural is a 'less elaborated mode of meaning'. In the figural, text is de-cathected: there is a 'plastic re-working of text into scenario'. The bound system of verbal representations is reworked by primary process, which first deconstructs and then reconstructs as 'the figure captures the energy'. At stake is a shift from system, from a 'geometry of linguistic relations', to field, to a 'topology of plastic relations'.[53]

Now let us follow Lyotard in his distinction of repression (*Verdrängung*) versus foreclosure (*Verwerfung*), the latter setting up *l'oedipe juif* as paradigmatic late modern subjectivity. Repression and foreclosure involve two vastly different Oedipal scenarios – one Greek and pagan and the other Jewish. Two different ways of playing out a story with the same beginning. Both Greco-pagan and Jewish dramas start with the wish to merge with or possess the mother. Both feature a subsequent moment in which the child notices that the mother is 'castrated'. At this point the child begins to fear castration by the father for his wish to possess the mother. In response to this fear he symbolically kills the father. Only now do the stories diverge. After killing the father there are two possibilities. The first is repression, in which the self introjects the father as part of the triangle, as a trace in the newly constituted symbolic of the unconscious. The second possibility is *foreclosure*, where the self does not accept, where subjectivity denies that he has ever symbolically murdered the father. The second possibility arises due to already existing de-cathection of the unconscious. Its consequences are a further shift of psychic energy out of the unconscious: as the traces of mother and father are torn out of the unconscious, they are *foreclosed* and excluded from it.

In the initial stages of repression and foreclosure, *Verdrängung* and *Verwerfung* are identical. Primary identification may well be the same in both. Repression and foreclosure, then, are two different modes of secondary identification. Even secondary identification has identical initial stages in both. In both repression and foreclosure, subjectivity murders the father for fear of castration. And in both subjectivity negates that murder. Repression and foreclosure are, indeed, two different ways of negating that murder. In repression, however, the murder is admitted to before it is negated, while in foreclosure it is straightforwardly denied. In repression the negation of the murder to which Oedipus has admitted takes place through expiation: through the expiation of Christian guilt for having murdered the Christ; through Oedipus's expiation at Colonus. This expiation, this penance bringing reconciliation, is a good deal more costly than Hail Marys and Our Fathers. The dues to be paid for reconciliation in the Greco-Christian Oedipus's symbolic are subjectivity's blindness and castration. On the other hand, for *l'oedipe juif* who denies this murder there is no expiation, there is no reconciliation. Both Oedipuses, Jewish and Greek, emerge through an archaic cathection of energy on to the external father. The Greek Oedipus de-cathects this external father and represses him as a trace on to the imaginary in a sort of compromise formation. The Jewish Oedipus for his part never de-cathects the external father. He pours ever more psychic energy on to him and projects him out from the immediate family into an infinite distance. Once de-cathected, the Greco-Christian Oedipus is patrophagous, having and introjecting the father. Its secondary identification is played out through *having* the father, literally introjecting him in communion by means of the body and blood of Christ or via the totemic meal. The Jewish Oedipus, bereft of ritual, will not introject, will not have the father. He wants to *be* the father in an entirely other process of secondary identification.

After secondary identification, for *l'oedipe* and *l'oedipe juif*, there are two starkly contrasting geographies of the *return* of the father. The *Wiederkehr der Verdrängt* for Oedipus comes from the direction of the inside, in dreams and in myth, as the heavily invested trace of the father becomes a governing symbol of the primary process, whether in the symbolic of subjectivity's unconscious or in the mythic symbolic of collective memory. But Jewish Oedipus undergoes a vastly different experience. Here the return of the father is the return of the foreclosed. Here the father, and Yahweh, returns from the outside with an unreconciled and unpresentable violence. The result is schizophrenia. Schizophrenia in which wishful fantasies, unre-pressed and fully conscious, are allowed into the system of the pre-con-scious ego. Now the pre-conscious of *l'oedipe juif* begins itself to operate on principles no longer of subsumption and reflection and inference but in-stead of displacement and condensation. *L'oedipe juif*, never capable of thing-presentations – denied the ability to imagine, to figure – now experi-ences the revenge of the figural in its full violence. *L'oedipe juif*, unable to figure, in an ultimate irony becomes the hostage in his conscious mind of the figural. He blurs, his visual experience awaking a world of double meaning. He condenses. He displaces. He is the schizophrenic. Jewish Oedipus, at first exclusively verbal, denying all through his particular libidinal economy, unable to think or dream in images, is the unconditional enemy of the specular, is the champion of the verbal sublime in opposition to its specular double. His secondary identification at the same time ex-cludes the father into the infinite and wants to be the father. In this simultaneous abasement and flying too high, in this dialectic of nihilism, in a state of full consciousness, he is blinded. Late modern subjectivity, as aporetic Antichrist, as *l'oedipe juif*, is constitutionally schizophrenic.

The Jews have experienced an entirely different 'collective Oedipus' from other religions. All religions, Lyotard notes, commit deicide as a response to the terror of the castrating father. Other religions are more or less 'chthonian', comprise cosmologies grounded in origins as springing from the earth. Other religions are grounded more or less in a set of mythic formulae, ordering institutions according to the classifications of matriar-chal, fraternal and totemic origin. Other religions are contingent on the unconscious repression of deicide's memory. This memory, as transposed symbol, is the basis for myths of origin, for rituals and narratives of earth creation and earth birthing of generations of gods and men.[54] Judaism is different. In *Moses and Monotheism* Freud spoke of an initial similarity with other religions, of the original and lawless domination of the *Urvater* over the hordes. After the murder of the *Urvater* there is normally established a religion of the brothers and the mother, a matriarchal and fraternal totemic religion. The repressed father in chthonian religions is an effaced signifier, bestowing meaning as mana to matrices of mythic signification. But this itself is contingent on the admission and expiation of this murder. In Judaism, with denial and no expiation, the father is not repressed but foreclosed. It is His return which (re-)establishes monotheism.

Thus Judaism, unlike other religions, is without a narrative of earth creation. According to Bultmann the sections in Genesis about the creation were only adapted from the cult of Baal as an afterthought.[55] Instead the crux of Genesis and the other books of the Pentateuch is the *history of* the Jewish people. In this religion without earth, in this supremely otherworldly religion, in which the world is so unimportant that their God never even claims to have created it, history is its driving force. Judaism forecloses speculation as to the origins of God and the world. The real space, Lyotard intones, where the Jewish God rules is history. 'God makes his work known in the history of Israel.' Thus Genesis I is less a speculation on origins than the first chapter in the history of God's work via the history of the Jewish people. Thus in Judaism there is no origin, there is no *arché*, there is no fulfilment. In chthonian religions there is fulfilment of the gods' will: there is realization of cosmic law, either in war or in tradition, constituted through the 'cannibalistic introjection of the father' and yielding a filiation of 'blood symbols', in a generational acting out of a drama. Even in Christianity there is the fulfilment of God's will through Christ and the New Testament. The Jew, with the world devalued and fulfilment *verboten*, is meant not to know the world. The drive to know the world, in the eyes of, for example, Levinas, is irresponsible. The meaning of nature or reality is unimportant. The Talmud is thus the refusal of fulfilment: it inscribes the never fulfilled character of the paternal order. The Talmud instead begins the writing, the endless interpretation of the 'discourse of the absent one'.

Violent surplus cathection of the absent father is at the same time a massive libidinal investment in the superego. The conscious ego, deprived of thing-presentations for reality testing, is disinvested, with the resulting superego cathexis. Freud addressed this in his writings on 'melancholia', and argued for the paradoxical obtaining of pleasure through such instinctual renunciation. Superego cathection involves narcissistic identification with (wanting to be, not have) the father and further de-cathection of the mother. Melancholia involves, then, the cruel deprecation and revenge on the ego by the superego: the ego, now weakened, being the place of 'the lost object'. Part of the libido freed from de-cathection of the unconscious is cathected on to the pre-conscious ego through a different type of narcissistic identification with the lost object. Now this lost object is indeed the mother, it is the de-cathection of the entire unconscious field: the entire silhouette of the mother. Instead, the mother is lost. And melancholia, that particular brand of psychosis characteristic of the Jewish Oedipus, becomes 'the never ending mourning for the lost object', for the mother. Here the mourner, *l'oedipe juif*, can never atone for the debt it owes to its conscience, to the father.[56]

The Jew is thus the *Melancholiker*: the unhappy modern subjectivity of Wolf Lepenies's classic *Melancholie und Gesellschaft*.[57] He is modern subjectivity in eternal mourning for origins, for mother, for place, for earth. He is modern subjectivity in constant and unbridgeable debt to conscience. This figure is instantiated in Georg Simmel, in Walter Benjamin, in contemporary German thought as rendered in the vision of the *Stadtmelancholiker*. And this is a figure of the city and not architecture, of mobility and not stasis. At the same time as mourning for lost origins, as accepting unconditional responsibility, this melancholic and aporetic, this riven subjectivity, denies origins and ignores responsibility. At the same time as being Levinas's hostage, he is Simmel's *flâneur*.

Conclusions

This chapter and the last were a detailed exploration of contemporary subjectivity and cultural change through the prism of reflective judgement. We introduce the notion of reflective judgement, through its exposition in the context of Kant's work, whose aporetic nature must be seen in contrast with Hegelian visions of reconciliation. We investigate the 'lack', the 'aporia', the darkness at the heart of human subjectivity entailed in reflexive judgement. We then attempt to sociologize the notion, drawing largely on Hans Georg Gadamer's philosophical anthropology, in which 'man', constituted by tradition and memory, is seen as a reflexively judging animal. Judgement is a matter of estimation, measuring, proportioning, evaluating, and human beings would then be proportioning animals, operating with primitive classifications. Here the classifying categories would need to be seen as essentially figural, indeed as configurations. These configurations come to form a sort of matrix through memory. Once such a matrix or horizon is formed, these classifying configurations cope with other configurations in their environment.

Chapter 9 was a sociological reflection on Kant's notion. Here we consider how reflexive judgement is a critique of determinate judgement. This is an essentially aesthetic critique, but at the same time one which is fundamental to any sociology of practice. The particular sociology of practice here features not intersubjectivity, but poesis. As such, we shall see, it is of a piece with cultural theory's notions of deconstruction and difference. Both the latter and the more constructivist sociological notions share a set of essentially *tabula rasa* assumptions, share an essential and one-sided groundlessness. We attempt to provide the ground for this figural sociology of practice by reconceiving it with regard to collective memory, a permanence revealing the characteristic finitude of aesthetic subjectivity.

What sorts of objects, one might ask – including works of art and other cultural artefacts – what sort of events are at issue in reflective judgement? If, in determinate judgement, objects are in some important sense means to other ends, in reflexive judgement the objects are 'finalities', or ends in themselves. As non-instrumental finalities in themselves, not subject to the 'interests' of theoretical and instrumental reason, these artefacts and events are imbued with a different order of meaning from the determinate meaning of logic or calculative reason. These objects – whether 'beautiful' or

'sublime' – are a dark glass, a stained window opening out on to a constellation of meanings sustaining human existence and social practice. This
fundamentally aesthetic order of meaning is the condition of existence
logical and calculative meanings.

What sort of meaning is at issue here? What kind of subjectivity? On the
one hand meanings of the 'sublime', of 'lack', of darkness and contingency.
On the other of the beautiful, of plenitude, light and reconciliation. Chapter 10 explored how this aporia is played out in human subjectivity. How
the plenitude of the beautiful and the 'lack' of the sublime are expressed
through the sensual motifs of the eye and the voice and ethno-cultural
motifs of the Hebraic and the Hellenic. This is explored through psychoanalytic concepts, in which determinate judgement and reconciliation re-
surface in the visual and Hellenic, while sublimity and lack is the principle
of the aural and the Judaic. If the Hellenic is taken to stand for high
modernity, then the indeterminacy of the Judaic represents the other,
alternative modernity. But, drawing extensively on Lyotard, another dimension emerges. This dimension is neither visual nor aural, but tactile; it
is neither Greek nor Jewish, but aggressively non-Western and 'primitive'.
It is the realm of not discourse, not icon, but the more indexical 'real'
of the figure. Again the second modernity is not only the groundlessness of
the sublime, the lack, the Hebraic, but at the same time the ground of the
figure, the material, the indexical.

Thus we pursue our description of the landscape of the other modernity,
in which we are reflexively judging animals, whose categories, configurations and narratives through which we judge are built through memory.
This memory is unconscious and well as conscious: involved in primary
process and secondary processes of the introjection, cathexis and discharge
of psychic energy or libido. What, then, is the place of this sort of subjectivity in today's contemporary economies of signs and space, in today's
global informational culture? Here determinate judgement takes on its
information age form of digitization. And our memories become the
future-colonizing collective memories of technological organizations. What
scope for the poesis, the aesthetic and ethical sociality of reflexive judgement, when the objects and events they are presented with are already
'framed' through digitization? What happens when they are doubly
framed, doubly synthesized under the banner of determinate judgement,
doubly digitized, first as information and second as communications? What
happens when our habituses (and hence *collective memories*) as well as the
figures of our unconscious minds are themselves digitized, themselves
framed by determinate judgement? Does this spell the final triumph of
technology, of instrumental rationality? The very tentative answer given is,
on the one hand, yes: that informationalized techno-capitalism does use its
expanded memory as a sort of collective 'cyborganization', colonizing the

future, and calculatively one by one eliminating the risks and insecurities in the future of capitalism. The answer, on the other hand, is no. The unanticipated consequences of this expansion of determinate judgement in human-machinic memories are paradoxically the further disorganization and complexity creation of global capitalism. And, finally, the only way of risk and complexity reduction, the only way to reduce indeterminacy in the future, is the creation of massively complex and indeterminate expert-systems and techno-organizations, i.e. the creation of what are effectively 'disorganizations'.[58] Hence, the outcome of all this massively expanded capacity of digitalized determinate judgement is increased *in*determinacy and the opening up of new zones for reflexive judgement. But let us not get ahead of, let us not pre-judge, our story. And let us turn in some detail to these issues in the reflections on the explosion of the second modernity in the technological culture of today's global information society. Let us turn to some detailed reflections on 'the object' which comprise the final section of this book.

Part V

Objects

11

Objects that Judge: Latour's Parliament of Things

The whole of parts I, II, III and IV has addressed the second, the other modernity, the modernity that emerges and runs parallel to the high modernity of the Enlightenment. This second modernity operates not so much irrationally, but through a different rationality. A great deal of cultural theory and a great deal of sociological writing has addressed the alternative rationality of this other modernity. As I have argued at length, however, this second modernity has predominantly been understood in a deconstructive vein, in a sense in which 'all that is solid melts into air'. Cultural theory has understood this chronic contingency in terms of difference, sociology in terms of reflexivity. I have argued throughout this book that both cultural theory and sociology in their focus on such deconstruction have forgotten a fundamental and equally important dimension of the other modernity. This is the dimension of 'the ground'. This book has thus far consisted primarily of a set of explorations of this ground. In part I we investigated the ground in terms of place, community and the labyrinth, in part II in regard to sociality and the sociological symbolic. In part III we studied the ground as life-world intersubjectivity, the semiotic index and a hermeneutics (not of suspicion but) of retrieval, in part IV art, memory and sensation.

Part V of this book takes an entirely different tack. It takes as paradigmatic the nature of *the object*. Once we look at the nature of the 'object', the 'thing', in any detail, we are forced to reconsider the binary oppositions of both first and second modernities. In inquiring into the object – and we do so through the writings of Bruno Latour, Paul Virilio and Walter Benjamin – we, in the first instance, necessarily problematize the opposition between humans and non-humans. In the work of these writers objects take on the characteristics of humans: they judge, they form networks, they speak, they work performatively. When objects thus begin to take on agency, the distinction between humans and non-humans, subjects and objects is called into question, needs to be reconfigured. At issue is a phenomenon constitutively beyond the scope, the range, of the second modernity. At issue is the *technological culture* of our global information societies. This emerging constellation is something vastly different to either first or second modernities.

First and second modernities work through binaries. The first, high modernity works from a binary of 'above and below': for example, the subject as suspended above the object; mind as above, and body as below; human beings and nature; man and woman; culture above and technology below; West and East. The second modernity works from binaries, not of 'above and below', but of *inside and outside*. Hence 'the same' on the inside and 'the other' on the outside; the sphere of necessity on the inside, the sphere of freedom on the outside; cognition on the inside, ethics on the outside. Even man and woman and West and East are reconfigured. Now woman, previously 'below' man, becomes man's unknowable outside. The East is no longer inferior to the West, but now the West's ungraspable other. Ditto with culture and technology. Before it was culture above and technology below, now technology is in the realm of 'the same' on the inside, and uncategorizable culture on the outside.

In the global information society there is not this 'difference' of above and below, of inside and outside, but instead an increasing *indifference*, especially of technology and culture, humans and non-humans. In the first modernity humans were counterposed, as if suspended above, to non-humans, and subjects to objects. In the second modernity humans are no longer suspended above but are 'in the world' (Heidegger) with objects. But humans (Dasein) still construct themselves on the horizon of a constitutive outside: of temporality and death. In the new technological culture, the age of intelligent machines, humans are increasingly *indifferent* from non-humans, from machines and from nature. As for death, it is no longer on the outside but has broken into the inside, in which it circulates as risk, as calculated insecurity, as apocalypse and disaster. This collapse of the difference of both first and second modernities into an emerging and generalized indifference is reflected in the implosion of culture into the knowledge-intensive and information-producing economy, the erosion of national boundaries. It is reflected in the vast agglomerations of indifference in the 'generic city', paradoxically more widespread in the East (Singapore, Shanghai) and South (São Paulo) than the West. This proliferation of indifference of the technological culture and global information society poses searching questions to first modernity early humanism and second modernity late humanism. We explore this in the final section of this book through a sustained inquiry into the nature of the object.

Towards a Non-modern Constitution

Bruno Latour argues for the rights of the object. He is the spokesperson for
the 'parliament of things'. Latour argues that modernity has systematically
refused to consider the rights of the object, partly because of its systematic
propensity to think in terms of subject/object dualism. He holds that we
can come to recognize the rights, the autonomy, the agency of the object.
We can do so if we can recognize that the modern mode of classification
never corresponded to what was really going on in thought and in practice,
and never recognized the consequences of these practices. Latour argues
that 'modernity' was never any more than a mode of classification, a mode
of sorting, or better an ideology that accounted for how we classified and
sorted. He argues that we must break with the time-honoured sociological
chronology in which *la pensée sauvage* of primitive classifications is displaced
by a dualistic *pensée moderne*, by a dualistic mode of modern classifications.
That we must instead come to terms with what is our very non-modern
mode of classification, and recognize at the same time that *we have never been
modern*.[1] It is only then that rights and representation, that rights to speak
and be represented, will have been granted to and claimed by the object.

Latour understands modernity, and its pre-modern predecessor and
non-modern successor, in terms of differing 'constitutions'. These constitutions are juridical frameworks which often do not correspond to *de facto*
practices. It is important to note that he speaks of a 'constitution' instead of
'mode of classification' here. And that is because these frameworks are not
just about classifications and epistemology, but also about *political* representation. Latour holds that this distinction between political representation
and epistemological representation is one of the modern constitution's
tendentious dichotomies. He is not the first to make this comment. Gayatri
Spivak, in her classic article 'Let the subaltern speak', points to the ideological nature of this dichotomy, which indeed tends to limit the chances of
subaltern speech.[2] Like Spivak, Latour holds that modernity's phoney
dualisms are rooted in the bifurcation of these two forms of 'representation'
and 'delegation', i.e. of political representation in parliaments and the state,
on the one hand, and of epistemological (or classificatory) representation
and delegation in the sciences, on the other.

Latour speaks of modern and non-modern constitutions, each with four
'guarantees'. There is also an implicit notion of a pre-modern constitution
as well, though its less codified conventions would not amount to guarantees. Each of his constitutions addresses four, so to speak, ontological
realms: the subject, the object, language and being. The realm of the
subject is also that of society, communities, culture and the state; the realm
of the object is that of things, technologies, facts and nature; the realm of

language includes practices of discourse, mediation, translation, delegation and representation; and, finally, the realm of being includes God and the gods, the immortals, the totemized ancestors – it includes questions of existence. For Latour every epoch's constitution must have conventions and guarantees in these four ontological realms.

The four guarantees of the modern constitution for Latour are: (a) that nature (i.e. things, objects) is 'transcendent', or universal in time and space; there to be discovered; (b) that society (the subject, the state) is 'immanent', i.e. it is continually constructed 'artificially' by citizens or by subjects; (c) that 'translation networks' between these first two realms are 'banned', i.e. the 'separation of powers' of these realms is 'assured'; (d) that a 'crossed out God' acts as 'arbitrator' of this dualism.[3] Now in fact, as distinct from in law, what this constitutional dualism permits and encourages is the invention and innovation of a host, a proliferation of quasi-objects, of hybrids that totally violate modernity's categories and guarantees. We moderns close our eyes to the hybridity of the machines, the technologies and other quasi-objects, of the 'monsters' that are thus produced. We moderns tend to classify them into the conventional dualistic categories. But none the less we produce these hybrids, these monsters, on a scale never previously envisaged. Further, our dualistic (anti-hybrid) categories have facilitated the production and innovation of these proliferated quasi-objects. The point in time has come now, Latour says, where these quasi-objects, these monsters, like gene technologies, thinking machines and ozone layers, have become so omnipresent that we can no longer deny their existence. Hence we should recognize now that we are not modern and that we never have been.

The point, paradoxically, is that it is this dualism that has allowed the proliferation of hybrids that violate its principles. Let us investigate this. The central dualism of modernity is that nature is transcendent while society and the subject are immanent. To be transcendent means not to be constructed, it means to be universal in time and space. It means somehow to be real as in social-scientific realism, to be objectively true. Modernity's constitution holds nature, scientific facts and technologies and other objects and things to be in this sense transcendent. However, the sociology of science, for example, has demonstrated the mythic character of this in demonstrating nature's immanence, in showing how facts and theories themselves are constructed. Nature, moreover, is not fully transcendent, but also partly immanent, in the sense of spatio-temporal universality. Scientific theories and facts only have a certain duration in time and a certain scale of outreach in space. The constitution holds that society and the subject are immanent in the sense of being constructed. That individual and collective subjects are artificial and hence fragile, lasting only a moment, the moment of their construction. The truth is otherwise, Latour claims. Society is partly transcendent: such collectivities of humans are durable in time largely 'through the enrolment of ever more numerous nonhumans',[4] i.e. through the enrolment of nature, of objects, of things and technologies. Thus what look like modernity's transcendental objects (and nature) are in fact non-modernity's mix of transcendence and immanence; indeed, they are not fully fledged objects but what Michel Serres calls 'quasi-objects'. What look like modernity's immanent, exclusively 'here and now' subjects (and societies) are themselves partly transcendent through their own extended duration in time and outreach in space: they are not fully fledged and immanent subjects, but partly transcendental 'quasi-subjects'.

The modern constitution thus legislates through two guarantees for these two separate realms of subjects and objects, of society and nature. Let us consider the constitution's third guarantee, regarding language or discourse. This guarantee 'forbids' the existence of 'translation networks'. What this means is that language or representing or signifying practices are involved only in 'work of purification', to the exclusion of 'work of mediation'. This guarantee too has opened up space for its own violation. Thus 'the official work of purification', though denying the latter, has permitted 'the unofficial (linguistic and representational) work of mediation'. The assumptions of the modern constitution that 'science and technology are extra human' in fact hides the repressed and unofficial work that multiplies the 'intermediaries' that are neither fully human or non-human.[5] The sort of discourse that is needed, Latour argues, is a 'symmetrical anthropology', a set of inscribing practices that contest the asymmetry of both realism and constructivism. Positivism and realism here only look at the causality by the transcendent object, while constructivism – including most anthropological and science studies work – only looks at construction by immanent subjects. Both of these reproduce the separation of the realms. Latour's symmetrical anthropology will give a place for the causal agency of both subjects and objects, or rather of both 'quasi-subjects' and 'quasi-objects'.

Let us examine Latour's constitution for non-modernity, realizing that guarantees in the third and fourth, discursive and existential, realms – guarantees in the realms of language and of God and the religious – are as important as guarantees regarding subjects and objects, societies and nature. Thus non-modern constitution's guarantees in realms one and two are instead of the 'non-separability of quasi-objects and quasi-subjects': of their population of a 'third kingdom', whose place is between the transcendent and the immanent. In this kingdom 'nature and society are one and the same production of successive states of societies-natures, of collectives'. Here every institution that interferes with the 'continuous deployment of [such] collectives and their experimentation with hybrids would be deemed pernicious'. Now the 'work of mediation' is no longer marginalized, but takes its place 'at the very centre'. Now the networks (of quasi-subjects and quasi-objects) 'come out of hiding'.[6]

The realm of language is just as important. Discourse in modernity involves purifying language, while non-modern discourse comprises practices of mediation. The key to non-modern language use is to destroy the ban on translation networks, to end the ban on our 'freedom' to 'combine associations'.[7] The modern constitutional guarantee that language must engage in work of purification also 'outlaws the archaic': it legislates the forgetting of history. The non-modern constitution will enable language to bring back history in a set of new associations combining the archaic and the new. Finally, in terms of existence, the modern constitution separated God out into a purely sacred realm, while the other three realms were placed securely in the profane. In its fourth guarantee, non-modernity will counteract modernity's Faustian subject by bringing the gods back into the realm of the profane. The non-modern constitution brings God, the religious, being, the existential, right back into this middle kingdom of quasi-objects, quasi-subjects, of hybrids and networks. These measures of retrieval of history and being, as well as recognition of the spatio-temporal durability and partly transcendent nature of the middle kingdom, will counteract the 'wild and uncontrollable' overproduction of hybrids; will lead to 'an enlarged democracy that regulates and slows down the cadence'.[8] Hence in the non-modern condition, the previously Faustian subject will be reconstituted in a new modesty, a new finitude.

Latour's non-modern constitution is made up of 'actants'. The notion of actant comes from Benveniste's theory of narrative. Here humans and non-humans play rolls in such narratives. Insofar as they play such roles they are 'actants' in the narrative. Latour's non-modern quasi-objects and quasi-subjects and even his discourses figure as such actants. 'Discourses is a population of actants that mix with things as well as societies'.[9] These actants – these monsters, these hybrids populating the middle kingdom – all translate, mediate and extend the networks, they 'trace networks': they build the 'actor-networks'. At points Latour speaks of various types of actants: quasi-subjects, quasi-objects, discourses and even 'existential' actants. But on a more fundamental level, non-modern (like pre-modern) actants are comprised of four sorts of 'properties', four sorts of 'ontological substance'. Each of these monsters, each of these actants, is comprised of subject properties, object (or nature) properties, discourse properties and existential properties. And each is comprised of different measures of each. Thus machines are hybrids, with accentuated quasi-object properties, or poems as actants have most pronounced linguistic and existential properties.[10]

In modernity each of these properties occupied a separate realm. God is 'crossed out' from the world and is only fully transcendent in the Reformation (and Counter Reformation): God was at that point separate and fully differentiated from the social, from nature and from language. Subject and object took on their autonomy, as did language, as we see in the various theories of semiotics – from Saussure to Peirce to even Barthes – and their assumption of the autonomy of the signifier. This followed a much less differentiated pre-modern constitution; in which the 'natives' 'saturated mixes of the divine, the human and natural elements with concepts'.[11] This is well known from classical theories of modernization. But Latour asks the further question: what is it in the West that allows this dualism, this hybrid proliferating dualism, to emerge? His answer to the question of the 'Great Divide' is that we in the West are the only culture 'which mobilises nature. We mobilise nature, not as signs, but as it is. And we mobilise nature through science.'[12] Thus Lévi-Strauss writes that the savage mind 'arrives at the physical world by the detour of communication', whereas the West 'arrives at the world of communications by the detour of the physical'. The savage mind 'recognises physical and semantic properties simultaneously' and 'mistakes mere manifestations of physical determinism for messages'; it 'treats the sensible properties of the animal and plant kingdoms as if they were the elements of a message'; it discovers 'signatures' and thus 'signs' in them.[13]

Morphism Weavers and Object Trackers

The modern constitution has also constituted a mould for the social sciences. Here, conventionally, realists and naturalists have identified and attributed centrality to a set of 'hard objects', universal in time and space, and cast them as 'causes' for determining the fate of human categories. These 'hard objects', such as the economy, genetics and biology, are precisely those, Latour notes, whose universality is decided by the sciences and technology. For realists these hard objects become causes that explain the 'soft' dimension of the subject, such as religion, consumption, popular culture and politics. For their part, constructionists had traditionally seized on the 'softer' parts of nature and understood them to be constituted by the subject. Thus Mauss and Durkheim's classifications are 'screens for the projection of social categories'.[14] These 'hard parts' of the subject are the 'social factors' that explain the 'softer side' of the object, such as gods, machines, arts and styles.

Now science studies, however, has changed all this. Here the radical constructionism of analysts such as Steve Shapin and Karin Knorr-Cetina submitted even the harder parts of nature to social explanation. Science studies turned epistemology *de facto* on its head. They were effectively a radical challenge to the 'asymmetrical' anthropology of epistemologists like

Bachelard and Canguilhem, whose 'epistemological break' is based on assumptions of asymmetry between true and false sciences. The epistemological break emerges only when the 'object alone remains, excised from the entire network that gave them meaning'. For these epistemologists, 'truth is explained by nature, falsehood by society'.[15] Science studies introduces a measure of symmetrical anthropology here in its retention of 'causes which serve both science and ideology, truth and falsehood'. That is, both truth and falsehood are explained by social causes. But science studies overcame the epistemologists' asymmetry only to find itself embroiled in another asymmetry. In totally empowering the constructing subject, it has taken all rights away from the object. Hence David L. Bloor and his colleagues break with naturalism only to speak of the pure immanence of the subject, and thus are blind to the proliferation of quasi-subjects and quasi-objects. Hence Knorr's constructivism, in its presumption that social interests condition the representation of nature, repeats the radical constructionism of the early Durkheim and Mauss,[16] discovering that the sciences too were social, were unjustified in then inferring that all of nature was merely constructed.

Latour is not a constructivist. Constructionism for him comes under that same old modern constitution that realism did. Latour makes two moves which separate him from constructionism. First, he does not understand objects so much as being caused by subjects, but instead sees them as bearing certain properties that subjects bear. Objects for him thus have agency: not causal agency like in naturalism, but more the sort of agency that subjects have. They have rights, responsibilities, they can judge and measure, they can mediate. Just like subjects can. So Latour's objects are not primarily caused by subjects. Instead they are *similar* to subjects. Second, Latour is not exclusively a sociologist of science. He is a sociologist of science *and technology*. His focus in his comparison of Hobbes and Boyle, for example, is not Boyle's theory, but the vacuum pump, the technology that mediates the theory. The same for his work on Pasteur: it is the laboratory, not the scientific facts, which is primarily at stake. Michael Callon, for his part, has similarly focused on the texts written about the experiment.[17] Now *technologies* have never had the transcendental status that science and scientific facts and theories have had. Technologies have always been very difficult to reduce to poles of subject and object. Previously they have with difficulty been reduced to the object role, as in, for example, 'technological determinism'. But with the growing centrality of genetic and information technologies this is increasingly impossible. Technologies become increasingly hybrid: neither subject nor clearly object. Sociologists of science may be tempted by the constructionist option. Latour as sociologist of science *and technology* can no longer be constructionist. He must be nonmodern.

So Latour's objects are not only constructed. They themselves do not so much cause as themselves construct. They construct through 'mediation' and 'delegation'. How does Latour understand this? He understands human social practices, in science and everyday life, in terms of a process of 'sorting'. This is reminiscent of Durkheim and Mauss's and Bourdieu's understanding of human beings as 'classifying animals'. This recalls Kant's third critique, in which, as we saw in chapter 9, determinate judgement is one (very important) variety of reflexive judgement. Determinate judgement is especially important in Latour's modern constitution, whose 'work of purification' involves 'civilizing the hybrids', 'sorting' them, by placing them forcibly into either society or nature. Latour insists that we see this form of dualistic mediation as only one form of mediation, and that the human or 'anthropos' must no longer be defined as a pure determinate judging subject up against a Sartrean 'practico-inert', but instead humanism has to do with our non-modern work of mediation. Humans, says Latour, are 'analogy machines'. The human is a 'weaver of morphisms': not just of anthropomorphisms, but also of 'zoomorphisms, theomorphisms, technomorphisms and ideomorphisms'. Not only do we use non-humans as representations or analogues, but non-humans themselves become analogy machines, themselves become weavers of morphisms. Classical humanism has conventionally stripped things of their powers, cut them off as 'delegations and senders'. But non-modern humanism instead 'shares itself' with these 'other mandates', through the 'redistribution of action among all these mediators'. 'The human', Latour continues, 'is in the delegation itself, in the pass, in the sending, in the continuous exchange of forms.' 'Human nature is the set of its delegates and representatives, its figures and its messengers.'[18]

This is, I think, the key to Latour's theory and the book. He is saying that objects themselves are judges; objects themselves engage in reflexive judgement, in the weaving of morphisms. To weave a morphism is more than just to represent: it is also 'to pass', to 'send'. It is – in the idiom of computer graphics artists – to 'morph' something,[19] i.e. to create your morphism and then to communicate it. It is through this communication to weave a net or a network. For Latour judgement is always at the same time communication of that judgement. It is never pure representation. Or pure fact. It is a statement and its sending. In its effects it is more like a speech act than just a predicative utterance. It is *parole* understood not as speech but as message: it always includes the sending. And the sending weaves a net, helps to construct a network. Here quasi-objects are among the most important of these 'mediators'. Mediation itself, of course, means much more than just representation. Representation involves the sort of practices occurring in sculpture, painting, the novel, the poem. Even film is more a matter of representation than mediation. But characteristically late-modern global forms of culture break with the logic of representation. Or, rather, such late-modern culture, quite rightly understood in terms of 'the media', can never represent without sending, without transmitting or communicating. Indeed, contemporary 'economies of signs and space', especially in their capacity as information, have a lot more to do with transmission than with representation. That is, in contemporary culture the primacy of transmission has displaced the primacy of representation. Contemporary culture is thus a culture of movement. A culture of moving (quasi-) objects.

And here is where Latour may become unwound in a contradiction. Although in his non-modern utopia we come to understand that we and non-humans are analogy machines, are reflexively judging entities, this is not what he suggests we do a social scientists. In this sense I think his theory itself is insufficiently reflexive, i.e. it cannot be applied to itself without contradiction. What Latour asks us as social scientists to do in non-modernity is not reflexively to judge and send, but instead to 'track the object'. What I am arguing is that cultural activities of analogic judgement are themselves typical of not non-modernity, but *modernity*. Latour recognizes this but then says we cover it up with a dualistic ideology of determinate (logical) judgement. But as we move into the proliferated hybridity of the global informational order, we may be involved in an entirely different set of cultural practices: *we become engaged in 'object tracking'*.[20] Thus, ascertaining that actants are simultaneously real, social and discursive, Latour encourages us to 'follow the quasi-objects to the end'. He encourages us to begin from the middle kingdom of the monsters and hybrids and track them to see how they are hypostatized as immanent or transcendent. If we track the object, we discover the network. He endorses Michel Callon's dictum that we put ourselves 'at the median point where we can follow the attribution of both human and nonhuman properties'.[21] That we thus track the work of mediation, of how quasi-objects in the middle kingdom become stabilized as subject and object. He says we should 'follow the work of proliferation of hybrids' and 'shadow the quasi-object or networks'.[22]

This 'shadowing' or tracking sounds a lot more like the work of a detective than the work of a judge. And perhaps this is what we are about in global informational culture. We non-moderns are perhaps not 'judges' at all, but 'trackers'. We are less concerned with the representation than with the sending, the signal. We are no longer pre-moderns of symbolic, not like the moderns iconic, but have moved into an *indexical* order of non-representation. Where we follow the object. Where not only social scientists, but all of us are object trackers. Whether when net surfing or 500-channel surfing, we uncover the hypertext, or open the doors and the drawers in interactive graphics on CD-ROM. In each case at issue is not so much representation or the symbolic, but information and sending. We trace the network through the Web site. There is neither aurality (the

symbolic) nor vision (the iconic), but tactility, indexicality at the heart of the
signal and the information economy.[23] Not only do we track the objects,
trace the networks. But as we will see in our discussion of Virilio below, the
objects can track us. The networks can be our prisons. In our discussion of
Benjamin below we will look at how object-tracking can be an allegorical
and metonymic practice as we reflexively dis-embed objects from contemporary culture and then re-embed them in our own allegorical ordering, an
ordering that is non- and post-narrative. An ordering of tracking that has
not so much to do with the representation of linear narrative or even the
problematization of representation by non-linear narrative. It has to do
instead with the *irrelevance* of representation: the irrelevance of narrative. It
has to do with what Lefebvre calls a 'path', a material path, an indexical
and tactile path that we trace and then that we lift out and reconnect. This
may be how we make sense and make meaning in contemporary culture.
And note that much of the time we make sense through practices of
orientation that do *not* involve making meaning. We non-moderns are not
mediators but materialist 'trackers', pathfinders. We find not Kantian rules,
but 'paths'. We create our hybrids not through mediating as analogy
machines, but as trackers, as allegorists.

C'accuse

'Mediation', 'representation', 'passing', 'sending', but also 'delegation', 'betrayal', 'translation'. Latour's language is as much political as it is epistemo-
cultural. This is his whole point. Modernity's subject–object dualism is
most of all a separation of political practices on the one hand from epistemological activities on the other. For him non-modernity should have no
such separation. Neither did pre-modernity. Paradigmatic for the entire
book is the juxtaposition of Hobbes's seventeenth-century politics with
Boyle's seventeenth-century epistemology. Latour notes here that the two
realms had not yet been fully separated: that science and the state were still
understood on very much the same model. Hobbes's idea of the state was
not just based in possessive individualism, but also, as Leo Strauss notably
argued, grew from an episteme set by Galilean physics: the notion of things
as atoms being generalized to citizens existing in mutual hostility in a force
field. Thus for Hobbes the 'calculation of human atoms' leads to the
'contract' of 'authorization granted by all citizens to a single one to speak
in their name'.[24]

Latour's focus is the reverse of Strauss's: it is on how science takes up the
political model. It is not on the Boylean in Hobbes but on how Boyle is a
Hobbesian. His assumption is that for people and things to possess agency,
they must be represented. Hence scientists are 'translators, intermediaries'

for the 'parliament of mutes in the lab', much in the same way that the 'sovereign' translates or represents what the 'citizens would have said on their own'. In order for representation to be possible so must be its obverse side, 'betrayal'. In this sense a false theory would betray the world of things as much as a sovereign can betray his or her citizens. Because the scientist's and the sovereign's activities take place in a dimension of immanence as well as one of transcendence, they often only look to be betraying their constituents. Thus scientists only seem to be 'betraying external reality' 'because they are busy constructing their own societies and nature at the same time'. And the sovereign only looks to be betraying the humans because he is also 'churning together the enormous mass of nonhumans that holds the Leviathan up'.[25] Thus the Leviathan not only represents, but it 'mobilises commerce, inventions, the arts ... it mobilises the countless goods and objects that give it consistency and durability'.

Latour in this sense uses the political theory to argue for representation for the 'parliament of things'. He then takes his case for the agency and rights of things into the realm of law. He argues that – like the rights-bearing subjects – things too are largely constituted in law. He first addresses the issue of 'the witness'. In Boyle's laboratory, Latour observes, the thing became true as scientific fact when presented to small numbers of 'witnesses' who 'represent nature as it is'. These 'little groups of gentlemen take testimony from natural forces and then testify to each other that they are not betraying the silent behaviour of objects'. Now we see 'what a natural force is, an object that is mute but endowed or entrusted with meaning'. These 'facts are produced and represented in the laboratory, in scientific writings; they are vouched for by a community of witnesses'. Here in the laboratory experiments, on the one hand, the facts are constituted immanently. On the other hand, the facts are also transcendent in that 'scientists are scrupulous representatives of the facts', and that what are really speaking are 'the facts themselves'.[26] Moreover, things themselves become witnesses in Boyle's laboratory. More reliable than human witnesses was Boyle's vacuum pump. It judged, it measured. It was endowed with meaning as a translator for the facts, for the scientific phenomena, for the non-humans, the things in the lab. The community of scientists is much less important for Latour as witnesses than is the instrument, the thing.

Paradigmatic for the thing and for the quasi-objects is Boyle's vacuum pump. It is Latour's paradigmatic technology, which is not a scientific fact but represents or embodies scientific facts. Scientific facts are not technologies. Scientific theories are not technologies. Most things are not technologies. Only things that primarily serve as *means* are technologies. Technologies serve as means through making things. The sort of technologies most important for Latour are also those which represent, judge and communicate. There were few of these around in the seventeenth century. Boyle's vacuum pump was one. At the turn of the twenty-first century, however, such judging and morphism weaving machines, such communication and network building machines, are at the hub of our post-industrial economies. This is why Latour's work may be of greatest relevance as a sociologist not of science, but of technology. Technologies, then, are Latour's paradigmatic quasi-objects. Thus Boyle's non-human witnesses were 'endowed with meaning'. And the new form of (scientific) text, the new form of discourse, 'the experimental scientific article [was a] hybrid between biblical exegesis', on the one hand, and 'the new instrument that produces new inscriptions', on the other. The vacuum pump thus testifies and inscribes. Laboratory practice centres on the 'signature of scientific instruments'. Moreover, the instrument is absolutely essential to the 'change of scale', the extension of universality of a scientific theory or fact. Boyle's Law, then, does not become universal but extends as far as its 'network is extended and stabilised'; 'its speed of propagation exactly equivalent to the rate at which the community of experimenters and their equipment develops'. For the theory to be true in a given place, the air pump must be in the lab. The universality of a theory is dependent on the expansion of 'competences and equipment'.[27]

Michel Serres has commented on the vast amount of historian's ink spilt on how subjects constitute objects, whereas the constitution of subjects by objects is 'drowned out' by the 'noise of discourse'; texts are surrounded by noise and attention, whereas 'pumps, stones and statues' lived their history in 'utter silence'. Serres notes that the subject bears witness in texts, in language, through 'testimony, traces or narratives', but for the constituting object 'we [only] have witnesses that are tangible, visible, concrete, formidable, tacit'. In its origins the object, as *Ding, res, chose*, only 'existed according to the debates of an assembly or after a decision issued by a jury'. The *res* was 'the object of judicial procedure or the cause (in the sense of agency not mechanism) itself. For the Ancients the accused bore the name reus' because magistrates were suing him. So the thing in pre-modern 'law of property' is not only the stake but the cause (*chose*), and 'the tribunal stages the very identity of cause and thing, of word and object, or the passage from one to the other by substitution'. Latour encourages us to follow Serres's metonymic, hence allegorical (and object-tracking), suggestions by urging the non-modern redistribution of accusations that replace one type of 'cause – judicial, collective, social –' by another type of 'cause – scientific, non-social, matter-of-factual'. The new mode of sorting, of morphism weaving, in non-modernity is thus a 'series of substitutions and displacements' that 'mobilise people and things'.[28] This agency redistributed to things not just makes them witnesses that help courts make judgements, but makes it possible for them to accuse, to become prosecuting attorneys. But things here may depart from Latour's optimistic scenario. And things constituted as *goods* can become the *'bads'* of the risk society. Veritable detective-machines, things such as video cameras or police computer files, track the quasi-subjects: objects accuse subjects. Constituted through a set of metonymic displacements, objects can track the quasi-subjects. They lift them out, they dis-embed and re-embed them allegorically and bring them before the court of justice of the things.

But from where can judicial decisions take place? How high is the judge's bench? Latour here draws on the work of Boltanski and Thevenot to break with dualistic notions of justice from modernity's constitution. Here critical tribunals, and especially science, figured as 'sources of denunciation' in cases of scientific and social justice. What Boltanski and Thevenot do in *De la justification* is to deconstruct such planes of 'critical indignation' by merely comparing them as 'ways we have of bringing affairs to justice'. Here the critical spirit becomes no longer a transcendental instance but 'a topic, a competence'. Critique loses its role as an 'ultimate reservoir of denunciation', and takes its place as one of a number of places from which justification of a decision can be uttered. Justice then becomes no longer a foundation, but an 'added force'. Judgement functions not by denunciation, but by 'triage and selection', by 'arrangement, combination, combinazione, combine, negotiation and compromise'. Against moral indignation, this non-modern morality is 'an unofficial morality that constantly selects and distributes the practical solutions of the moderns'. It is 'active and generous, following the countless meanderings of situations and networks'.[29]

Boltanski and Thevenot focus here on the 'objective stakes of our disputes', on objects engaged in tests of judgement. At issue in effect is a form of 'phronesis', but one in which objects play as large a role as the intersubjectivity of disputants. Here, as stakes and as contents, objects in the world of disputants themselves select the tribunal, select one mini-tribunal among many that can serve as a source of justification, as a 'competence'. This is only a partly embedded, a partly situated, ethics, a partly immanent ethics, as there are still smallish 'hills', from which justification can be made which gives the judgements extra added force. These mini-tribunals of non-indignant moral judgement are a 'competence' (and for Boltanski love and justice are understood as competences) but also as a 'topic'. During the 'wanderings' of quasi-subjects and quasi-objects through the networks, these topics or topos appear like a thousand plateaux, a set of mini-instances from which subjects and objects can select as competences – as added force – in disputes concerning their rights and the distribution of agency. Subjects such as us tracking objects. Highly intelligent objects tracking subjects. All following the meandering paths of networks, of rhizomes, in cases where branches break off from the network.

Using these plateaux as extra added force, as competences in the mini-arbitrages between objects and objects, subjects and subjects and objects and subjects. This is not just phronesis, but also prosthesis: also part and parcel of what Lury calls 'prosthetic culture'.[30] The issue is, however, a question of who is tracking whom, of who is prosthetically grafting limbs on whom, in not the either/or but the 'both and' of Latour's non-modernity.

Networks: Spiralling Time and Space

The radical transcendence of scientific truths for Latour becomes only an added force, a 'competence', a 'small cause' with 'large effects'. The massive expansion in scale of the networks flows from the smallest causes. The causes that scientific truths make possible are quasi-objects, not the truths themselves but the 'technologies', like the vacuum pump or computer. From this 'minimum of means' is 'generated a maximum of differences', a maximum of 'scaling effects'. This spatial expansion comes from the enlistment, the recruitment, of quasi-objects by networks for their own spatial expansion. Such enlistment of quasi-objects also went on in pre-modern times, in which ancestors and non-human totems would be recruited to stabilize and expand networks. The difference is only in scale. Whereas traditional networks formed only local loops, the particular type of non-humans (i.e. technologies) enlisted by moderns have enabled the invention of much longer networks. Pre-moderns also wove morphisms, 'weaving together the threads of nature, society, the subjective and reality'. But this very mix, this saturation, this complexity – as opposed to modernity's dualistic simplicity – encouraged not adventure but great prudence. Here 'every monster becomes visible and thinkable', posing major problems for the 'social and natural order'.[31] Theories and scientific facts for Latour are thus neither universal nor relativist, but 'relatively universalistic', just like empires, depending on how far the networks spread.

Non-modern networks pose fewer threats because they do not destroy locality. The increasingly global networks, Latour argues, do not 'de-territorialize' because they do not spread across and cover the totality of space, but are only universal in the 'sense of networks of gas lines or sewer pipes'. They are only 'lines' connecting points or localities. They are only 'nets thrown over spaces'. They do not erode the local but instead are connections of localities. Technological networks like railroads are 'local at all points', at all local stations composed of 'particular railway workers, ticket machines and stations'. These relatively universal networks are composed of, on the one hand, 'particular places' and, on the other, 'a series of branchings'. 'Between the lines and the network there is strictly speaking nothing at all'. The networks then 'spread out in time and space without filling time and space'. What Latour is taking about is not a 'topography' of the 'total state' but a 'topology'. Topography covers surfaces but 'topology', according to *Le petit Robert*, addresses the qualitative properties of the relative positions of geometrical beings. Thus the topology of a totalitarian state is of a certain 'scale obtained through the construction of a network of statistics and calculations of offices' and the like. And capitalism itself should be understood not so much as a world system, a world topography, but as a 'skein of somewhat longer networks . . . on the basis of points that become centres of calculation'. The model of technological networks is extended to account for the totalitarian state, capitalism and science itself, also comprised not of any de-territorializing essence but of 'frail and tenu- ous networks' 'with their itinerary of [not machines, but] facts'. This new topology makes it possible to go anywhere 'without occupying anything except narrow lines of force'. Further, Latour insists, the 'branch lines must be paid for'. Boyle's theory is only valid as far as its network extends, as far as vacuum pumps are bought and scientists are trained in a set of competences. Satellite television is universal as far as I have paid for 'antenna, subscription and decoder'. There is a certain 'price of extension of networks for measuring and interpreting'.[32] The quasi-objects who measure and interpret must be bought and the quasi-subjects who also measure and interpret must be trained.

Modernity's dualisms become non-modernity's 'added force' in actor– network temporality. With regard to temporality here the idea of *revolution* is integral to modernity's constitution. The idea of revolution, like the exalted tribunal of critique, is transcendental: the truth only emerges with the revolution. Everything before the revolution is consigned to the dust- bins of history. Man's real history only starts in *l'an 1* of the revolution. This is the case for both political and scientific revolutions. Both of these partake in modernity's assumption of irreversible time. Time is irreversible because the past has disappeared: it has no value, no meaning. For there to be meaning we must go forward. Revolutionary temporality is based not in 'events' but in 'essences', in transcendental essences that emerge: in the 'universal transcendence of local and fabricated laws'. Thus political revo- lution concerns nature, concerns 'natural rights'. Revolution concerns the emergence of 'universal and necessary things that have always been present, lacking any historicity'. This is Marx's essence that has no history yet emerges in history. It is Habermas's dismissal of the past as a time of confusion before being, things, men and language were sufficiently dif- ferentiated for meaning to be possible. The irreversible temporality of revolution comprises also the sort of homogeneous time 'that passes' and 'accumulates', as Charles Péguy wrote, 'in savings banks'. And the theory of progress, Latour agrees, amounts essentially 'to such a theory of time in savings banks'. Time as 'irreversible arrow', as 'capitalization'. In Marxism in any given mode of production, time accumulates, as do the means of production. When the accumulation of time and productive forces is no longer functional for productive relations, the latter burst asunder and a new mode of production emerges, with a new accumulation of time, while the old temporality is devalued and discarded. Thus, as Nietzsche mentioned, modernity's devaluation of the past results in a 'historicism', marking the emergence of the museum in which moderns 'keep and date everything because they have definitely broken with the past'. What could be further from the memorial, from the hermeneutic notion of the museum as a repository of collective memory? This idea of museum as 'expert system' in which the time of the past is accumulated and saved. Any idea of institutions and objects with pasts is destroyed.[33]

Non-modernity rethinks revolution as an 'in potentia', as itself encouraging a 'retrospective attitude'. Revolution too becomes an 'added force' in an eminently reversible history. Non-modernist time is not irreversible, but contains 'a past which remains and even returns'. Time is no longer an arrow but a 'spiral', in which 'points from the past' are often closer to us than the present. Time can be revisited, repeated. We are, as Péguy wrote and Serres concurs, 'exchangers and brewers of time'. We 'go down sideways and grab hold of the event . . . in its intensity'. The old irreversible time came from 'binding together elements' or quasi-objects into a single temporality, whereas now we recognize a 'multiplicity of times'. Nonmodernist sorting must 'mix up different periods, ontologies and genres'. Indeed, Latour argues, it is the 'connections' and how they 'are sorted out' that make time. 'The networks' construct both irreversibility and reversibility. Non-modern time is neither the pure essence of nature nor the pure contingency or event of society, 'but a gradient that registers variation in stability of entities from event to essence'. At issue is a 'spatio-temporality' of 'successive helixes' on a spiral, each one 'more eccentric' as the size of the network grows. What changes with the modern sciences is 'the extension of the spiral, the scope of enlistments it will bring about, the ever increasing lengths it goes to recruit these beings'.[34]

This treatment of temporality brings out the best and the worst in Latour's non-modernist futurology. The best in the sense that this book is extraordinarily instructive in rethinking today's global informational order, its allegorical and indexical subjects and objects, their judgements and communications, their indexical tracking. The culturation of the economy is also the production of 'reflexive objects' like software and surveillance video cameras: contemporary advertising produces not products for audiences but audiences for products. Latour's proliferating hybrids of 'frozen embryos, digital machines, sense equipped robots, hybrid corn, data banks, whales outfitted with radar sounding devices, gene synthesisers' are the very travelling objects of the global information society. His 'monsters' inhabit the socialization of the natural, in which the contingent subject is preserved in the duration of the object. Nature, previously universal in time as object, itself becomes relatively contingent in 'the ozone hole, global warning, deforestation'.[35]

Latour also represents the worst in our informational economies. He gives us only one side of the other, the second modernity, that of difference: the side of innovation through eternal deconstruction. In doing so he systematically ignores the dimension of the ground. His idea of the past and reversible time is primarily of the 'exchanging and brewing' of past 'events', in the interests of innovation. For him events are more of the essence than duration. We are to mix and match events in polyglot pastiche, rather than think in terms of duration. This is a hermeneutics of return, not a hermeneutics of retrieval. 'The event', as in Freud's hermeneutics of suspicion, comes back as return, though in a mix and match sort of sense. Duration, as we noted in discussion in chapter 9 of Gadamer, is always with us to be retrieved. It is this that allows meaning to be in the past. Latour's quasi-objects, in contrast to Gadamer's monuments, do not have pasts to be retrieved: they are resources for the future.

The same is true for 'non-modernity's' grounded justice and ethics. Here the 'added forces', the 'little mounds of justification', are not understood as integral to embedded practices, but instead as 'competences', as 'small causes'. Again there is the forgetting of the past, the neglect of the historical dimension, the impossibility of phronesis, of a situated ethics. For Latour there is instead an ethics of innovation, of difference, of 'imbroglio sorting'. This almost Popperian centrality of imbroglio sorting and competences leads beyond an ethics of innovation. It seems to lead in the direction of instrumental rationality, in which quasi-objects and even quasi-subjects are primarily instruments. Thus 'collectives' 'mobilize' these competences and these quasi-objects as instruments furthering their own 'stability and expansion'. 'Some collectives mobilise ancestors, lions, fixed stars and the coagulated blood of sacrifice', and every collective 'mobilises heaven and earth in its composition along with bodies and souls, gods and ancestors and powers and beliefs'. We mobilize a different set of quasi-objects. We mobilize *technologies* in the interests of the expansion of increasingly global collectivities. Whereas pre-modern mobilization and recruitment led to simple reproduction, modern and non-modern mobilization leads to expanded reproduction of the networks. 'The fact that one collective needs ancestors and fixed stars and another genes and quasars is explained by the dimensions of the collective to be held together.' The assumptions here are clearly of instrumental rationality and a network functionalism. 'Science and technology are remarkable not because they are true...but because they multiply the nonhumans enrolled in the manufacturing of collectives.'[36]

12

Bad Objects: Virilio

In part IV, on judgement, we saw that Kant's idea of judgement was based on the juxtaposition of *instrumentality* and *finality*. Kant's first critique of pure reason addressed objective knowledge in the sciences. Objective knowledge, we saw, deals with nature, deals with objects as 'instruments'. So does commodity exchange on the market. A whole history of German social thought – from Hegel to Marx to Weber to the Critical Theory of Adorno, Marcuse and Habermas, to Heidegger – has understood this sort of objective (positivist) knowledge and commodity exchange effectively in terms of 'instrumental rationality'. In juxtaposition to this, Kant counterposed the idea of *finality*. In aesthetic judgement, Kant said, we treat nature and the object not as an instrument, but as a 'finality'. That is, not as a means to an end, but as a medium carrying its own end in itself. Kant's theme of finality is apparent in Marxian use-value, in which – in contrast to exchange value – we engage with work and the things around us not as means to ends but intrinsically. The idea of instrumentality – through the length of this book – is the driving theme of the first modernity. The idea of finality is that of the second, the other modernity. Finality has a different logic, a different rationality, from the first modernity.

The whole of this book has dealt with two types of social relations – those between persons and things and those between persons and persons. Parts IV and V largely deal with relations of persons and things, with 'I–it' relations. Parts II and III largely with relations between persons and persons, with the 'I–thou' relation, with intersubjectivity. Part I dealt with a combination of the two. Like 'I–it' relations, relations of intersubjectivity can involve instrumentality, on the one hand, or finality, on the other. If 'I–thou' relations are institutional, to the extent that the end of these institutions is the functioning of society, then they are instrumental. Thus a number of normative institutions are shot through with the instrumental logic of the first modernity. Michel Foucault's work was dedicated to the explication of this. To the extent that the 'I–thou' relation takes the form of a grounded intersubjectivity, of an embedded life-world sociality, then this relation is a finality. This embedded intersubjectivity as finality has been integral to the second, the other modernity.

Part V of this book deals mainly with the 'I–it' relation, with the theory of the object. But as we saw in the previous chapter, it does so in an age in which the distinction, the dualism, the aporia of instrumentality and finality has been exploded. Bruno Latour, we saw, accepts this dissolution of the aporia of the second modernity – the disappearance of the cleft between meaning and beings, between freedom and necessity – with few regrets. I wish that I could be so sanguine. In the other thinkers considered in part V – Paul Virilio and Walter Benjamin – there is a different attitude. Virilio and Benjamin, with Latour, keenly grasp that we live in an emerging era that irreversibly destroys the foundations, the ground of the other modernity. Yet both Virilio and Benjamin regret the dissolution of finality, the disappearance of the aporia. In both thinkers the ground appears in mourning, as memory, as community, as place. Virilio, a Christian, and Benjamin, a Jew, have a great sense of mourning for the ground. But this thematic has, I think, also the highest relevance for those cynical seculars, the religiously unmusical among us. This mourning for finality, for being, for, indeed, difference may be necessary to any meaningful sense of memory, of community, of ethics, indeed for any meaningful politics today.

From the *Cité* to the War Machine

Paul Virilio paints for us a scene of a time that once was, of an *âge classique* of the walled city. Before the rise of this ancient city was an archaic age, a time of 'tumult', a time of the tribes, in which barbarian hordes wreaked devastation. This was the first age of war *per se*, the age of the coming of the state, the first organization of the 'territiorial economy'. The *âge classique*, in contrast, was an age of politics, surely in Hannah Arendt's sense of the political as the intersubjectivity of community and communication in the polis. But most of all in Clausewitz's sense in which the political is consti-tuted in international relations, and protects society from other nations. The *âge classique* was also the age *par excellence* of the city. And Virilio's city is all about space. The city and not the village and the tribes is the location and ultimate origin of place. For Virilio space is place. Virilio's classic city is not that of Mumford and the historians of architecture: it is not the classic city of winding streets and monuments. It is instead a city whose main virtue is the enclosure. Whose main architectural virtue is the protection of the enclosure from the outside hordes.

War in the *âge classique* was not a matter of speeding up, but instead of slowing down. It was a question of slowing down the attacks of the barbar-ians on the city: a question of the protection of 'urban sedentariness'. The organization of war was also the organization of urban space inside.[1] The paradigmatic objects for the ancients were the 'obstacles' protecting and thus permitting this organization of the city: the catapults and projectiles, but even more crucially the durability of the 'mineralization' of the buildings, the watchtowers, blockhouses, walls and ramparts, the other fortifications that separated inside from outside, that enclosed *zoon politikon* from the attacking tribes. This was the age of politics: politics, of course, not as *la politique*, but *le politique*. But when the barbarians outside finally bring down into piles of rocks the walls of the city, when the battering rams and shells and arrows devastate the city, the *âge classique*, the age of politics, is over. Now Hobbes's war of all against all becomes the rule, not figuratively as possessive individualism, but literally as pure war, as what Goebbels called 'total war'. Now the age of 'speed' comes to displace the age of politics. Now the paradigmatic objects – the projectile, the tank, the logistic truck, the movement of troops along roads – are no longer inscribed in urban sedentariness, but in the movement of war. Politics as *le politique* yields to 'strategy', 'geopolitics' makes way for 'chronopolitics'. Politics had been concerned with the parcelling out of geographical space, of 'the organisation of population into a territory'. Now the destruction of the political brings with it the triumph of temporality over place in a generalized 'vectorization', of movements of weapons, technologies, troops and populations. Once populating space, human beings now became increasingly concentrated in time, in the time of these movements.

What sort of order is this order of speed which has destroyed the city walls? In military terms there is a shift from 'strategy' to 'logistics'. The strategist had 'governed the city, through organization of a theatre of operations with ramparts and the whole military-political system'. The strategist was part of the military elite, a horseman of the military caste in Dumesnil's Indo-European triptych of warriors, peasants – concerned with the economy (*oikos*) – and priests, whose business was the sacred. The new age of logistics is not for Virilio that of the hegemony of the peasant and the commodity as technology. Instead the age of logistics, and 'logic' is inherent to logistics and not strategy, is the fusion of the old warrior and priest castes into warrior-priests, under the hegemony of the priests. In modernity's age of logistics priestly power constitutes military might. Now cosmology is no longer grounded in the geocentrism of the earth, on the one hand, and the theocentrism of God/the gods on the other. The new priests bring with them a new cosmology of Kantian and Newtonian universalist time-space. The new class – the new military class – operates primarily in the register not of strategy but of knowledge. Now there is a method of calculation of the war economy – and the subsequent shift of workers and material from plowshare to sword production – into the state budget. Thus must be understood Clausewitz's obsession with logistics: with the crucial role of recruitment, mobilization and the transport of men and resources.

The age of logistics marks the emergence of the mass and 'democratic' – non-mercenary armies of the Napoleonic Wars, which were eminently technical wars in the movements of artillery, the use of telegraph.[2]

Total war foregrounds the logistics of shifting munitions, of transportation. It signals the advent of the tank. While trucks are moving and bringing ammunition, flying shells are bringing death. At issue is a general 'system of vectors of production, transportation and execution'. The military class is now dominated not by the warrior ethos but by the 'war *machine*'. The military class is concerned above all with efficiency, with the accumulation – in both Marx's and Heidegger's sense – of a standing reserve, recruiting both men and the machines of war – rifles, uniforms, bullets – but especially with the ability to *move* that standing reserve. The war machine comprises both that accumulation and this movement: the war machine is less about explosives than the speed of delivery or 'vectorization' of those explosives. Collective memory structured the horizon of the strategist of the ancient city. The new military class is possessed instead with a 'negative horizon': an unbridled intelligence with no sense of limits. Even death is not outside its limits or its technology. For the new military class and indeed all the classes the struggle of interests in the economy is only a superstructural reflection of the war of all against all in the era of total war. Now the 'geocentric' cosmogony of earth, mother-earth, of the mother and the generations is effaced. The 'riddle of nature' is displaced by techno-centrism and the 'riddle of technology'.[3]

The *âge classique* was an era of 'politics' in the sense that conflicts were regulated under law. The politics of classical democracy, however, has been replaced by the 'trans-politics' of the age of pure war: by not democracy but 'dromocracy'. In Greek the street is called a run (*dromos*) and *dromo* is a race. The *dromos* or street functions to 'drain the population as fast as possible to the city gates, to the outskirts'. Classical democracy operated under the sign of reversible time. Time was reversible in the classical ethos of the continuity of history, in the ethos of 'dialogue and dialectic and the time for reflection'. Classical humanist reflection and dialogue presume the reversibility of time, presume the chance to go back into the past, to bring the past to bear on the present. Modernity's war machine, for its part, heralds the depletion of time, the explosion of humanism by the supremely irreversible vectors of trans-political speed. These unidirectional vectors abolish not only humanist duration and reversible time, but also space and territory: like Latour's branch lines they are topological rather than topographical, i.e. they don't take up territory.[4]

Virilio's notion of 'the good life' in *l'âge classique* is bound up with this metaphysics of enclosure and interiority. Thus his very early work and later exhibition published in *Bunker Archeology* studies the circle of blockhouses

comprising France's Atlantic Wall during the Second World War. The
blockhouses and the Atlantic Wall protected the enclosure of national
space from the enemy outside. It separated continental space from maritime space. Virilio's polis, his notion of the good life, is in this sense not
as political or dialogic as Hannah Arendt's. Virilio's good life is not primarily concerned with intersubjectivity in Arendt's sense or, like Alistair
Macintyre's Aristotelian practices, assuming a teacher–pupil relationship.
Virilio's good life is instead about enclosures, on the one hand the city, and
on the other the individual. What is destroyed in modernity's dromocracy
is the interiority both of the city and of the individual. It is the subjectivity
and interiority of the individual and not intersubjectivity or dialogue that is
his focus.[5] Thus, as Arthur Kroker observes, the focus of Virilio's work is on
the 'reduction of experience to dromocratic consciousness'. For Virilio this
shift from classical interiority to modern exteriority is also a shift from the
primacy of the word to the principle of sight. The body, formerly a living
metabolism, becomes a 'metabolic vehicle', becomes an 'abstract vector of
speed'. At the same time the interiority of the soul is destroyed in the
'invasion of the body by technology'. The consequence is the 'exterioriza-
tion of the human sensorium' – through a set of prostheses into first the war
machine and later virtual machines. Virilio is a Christian and there is a
profound dimension of the religious in his work: a 'lament', as Kroker
notes, 'for the religious imagination in the age of secular dromocracy'; an
insistence on the recuperation of 'a value-driven ethics of remembrance,
from a refusal of the technological imperative'. Virilio brings us back to the
interiority of the confessional, to revelation and the word of God, to a
Thomist aesthetics of apperception.[6]

Dromocracy and the age of the war machine are not the end of Virilio's
story. More recently there has emerged an apocalyptic reversibility, a self-
cancellation and exhaustion, in which the principle of movement turns into
a principle of stasis. Now speed moves into a different register: from the
movement of people and material objects in space to the movement of
images and signals at absolute speed. This new age of individuals static
behind their terminals reveals the flipping, the reversing of acceleration
into the inertia of escape velocity. There is now a decline of salience of state
vectors, of war vectors, of the social relations of war, to the gain of the
'chrono-photographic sphere of speed and communication'. There is a
'cinematic derealization of war', as movement 'becomes subordinated to
the logistics of optical phenomena'. Now the remnants of collective
memory incorporated in the heat of war are displaced by total forgetting
and the cold surfaces of 'digital violence'.[7]

What is this new age of 'polar inertia'? The pole, he notes, is an absolute
place that does not move when the earth rotates. In the age of information

every city, every airport, becomes more and more the same place, the same
absolute place of polar inertia. Movement in Newtonian time-space becomes relativized and inertia in the new cosmology of absolute speed. Now
the exponential development of simple modernity's vectorization exhausts
itself and the field of Newtonian time-space, the field of movement of
dromocratic urban streets, shrivels up in transformation into the electromagnetic field, the field of perception, of optics, of the speed of light. A
general exhaustion of vectorization, of the accident, a breakdown of the
dictatorship of movement in the age of the perceptual field is the condition
of polar inertia. This breakdown has nothing to do with necessity, substance or truth: it is the accident of accident, contingency's contingency.
This breakdown in movement and emergence of polar inertia becomes the
paradigmatic mode of experience for not just the middle classes, privileged
and included in the 'live zones' of the information and communication
loop. It is also the experience of the underclass, the pariahs of the 'dead
zones': squatters live the inertia of the ghettos, the favellas, in the general
breakdown of vectorization. Polar inertia heralds the intensification of
the 'aesthetics of disappearance', which had already emerged in the
dromocratic age. Such 'disappearance' stands in contrast to the *revelation*
that was promised in a previously hegemonic 'aesthetics of apperception'
and hence appearance. Greek civilization thus foregrounded a politics of
appearance whose object was to 'promote an image of the world' through
the art of defence of the city. In the age of general vectorization, however,
the image exists not insofar as it appears, as in classic painting, sculpture or
architecture. It exists insofar as it vanishes, escapes, disappears.[8] Thus the
view from a car or a train moving at speed, or the speed of the cinematic
image, is an experience of perceiving through disappearance, in which
substance becomes contingency, and the scene obscene.

Death: Bads, Contingency, Theodicy

Any theory which understands modernity so integrally in terms of military
movements and violence must be bound up with a problematics of death.
Virilio's statements on death can be puzzling. He speaks of a 'death
machine' lurking behind 'technology'. He speaks, for example, not just of
the death of individuals, but the death of a city, intoning that 'a captured
city was an exterminated one' 'in its stones and in its flesh'. The juxtaposition of death and extermination are reminiscent of Baudrillard, who
counterposes the terms in *Symbolic Exchange and Death*. Here death is only
possible where there is the reversibility of the gift or the symbolic. When
economic exchange displaces symbolic exchange, the irreversibility of extermination replaces death. Virilio's death machine and extermination

would then spell the end of death and simultaneously the dissolution of excess. Now excess itself is no longer outside and in the general economy but incorporated into the mechanism of the restricted economy of total war. Virilio speaks of the gates of the ancient city[9] and paths from the gates through which citizens walked to bury their dead. This excess of death outside the city gates gave life and order to the rhythmic web of symbolic exchanges existing within. It also provided the mould for reversibility in the symbolic trace of the ancestors, through which memory and history returned to provide a substrate for the city's imaginary. In the city's destruction through generalized vectorization, death is incorporated into technology itself, its excess no longer providing an ungraspable 'real' constituting a positive horizon for the collective imaginary and symbolic. The era of the death machine is thus the era of the *'horizon négative'*.[10]

For ancients, 'metabolic speed', the speed of the living, was given a frame by this excess of death. 'Technological speed' of generalized vectorization is, however, 'the speed of death'.[11] Now metabolic speed is itself invested with death as technology, as we become 'metabolic vehicles' in the age of pure war. These hybrids, these monsters, incorporate death in the political economy as we calculatively work out a series of health regimens; as we obsess with our bodies in the attempt to control death, to subsume death under technology. Death on the outside of the city gates previously imparted sense and form to religious and philosophic activities, to the arts and to politics. Now entire sectors of our social and market economies are devoted to the technologization of death.

Virilio understands death as 'an interruption', an 'interruption of knowledge'. For the Greeks 'epilepsy' – as an interruption – meant 'little death' and 'picnolepsy' the frequent alteration of consciousness and unconsciousness. Interruptions such as sleep and dreams structure consciousness, as the outside structures the inside. Thus the temporality of interruptions structures the temporality of duration of consciousness. For the Greeks, 'the consciousness of death is the origin of consciousness'. We 'idealise and idolise consciousness because we are mortal'.[12] This is surely the point of not just Bergson but also Heidegger's *Being and Time*, in which the temporality of understanding, including projection, is moulded for us mortals, for us *Sterbenden*, by death itself, by death as the interruption existing outside of duration's temporality. In this sense time structures being. Time (as death) structures in particular the being of Dasein, in particular the being in the world, and the temporality (the duration) of being in the world of Dasein.

If the *conscience individuelle* is structure by interruption, all the more so for the *conscience collective*. Interruptions mean 'stopping', and thus interruptions like the Sabbath or the commemoration of Martin Luther King's death are stops, are full stops as punctuations in which we take off from the time of work life to partake of the nation's symbolic. Thus also in the geopolitics of the *âge classique*, interruptions in space like ramparts and chastity belts helped to constitute the normal temporality of the city. Virilio can then lament the abrogation of the death penalty as a further erasure of the collective imaginary. In the ancient city, the king was the chief strategist involved in integral social relations with death. Priests and warriors were 'dealers in death': the former dealing death, the latter interpreting it. In the polis, death as well as the material economy were constituting margins of the public sphere, making possible the space for existence of *le politique*, of *das Politische*. Politics is thus in the very best sense of the word 'an interpretation of death'.[13]

Necessity and substance are the stuff of life and duration in the same sense that accident and contingency are the stuff of the interruption and death. For Bergson, speaking of the human subject, we are the substance and the accident is death. Virilio thus understands 'the accident' under this general heading of death and the interruption. He addresses the object: 'We are not interested in the object, we are not conscious of the object unless we are interested in the object's accident', unless we are interested in 'the death of the object's substance'.[14] What Virilio is saying here is that the object only possesses substance, only possesses singularity, when its meaning is structured by death. Thus ramparts, walls, blockhouses, as well as ritual monuments, mausoleums, churches, graveyards, buildings of the state, are given meaning, given singularity and substance through the death (and its reversibility) that falls outside the frame of this web of objects. Death as contingency, death as accident, circumscribes these objects and their necessity, their substance and duration. In Aristotle's antiquity substance was necessity and accident was contingency. Yet as Kipling knew, 'the first victim of war is truth'. In the age of total war, technology contains its own accident: the ship the shipwreck, relativity theory the bomb. Now accident is part and parcel of substance. Death, contingency and accident are everywhere: they are the *identity* of the object.

The implications of this for the sociological understanding of risk and contingency are vast. The notion of reflexive modernization also involves reflection on the limits of reflexive monitoring of the self and of social processes. It involves reflexive monitoring and unintended consequences. The more we reflexively monitor the more a set of unintended consequences are produced. In 'second-order reflexivity', if we become *really* reflexive, then, as Max Weber instructed in his ethics of responsibility, we live with our finitude and accept the inevitability of these *Nebenfolgen*, of the risks of the risk society. Now Latour, for example, as we saw, will agree with this. His instructions are to break with dualisms comprised in the Faustian control of reflexive monitoring. He says that the unintended consequences of the former were in any event responsible for the wonderful array of innovations, in scientific facts, technologies and goods more generally, that have built the expanding and increasingly globalized actor-networks. He also instructs us to live with this hybridity.

Virilio, is attuned, however, to a radically disparate dimension of the risk society. Virilio is attuned to the risk society in a sense closer to classical sociological theory of Weber and the late Durkheim, in which theodicy, the cultural interpretation of suffering and especially death impart a symbolic order to lived social experience. Here again the outside – theodicy, contingency, the bad – structures the (social) symbolic and imaginary orders on the inside. Latour is the ultimate optimist, seeing reflexive monitoring, i.e. the dualism of modernity's constitution, as yielding a whole range of wonderful and innovative goods. Virilio, like Ulrich Beck, recognizes the centrality of the 'bads' as side-effects that modernity's constitution can produce. Yet Beck does proffer a strong dimension of goods in the era of reflexive modernity. Indeed, he holds out the optimistic possibility of surmounting the bads with societal reflexivity. Beck's societal reflexivity is not monitoring *per se* and is a sort of collective and informed reference of society to itself, through a process more resembling institutional bricolage than monitoring. Virilio, with his dimension of classicism and *Kulturpessimismus*, sees the whole set of affairs as comprising *bads*. Missiles, projectiles, catapults, shells and other dealers of death are paradigmatic for him of modernity's objects.

We noticed above that Latour ingeniously attributes the power of judgement to quasi-objects. So does Virilio in a darker scenario. As we saw in chapter 11, detective-machines now track the quasi-subjects: objects accuse subjects. Constituted themselves in metonymic displacements, objects can track the quasi-subjects. They lift them out, they dis-embed and re-embed them allegorically and bring them before the court of justice of the things. Modernity becomes the death machine. Risks and bads are not unintended consequences, but at the heart of technology. As death and contingency colonize the object, it loses singularity. It becomes a commodity. Goods in the risk society are bads by another name.

In antiquity, the bads of death structured the good, the good life inside the city gates. With the general colonization now of the inside by death and the bads, the good life is reduced to the utilitarianism of mere goods. These goods, these objects, intellectual property as goods, as empty algorithmically calculated goods, accumulate at an ever increasing rate in the 'chip sector' of post-industrial economies. This chip sector – comprising microprocessors, software, computers, multi-media, telecommunications and increasingly entertainment and a large portion of education – is one of the two main cutting edge sectors of the post-industrial economy. The other is what might be called the 'risk sector' – comprising biotechnology, genetic technology, hospitals, medicine, insurance, pharmaceuticals and increasingly chemicals, food processing and distribution, sport, leisure and tourism. Objects as calculated bads accumulate at an ever greater rate in the risk sector. At one time the most significant objects – monuments, memorials, churches, mausoleums, walls, ramparts, gates – were those that mediated between life and death. These paradigmatic objects were not inside the frame of symbolic exchange, the good life and the city. They were also not outside the frame, as were death, the bad and contingency. Instead, these mediating objects *were* the frame itself. They were the 'tain of the mirror'. These design and architectural objects were not representations like painting and sculpture. One side of them was surely symbolic, but the other eminently practical. In this sense the partly indeterminate judgement inside the gates of the city experienced infinity, death and the freedom of the outside through the dark glass of these objects. But they were not just, as some might think, in terms of Kant's third critique, only aesthetic objects. Indeterminate judgement, indeed reflexivity itself in Kant's sense, needs to work through these objects. These objects which we live in and by are the condition of reflexivity. Foremost among these objects is perhaps the mother as lost object, mediating between contingency and our organization as organisms, bodies and psyches. The mother as lost object, the generations and collective memory, are 'the real' that constitute this gateway. Even our reflexive recognition that death has entered the gateway does not relieve us of the responsibility of the impossible retrieval of this past, of this lost object.

From War to Cinema

At some point in the twentieth century power comes to operate no longer primarily through the 'war machine', but instead through the 'logistics of perception' of the *vision machine*. Now the battle field and material field of Newtonian time-space is replaced by the *perceptual field*. Whereas for Foucault technology is discursive and bound up with knowledge, for Virilio technology is bound up with the object: first the material object in the age of dromocracy and then the perceptual object in the age of 'dromoscopy'. This is still, indeed even more, an age of speed. But now the vectorization of movement cedes to a generalized optics. The vision machine is of a piece with today's digitized electromagnetic fields. Its basis, its model, is crucially the perceptual field. The perceptual field is always encountered, always experienced, not through the 'real interface' of the material field, but via a graphic interface. The perceptual field entails the de-realization of dromocracy, of the war machine. A logistics of the real yields to a logistics of perception.

The vision machine helps us to see what we otherwise would not see. It involves vision at a distance or 'tele-vision'. But perceptual fields are by no means always televisual fields. The new age of optics always involves perceptual fields. Vision machines are technologies in which we first focus on a perceptual field, but also see *through* – as through a window – a perceptual field. In this sense painting is not a vision machine and a painting is not a perceptual field in this sense of optics. You do not see through a painting. A painting is opaque and somehow material. The vision machine is always transparent, or what Virilio calls 'trans-apparent'. The first simple vision tools, the first simple or 'ocular' watching machines, came from the necessity of war: for example, watchtowers and the anchored balloon. But there was no perceptual field *per se* here and hence no vision machine. The original '*lignes de foi*' ('lines of faith' literally) for rifles were also ocular watching machines, but not yet vision machines because they operated in the material or real, not the perceptual field. The beginnings of the vision machine are instead in the 'geometrification of looking'.[15] In the camera the object was geometrically targeted through peep sights and then lenses. 'Objectivication' – and the lens in French is '*objectif*' – became the principle overriding faith and the 'interpretive subjectivity at play in the act of looking'. This was the geometrification of the gaze, the window out on to the real world through the perceptual field, 'the eye's function becoming a function – with the development of telescopic sights – of the weapon'.

Precursors of the vision machine include the stained glass church windows, and the perceptual fields opened up by the show windows, the *vitrines* of department stores in which commodities could be arranged. More prescient were the world fairs – precursors of today's holographic theme parks – whose spectacle involved such radical 'derealization'. War, for its part, was always unreal and irreal in its apocalyptic dimension, but it only became derealized in this spectacular sense (i.e. of transformation of material fields into perceptual fields) through the presence at a distance of the *son et lumière* of the trenches and shells of the First World War. Only then did the logistics of perception come to rival the Napoleonic logistics of movement[16] and the horizon of war emerge as enucleated in Bataille's specular sublime. The principle of war, however, became properly displaced by the optics of the perceptual field only with the emergence of cinema itself. This mechano-optical watching machine embodied no longer the 'passive optics' of Galileo's telescope, but instead the 'active optics of the synthetic image'. This was also a step further than the camera. Nièpce's camera – like the painting – produced a trace of one material object on another material object, i.e. a light-sensitive material, in his case paper coated with asphalt. Marey's chronophotography produced not matter but light, celluloid-filtered light. It thus transplanted the commodity system into 'immaterial fields of perception'.

The implications for time and memory are important. Cinema is like war in its technologization of memory, in its instrumentalist robbing of memory's substance. Memory is a '*science* for those who make war'. Memory now is no longer based on common experience, but becomes 'parallel memory, paramnesia'. Thus cinematic memory is a visual hallucination like dreaming: it is a 'luminous resurrection of the past'. This is forgetting technologized as memory, and is only accentuated later in digital memory. The image, the figure, is not, *pace* structuralism, a variation of the text or discourse. Indeed, the reverse is true. Printing is also the recording of images on ink-sensitive paper. Writing like photography is thus 'inserted' in time which is 'exposed rather then simply passing'. Writing like the photograph is just another form of printing, in which the 'means of communication slow down and retain the immediate, fixing it in an exposure time that escapes daily wear' and hence is 'taken as truth'.[17] Nièpce's camera obscura, his dark chamber, created a negative image on the asphalt-coated paper and needed an exposure time of eight hours. How different is the exposure time of the lens of the movie camera, at 18 or 24 frames per second, whose 'aesthetics of disappearance' dissolves belief in truth and substance.

The perceptual field, the logistics of perception, is right from the start not about objects, not even about images of objects, but always about radiation and mostly about light. Nièpce wrote to Daguerre that 'light acts chemically on bodies. It is absorbed, it combines with them and communicates new properties to them. In doing so it enhances the natural consistency of some bodies.' The first photographs on Daguerre's early nineteenth-century 'heliographic plate', then, were 'solar writings': important not in representing objects as images, but in revealing the writing of the sun. And Nièpce described his invention as the introduction of 'photosensitivity' 'to a world completely bathed in luminous fluid'. Further, the heliographic plate 'does not reveal assembled bodies . . . but lets itself be "impressed"; it capture signals transmitted by the alternation of light and shade'. This constituted a 'depreciation of solids whose contours are lost'. The beneficiary is the 'point of view', the perceptual field itself.[18] Thus even the earliest perceptual field was primarily a question of, first, the point of view of the viewer and, second, a question of 'signals' attached to radiation.

The perceptual field and the logistics of perception invariably involves emitted signals carrying information to a receiver and a 'point of view'. Like the photon's energy in the electromagnetic field, the early vision machine's perceptual field and its 'sun worship' spelt the 'eclipse' of 'objects and solid bodies' as the central subject of systems of representation by the 'plenitude of a certain energy'. The very architecture of early cinemas – the great palaces established by the German immigrant known in the USA as 'Roxy' – was a world of not objects, but darkness and light. Thus, Virilio writes, 'the auditorium plunged into artificial darkness', 'dissolving' the 'bodies' in it. The 'matter provided to cinema goers is light'. Cinema is a matter not of 'public images' but instead 'public lighting'.[19] This was already the undercutting of Galilean, Newtonian and Cartesian space, in which masses constitute moving points in time and space. Now the 'matter' for cinema goers becomes 'light', the object and its mass become energy.

This perceptual field is a 'clear field', destroying the previously existing aura, the singularity of the object. Benjamin wrote that 'photography prepares a salutary moment by which man and his surroundings become strangers to each other ... opening up the clear field where all intimacy yields to the clarification of details'. This is the precursor of the virtual age of digitization and high definition. Benjamin understood and Virilio notes, 'this clear field is the primary promotional field of both propaganda and marketing, of the technological syncretism within which the witness's least resistance to the phatic image is developed'. Documentary films have self-consciously constituted a trace or memory that is not just the history of an event but 'provides a cast of anonymous extras with whom one can identify and provokes a specific emotion in the viewer'. At issue are 'images of the *fatum*, of something done once an for all'. The 'induce a feeling of the irreparable and through a dialectical reaction foster a violent will to engage the future', a will undiminished 'by any apparent *mise-en-scène*, any aestheticizing discourse'.[20]

Thus photography and especially cinema are in the first instance de-stroyers of aura, destroyers of integral memory while creators of memory for what Virilio calls instrumental purposes. Photography and cinema are opposed to any aestheticizing discourse. Their triumph of light and point of view over the singularity of and intimacy with the object is at the same time the triumph of technology over *poiein*, of know-how over doing. There is none the less, Virilio notes, a sort of 'dialectical logic' to the mechanical vision machine. A logic which, unlike the formal logic of painting's auratic object, no longer works from the opposition and mutual exclusion of art and techne. This dialectical logic is that not just of technology. It entails a gaze that is a lot more than only geometrical, a point of view in excess of the merely transcendental subject and the geometry of the sun's radiation. It entails also a 'gaze of the West that was also the gaze of the ancient mariner, fleeing the non-refractive and non-directional surface of geometry for the open sea in the quest of unknown optical surfaces... [in quest] of an essentially singular world as the initial foundation of the formation of meaning'. The logistics of perception does not exclude *poiein*, but instead, as techne, carries *poeien* within it. Thus the 'sea's horizon', unlike the purely

negative horizon of techne, emerges as a 'poetic accident'. Once the enclosure of continental territory has broken down, and technology as death has
invaded the city, we must escape into maritime space: we must escape, we
must like 'Fortune, fleeing like a prostitute', escape the determinacy, the
reflexive monitoring of the now geometrical enclosure for the sea. The
same is true of the ship itself, in which 'the vessel inaugurates an instrumental structure which tested and then reproduced destiny's always far from
equilibrium, its eternal unpredictability. . . via man's capacities for reaction,
courage, imagination'. This is 'the unexplored side of the failure of technical knowledge, a poetics of wandering', in which 'the shipwreck did not
exist before the ship'.[21]

Thus is much more than an idea of reflexive monitoring and unintended
consequences. Here the unintended consequences, the 'failure', accident,
contingency, fortune, are built right into and integral to the geometry
of technology and reflexive monitoring. Accident, failure is poetic; is on
the side of art and imagination. We are already outside the logic of
Kantian time-space and thus of determinate and aesthetic judgement.
This is already the age of the perceptual field, of optics, of logistics, of
perception. And the rules to be broken through alternate logistics of
perception, through different modes of scanning and alternative rule-
finding, are also optical. Dialectics and struggle are displaced into the
perceptual field. At this point there is still a place for avant-gardes. Indeed,
the logic of the avant-garde can only come from this dialectical optics.
Thus Degas's nude effectively glossed the techne of the documentary.
Degas's nude was not for an audience but partook – like Manet, like Italian
neo-realist cinema – of documentary. Hence can be understood the im-
pressionists' – who exhibited in Nadar's studios – fascination with photography. But this was only characteristic of the early days of the vision
machine. With the advent of the fully fledged digital and electromagnetic
vision machine, 'the West's wings of desire, its sails, oars, a whole apparatus
of technical know-how . . . [increasingly] swamp the (heretofore) unpredictable rules of poetic accident'.[22] Virilio's instrumentality of the image has its
final triumph.

From the Mental to the Instrumental: the End of the Gaze

There is in recent decades a transformation of the perceptual field from a
regime of mechanical technology and direct light to an electromagnetic
field of digital technology and indirect light. This is at the same time a shift
from the '*image mentale*' to the '*image instrumentale*'. Here the point of view of
the subject is eroded in an objectification and instrumentalization of the

perceptual field. This was already emerging with the mechanical image whenever it took on the role of 'public image'. Thus the terror effect of physical and metaphoric light in the French Revolution, of Marat and the mania for denunciation, the mania for 'tracking down darkness', 'digging up the dead', with nothing left in the opacity of the sacred. This inquisitorial spirit of bringing to light continues with the mid-nineteenth-century emergence of a mass press 'of informers'. Indeed, Felix Nadar innovated aerial photography and electric-illuminated nocturnal photography in his work for the French secret service.[23] And investigative techniques were central to the institutionalization of the public image, in the photographic printing of the three great authorities – medicine, army and the police. In courts of law subjective evidence and the 'scenic effects' of great performing lawyers were on the decline in the face of objective or documentary proofs – in the fingerprint, the photo, and later video evidence and DNA. The human eye was no longer recognized as giving signs of recognition.[24]

Documentary films were themselves a party in this. Their precursors were Géricault and the Romantics' early nineteenth-century enthusiasm for '*l'art vivant*', for the pictorial spectacle of vividly detailed battle scenes and historic events in panorama. Similar was the effect of Daguerre's diorama, and rotundas, of whose great potential propaganda value Napoleon was aware. Thus can be understood the 'Medusa syndrome', in which the 'gorgon's eye' 'will dispose you, make you lose your own sight, and condemn you to immobility'. This is instantiated in the documentary films used especially in Britain after the First World War for propaganda and carried on in the mass observation of the interwar period. These efforts negated Hollywood's 'subjective cinema'. Their objective use of the camera 'breaks with an aesthetics of sensitive perception that still depended on the degree, nature and importance of the cinemagoer's past aesthetic experience, memory and imagination'.[25] The candid camera of documentary – without any *mise-en-scène* or any *prise de vue* – spelt the 'evaporation of visual subjectivity' into 'an ambient technical effect'. The documentary in its objectivity has no *mise-en-scène* from the producer side. There is no scene at all, but the accident of the ob-scène. There is no subjective point of view shot; that is, there is no *prise de vue*. There is instead the *surprise de vue* of the candid camera. The viewer also loses his or her point of view. The production comes from no horizon at all, more from a negative horizon, a negative imaginary. The publicity image, like the documentary, no longer has 'photography's memory of a more or less distant past, but instead a will to engage the future and not just represent the past'.[26]

Virilio writes: 'Il n'y a donc pas que l'obscure clarté des étoiles à venir du lointain passé de la nuit du temps, la faible clarté qui nous permet d'apprehendre le réel, de voir, de comprendre notre environnement présent provient elle-même d'une lointain mémoire visuelle sans laquelle il n'y aura pas d'acte du regard.'[27] The 'obscure clarity of the stars to come from the long-time past of time's night' is the obscure clarity of memory that permits us to apprehend the real. It is only this that allows us to see. Our understanding through vision of the present environment has its source in a long-time visual memory, without which there cannot be the act of the gaze. The shift to the objective and instrumental image, evaporating both subjectivity and visual memory, means also the destruction of the gaze.

Such is the 'virtual image' of the new vision machine. Unlike the material image of painting, where there is a man behind the brush, and unlike the still subjective and mental image of cinema, where there is a man behind the machine, now there is a machine behind the machine. Now the sender is literally a transmitter, a sending machine, and the receiver is a physical technological receiver. The vision machine – television and ''informatique' – operates through blindness, indeed through blinding: 'une population des objets est en train de vous dévisager'. The virtual image is instrumental in its means–ends rationality, in its collection of information of surveillance on individuals in what is not a graphic, or even any longer a photographic or cinematographic, but an 'infographic', society. Today's image is instrumental most of all because an instrument is producing the visions and an instrument is doing the seeing. Thus computers and other information machines – present in manufacturing industry in robotics – function not only in recognition of relevant signals, but also in analysis and interpretation. This is full automation of perception, in which instruments are using instruments, and instruments are receiving from instruments. This is full 'synthetic perception', the triumph of expert-systems.[28]

If the situated and graphic image was 'real' in its truth, in its temporal duration, the cinematographic and mental image is 'actual' in its fleetingness, a bit like the succession of appearances in phenomenology. The infographic and instrumental image is in contrast 'virtual', in its utter fabricatedness and in the active optics of instruments. Like the 'model' in Baudrillard's hyperreality, it is operational: created by the numerical imagery of technoscience. The instrumental and virtual image involves fully the 'prostheses of automated perception', a 'machinic imaginary' from which we are totally excluded. Unlike the old public space of intersubjectivity, of communication and reflection, the machinic imaginary is like a 'foreign interlocutor': now no communication is possible, as the dialogic public space of Parisian eighteenth-century cafes described in Richard Sennett's *Fall of Public Man* is replaced by the surveillance of the 'public image'. This comprises also a shift from classical 'formal logic' and modern dialectical logic of moving images to the 'paradoxical logic' of the virtual and instrumental image. In the formal logic of the image – in painting, sculpture and engraving, God is prime mover and the mode of truth is revelation. The principle of movement subsequently shifts to matter and science governs the mode of truth in dialectical logic. This is dialectical in two ways. First, in the above described retention in tension of both techne and poiein. But also in its partly reversible temporality: in its partial retention of past time, in deferred time (*temps différé*), in which 'the presence of past puts a durable impression on plates or film'.[29]

The virtual image is paradoxical in several ways. It is the logic of neither art nor science but of the more strictly instrumental 'technoscience'. Its mode of truth is neither revealed by God nor discovered by science. Instead there are no clear distinctions between true and false: indeed the distinction of true and false is no longer even problematized. Most paradoxically, however, an image that has the status of accident comes to dominate reality. Further, the high definition of this accidental image becomes more real than the real. The older polarity of the 'figurative' and the 'real' was based on a clear distinction between the two, in which the transference ('*transfert*') from real to figurative was intentional. This is true both in classical painting and in cinema and photography. Now, however, transfer is no longer from real to figurative, but from 'actual' to 'virtual'. The actual is fleeting, more difficult to pin down, has a weaker reality effect than the virtual. And the transfer from actual to real is not intentional but accidental. There is no *mise-en-scène*, there is no apparatus of *prise de vue* or shot but an apparatus of *surprise de vue* in, for example, time-lapse video, or Web site trading on futures markets. There is a quasi-fusion of the object with its equivalent image. This hegemony of the accidental image is also the dominance of tele-presence, the greater reality of presence at a distance. Unlike the *mise-en-scène* of painting or cinema, tele-presence entails not representation but presentation. There is no re-presentation, but far away events are registered through an '*accident de transfert*' which 'supplies their existence in the here and now'. The virtual image is the local hegemony of an accidental image recorded at a distance. This image picked up in real time dominates over viewers' mundane real space.[30]

Cinematic experience presumes the mobility and motility of the human eye. Here 'vision comes from far away, it is a sort of travelling, a perceptual activity which begins in a past to illuminate the present, to define the object of our immediate perception'. Human vision thus presupposes 'retinal persistence', a memory-centred mental persistence encompassing the entire nervous system. Human vision in the cinema presumes duration, the stepwise building of suspense. But what about *in*human vision? Inhuman vision is based not on the eye's mobility, but on light's movement of light, on light's finite speed. Time is no longer measured by Newtonian intervals of movement in space but via the frequency of light. Reality is traced by the path of light. Inhuman vision and television is based, as Hitchcock noted, on a temporality of not suspense, but 'surprise': cinematic 'extensive time' yields to the short attention span of tele-visual 'intensive time'. Intensive time is, as spatio-temporal categories are relativized, no longer time at all. It is instead speed, absolute speed. The intensive time of speed foregrounds the infinitely small duration. It discovers – 'outside the imaginary of exten-sive eternity' – 'the final figure of eternity', in the post-Einsteinian cosmol-ogy of absolute speed. Gone are the geometric optics' observables and non-observables, as light triumphs over matter. Exposure is no longer duration and extensivity: exposed instead is the 'intimacy of the object'. At issue is 'relative illumination', as 'the stamp of the absolute has shifted from matter to light . . . to light's finite speed'. What 'serves to see, to understand, to measure and therefore to conceive reality, is not so much light as its velocity'. Blindness is at the heart of the vision machine: the active optics of the video-computer functions like an 'electronic occipital cortex'. The delayed time of communications yields to the instantaneous emission and reception of 'non-communication'. If there is no difference between emis-sion and reception then distinction between real and figurative no longer makes sense. 'The horizon of sight is contaminated', and, as Baudelaire observed, 'intoxication is a number'.[31]

Polar Inertia: the Last Vehicle

The blindness at the heart of the vision machine is the blindness of 'polar inertia'. Previously, the passive optics of the telescope and cinema as technologies was supplemented by the active optics of the eye. Now the electromagnetic field's technology of active optics leaves space for only a passive optics of the human eye. Inertia becomes the 'primary horizon' of human activity: inertia cast not as infirmity but as progress. Polar inertia describes a transition from '*aménagement* [sorting, dividing up and provisioning] *du territoire*' to the 'control of the environment'. The real time of videoscopy now marginalizes both the real and time. Absolute speed displaces from centre-stage to the margins both time and space, both the real and the figural. This is because the real of real time is more real than the real. And the time of real time is faster than time. It is absolute *speed*. The eye in polar inertia comes from nowhere and goes nowhere in time, with the disappearance of memory. In space it stands still, losing mobility and motility, as movement is transferred to the absolute speed of the electromagnetic field. This real time of 'tele-action' – and agency is displaced into indirect light – takes over from the real space of im-mediate action. In tele-action the 'population of things' arrives without ever leaving. There is a shift from the limited arrival of the means of transport and communication to the generalized arrival of instantaneous telecommunications.

Virilio here is speaking from the point of view of both post-Einsteinian optics and cosmology, anticipated by Malevich among others in the arts. The 'interface of observation', he argues, in all modes of seeing gives things their 'objective existence'. Thus sunlight gives painting and photography and direct electric light gives objects in cinema an opacity, gives them a truth beneath their surfaces. But the 'indirect lighting of the radio-electric field (of electro-optical lighting) of fibre-optic cable' confers on the surface itself an objective existence as the opacity of truth is dissolved. At issue in the vision machine is a certain 'topography', or 'teletopography'. Now reality and the object consist under 'the intense lighting of videoscopy' only of '*minimal* surfaces'.[32] This minimal surface is on the one hand given an extraordinarily high intensity, and on the other rendered transparent. Here the 'space of a distance [in the cathode screen] transmutes itself, under our eyes, in this luminous energy, this power of illumination'. There is a history of the extension of this artificial transparency. For a long time it existed on the margins of society, in, for example, the mid-seventeenth-century lighting up of the city streets in Paris for reasons of security and commerce. Of a different order, however, are the spectacles of the fire of Rome, the pyrotechnical artifice of the Enlightenment. These resemble much more the indirect lighting of (not electric light but) electro-optics. This is the 'unveiling of a scene', the revelation of a transparency: a passage from the ordinary and direct light of 'public space' to the indirect and more than ordinary light of the 'public image'. In the light of public space the activity of the eye and the 'I' of the perceptual field are at centre-stage. The light of public image involves the eye's passivity. This 'more than ordinary light' of ancient and early modern times was already a 'commutation of sensible appearances': the 'spectacle of transparency, l'éclairement public', was crucial to culture, to the 'collective imaginary'.[33] I was one of a handful of Westerners (accidentally) to be in Leipzig in then East Germany in November 1989 on the night of the demonstration, march and candle lit vigil on the Stasi headquarters. This candle light was at the same time the light of revelation of the German national imaginary. It was the *unheimlich* moment of its disconcealment. It was a night of disconcealment and bringing into the open also of who was spying on whom, and the gross injustice of the system. But it may most of all have been disconcealment of the marchers themselves – the masses of Greens, of anarchists, of young marginals – but also of the national dimension of the eastern German repressed, chanting no longer 'Wir sind das Volk', but instead 'Wir sind ein Volk'. But this is not to diminish this moment of aesthetic apperception engraved on the national imaginary.

Today's numerical light is 'capable of piercing the shadows [*percer les tenèbres*] of the real, of being the vehicle via the most realist appearances of an unknown transparency, a synthetic illumination . . . comparable to fractal geometry'. These paths and their 'trans-appearance' signal a 'form-image': form that has no form, image of what has no image, figure – like in subatomic physics – of a dynamic emptiness. These paths of 'trans-appearance' and transparency transform time-space distanciation into immediacy. They are the transparency of an emptiness. These paths – that Virilio calls a '"path" without a path'[34] – can be understood, it seems to me, as interactive trajectories or path, a 'telebridge' between a growing number of surfaces, one in which all distances become relative places of projection. They are unlike the paths of Heidegger's *Holzwege* or Henri Lefebvre's urban paths. Both of the latter are primarily not visual, nor aural, but instead tactile, closer to the semiotic index. For Lefebvre these tactile paths operate on a more basic level than that of meaning, i.e. on the level of orientation. Dasein and human beings use meaning to orient themselves. But Lefebvre speaks of the orientation of spiders on paths. This is orientation without meaning. The 'signal' in semiotics, and often other indexes, also serves to orient without attaining the status of meaning (*Sinn, sens*). Pierre Bourdieu's habitus is also structured as a mode of orientation, prior to meaning. Here meaning is one very important mode of orientation, just as logical meaning is an important subset of meaning. That is, just as determinate judgement is an important subset of meaning. The point, however, is that the subject of Virilio's paths that have no path is not the habitus, or even the spider. The subject of the path is the absolute speed of light. And the consequences are not human orientation, but species *disorientation*. Further, Virilio's paths imply – as we shall see below – a very specific type of interactivity. At issue is neither time-space distanciation nor time-space compression but time-space destruction, time-space relativization, the increasing irrelevance of the time-space problematique in the electro-optical economy of speed.

This is the age of the 'last vehicle', a static, 'audio-visual vehicle'. In time-space compression, characteristic of the former age of movement, time intervals between departure and arrival progressively became smaller and smaller. Things and people begin to arrive sooner and sooner after they departed. Einstein spoke of the limited versus general theory of relativity, Bataille an *économie restreint* versus an *économie generalisé* and Bourdieu of fields which were either *restreints* or *generalisés*. Virilio for his part speaks of a limited arrival (*arrivée restreinte*) of human and material vehicles through our various ports: through our harbour-ports, train stations, through the motorway exits (*portes*) partly replacing the old city gates (*portes*), through airport gates (*portes*), through the doors (*portes*) of our houses and flats and offices. But now there is the *general arrival* of non-material things, including people (their images, their voices, their messages, their names and e-mail addresses, their Web sites), through our 'teleports'. This generalized arrival does away altogether with the interval between departure and arrival. There is no interval from gate to gate, from *porte* to *porte*. There is, in other words, in the age of polar inertia a generalized arrival without departure at all.[35] There is thus an instantaneous interface, unlike the time it takes to interface with things and people as they travel through a succession of gates, ports and doors. Thus war news travelled once for a month from a 'correspondent', by post from, say, Russia to a newspaper in California. Then transmission sped up; in the Vietnam War to more or less overnight. Finally, the Gulf War was transmitted in real time on TV. The same is true of reports of politicians' speeches. These are now often made on television in interviews, not reported by the news but taking place in real time on TV. Again, arrival of information without departure, as time-space space compression implodes upon itself. The generalized arrival means that everything can arrive from everywhere, as well as from past and future at the same time. Whereas the material vehicles of the former Newtonian dromocracy did the moving, now the audio-visual vehicles stay still and are moved to by the masses of non-material objects (and subjects). But the things that move to the inert vehicles are other audio-visual vehicles. All audio-visual vehicles are transmitters, all are receivers. All broadcast, all receive.

Transport for the last, audio-visual vehicle, is thus no longer transport at a distance but '*transport sur place*'. My transmitting teleport, my audio-visual habitacle, comes to yours in my broadcasts, my e-mail, without moving. This electronic *transport sur place* is simulated in leisure and amusement parks where on roller coasters and the increasing number of simulator rides – space ships, back to the future rides – we go somewhere without going anywhere. Polar inertia means the loss of activities to the hegemony of sensations. The turn of the twentieth century working-class 'theatre of physiological sensations' accompanied the loss of physical activities in increasingly cramped cities. The classic amusement parks – Coney Island, Blackpool, Chicago's Riverview – belonged to the age of the mass working class and 'dromocracy'. You actually moved on rides. Today's amusement parks replace physical activities by mental and imaginary sensations: they replace point of view by a certain *perte de vue* (loss of view).[36] What remains is only optical illusion. The older 'Fordist' amusement parks were in or close to proletarian city centres or holiday resorts. The new amusement parks are past the suburbs into the 'ex-urbs'. They are themed: they are also owned by the studios. Thus Universal has City, and Disney Studios is the symbolic basis of Disney World. Thus the take-over by Time-Warner of the massive American Six Flags. Now increasingly the simulated rides and studio pervaded rides. You experience the magic of the studio no longer merely through the flat interface of the cathode screen, but through virtual reality, through the holographic experience of the studio amusement park. If the themed heritage industry and 1950s rock 'n' roll cafes brings the past live back to you, the studio amusement park brings the future back to you. The shift from dromocracy to polar inertia is ever more pervasive. You don't go to the cinema: the cinema comes to you. In the polar inertia of audio-visual habitacles, omniscient, seeing not just everywhere in space at great distances, but also God-like into the past and future. The past, present and future in which Newtonian time-space circumscribed our action is no longer with us. The past and the future (and not only objects at a distance) are with us here and now in real time.

What sort of architecture, what sort of 'architectonic', does this entail? Virilio here makes use of the French-language distinction between *immeuble* and *meubles*. *Immeuble* means fixed property in buildings, and also literally means unmovable. *Meubles* means furniture, but also movables. Thus where previously the automobile was a vehicle of transport along distances, the car of polar inertia functions more in *transport sur place*. The car becomes a '*pièce détaché*' of the *immeuble*, of your house, of your habitacle, as a much smaller proportion of your incoming and outgoing traffic takes place through its usage. Further, the car (a motorized *meuble*) itself comes to resemble more and more your house, your *immeuble*, with its telephone, its CD player reduplicated from the home. The motorcar is such a slow means of transport that drivers must resort to other means of communication while driving. The car becomes increasingly an audio-visual vehicle and becomes attached as one of the home's many teleports. Now the speed of the automobile, indeed automobility in all its forms – terrestrial, maritime and air – transforms the architecture of the city, while audio-visual speed (with the disappearance of the architectonic) only transforms the 'interior architecture' of the intelligent home, the smart building.[37]

Virilio obsesses about the chair, paradigmatic as piece of furniture or *meuble*. The doubly movable *meuble*, the wheelchair, was introduced in 1820, followed by the self-moving chair, the '*meuble qui se meut*', the automobile, the early prototypes of which were like children's cars. They and the electronic wheelchair were effectively prostheses for the motor handicapped (*infirme-moteur*). The prototype for the chair in the audio-visual regime was the cinema itself. This was the 'emancipation of the chair'. And Hitchcock said, 'Cinema is first of all some armchairs with people in.' Now, however, the chair is increasingly the focus of a cockpit, a habitacle such as the video cabins in pornography shops. Now air and vision converge in the weightlessness (leaving behind the mass, space and time of Newtonian cosmology) of the pilot, the astronaut, and also of the satellite, film frame, photogram and videogram. The ideal-type of last vehicle functions in a weightless *transport sur place*. *Transport sur place*, contends Virilio, involves not

movement through territory, but instead control of the environment. Thus
the first idea of flight for aeroplanes was not to go from A to B, indeed
not to go anywhere but up in the air. And Marey, the inventor of
chronophotography in 1884, was also president of France's Société de
Navigation Aerienne. The 'conquest of an incomparable spectacle' captures the feeling reported by NASA astronauts of omniscience. The idea, of
course, is not just omniscience but control. God is both all-seeing and all-
powerful. Even television in its infant invention of the iconoscope was not
intended for mass communications or indeed for communications at all. It
was meant literally to augment the scope of vision. Thus also the idea of a
camera on a rocket to observe the universe.[38]

The habitacle, the weightless teleport in the age of general arrival
without departure, gives us powers of surveillance. The habitacle as interface is a variety of glass window or *vitrine*, a '*vitrine électronique*'. This *vitrine* is,
however, more than a cathode screen, more than a flat interface, but also
a shop window, comparable to the shop windows behind which Amster-
dam prostitutes flaunt their wares.[39] These habitacles for Virilio are not at
all about communication or any possible dialogics. They are about *observation* – even communications in electronic text serve the function of observation. Observation and omniscience of past, present and future and the
ability to have immediate view of all other habitacles, all other broadcast-
ing/reception sites in all places and times. If we can see all the other shop
windows, they too can see us. They too can bring us at the speed of
light down the pipes instantaneously into their habitacles. We are not
only omniscient subjects, we are the transparent horizon of the *surveillés*,
the objects, blasted through in our shop windows to the others. This is
the triumph of total spatio-temporal transparency, of the transparency of
the horizon. Even more than the shop window encased prostitute, would
not the ideal typical habitacle be the glass encased cube? Would it not be
the glass cube displaying Jeff Koons's basketball in the Cologne Kunsthalle
or even better Damien Hirst's dead sheep? The habitacle is the glass case
and we are the residing object, the prostitute, Koons's basketball, Hirst's
sheep's head in its glass-cased tomb. We are the last vehicle in the age of
polar inertia.

Time of Exposure

In Virilio's modernity a logic of time displaces a logic of space as *strategy*
displaces politics. Now initially 'strategy' is a question of movement, of
mobilization, of recruitment of human and non-human resources as
quickly as possible. Subsequently what emerges is that strategy becomes
less how fast you can move people and things but how far – as war is

transformed into cinema – you can see the enemy. Thus observation becomes the stake in strategies. This said, with the decline of the arms race and the rise of the *feindlose Staat,* observation as strategy takes a new twist.[40] Now the stakes are often economic profits, and what observation into the past and future as well as of distant places will give is information. Most important for Virilio is the contemporary drive to omniscience – to perfect knowledge of past and future, and everywhere – as the Faustian aim in the age of the vision machine. If, in modernity, power worked through getting as far as possible faster, in the new dromoscopic era power operates through having the most information. The vision machine is the omniscience machine.

Observation in this context is fundamentally a question of light, a question of how light exposes. And what light exposes. Hence Virilio writes that no longer do we have a 'time of chronology and history' but a 'time of *exposure*', a 'time which exposes itself to the absolute speed of light'. When exposure depended on direct light in cinema and photography, observation of distances and times was increased but still very limited. Only when the time that is doing the exposing is the absolute speed of light do we have the most incredible time-space increase in observation. Indeed, with the speed of light now perceived as the cosmological horizon, time itself is relativized as it is exposed to speed, to the speed of light. It is speed, or light as speed, that becomes 'revelatory' 'in the photographic [and not just the photographic] sense of the term'.[41] And Einstein's theory proposed the relativization of time, space and mass, in the context of the universality of the speed of light. Einstein's idea was that velocity (hence time and space) was relative to the observer, and thus seems in the first instance to be a 'standpoint epistemology'. Only this was not true for the velocity of light, which is the same in all reference frames. In this sense 'space-time must instead be space-speed which relativises duration and the expanse of material to the sole benefit of light'.

For Virilio it is not just light but time that is at work in exposure. Thus time as movement of masses at one point in travel operates to expose as we see more and more distant places through trains, cars, boats and planes. Time in photographs exposes the past. But it is time as the speed of electromagnetic waves that totally revolutionizes exposure, and makes the transparency of polar inertia possible. 'Time no longer – as in Kant – passes', Virilio says, 'time exposes'. It instantaneously, and not over a period of time, exposes great distances and the past and the future, like the 'divine gaze' of 'ubiquity and simultaneity where the past, present and future are co-present in a unique perception'. Already in the cinematic age time begins to function, no longer through passing, but instead through exposing. The past–present–future of time passing changes register into the real time and delayed time of exposure. Cinema and photography expose in delayed time. The speed of light, the photon, exposes in real time. Speed is light. Absolute speed is the speed of light. At the heart of this is the 'photonic mise au point (exposure)' of the sub-atomic physical world'. Not the light of solar time but 'the absolute speed of the photon, the action quantum of light – and the intensity of light – is the standard and ultimate limit of the perceived world'.[42]

Einstein's work was in optics, a branch of physics in which he found that classical mechanics' explanations were no longer adequate. Classical optics dealt with waves as the means of the transmission of energy. Such energy could be transmitted from one body to another and absorbed either by vibration of a material medium such as in water and sound waves, or by variation in the intensity of field vectors in an electromagnetic field in the case of electromagnetic waves such as light. Sound waves are longitudinal waves travelling through a material medium by forcing the molecules of the medium apart and together. And light waves are transverse waves which displace not a material medium, but field intensity vectors at right angles to the direction of the waves. Light waves are just one type of electromagnetic wave: others are, for example, radio waves, X-rays and gamma rays. Light is just one of a number of frequency bands of electromagnetic radiation. At issue is the study of electromagnetism, i.e. the physical nature of waves in electromagnetic fields. The velocity or speed of an electromagnetic wave depends on its wavelength and its frequency. Subsequently, physics and optics began to focus not so much on waves but on elementary particles, such as the photon, electron and neutrino. But these elementary particles, including the photon, do, when in motion, have wave properties.

In classical physics energy was primarily a wave phenomenon. But quantum theory discovered the emission and absorption of energy in tiny discrete amounts. One bundle of such energy is known as a quantum. These bundles of energy behave like matter but spread out more. The unit of analysis here is the atom, which gives off light or other radiation (i.e. energy) in particular frequencies, these frequencies corresponding to the definite energies of the quanta, e.g. photons. The electrons of a given atom have only certain allowed energy levels. The wavelike properties of the motion of the electrons explain their energy levels. When an electron changes from one level to another, quanta of energy are released. In this context Newtonian physics works fine, but only for large-scale systems and at reasonably slow velocities. At issue, however, in contemporary telecommunications and microelectronics are small-scale systems and very fast speeds.

Time as the speed of light, then, exposes not just information but also the habitacle, exposes the glass cage (compare Weber's iron cage). How do electromagnetic waves do this? In radar, for example, radio waves expose the nature of remote objects. Emitted scanning radio waves from a source reflect off the surface of the object and transmit pulses of electromagnetic waves that are picked up by a receiver. These are then processed electronically and converted to visible form on a screen by a cathode ray tube. Radar units use microwave frequencies mostly above 100 megahertz (million cycles per second). Radio itself transmits and receives electromagnetic radiation in the radio frequency range, at the speed of radio waves, i.e. their wavelength times their frequency. James Clerk Maxwell developed in the nineteenth century the mathematical theory of radio waves. Heinrich Hertz devised the apparatus for generating and detecting them. John Ambrose Fleming designed the vacuum electron tube, which can detect electromagnetic waves and electronically convert them to sound. In radio, of course, sound waves must be converted into electromagnetic waves – as in the telephone the electric current varies in accordance with sound waves – before broadcast. Subsequently, the vacuum tube and cathode ray tube were replaced by microelectronic devices: transistors and then semiconductors. But these electromagnetic waves are not themselves this – voice, text, image, moving image, holographic – information. Radio waves are information-bearing signals, but the information itself is carried in sidebands added to the carrier wave.

What is involved in this shift to the new time of exposure and the optics of the signal is the hegemony of observation. That is, the shift from delayed time to real time spells the end of representation and communication in the interests of environmental control through observation. Classic optics with its delayed time, with its 'interval', makes possible '*communication*', while electro-optics, in which interval cedes to interface, gives primacy instead to '*commutation*': commutation of distance and the time interval.[43] For there to be communication, notes Virilio, there must be an interval between sender and receiver. The sender must emit his or her speech act, the receiver must accept or reject, the sender must develop arguments for the receiver to accept the speech acts. All this takes time. It takes a certain distancing. But with the commutation of interval and distance, the sending is at the same time receiving. There is no time to accept or reject. The speech acts are not discursively justified. They are violently imposed. The replacement of interval by the immediacy of interface entails the erosion of communication by observation, the erosion of dialogue to the benefit of control over the environment. And the other habitacles under our observation come increasingly to comprise this environment under our control. On this model interactivity is not communication. It is mutual exposure. Mutual exposure of glass cages. Like aesthetic representation, speech-acts and communications represent, re-present ideas or intentions. But with commutation of distance and interval, with the shift from representation to the real time of signal and interface, there is not narrative, not representation, but *presentation*, the presentation of self through the glass (not iron) cage.

If Weber's iron cage was the representation of bureaucracy, today's Goffmanesque *glass* cage is the presentation of commerce. To present self is to sell self. And this presentation is of the highest definition. Now the conversion of signals, of information-bearing electromagnetic waves, into images is through semiconductors and is at the same time the numeration of the image, its calculation pixel by pixel. Definition is no longer dependent on purity of lens but on the speed of calculation of the linked computer.

This book has largely been about the ground, not so much the groundlessness of the other modernity's groundless ground. Virilio imagines this partially via the history of physics. The centre of the earth, the mother, the generations, was the ground of meaning for the ancients. But this ground in the Copernican revolution became just another body, i.e. became relativised. It is the spatio-temporal interval that becomes the new ground in the age of movement. This is the age of masses, distances and velocity. What phenomenology did was to put into question these Kantian–Newtonian assumptions of cause, identity etc., to put into question the unknowability of things themselves. Now the ego becomes a ground, in a vastly different way for meaning. This again was found to be unsatisfactory and the ego to be not a transcendental ground but instead an accidentally singularized body, suspended in the temporality of duration, the temporality of a life-world. If the ego is no longer a ground but now a body, the life-world duration and experience (*Erfahrung*) become the ground. But even this Bergsonian or Heideggerian time as ground, itself is relativized as a body in the age of speed. Such a time of duration and being-unto-death is a body in the context of another ground. This ground itself may be an absolute singularity of the accident of accidents, the birth of time and the centre, the ground now moving to the 'time zero' of cosmology. This is the horizon for the shift from corporeal activity to the real time of interactivity, to the interactive trajectory, the *trajet* without *trajet*, the path without path of absolute speed.[44]

The Symbolic in Fragments: Walter Benjamin's Talking Things

Walter Benjamin takes the theory of the object into a wholly different register from Latour and Virilio. He takes the notion of the object into another dimension. This is partly, we shall see, because he takes language very very seriously. Further, Latour and Virilio – like so many of us, ensconced in the fast-capitalist networks of the global information culture – pay scant attention to the past: they reflect very little on memory. Benjamin's eyes are always fixed firmly on the past. Let us reflect on Benjamin as we begin to bring this book to a close. First, we will find him acutely aware of the aporia, of the irresolvable tension in modernity, between the first modernity's 'instrumentality' and the other modernity's 'finality'. For Kant, as we saw in chapter 9, things could be grasped objectively, as in the first critique, through the logical categories, as instrumentalities, or they could be encountered, as in the third critique (on the lines of aesthetic experience), through judgement as finalities. For Benjamin the object may possess the quality of 'aura'. Benjamin's idea of aura, we will see, is firmly in the tracks of Kant's idea of finality.

   The first part of this chapter addresses the auratic object, the object as finality in Benjamin. The particular object that Benjamin addresses in this context is language. Here we will explore the dimensions of the other modernity's ground, in a detailed analysis of the linguistic experience of Benajmin's 'storyteller'. We will further explore this in his essays and writings on the theory of language, which counterpose the instrumental use of language against language as a finality possessing its end inside itself as its aura, as its 'magic'. Yet Benjamin is well aware of the dissolution of aura, of the explosion of the aporetic difference between instrumentality and finality, in the much more general indifference of contemporary cultural experience. In this sense Benjamin was prescient. Benjamin discusses this indifference in the '*Chokerlebnis*', the chronic, sped-up, disorienting, jolting experience of the assembly line and the media. Yet this wasteland of indifference is already the setting for Benjamin's book on German tragic drama and his reflections on Baudelaire's Paris. Now the objects are no longer language: they are urban ruins, arcades, disused commodities, the figures of the city. And the subjectivity experiencing these objects is the melancholic. This will be the focus of the second part of the chapter. Here we will focus on Benjamin's melancholic in the midst of the jolting experiences of the rapid succession of objects in the wasteland of technological culture.[1] We will see how the melancholic, through the language, through the gaze of these very objects, can, at the same time, allegorically, retrieve memory and redeem aura.

Aura

Craftsmen and Fairy Tales: the Ground

Walter Benjamin gives us a strong theory of the ground. This is predominant in the Romanticist phase that constitutes his early work and resurfaces in his late classic essay 'The storyteller'. The paradigmatic later work *The Origins of German Tragic Drama*, the work on Baudelaire, the arcades and nineteenth-century Paris, the essays on surrealism and photography and even the 'Theses on the philosophy of history' underscore the groundlessness of the ground. But 'The storyteller' develops all the elements for a theory of the ground. Let me address these themes in the order that Benjamin introduces them in 'Der Erzähler'.

Benjamin opens this rich essay by addressing the communicability of experience: the 'ability to exchange experiences'. The disappearance of the storyteller has taken this, 'the securest among our possessions', from us. We have encountered in discussions of phenomenology above the idea of experience, in particular counterposing *Erlebnis* and *Erfahrung*. The experience of Benjamin's storyteller is in the register of *Erfahrung*. Benjamin uses the word experience repeatedly in the first few pages of 'The storyteller'. He speaks of 'the ability to exchange experiences'. He notes that 'experience has fallen in value': that we are 'poorer in communicable experience'. He observes that the flood of books after the First World War partook not at all of 'the experience that goes from mouth to mouth'; that 'strategic experience, economic experience, bodily experience and moral experience has been annulled by tactical and mechanical warfare, by inflation and by political power'. What does he mean here by experience? This 'experience [*Erfahrung*] that is passed from mouth to mouth'?[2]

In each case here the German word for experience is not *Erlebnis* but *Erfahrung*. Gerhard Schulze, in his influential *The Experience Society*,[3] characterizes contemporary society not by risk or post-industrialism, but as being the society of immediate experience, of immediate and subjective experience. This is *Erlebnis*. *Erfahrung*, on the other hand, is a kind of experience that is neither subjective nor immediate, and in both of these senses grounded. What is at issue is *Erfahrung*. The fullness of *Erfahrung*. The experience that the storyteller passes from mouth to mouth as well as the past experience of the storyteller himself is a matter of *Erfahrung*. Indeed, the experience that is passed and the experience that the storyteller has, i.e. the way in which he experiences, are inseparable. If we analytically separate them *Erfahrung* loses its richness, loses its plenitude.

In contrast to the *Erfahrung* of the storyteller stands, for Benjamin, the *Erlebnis* of the novel and of information, of information that appears in the newspapers. *Erfahrung* for Benjamin is intersubjective and 'comes from afar'. Its intersubjectivity is dialogic in a very important sense, one that is vastly different (indeed counterposed) to Habermas's idea of intersubjectivity. It is also seriously embedded. Seriously situated. It is situated in a sense that cannot facilely be disembedded and re-embedded. In this chapter we shall speak of two Walter Benjamins: the Benjamin of romantic *Sprachphilosophie* and 'The storyteller', whose regulative concept is 'aura'; and the Benjamin of *German Tragic Drama* and Baudelaire's Paris, whose regulative concept is 'allegory'. Benjaminian *allegory*, we shall see, possesses a very important, albeit aesthetic, dimension of disembedding and re-embedding. But this is not possible in *aura*, in which artefacts, fragments and other objects are situated in a way that cannot become disembedded. With disembedding and re-embedding – of baroque and modern allegory – the plenitude of experience is necessarily lost. But when Benjamin speaks of the economic, strategic, moral and bodily experience that we are deprived of with the retreat of the storyteller, he is also talking of the de-situating of experience, so that *Erfahrung* becomes *Erlebnis*.[4]

Communicable experience, via the storyteller, must 'come from afar'. Unlike the dis- and re-embedding of contemporary time-space distantiation, which seems to possess a certain surgical cleanliness, the movement of coming from afar must leave its tracks, its path. Unlike 'information' which can disembed and re-embed, 'it does not aim to convey the pure essence of the thing'. 'Instead it sinks the thing into the life of the storyteller.' Instead 'the traces of the storyteller cling to the story'. This is an 'artisan [*handwerk*] form of communication' and the traces cling 'the way the hand prints of a potter cling to the clay vessel'. The storyteller's 'tracks are frequently evident in his narratives'.[5] Unlike the novel, which is separable from the novelist, the story (*Erzählung*) is not separable from the story teller. There is none of the neatness here of leaving one bed and moving to another. It is instead a matter of dragging the bed along behind. That is what the storyteller does. The two archaic – literally archaic in the sense of pre-ancient – types of the storyteller are the 'trading seaman' who comes from afar in space, and 'the resident tiller' who comes from afar in time, who is local yet deeply rooted in the past. If this 'peasant and seaman were the master class of story telling', Benjamin notes, the 'artisan class was its university [*höhe Schule*]'. The trade structure of the Middle Ages thus comprised on the one hand he who comes from afar, the travelling journey-man, and he who is master of the past, 'the resident master craftsman', under the same roof, both imparting the craft of storytelling to their apprentice.[6]

This coming from afar of communicable experience contrasts with the immediacy of experience of the 'novel' and in 'information'. Benjamin contrasts the novel and information to storytelling as 'forms of communication'. Information and the capitalist press – and this is valid for today's information society – confront storytelling in an even 'more menacing' way than the novel. Indeed, they bring about a crisis even in the novel. Information is no longer 'intelligence', no longer experience from afar. Benjamin evokes *Le Figaro*'s report of an attic fire in Quartier Latin, in which information 'supplies a handle for what is nearest'. The authority of information is vastly different from that of the story. The authority of information comes in its 'prompt verifiability'. It must 'sound plausible'. News, notes Benjamin, always comes 'already being shot through with explanation'. I think most of today's information society information comes already shot through with explanation. This is at the same time the impoverishment of storytelling and stories. A 'story if reproduced' 'must be kept free of explanation'.[7] Information might well be 'democratic', yet it still in a very important sense is monologic, and will not pass much further in time and space.[8] The story which cannot be explained, but only interpreted, lasts a lot longer than yesterday's papers, and 'achieves an amplitude that information lacks'. 'The value of information does not survive the moment in which it was new.' Information must surrender to the moment completely 'and explain itself without losing any time'. For its part, 'the story does not expend itself. It preserves and concentrates its strength and is capable of releasing it even after a long time.'[9]

The story obtains its validity elsewhere: its distantiated origins give it a certain authority. Coming from afar gives it authority, partly via the legitimacy of tradition, of repetition, of recounting. And 'der Erzähler', literally 'the recounter', is the literal German here which does not have story, *Geschichte*, in its root. But this legitimacy, this validity or authority, goes beyond tradition and resides in a more fundamental sense in the 'aura of the storyteller'.[10] Here aura has a religious or symbolic dimension that is more fundamental than tradition and is integrally connected with death. The story gains in authority through death. Thus Benjamin recalls the mediaeval pictures 'in which the deathbed is turned into a throne towards which people press through the wide open doors of the death house'. Death, he notes, was then not hidden away: indeed, every room of every house bore traces of the dying. And the communication of the dying man's wisdom, his experience, his stories, only 'assumes transmissible form at the moment of his death'.[11] Even the 'poorest wretch' dying has this authority; that is, 'the source of his story'. The living storyteller, coming from afar, 'borrows his authority from death'. His story, punctuated by a series of deaths, 'refers back' to what Benjamin understands to be a 'natural history'.[12] In this natural history, rooted in the temporality of the generations, death and time itself are reversible, and the dead are at the same time with us.

This 'natural history' and its aura are also somehow 'earthly' and 'maternal'. They are 'created'. Thus 'the righteous man' – and 'the righteous man encounters himself in the storyteller'[13] – 'is the advocate for created things at the same time that he is their highest embodiment'. He 'has the maternal touch which is occasionally intensified into the mythical'. At issue here is 'creation', 'a bridge established between this world and the other'. The 'righteous man' in the stories of Leskov, Benjamin's archetypal storyteller, 'is an earthly powerful maternal male figure', who like 'the whole created world' speaks 'not so much with the human voice', as 'with the voice of nature'.[14] What Benjamin is indicating here is that the story, and storyteller – who is a righteous man – receives authority from the generations, from a sort of symbolic politics of the earth, of 'the mother', the maternal. Aura here is a matter of the symbolic itself. In the 'Work of art in the age of mechanical reproduction', Benjamin does indeed speak of aura in terms of authenticity. But authenticity here was a matter of neither existential meaning nor the originality of the 'auteur', but instead simple non-reproducibility. And the uniqueness at issue is again not aesthetic originality, but a quality 'inseparable from being imbedded in the fabric of tradition'.[15] It is tradition (and not high modernist originality) that is inseparable from and necessary for aura. The authority of the story is derived from death as situated in a natural history of maternal and earthly creation. The authority of the storyteller leads back not to a lost object or lack, but to the plenitude of the object, the plenitude as well of the symbolic.

The novelist, in contrast, 'warms' the reader's 'shivering life with a death he reads about'.[16] What could be more opposite to the hearer of the storyteller, who is guided by the 'counsel' of the storyteller. The story-hearer's life is not shivering to begin with, it is much sturdier, though still in need of 'counsel'. But the novel, which though not auratic is still singular, cannot provide counsel. It is the death read about in the novel that takes the place of such counsel. The novel does not provide orientation to the reader (as the story does to the hearer): it can do no better than to provide solace or warmth. How does this death provide warmth? The 'novel gives evidence to the profound perplexity of the living'. The novelist is 'isolated'. He is 'uncounselled'. The novel's characters and readers are similarly 'devoid of counsel', do not contain 'the slightest scintilla of wisdom'. The novelist does not speak from his experience, from his situation. He is isolated. What the novelist writes is 'incommensurable' with regard to the representation of human life.[17] The storyteller works from his experience to the listener's experience. The novelist and reader do not communicate experience, and are not situated in their own experience. Both reader and writer are lifted out from their experience.

If the story give counsel through the communication of experience, the novel centres on 'the meaning of life'. The story-hearer, organically connected craftsmanlike to his experience, is not concerned about the meaning of life. The story-hearer cannot get and surely does not want that sort of distance on life. This quest of the perplexed and uncertain novel reader to devour the novel voraciously in his quest for the meaning of life is only possible, as Georg Lukács noted, when meaning and life are counterposed to one another, when meaning as 'essential' and life as 'temporal' become separated.[18] Death in the novel lets the reader intuitively grasp the meaning of life, in that death is the end of temporality. In its closure (as in classic narrative), death imparts to the reader the meaning of life when the novel ends or the character dies. Thus the novel imparts meaning through death as closure, while the story imparts meaning through death as continuity. The novel imparts meaning through death as 'finis', as irreversible time. The story imparts meaning through death as eminently reversible time: indeed, through the reversible time of history.

The story works from a number of deaths, the novel from a single death. Both story and novel emerge, Benjamin observes, from the epic. The epic, which unlike the novel is quite integrally historical, comprises a very strong dimension of memory. Indeed, 'memory is the epic faculty par excellence'. Memory for the epic 'absorbs the course of events . . . and with the passing of these makes peace with the power of death'.[19] In the novel and the story, the two elements of epic memory are differentiated. In the story memory becomes 'reminiscence', and in the novel 'remembrance'. Reminiscences are short lived, while remembrance is 'perpetuating'. Remembrance is 'dedicated to one hero, one odyssey', while reminiscence is dedicated to 'many diffuse occurrences'. Through reminiscence the story hearer receives counsel in the 'moral of the story'. The single remembrance in the novel imparts to the reader not the moral of the story but the meaning of life. This becomes available only through remembrance, i.e. when, 'the subject' has 'insight' into the 'unity of his entire life . . . out of the past lifestream which is compressed in memory'. This unity of remembrance is the experience of death (as irreversible finality). The reader must read the novel in terms of the already known death of the protagonist. This is vastly different from real life. But only then can the reader grasp the meaning of life from the novel. The reader most of all shares the experience of death (as finality) with the characters. 'How the characters make him understand that death is already waiting for them ... is the question that feeds the reader's consuming interest in the events of the novel'.[20]

The novel, Lukács said, is the form 'of transcendental homelessness', and 'time' can only be 'constitutive' in this context.[21] That is, only in a situation of transcendental homelessness can time – in the sense of death as finality – become constitutive of the meaning of life. Heidegger's notion of time and death thus becomes no longer a philosophical universal, but a sociological characteristic of modernity. That is, time is the transcendental horizon of subjectivity, and of being, only in modernity. What time is to the novel history is to the story and storyteller. Time is integral to a quintessentially modern episteme. Time as irreversible, as abstracted from practices, as abstracted from history and tradition, would be thinkable only as a topic in modernity's aporia, in modernity's perplexity. Newton's homogeneous space-time is then of a piece with the temporality in which death constitutes duration in the novelistic time of Bergson, Proust and Heidegger.

What mode of temporality does modernity's time disrupt? What was the mode of temporality for Benjamin's storyteller? Being here would appear not in time, not in a being unto death, but in the very unapocalyptic rhythms of history. Being would appear in tradition. The storyteller and the craftsman share this temporality. The storyteller, like the righteous steady craftsman, is not an ascetic 'but a simple active man', not a holy man, mostly a secular man, his the 'sturdy nature' of the craftsman.[22] His rhythms are slow, not apocalyptic, more traditional than charismatic. The storyteller works not through the strong intentionality of the novelist, but through the habitus and through habit. To listen to a story requires not the vigilant reflexive monitoring of late-modern self-identity, but 'a state of relaxation'. It requires not the alterness necessary in an age in which what is solid melts into air, but 'a state of relaxation', indeed 'a state of boredom as the apogee of mental relaxation'. Such relaxation is only possible in 'the listener's self-forgetfulness' that arises 'when the rhythm of work has seized him'. Only then 'does the gift of retelling come to him all by itself'. This is the 'web', the web – 'now becoming unravelled at all its ends' – connecting listener-tellers in which 'the gift of storytelling is cradled'.[23] This is the slow and repetitive temporality of the story. It works only through being repeated. The temporality of the *Erzählung* is also that of the crafts. The novelist is an artist, writing against the imminent temporality of his death. He has no time. The craftsman has lots of time. The craftsman is not creating something like the artist/novelist. He works not creatively but as a natural being imitating other things of nature. He does not create but lets things of nature achieve their own perfection. He does not, like the novelist, write against death. He works in an eternal time, so he has plenty of time. He does not the novelist's worries about closure, but instead partakes in 'a patient process' in 'which a series of thin, transparent layers are placed one on top of the others' – 'a patient process of nature', a 'product of sustained, sacrificing effort' typical of an age 'when time did not matter'.

The storyteller's assumptions of eternity are but a more secular version of those of 'the chronicler'. The storyteller partakes of not the novel, but the epic, and 'historiography constitutes the common ground of all forms of the epic', though none more surely than the chronicle. The chronicler is the mediaeval precursor of the historian. But the historian is enclosed in modern bounded time and hence is chained to the logic of explanation. The chronicler, for his part, narrating from a 'divine' and 'inscrutable' 'plan of salvation', does not need to explain events but only to interpret them. The storyteller's 'epic mind' initiates the web, of the retelling (*erzählen* shares similar roots with the tale and to tell) not just of the one story, but of all the stories. 'One ties to the next', in an endless time, perhaps best known in the great Oriental storytellers. 'In each there is a Scheherazade who thinks of a fresh story whenever her tale comes to a stop.'[24] For the historian and the novelist, the heavens and the earth 'have grown indifferent to the fates of the sons of men and no voice speaks to them from anywhere'. Now stones, for example, 'are measured and weighed and examined for their specific gravity and density, but they no longer proclaim anything to us. Their time for speaking with men is past.' But the storyteller keeps faith with the 'naive poetry' of things. His is not just a temporal web from teller to hearer, from master to journeyman to apprentice. It is also a spatial web, a vertical webbed ladder. A 'web' that is both the golden fabric of the religious view of the course of things and the 'multicoloured fabric of a worldly view'.[25] A web that is a 'ladder extending downward to the interior of the earth and disappearing into the clouds', which is 'the image for a collective experience to which the deepest shock of every individual experience, death, constitutes no impediment'.[26] This is Benjamin's symbolic, a natural ladder, ascending from the earth. Its inside is not constituted by death. Instead death is exchanged and circulates in its very web.

What is the place of 'revelation' in all this? This is not an easy question. The storyteller *per se*, in comparison to the chronicler, is not a holy man. Yet Leskov, Benjamin's paradigmatic *Erzähler*, was a Christian and saw storytelling as a practical activity as a possible route to sainthood. Leskov understood Christianity itself on the model of the fairy tale. Thus the resurrection was a 'disenchantment' of myth, a wakening from the 'nightmare of myth'. Christ here takes on the role of a sort of middle, a not yet 'broken middle', a middle and mediator between the mythic (and perhaps Jewish) extremes of sacred and profane. On this model, revelation would transpire through gentle counsel of humans and naturalistically letting other things be. This is a sort of non-violent disclosure, whether Christian or non-Christian, of the meaning of being. For Benjamin by implication one could only pose the question of the meaning of being in modernity, with its abstract – whether contingent or homogenous – time, and its comprehension of death as contingency, ambivalence or margin. In the *Erzählung* being would disclose itself not at all through posing the question of the meaning of being, but gently in counsel and the gentle relationship towards the natural language of things.[27]

If myth has to do with lineage, then the *Erzählung*, which is perhaps more 'tale' than story – whether epic, chronicle or fairy tale – comes perhaps not from more inclusive social formations: hence it is institutionalized in what Gadamer called 'the memorial'. Benjamin's storytelling as memorial here is less institutionalized than the monument, and surely Benjamin's web of stories is very, very 'low church', and as immanent as transcendent. The memorial of the storyteller consists of memory as a 'dialogue with the past'. This form of memory is vastly different from memory in the novel. Novel-istic memory is interior and monologic: it is the personalized, psychological memory of one lifetime only, forgetting the past and the generations. Benjamin's work on allegory features deathly landscapes of the seven-teenth-century German baroque and nineteenth-century Paris. There is correspondingly a presence of *life* in Benjamin before the demise of aura. The force of life pervading Benjaminian aura has little to do with *Lebensphilosophie*. Indeed, *Lebensphilosophie*'s contingent, subjective time kills this sort of auratic life as substance of the 'living community'. The commu-nication of experience of the storyteller is a set of life exchanges, in which the friendly nature of the fairy tale becomes a life force in the world.

But with the demise of aura, the displacement of *Erfahrung* by *Chokerlebnis*, what role is left for the modern storyteller? The new breed of *Erzähler*, says Benjamin, 'sees a new beauty in what is vanishing'. He works through the 'proverb', and perhaps the nineteen sections of *Der Erzähler* are nineteen proverbs, each an 'ideogram of a story'. Modernity's tale, its proverb, is thus 'a ruin which stands on the site of an old story, in which a moral twines about an event like ivy around a wall'. The new storyteller must none the less not share the immoralist's concern with the meaning of life, but instead continue as a moralist of *kleinen Vernunft* operating in an age of time or even speed, telling tales in an aesthetics of disappearance.

Language Magic: Revelation, Organic Totality

Benjamin is reticent about revelation – and redemption – in 'The story-teller'. He is much less so in his early work. Winfried Menninghaus thus argues in his seminal *Walter Benjamins Theorie der Sprachmagie* that Benjamin's work from beginning to end constituted a 'rettende Aneignung der Sprachmystik', a redemptive appropriation of language's mystery.[28] This is most of all clear in his very early work which was rooted in Romantic *Sprachphilosophie* – a language philosophy that, in comparison to the Anglo-American ordinary language philosophy, might be understood as *extra*ordinary language philosophy. The young Benjamin, writing his PhD thesis on German Romantic art criticism, was not part of the fashionable Nietzschean academic groupings of the early Weimar Republic, of people like Gundolf and others close to the Stefan George circle. His work, in comparison, seems almost 'traditionalist' and implicitly critical of the Nietzscheans. The academic jobs in the *Geisteswissenschaften* that opened for Jews in those years were often filled by these Nietzschean radicals. Benjamin's work, though always supremely idiosyncratic, in important respects seemed to be more in line with conservatives'.

Benjamin's early programmatic writings on language, such as 'Über die Sprache überhaupt und über die Sprache des Menschen', were based on the assumption – following Johann Georg Hamann and Wilhelm von Humboldt – that language has its own spiritual essence (*geistiges Wesen*). The ontological assumption here – rather similar to life world phenomenology – was that all beings – humans, events and things – have a spiritual essence. And that this essence is communicated in language. We must note, as Benjamin observes and Menninghaus insists, that such communication takes place not *through* language but *in* language, not *durch die Sprache*, but *in der Sprache*. That is, Benjamin stood opposed to what he called the 'semiotic' use of language, in which the sign as an instrument refers to a meaning. Instead, for him, the sign must carry its meaning *in* it. Now what is the specific essence of this particular being, language, which – unlike people, things and events – is primarily doing the communicating of the essences of the latter? Language – and not these other beings – has its own essence in some kind of mediation. Benjamin and *Sprachphilosophie* insist that this essence as mediator lies in what is left over after language plays its instrumental function. Language may thus mediate, but it is never simply a *Mittel*, or a means. It is instead a medium. Language as means can only communicate instrumentally *durch die Sprache*, but language as medium can also mediate *in der Sprache*.[29]

Benjamin's two main influences as *Sprachphilosophen* were not integral to the Romantic movement *per se*. Johann Georg Hamann was an eighteenth-century Protestant thinker, who quarrelled with Kant over the latter's notion of intuition, which Hamann understood with regard to the forms of language. Hamann's thought on language was in the mould of Lessing's dichotomy of 'accidents of history' on the one hand and 'knowledge of God' on the other; and of Herder's essay on the origin of language. Thus

Hamann counterposed history as a 'continuing sign' and the world as the 'language of God'. For Hamann language did not *have* a content, instead it *was* a content. Hamann was a major influence on the Sturm und Drang figures, on the next generation of Romantic thinkers – on Schelling and Hegel and less directly Novalis, Schleiermacher and A. and F. Schlegel. But the Romantics were more secular than Hamann. Indeed, the strong dimension of the occult in Benjamin's work owes more to Hamann than the Romantics – and especially to the central place of revelation (*Offenbarung*) and 'the name' in Hamann's thought.[30] Benjamin was later to bring this idea of the occult into the everyday: this would be integral to his break with high modernity's novelistic for the allegorical mode of life of 'low modernity'.

For Hamann God both gave man language and gave him the truth through language. With Hamann, Benjamin contrasted speech as instrumental with speech as 'revelatory'. Thus God gave man language in order and in which to reveal the God-given essence of things. God gave things essences. And God gave man – partly as his essence – language. Man's essence can thus reveal the essence of things. Or man's essence, language, is to reveal the essence, the Godly dimension, the spiritual essence of things. Hamann's writings were not specifically in the philosophy of religion. So revelation was not just something Godly, not just something that took place through the word of God, but became a quality of all human speech. Man's language, of course, was not always revelatory: more often it was instrumental and merely designated the verbal content of predicative utterances. Language was thus on the one hand 'the mere cladding of arbitrary signs', but on the other 'cabbala'.[31] This mystical spiritual nature of language, its 'cabbalistic' dimension, of course of Jewish origin, was used by Hamann, and also by the next generation of secularizing Protestant Romantics, especially Novalis and Schlegel. The latter used it rather restrictively, only in contrast with the instrumental operation of language. With Benjamin – who later came under the influence of Jewish thought – it retains much more of the occult dimension.

Hamann spoke of the cabbalistic *topos* of the 'revealed name'. This was the central secret of Judaism. The unspoken, secret, name of God is for Benjamin the '*Inbegriff*' of cabbalistic, 'magical' communication. Man 'communicates a spiritual essence when he names the thing'. To name a thing is to allude to the mystery of the name of God. Naming for the young Benjamin is not mimetic, but instead invokes 'die Sprache der Sprache', or the essence of language. If the essence of the thing is in its name, the essence of language – its 'content transcending content' – is the secret name of the Godhead. The previously hidden essence of a thing, i.e. the deeply mediated essence of a thing, becomes immediate in the cabbalistic, the magical dimension of language.[32] But the deeply mediated essence of language itself is the secret of God's name.

A number of themes in *Sprachphilosophie* came down to Benjamin in the work of the more secular and humanist Wilhelm von Humboldt, a contemporary of Goethe and Hegel. Humboldt's subject was not so much revelation as national languages: national languages each with its own linguistic essence. This was also a content-transcending dimension of a language: its authentic content, its 'innere Sprachform'. This spiritual essence would have a *sprachbildenden Kraft*, a language-forming power. Humboldt was a believer in the inalienable value of the individual, and the development of human powers. For him man's *differentia specifica* was in being not the Enlightenment's conceptual or Aristotle's political animal, but a language-using animal. Language expresses the spiritual essence of a nation. There is an organic totality, a 'life', in a national language, a notion evoked in the nineteenth-century philology and historical linguistics of the Grimms. Herder, Hamann and Humboldt spoke of the 'physiognomy of innere Sprachformen'. Language expressed a specific *Denkart* or thinking style, involved in the practices, linguistic habits ('die Sitten der Rede'), of a community. Cabbalistic language for its part was especially prevalent in how national languages spoke of nature, history, art, religion and Sittlichkeit.'[33]

Even Benjamin used this idea of totality, with its implicit organicism and notion of life, saying that the verbal content of language is an 'extensive totality', while its inner content is an 'intensive totality'. Romantics like Novalis saw in language's cabbalistic dimension a 'mystical and eternal grammar', a 'physiological stylistics'. Benjamin wrote in the 'Task of the Translator': 'the true translation is *durchscheinend*; it does not cover the original; doesn't put the original under the light, but lets pure language, strengthened through its own medium, only more fully reflect onto the original'. Translation is thus 'the expression of the innermost relation of languages to one another'. A national organic totality is also a way, a form of life, it is indeed a 'style'. At issue here is not 'lifestyle' but style (*Stil*) as spiritual essence, as the 'signature of a particular Weltanschauung'. Thus the German notion of '*Art*' or '*Mode*' as 'mode' or 'way' is seen through language. Translation is not so much a question of what is meant (*gemeint*) but a capturing of the way of meaning, 'Art des Meinens'. The content-transcending content of a language is its way of meaning, its style. For Benjamin, following Hamann, what counted was not the isolated word but the *Mitteilungsmode* (mode of communication), the national or individual *Denkart*, way of thought. The notion of physiognomy used here tied style integrally into 'life'. A language appeared for Hamann as style not in its instrumental, but in its revelatory, mode.[34] Here style, lifestyle, resides not in disembedded semiosis but in forms of life.

This idea of style as revelatory and content-transcending dimension of national languages, Benjamin extended to the discussion of the artist, the poet, speaking, for example, of Proust's style as the signature of the individual *Weltanschauung*. In this early *sprachphilosophisch* work Benjamin absolutized the distinction between '*Das Gemeinte*' (the meant) and the '*Art des Meinens*' (way, style of meaning). At this point Benjamin followed the Romantics in championing symbol at the expense of allegory; of championing Mallarmé's symbolist *poèsie pure*, poetry counterposing the *Eigengewicht der Wörte* to their *gedankentransportierende Funktion*. Later Benjamin was to break with this introspective modernism as well as romanticism as too esoteric. He was to break with this romantic idea of the pure language of the work of art, as 'an internal *potenzierenden Selbstreflexion*'; to break with 'the pure language "of the name"'. His later work would forsake Mallarmé's esoteric introspection for Baudelaire's exoteric 'extrospection', Mallarmé's symbol for Baudelaire's allegory. In this recasting of allegory not just the *Art des Meinens* but the prosaic material *gemeint*, the referent, became worth deciphering. Benjamin's magic of language (*Sprachmagie*) was no longer confined to the lofty heights of romanticism and symbolism, but came to inhabit the lowest, basest levels of the material world. Benjamin as he wrote *Gerschom Scholem* would deflect his '*Denkkraft*' from pure language to the '*tradierte Worte*', to the '*verkrustete Oberfläche*' of vulgar language, and in the streets, objects and figures of 'low modernity', he would 'excavate a *verschlossene sprachliche Leben*', a hidden linguistic life.[35]

Allegory: the Aesthetics of Destruction

Through the whole of his work, Benjamin opposed modern Kantian 'practical' understanding, and with Romantics such as Schlegel endorsed instead the 'speculative' understanding of antiquity (see chapter 10). Modern practical understanding conceived of art and knowledge as produced or constructed through practice, while ancient understanding conceived art and knowledge in terms of mimesis. This 'passivist' epistemology was wedded in Benjamin's early work to an auratic and idealist valuation of 'symbol'. But his later 1933 essay, 'On the mimetic faculty', proffered, unlike Schlegel's valuation of the beautiful in classical sculpture, a 'materialist' notion of mimesis. This was Benjamin's version of dialectical materialism. It was the theory of *Sprachmagie* displaced from the lofty spheres of subjectivity into the vulgar language of things, people and places of everyday life. The essay on the '*mimetisches Vermögen*' began from vulgar and profane mimesis: how similarities are produced in children's play.[36] Benjamin's dialectical materialism started not from the commodity as capital, because the commodity as capital had already come under the spell of the idealism of the value-form. It started from the thing, the material object that lay beneath the commodity. This dialectical materialism did not promise the scientific comprehension of the movements of capital. It was a lot more materialist than this. It did not subscribe to the subsumption of the material by the theoretical apparatus of scientific socialism. It was more materialist even than scientific socialism. It began from the power of the material object itself, in what is not objectivism, but instead a, so to speak, 'object-ism' that can never mastered by subjects through scientific categories. An object-ism that makes Marxist objectivism redundant. Benjamin's objectism instructs us instead to listen to the language, to the speech acts of the material objects themselves.

This is the stuff of modern allegory, of Benjamin's dialectical materialist invocations of nineteenth-century Paris. Always starting not from the theory, but from the material object, from the particular itself, and then renegotiating theory as allegory, the allegorist, operating in a mimetic mode, has the task of deciphering the material things of everyday life. This is a technique of '*Absetzen*' into a mosaic, into an independent series of motifs.[37] *Absetzen*, to lift out and place elsewhere, is a mode literally of disembedding. The allegorist thus deciphers the material, the everyday, the real inaccessible to the realist, through a process of disembedding. These disembedded particulars are then not so much re-embedded as deciphered in a process of transformation. Allegory involves – whether in the baroque allegory of Benjamin's *Trauerspiel* or in Baudelaire's modern allegory – a process of neither Marxian valuation nor Nietzschean revaluation (*Umwertung*), but instead of *de*valuation of things; it involves the *Ent*wertung der Dingen. Allegory has a 'destructive power'. Allegory, as we shall see below, is not a question of constructionism, nor of realism or even deconstruction, but rather of *destructionism*. It is not a matter of production, or of consumption, but instead of destruction.

At issue is the 'Herausreißen der Dingen aus den ihnen geläufigen Zusammenhängen', literally the ripping out of things from their normal connections. Indeed, a better figure for understanding this *absetzen* and *herausreißen* – this lifting out and ripping out – is not disembedding, partly because it does not involve further re-embedding. It is instead *unravelling* of the web of stories and of objects linked together by the storyteller, by the travelling craftsman. There is a double destruction at work. First, the unravelling and destruction of the web of auratic connections, and, second, the destructive transformation of the elements, of the nodes, of this web into another more fragmented mosaic of objects, of linguistic figures. It is a process of unravelling and then recasting in fragments. But who or, better, what is carrying out this allegorical alchemy, this destructive deciphering of the language of things? In Baudelaire's doctrine of allegory, the passive agents of destructive deciphering are the figures of allegory themselves: the poetic figures of allegory – evil, time, death, memory. Thus the significance of *le Mal* in Baudelaire's *Fleurs du Mal*. Here the *fleurs* are the things, the appearance, and *Mal* the meaning, the allegory. The *Mal* destructively re-deciphers the flowers, transforming their beauty into a entirely different aesthetics. Allegories, Benjamin notes, 'sind im Reiche der Gedanken wie Ruinen im Reiche der Dingen'.[38] Allegories in the realm of thought destroy flowers, transform stones into ruins.

Baudelaire, as melancholic and poet, sees not only stones and flowers, but the shock of the new in the panoply of capitalist commodities allegorically. They are destructively deciphered. Capitalist commodities, stockpiled in Marxian accumulation, in Heideggerian technology, are through surrealist allegory disconnected from their networks of circulation, are taken off the stockpile and instead placed on the junkpile of disused dresses, perfumes, baby carriages and toilet seats. These things are neither singular nor any longer commodities, but ruins, disused commodities. The allegorist is the surrealist, is the nineteenth-century poet. Indeed, the allegorist is modernity itself. It is capitalism's creative destruction, its role in melting the solidity of the stockpiles into the 'fremde Bedeutung' of the junkpiles.[39] For Baudelaire allegory is evil, but an evil whose transformed object subverts the homogenizing logic of commodity and technology. The object as evil, ripped out of the circuits of circulation and given a *fremde Bedeutung*, is the seduction of modernity.

The allegorist's cityscape was comprised not just of things but of people, of archetypal figures – idlers, students, gamblers, flâneurs, prostitutes. The experiential structure of these figures, especially of the gambler, mirrors the *Chokerlebnis*, who – in contrast to the auratic *Erfahrung* of the storyteller – characteristic of Benjamin's modernity *Erfahrung*, as we mentioned above has the 'ancient' temporality of the storyteller. This is the time structure of the full object, of wish fulfilment, of a plenitude in the 'Symbolik der Völker'. The modern time structure of *Chokerlebnis*, of not the full but the missing or lost object and deprived wish fulfilment. This is a *de facto* disqualification of temporal experience. The object is lost: the unravelling of the web of stories severs the past from the present. Now the next moment is always the first moment. The pleasure of Baudelaire's idler has nothing at all to do with wish fulfilment. *Chokerlebnis* is time in fragments. The web of objects and stories has been disconnected: the full objects displaced by unwanted and *found* objects, stories by allegories. This time of *Chokerlebnis* is more fragmented than novelistic time. The unity of novelistic time constituted a horizon for the meaning of being, in relation to which death was a constitutive yet contingent outside. But now the contingency, the ambivalence of death, is everywhere.[40] It stalks the streets of the city, it inhabits the commodity. Yet there is still a moment of revelation – revelation through the profane illumination of *Chokerlebnis*. Here being is disclosed not in the everyday activities of the web of stories or the webbed ladder of the generations. It is disclosed not on the temporal horizon of ontology and the novel, nor on the backward looking tracks initiated by the Oedipus. Instead it is revealed in these disconnected moments – as narratives of both story and novel are unravelled – these fragments of allegorical modernity.[41]

Chokerlebnis was also the experience of the industrial worker, whose time was disconnected into parcellary fragments. But there was a crucial difference between such Taylorist time and the experience of the pimps, hookers and gamblers as marginal figures of industrial modernity. The latter did not use time, but 'killed time' (*tuer le temps*), theirs was the gambler's contingent time of '*le jeu*'. Baudelaire's wastrels, parasites, operated not productively but destructively on the goods of the cityscape. They did not so much produce goods as transform goods into 'bads'. These humans on the margins are very similar to the non-human disused goods taken from productive stockpiles and displaced on to marginal junkpiles. These humans too have been allegorically displaced to capitalism's margins. They are like cast-off commodities without exchange-value, and without use-value. They are useless. The industrial worker is at the heart of industrial capitalism's 'live zones'. The idler, gambler, whore, adventurer is cast away into the *dead* zones of industrial modernity.

If Mallarmé's mode of perception derived from the auratic timelessness of transcendent beauty, Baudelaire's gaze was structured by the *Chokerlebnis* of contingent movement of the masses in the city. At stake here is a new hermeneutics, of neither suspicion nor retrieval, but of destruction. At stake is something vastly different from the mimesis of the beauty of classical ideal essences in sculpture and the lyric poem. In this classical mimesis, culture mimes nature. But in modern allegory, mimesis transforms the natural into the artificial. It transforms the world of natural things into artificial objects, commodities into disused artefacts. The allegory in Baudelaire's poem 'Allegory' is a beautiful woman.[42] Indeed, the *fleur du mal* itself is a beautiful woman. The *fleur du mal* is not the earth mother or Aphrodite's beauty of antiquity. The *fleur du mal* is the woman of the shadows. She is the whore. She transforms the natural of beauty, through her own natural mimesis, into artifice, into the artificial. She transforms the good into the bad, the good life into the 'bad life'.

For the ancients, 'language is the mother of reason and revelation'. The mother and the maternal as medium (and not means) is central to the iconography of the storyteller. But if the story and the epic are based on the geocentrism of mother and generations, what happens with the differentiation of the epic into tragedy, history and philosophy of later antiquity. Does tragedy mirror not so much catharsis as the uncertainty and perplexity of our own modernity? Does not the certain bequeathal of the mother turn into the perplexity and confusion of tragedy's Oedipus? Does not the fulfilled and geocentric medium of the auratic mother of tradition and the generations become the lost object of today's Oedipus, cast adrift from the generations and from the social itself into a chronic and interminable perplexity? Capitalist technology may be the basis for the creation of new social classes, but it always also acts as allegory, marginalizing social classes into the dead zones and wild zones. A process only accelerated in an age no longer of time but of speed. Now any horizon for the revelation of being – which is no longer the meaning of being – is counted perhaps less in fragments than in nanoseconds. Relegated to the wild zones by what is no longer Baudelaire's time-capitalism but global informational and speed-capitalism are the de-industrialised ex-working class in European council estates and the black ghettoes of the USA.[43] Away from the counsel of aura of the story, away from the meaning of being, where are the twenty-first century allegorists' fragments of revelation going to come from?

Alongside his doctrine of allegory was Baudelaire's 'doctrine of corre-spondences'. This, as Benjamin observed in Baudelaire's 'Spleen de Paris', was based on two types of correspondences: 'spleen' and 'ideal'. Ideal here is consistent with aura, with *Erfahrung*, with the motif of the storyteller. Spleen, on the other hand, is a black humour: the melancholic is splenetic according to the theory of the humours. Baudelaire's 'Spleen de Paris' is, observed Benjamin, a *mélancolie passagère* and spleen is *Chokerlebnis*, it is Hegel's unhappy infinity (*schlechtin Unendlichkeit*). Spleen, itself a figure of allegory, invokes the universal disgust of the urban melancholic: his ennui, neurasthenia, boredom of an endless time with nothing to do. Yet at the same time there is a threatening and fascinating *gout du néant*, a taste for nothingness, in spleen. Correspondences involve all the senses: they are in the look, the smell, the sound and the colour of things. The mode in which we relate to things characterizes our correspondences with them as sple-netic or ideal. Ideal time experience resembles idealist time experience, the storyteller's relationship to things involving trust, intimacy, familiarity: the *Eingedenken*, a mindful remembrance structuring our correspondence with things. The ideal is an auratic correspondence, in contrast to the time experience of the *Zertrümmerung* (shattering) *der Aura* in spleen.[44]

If Latour's things judge and Virilio's things – in one way or another – explode, then Benjamin's things not only talk, but see. Both spleen and ideal, both allegory and aura, concern also how things look at people: involve the gaze of things. Thus, in ideal and auratic experience the perceiver finds in things a *regard familier*, a *vertraute Blick*, an intimate look whose mindful remembrance guides us to far places in time and space. Benjamin writes that when we 'experience the aura of an appearance [this] means that it is invested with the property of a look . . . so that the unique appearance of a distance comes to bear in it'. These things, these appear-ances, are, observes Benjamin, the *Daten des Eingedenkens*, the data of mind-ful remembrance.[45] Auratic things thus incorporate involuntary memory or *Gedächtnis*. 'Das Idéal spendet die Kraft des Eingedenkens.'

Now spleen, as we saw, is a second type of correspondence, involving – in Proust, in Baudelaire – a *sectionnement*, a *Zerfallung* (falling into pieces), of time. In splenetic correspondence the eyes of things and people are not trustful, they indifferently mirror: they coldly penetrate; they neither ask nor answer. Spleen – despite the 'satanic extroversion of the splenetic' – is an everyday and practical time experience. It is a content, a dramatic content of what is an empty time experience. This practical and material content of splenetic experience is reworked through the destructive mimesis of the allegorist. Allegory is the form that reworks the content of spleen. Spleen comes to words in allegory. Spleen which is *Trauer*, or mourning, the practical experience of *Trauer*, is here transformed into the form of allegory, of *Trauerspiel*. And the figure involved in this 'satanic transformation of experience' – in contrast to the storyteller's communication of experience as wise counsel – is the melancholic. The melancholic is the allegorist.[46] The melancholic (possessed of the black humour himself) is the translator of spleen into allegory. The melancholic, with time to kill in the desolate cityscape, has only one divertissement open to him: and that is allegory. Benjamin writes, 'Auf dem Passionswege des Melancholikers sind die Allegorien die Stationen', a phrase which defies translation in its revelatory, indexical and 'objectist' invocations. The melancholic is a brooder. Indeed, Baudelaire called *Les fleurs du mal* 'un livre saturnien; organique et mélancolique'.

The melancholic transforms destructively the register of correspondences – the experience of idler, gambler and adventurer – into the register of allegory. And the objects it works from are dying objects, are disappearing stories. For the allegorist as melancholic, 'the relics come from the corpse, the contemplation of dying Erfahrung, which it (allegory) euphemistically calls Erlebnis'. If the form of ideal correspondences is in symbol and in the storyteller, the form of splenetic ones is in allegory. And the flâneur is a particular type of melancholic, a particular type of allegorist. The flâneur is the melancholic who works a particular type of raw material: the commodity. The flâneur sees the commodity literally as a fetish. Unlike for Marx's proletarian, the flâneur's fetishism is not due to his mistaking use-value for exchange-value or the commodity form for the social relations of production. The flâneur starts from the commodity form as his raw material and transforms it into a fetish. That fetish is the allegory. The flâneur starts from a content, in this case an empty content, the commodity. His 'allegorical intuition' then translates the commodity into the form of a drunken exhilaration.

The flâneur's translation of commodity into allegory is not a question of work or active transformation. It is passive, mimetic. The flâneur has a satanic *Einfühlung*, an empathy with commodities. Excluded from production, 'he lets himself be overwhelmed by the stream, by the current, the roar, the storm of commodities on their way to customers'. This is a satanic mimesis, reworking homogeneous time into a particular type of *durée*. The flâneur is a sort of hero, his unproductive heroic will differing vastly from the ancient hero's classical virtues. He is not the hero, but instead *performs* the hero; not through action (*Handlung*), but satanically through *Haltung* (bearing, posture, style).[47] The flâneur allegorizes commodities through transforming them into a drunken stream or rush (*Rausch*), overflowing his blasé attitude. The flâneur translates the commodity through his neurasthenic lifestyle into artifice, into ornament.

Protestant Ethic, Baroque Melancholy

Absolutism and Protestantism

The modern allegory that we have just described is a major change in comparison to Benjamin's original baroque allegory. Whereas modern allegory renders the corpse of *Erfahrung* from the inside, baroque allegory sees it from the outside. What modern allegory understood in the *Innenwelt*, baroque drama saw in the *Umwelt*.[48] The flâneur is a product of a later modernity, of the electric movement of commodities. He is a melancholic largely on economic grounds. The baroque allegorist, for his part, is a melancholic on religious-political grounds. It is to the baroque allegorist that we look for the emergence of that pathological constitution of the humours in which each and every thing, because it is lacking in any creative connection to him, becomes a cipher of a puzzle-like wisdom. At issue are things endowed with powers of speech: but they are talking things that at the same time are empty and dead. The question asked in Benjamin's thematization of modernity is: how do we obtain redemption when the good life, in terms of both the good and life itself, is no longer possible? In late modernity, as we saw, this destruction of the good life was accomplished by the commodity. But the way is paved for this in the early modern period by the rise of absolutism and especially the emergence of the Reformation. If the desolation of the good life by commodities resulted in the flâneur scavenging the cityscape, then the earlier desolation wreaked by absolutism and the Reformation resulted in the melancholic of *Trauerspiel*, of seventeeth-century German baroque drama.

In the 'Epistemo-critical prologue' to the *Ursprung des deutschen Trauerspiels* – which is about the origins, the conditions of existence, of German *Trauerspiel* rather than directly about *Trauerspiel* itself – Benjamin compares the baroque with the expressionism of his own day. Late nineteenth-century Romanticist critics had ignored the baroque. German playwrights of that era lacked the touch of genius of Spanish baroque writers like Calderon. These earlier German scholars saw the baroque 'themes of Haupt and Staatsaktionen as a distortion of ancient royal drama, its bombast [*Schwulst*] a distortion of dignified Greek pathos, and its bloody finale a distortion of tragic catastrophe'.[49] But the expressionist ethos of the early twentieth-century Stefan George circle accompanied a revaluation of the baroque, one writer in 1904 comparing it to the *Kunstgefuhl* of expressionism: as 'inwardly empty or deeply disturbed, outwardly occupied with technical problems of form which seemed at first to have little to do with the existential problems of the age'.[50] In both *Trauerspiel* and expressionsism there is the radical dualism of the deeply disturbed interiority of the artistic soul and the irrelevance of the outside world. In both the poet is concerned 'with lamentation and its resonance'. The allegory of both *Trauerspiel* and Weimar expressionism is only possible in an age of decadence, such as Luther's Germany, Baudelaire's Paris and the final decades of the Roman Empire. In such ages, Riegl noted, there is little artistic achievement, because the finely made work of art is dependent on the valuation of matter, of spirit also being immanent in matter, in the artistic materials of the world. In such ages there is little of artistic achievement, but instead 'an unremitting artistic will'. The extreme dualism of this Early Modern period of decadence was embodied in an absolutism in which the king was so exalted that nothing else of earthly history – not even the powers of the aristocracy – mattered.[51] This dualism also made it impossible for being to be present *in der Sprache*, in the materials of the work of art. Aura could be immanent in the prince and in God but not in the work of art, which could only exist – with both beautiful and sublime annulled – as allegory.

What is the nature of *Trauerspiel*? Benjamin answers this question first by counterposing *Trauerspiel* and classic tragedy: here he is also counterposing allegory and aura. Nothing could be more different than *Trauerspiel* from Benjamin's Aristotelian understanding of tragedy. *Trauerspiel*, to start with is, the study of extremes, from the very high to the very low, from bombast to hand-wringing lamentation – in contrast to the Aristotelian virtues' valuation of the mean, of the measured comportment and avoidance of extremes of the reasonable man. Tragedy was based on the fusion of the sacred and profane, on the immanence of the sacred in the profane. *Trauerspiel* in contrast presumed the radical separation of sacred from profane. The effect of catharsis was central to Aristotle and tragedy, connected to the cultic character of Greek theatre. Catharsis came from the purging effects of feelings of fear and pity on the part of the audience and their participation in the integral whole of the action. Reconciliation was central in Greek tragedy. The audience, feeling the perplexity, the aporia of fear and pity, resolved this through the pleasurable feeling of catharsis in the end. *Trauerspiel* for its part was not cultic. The audience was to consist only of the princely estates. In catharsis art brings the audience into the integral whole of the culture: it reinforces the good, the good life and reason in the audience. *Trauerspiel* is indifferent to the good life of the masses of the ruled under the absolutist state. It is indifferent to their participation in any cultural symbolic of the whole community. Tragedy encourages the virtues – as well as their mean and reasonable standard in the audience. *Trauerspiel* does 'confirm princely virtues, but also depicts princely vices, gives insight into diplomacy and manipulation of political schemes'.[52] *Trauerspiel*, like Baudelaire's allegory, seems to be more a question of the 'bad life' than the good life, more of evil than good.

Tragedy comprises a 'structure of dramatis personae' from 'a pre-historic epoch – the past age of heroes'. The perplexity of an initial conflict with the Gods yields to cathartic reconciliation with the fates. Here the representation of a primordial past is crucial to the living sense of traditional community. In *Trauerspiel* neither audience nor dramatis personae experience such reconciliation. Moreover, the nature of the action is so obscure, so meaningless in an already desolate world, that neither dramatic characters nor audience experience perplexity. At issue in *Trauerspiel* is neither the aporetics of Kantian judgement nor Hegelian sublation. When nothing matters, when nothing counts, there is no reason to experience perplexity. At issue is a culture truly after the apocalypse, after the tension of all the resolved and unresolved juxtapositions is played out. The time of perplexity is still in this sense the time when there is everything at stake. In *Trauerspiel* and allegory there is nothing at stake. Perplexity is pointless. In ancient politics legitimation of rule was partly through this tradition of living community and partly through reason as demanded by rising commercial elites and Socratic philosophers. In *Trauerspiel*, because of the very absolutism of power – with the impending collapse of even the theocratic doctrine of state – no legitimation at all is necessary. Opitz, Gryphius, Lohenstein and other *Trauerspiel* authors used the distant Orient, the imperial, absolute and theocratic power of Byzantium, as subject matter for plays. The action was so exotic, so distant from the audience, that little integral participation, little fear and little pity was possible. The audience instead was indifferent. Further, the tyrants in these 'Haupt und Staatsaktionen' could do what they wanted.[53] The arbitrary will reigned. No legitimation was necessary.

Absolutisms's indifference to the good life among its subjects is paralleled by the Reformation's indifference to good works among communicants. The *Trauerspiel* dramatists were Lutherans, assenting to the radical dualism of the Protestant doctrine: assenting to its (in contradistinction to Catholicism) refusal of the penetration of secular life by the symbols and rituals of religion. In Lutheranism faith did not have to be proved: there was a large dimension of fatality in 'the philosphy of Wittenberg'. Faith alone counted, as the world was too devalued in its drastic dualism even to be worthy of good works. Man for Luther was lower than the excrement from the Devil's anus. His good works could not count for the glory of God. Faith alone counted. Even Calvin saw no possibility of making better an empty world through good works. For him and Luther virtue did not matter: 'human activities were deprived of all value'; there was 'no distinction between human activities'.[54] Now, for ordinary people, the response to all this was upright living. It was Weber's spirit of – though good works did not count – showing that one was already predestined for the elect by upright living. For the era's 'great men', however, the response was '*melancholy*'. 'Those who looked deeper' than Weber's petits bourgeois 'saw the scene of their existence as the rubbish heap of partial and inauthentic actions.' Life itself protested against this gross devaluation that it experienced at the hands of faith. Life felt a 'deep horror' that the whole of existence (*das ganze Dasein abspielen*) might play itself out like this.[55] This is the context in which *Trauer* becomes the sensibility of the melancholy man.

Melancholy

In standard German dictionaries, *Trauer* is translated as mourning. But *Trauer* in its full significance in *Trauerspiel* is a question of lot more than this. *Trauer* involves contemplation. *Trauer* is the sensibility of the melancholic. It involves not activity or practical reason in Kant's sense, but a slothful attitude that is also an attitude of contemplation. This attitude of contemplation is obsessed not with intersubjectivity but with things. It is a passionate *in*activity which is obsessed with the language not of other subjects but of things. It wants to redeem disused things through contemplation. Things (and ourselves) will thus be redeemed through the effectively satanic knowledge of the melancholy, a revelation through satanic knowledge, from the 'depths of the earth', of the language of the things. From the rational pessimism of Stoic *apatheia* to *Trauer*, to mourning, is but a small step. As with mourning, there is a certain 'deadening of emotions; an ebbing away of waves of life'.[56] *Trauer*'s mourning works best through the mediation of Christianity. Judaism had already bequeathed the violent dualism of the wholly transcendental God and the meaninglessness of history and good works. Christianity compensated by giving Christ as the middle term, the communion and community, and a certain possibility of construction of the symbolic. *Trauer* is problematic for Judaism. You cannot mourn a middle that never was. Protestantism's erasure of the middle, the advent of the 'broken middle', formerly constituting the plenitude of the symbolic, brings the *Trauer* of mourning for the broken and dead middle, brings mourning for the lost plenitude of the symbolic.

Trauer is the mourning for the broken middle, for the lost object: a contemplative attitude, 'a pathological state', a deadening of life to the point of 'depersonalization'. And melancholia was a pathological state for both Aristotle and the early modern doctrine of the temperaments. *Trauer* is depersonalized, yet with mourning's characteristic 'passion', and 'tenacity of intention'.[57] *Trauer*'s passionate yet depersonalized attitude of mourning stands in a very special relationship with things, with the world of objects. Not only is life drained out of *Trauer*'s subjectivity, but the world of objects is also drained of life (*entleert*). If objects are *entleert*, are emptied of life, then objects 'lack an active and creative relationship to us'. This, we must note, is fully opposite to the sort of objects encountered in Heidegger's being in the world. There we can have two possible, both active, relationships with objects. Either they can be *zuhanden* (ready to hand) in a sort of craft relation with us, or they can be *vorhanden* (present at hand) and problematized in a Cartesian relation. Benjamin's objects are neither *zuhanden* nor *vorhanden*. As in Albrecht Dürer's engraving *Melencholia*, in which the 'utensils of active life are lying around unused on the floor, as objects of contemplation',[58] *Trauer*'s and Benjamin's objects are dead, his world is dead. We neither use nor scientifically scrutinize his objects. Instead, Benjamin writes, it is a 'Gesinnung in der das Gefühl die entleerte Welt maskenhaft neubelebt, um in rätselhaftes Genügen an ihrem Anblick zu haben.' *Trauer* is a sensibility in whose feeling the emptied world once more comes to life, in order to take a hieroglyph-like pleasure in its gaze. The 'simplest of objects becomes the symbol of some enigmatic wisdom'. Objects are lifted out of their world, not for Cartesian analysis, but for mystic contemplation. In *Trauer* and *Trauerspiel*, 'the great constellations of worldly chronicle seem but a game', 'worthy of attention only for the meaning deciphered from it, whose unhappy infinity secures the bleak rule of the melancholic distaste for life'.[59]

The prince, protagonist of baroque *Trauerspiel*, was a melancholic. For Albertinus, melancholy was a severe mental disorder and the 'court not so different from images of hell', itself known 'as the place of eternal *Traurigkeit*'. Gryphius's melancholic prince 'quailed before his own sword: when he dined, the mingled wine that is served in crystal turning to gall and poison'. The syndrome of Aristotelian melancholy, for its part, was a dialectic of madness and genius, the melancholic genius soaring to the loftiest of deeds before collapsing into its opposite, madness; his prophetic ability comprising at once 'the most intensive spiritual activity and its profoundest decline'. Melancholy was the basest, the least noble, of the four 'complexions', each of which in the doctrine of the temperaments was based in a humour. The sanguine temperament found in wet and warm climates was based in blood; the phlegmatic temperament, common in wet and cold climates, in water; and the choleric complexion of dry and warm lands in yellow bile. But what about the ignoble, most creaturely (*kreaturlich*), humour, melancholicus? This complexion, due to an excess of dry and cold elements, was based in black bile. His constitution in not *bilis naturalis* or *candida* but *bilis innaturalis*, the melancholic is the poorest of candidates for the good life and virtues of dry and warm climates. His practices bear the internal bads of vice, in the range of the vicious and pernicious rather than the virtuous and felicitous. The melancholic is 'envious, mournful, greedy, avaricious, disloyal, timerous, sallow'. Mediaeval Christianity had forgotten the dialectic of Aristotle's melancholic, and saw only his base and creaturely aspect. Though all four temperaments are fundamentally 'contemplative impulses', melancholy is the least spiritual, the most creaturely. It is Luther's misery of mankind in its purely creaturely state: satanic, yet lower than satanic. Spleen is decisive in the formation of black bile, and the hypochondriacal melancholic is splenetic. According to the ancients, spleen was the dominant humour in dogs, this motif dominant in Dürer's *Melencholia*. When this delicate organ deteriorates, the dog grows rabid.[60]

Aristotle's dialectics of melancholy was revived, however – via the mediation of Arabian science – in the school of Salerno, through Renaissance and Baroque motifs. This comprised, preserved by Arabia from Hellenism, the astrological significance of Saturn, 'the baleful, menacing star'. Saturn is the star not of Aristotle's mean, but of the extremes. It is the furthest and remotest of planets, hence the melancholic's inclination for long journeys and exoticism. Saturn is 'farthest from everyday life' and thus 'the originator of all deep contemplation'. It 'endows the soul with both sloth and dullness and the power of intelligence and contemplation'. The theological concept associated melancholy with the inert mass of the stone, with sloth – one of the seven deadly sins – or 'acedia'. This, due 'to the feeble light and slowness of Saturn', underscored the apathy and indecisiveness of *Trauerspiel*'s prince. But there is a third element connecting the contradictory terms of melancholy's dialectic. And this is the earth itself, the depths of the earth itself: for melancholy's contemplative wisdom is achieved through this very base and creaturely sloth via this earthly relation. The saturnine melancholic's wisdom is derived 'not from the voice of revelation'; his prophetic dreams are instead from 'geomantic slumber'. Saturn is also the god of agriculture; saturnian knowledge is a gift of the earth's treasures. 'For the melancholic the inspirations of mother earth dawn from the night of contemplation like treasures from the interior of the earth.' 'The earth, previously important only as a cold, dry element, acquires the full wealth of its esoteric meaning.'[61]

Melancholy's dialectic thus passes through a moment less transcendental and Hegelian than netherworldy and satanic. This is a truly negative
dialectic. Knowledge emerges less through Kantian or Godly practical
activity than through the speculation of evil. Benjamin's melancholic,
whether early or later modern, faced with the deserted landscape, deserted
by the religious and the political and left finally in ruins by the commodity,
finds knowledge and encounters revelation and the meaning of being
through the fragments of its ruins, in what is literally a *profane*, even satanic,
illumination. The gaze and the language of the things is a language of evil.
His destructive mimesis is indeed the devil's work. The angel of history is
no ordinary angel. Saturninans, born under the baleful, leaden planet, are
recognizable by their 'immersion in creaturely things'. The saturnine
and baroque courtier is characteristically unfaithful to men but loyal to
things, is obsessively attached to things, to the sceptre, crown, royal purple,
throne, the ornament more generally. The Saturnian is not interested in
intersubjectivity. He is not endowed with spirituality, or subjection to
higher laws. He has no ethics, but only the lower laws of the baleful
constellation. The adamic melancholic has a 'hopeless loyalty to the
creaturely'; he 'betrays for the sake of knowledge'. For *Trauerspiel*'s courtier,
'every loyal vow, every memory surrounds itself with the fragments of the
world of things as its very own, not-too-demanding objects'. Hamlet,
Benjamin notes, was the melancholic of Renaissance drama. Despite his
estrangement, he could achieve a redemption not unlike Christian reconciliation through attaining self-knowledge at the play's end. But for the
German and baroque melancholic, self-absorbed rather than self-knowing,
transcendental redemption is not possible. His sloth is too great, he is too
absorbed in the creaturely. His tenacious self-absorption can only redeem
the objects of his obsessions.[62]

Allegory versus Symbol Revisited

In the *Ursprung des deutschen Trauerspiels* Benjamin rejects Goethe's and
Schelling's valuation of symbol even over classical allegory, for its presumptions of unity of form and content and 'absence of dialectical rigour'.
Inasmuch as allegory points to truths outside itself, both dualism and
dialectic are possible. Paradigmatic for symbol was Greek sculpture, for
classical allegory the epic poem. Here there was a momentariness, a sud-
denness of revelation in classical sculpture's symbol, while epic allegory has
a prolonged temporality. Goethe devalued allegory, saying that in symbol
we see the general in the particular, while in allegory the particular is just
an example of the general. In symbol, when we 'grasp the particular in all
its vitality', we also grasp the general. In contrast, the more didactic

allegory starts not from the particular but from the general, from the concept. Benjamin will agree that allegory, unlike symbol, is edificatory, is in this sense more didactic. He will allow that in classical as in modern allegory there is a separation of meaning from being, i.e. unlike in symbol meaning is not immanent in being. Allegory is thus 'a successively progressing, dramatically mobile, dynamic representation of ideas'. Unlike the activity of symbol in the classical sculpture or modern romantic poetry, 'its contemplative calm immerses itself into the depths which separate visual being from meaning'.[63]

The point is that Benjamin, while allowing that allegory is rigid and logical, denies that it starts with a universal and chooses a particular as an example of it. He denies that allegories in this sense are semiotic or 'signs'. He notes that Schopenhauer understood allegories as 'inscriptions', as 'hieroglyphic', and that hieroglyphs are *not* signs. Allegory, he continues, thus concerns 'emblematics'. And emblematics are not general concepts. Indeed, they are not concepts or representations at all. Instead, 'nature is the subject matter of emblematics'. And 'the epic poem is indeed a history of signifying nature in its classic form, just as allegory is in its baroque form'.[64] That is, in classical allegory as in Benjamin's storyteller one starts from nature, from the particular. Meaning is not immediately present in this nature, it is not immanent in it, nor is it immediately to be discovered from it. From a long and patient process of deciphering, however, we may begin to cross the dialectical chasm between the natural and particular (i.e. the material) and the ideal or meaning. Allegory is just a different way of moving from the particular to the general.[65]

All this said, the difference between the classical allegory of the epic, legend and storyteller and modern allegory is that the former is auratic and the latter is not. In the former nature is live, while the latter is about fallen nature. History loses its life blood to become a mere 'stage property'. Modern (baroque) allegory is ornamental as 'the observer is confronted with the facies hippocratica of history as a petrified primordial landscape'.[66] Yet the gist of Benjamin's argument here concerns not the differences but the similarities between classical and baroque/modern allegory. He writes, 'the allegorical way of seeing is the baroque secular explanation of history as the passion of the world'. Yet modern and classical allegory, unlike the rule-finding and flexible symbol of third critique Kant, lacks freedom of expression as the 'form in which man's subjection to nature is the most obvious'. Symbol is about life and freedom, but for all allegory, 'everything about history that from the very beginning has been sorrowful, untimely, unsuccessful is expressed in a face – or rather in a death's head'.[67] The emblem is at the same time always a face, always a death's head. And with 'its seeds in the creature's graceless state of sin', 'nature has always been subject to the power of death, has always been allegorical'.

Thus ancient Greece and the Renaissance comprised an aporetic tension of symbol and allegory, of on the one hand harmony and life and on the other death. Of a Greek principle on the one hand and an Egyptian, hieroglyphic and hierocratic and mystic principle on the other. Hence, 'Homer's legends are also mystic orphic doctrine, principally from Egypt'.[68] Benjamin points to the importance of allegory and symbol in the Renaissance, during which humanist scholars (including Dürer) deciphered and worked on allegorical exegeses of Egyptian hieroglyphs. This involved close observation of objects as emblems, of writing in concrete images; hence the enigmatic hieroglyphs that covered in medallions Renaissance columns. Thus Alberti's concern with hieratic ostentation, with a 'natural theology of writing'. In the Reformation, however, the interest in symbol died as unadulterated allegory came to the fore. This was not so much language as objects, but nature, as objects and nature which speaks. The Reformation was thus the 'emblematic age'. But at issue here is a nature in which God does *not* reveal. God reveals in symbols, but symbols for their part cannot express mysteries. Instead at issue is a 'mystical philosophy of nature'. Baroque allegory's exclusive aim was the 'mysterious instruction' of its 'creatures'.[69]

14

Conclusion

Once we start taking the object seriously then the other, the second, modernity has to start asking itself some perhaps disturbing questions. To take the object seriously is to pose some very pressing questions to the problem of *ontology*. The second modernity, as we saw along the length of this book, as much as anything else ultimately shifted debate from issues of *epistemology* to issues of *ontology*. Ontology, unlike epistemology, does not address reality *per se*. Ontology addresses being. Ontology, unlike epistemology, does not foreground cognition, or cognitive meanings. Ontology addresses instead existential meaning. Whether in straightforward positivism or in structuralism, whether sociological, linguistic or anthropological, when the knowing subject stands in a subject–object relation with these social structures, we are in the realm of epistemology. Even when the subject constitutes or constructs the object of inquiry we are still in the realm of epistemology. We still are giving all powers to the subject of knowledge and de-problematizing the object. We are reducing the object to merely an object of knowledge for us. What cultural theorists have called the 'metaphysical tradition' has forgotten the problem of ontology. Indeed, the metaphysical tradition – like the contemporary positivisms, whether in sociology or in philosophy – reduces ontology to epistemology. Questions of being and existential meaning are ruled out of court. Language becomes a mere instrument. Objects are reduced to instruments to produce or accumulate, or, at best, to dissect and study as 'variables'. Uncontested at centre stage here is the knowing subject, who takes on quasi-infinite powers.

The first, high modernity was about epistemology. In very many respects – in the academy, politics, the world of business and markets – the first modernity is very much still with us. Indeed, it is a major power, a major dimension of the contemporary world. The second and other modernity from the very start – from the Romantics to literature and painting in late nineteenth- and early twentieth-century Paris to sociological hermeneutics – has been about ontology. The object in the second modernity has become ontological. It is possessed with being. It is no longer reduced to a thing whose sole function is the assertion of valid predicative statements. The object in the second modernity gains vastly in status. It is now not just a speck, a point to be known. It comes to take on an ontological structure. It comes to take on a structure of meaning. A meaning that is not reduced to epistemological and utilitarian functions. The object in high modernity was not a thing-in-itself. It did not possess an ontological structure. The object's ontological structure in the second modernity allowed it to take on epistemological functions, but also to be invested with affect, with desire, with care, to be lived by and lived with. As such, the object has been a highly mediated prism on to being, on to existential meaning.

In the first modernity the symbols of art and language became instrumentalized. Art, much like science, comes to depict things in the world. Art itself in this sense becomes epistemological. It devalues the status of its objects, as well as that of its own medium. The medium becomes a means, and the objects reduced to things to be depicted. In the first modernity language is understood as an instrument. The signifier is a tool to latch on to a signified, to point to a referent. The speech act is merely a means with a performative and pragmatic impact. The media of art and language are reduced to instruments or at best transparent windows on the world. Art and language are fundamentally epistemological. As pure means, art and language are deprived of ontological weight. They are emptied of being to be epistemological means.

In the second modernity, art and language become ontological. Art becomes not primarily a means of depicting, but opens up on to existential meaning. Compared to objects in general, art opens up in a far less mediated way on to being. The ontological structure of the work of art is different from the object. It is such that it may open up through the imagination on to being harmonically and in an ordered way. But its ontological structure comprises at the same time a dimension of anti-structure. Art may also open up on to being through overwhelming, through the 'rush' of the sublime. Similarly with language and especially poetic language. Language takes on an ontological density in the second modernity. Meaning is no longer solely epistemological or through language, by means of language. Meaning in the second, ontological modernity resides in language itself. Language and art also have a very special ontological structure in comparison to objects, in that they form the basis of our horizon. They are horizon constituting. They provide or explicate fundamental symbols in the structure of our horizon. They help to impart a certain permanence, a duration to collective memory. Art and language and their institutional embodiments are what suture the wound with which human beings face the world.

What about the subject? What happens to the subject in the shift from first-modernity epistemology to second-modernity ontology? The subject is the major loser. The subject previously, in humanism, having taken on attributes of infinity, now starts losing sacred substance. The subject becomes finite. The subject is no longer 'above the world' in a hierarchical subject–object relation with the things in the world. He or she is now in the world, situated in the world among the objects in the world. Subjects are no longer closed off: they are also no longer 'constructors' or 'constitutors' of objects. They are now also receptive, open, endangered and living among the objects, open through sensation to them in the world. Subjects are no longer disembodied thinking substance, but are instead bodies in the world, their finitude reinforced by the now recognized non-rationality of primary processes in the unconscious mind. The subject is no longer universal. He or she is no longer a subject of epistemology making universalistic statements about the things in the world. Subjects are now not universal, but singular. They approach objects in the world no longer from the infinite position of epistemology but from the finitude of experience. Subjects no longer know objects, they instead experience objects in the second modernity. The universal subject has thus become finite and singular.

The object itself is no longer the 'particular' complement of high modern 'universality'. It is no longer a particular instance of the universal. The object – and especially objects of art and cultural objects – gaining what the subject loses in substance and powers, is now no longer a particular. Nor is it a means to an end. The object, previously a particular, now becomes a finality. Thus the governing dictum of Kant's third critique, his *Critique of Judgement*, is '*Zweckmäßigkeit ohne Zweck*', finality without end. In the first modernity objects were utilitarian, they were not finalities or *Zweckmäßigkeiten*, but *Mitteln* or means. First-modernity objects were not *finalities* but *instrumentalities*. Objects were means with ends (*Zwecke*). As objects take on ontological depth, they lose their functions as means. They no longer function for ends. Indeed, objects no longer primarily function. The whole logic of means and ends disappears with the logic of universal and particular. Objects, when they are no longer means, no longer have ends. They also don't become ends. They instead becomes finalities. They become things-in-themselves.

Not only subject–object relations are transformed in the second, the other, modernity, so are subject–subject relations. Not just our relations with things, but social relations, relations of intersubjectivity, are transformed. Again the shift is from epistemology to ontology, from instrumentality to finality. First-modernity social relations are ideal-typically institutional, they are normative, they are functional for the reproduction of society. Insomuch as they are functional for reproduction of society or the social, first-modernity social relations are instrumentalities. Second-modernity social relations are, in contrast, finalities. They do not function to reproduce society. At issue is not 'the social' but instead what Simmel called *sociality*. Second-modernity social relations have ontological depth:

they do not betray normative functioning, but open out on to existential meaning. They are not normative to the extent that norms are means for the reproduction of society. They do not separate out value from fact. In the second modernity the 'social facts' of social relations are not the 'variables' so dear to positivism, but instead open out on to value-structure, on to ontological structure.

Now the entire juxtaposition of first and second modernity, of epistemology and ontology, of instrumentality and finality, comes under threat, we have seen, with the rise of the global information culture. The 'difference', the irresolvable aporetic tension, between first and second modernity, between instrumentality and finality, tends more or less to explode, to dissolve in the rise of the new technological culture. It tends to become dissolved into the general indifference of the information age. In the indifference of the information age objects tend to take on capacities previously associated with subjects: they take on powers of judgement, of measuring, translating and interpretation.

In the indifference of today's global information culture the object increasingly fuses with art, fuses with language. There comes to be a profusion of objects that are already cultural. Now capital has begun largely to accumulate by means of these cultural commodities. By means of objects that have as much in common with art and language (i.e. symbols) as they do with more traditional objects. By symbolic objects which circulate in markets and through markets come to constitute our horizon. In the global information culture there is a vast expansion of things that think, of objects with information and memory, of objects that talk, judge, police and seduce. Even biological things now take on informational status. The body is increasingly indifferentiated from other objects as body parts and genetic information units are circulated in the market.

In the second modernity, despite the ontological gains by the object and art and language, there still was a sort of 'late humanist' hierarchy, in which subjectivity was still privileged as a being different from other beings. The epistemological and universalist subject may have been displaced by singular and finite subjectivity, but the latter is still privileged in its capacity for interpreting the meaning, for explicating the ontological structures, of other beings. The second modernity's subject continues to be privileged in its capacity for reflexivity, i.e. for interpreting the ontological structure of subjectivity itself. But what happens in the global information culture when there is an increasing indifferentiation between subjectivity and machines: when machines come to become 'things that think', when subjects are increasingly found side by side with their 'extensions', with information and communication machines? In the global information culture the hierarchy of subjectivity and the object, of subjectivity and technology, is disrupted.

The same is true for the symbol and the object. In the second modernity's previous hierarchy, symbols, art and language formed the horizon against which objects were to be interpreted, revealed. Now an increasingly greater proportion of objects, of the things produced and marketed, themselves are language-objects and art-objects, are symbol-objects, are hybrids of art/language on the one hand and the object, the thing, on the other. Now these symbol-things, these symbol-commodities, come to constitute the horizon disrupting the old hierarchy. The horizon was constituted through art and language, against which the commodities (material objects) were interpreted. Now the material objects themselves are symbolic and horizon constituting. There is thus a pronounced tendency towards fusion in the global information culture of subjects and objects, objects and symbols.

What about being? In the other modernity, subjectivity interpreted objects in the space of the same, while language and art constituted the limit condition, the mediating space, of difference and 'text' between same and other. Being and death, for their part, occupied the space of the other. But with the shift to the post-apocalyptic culture, with the explosion of the boundary separating human and non-human, nation and foe, same and other, being and death itself are no longer on the outside, but circulate on the inside, as entities, calculable and digitized like other beings. The explosion of the symbolic is partly the work of death, of being. The restricted economy explodes into the general economy. The villain in J. G. Ballard's post-apocalyptic *Drowned World*, the albino Strangman, rides his hydroplane, surrounded by crocodile allies and his band of black gangsters. As Strangman says to the novel's biologist protagonist, 'they fear me because they think I am I dead'. With explosion of the boundary, the third space of difference, into the general indifference, death is no longer outside us but among us. In Ballard's fictions of the future, as in Benjamin's melancholic of the past, the aporias of risk have already been played out long ago. There is not a risk society but a post-apocalyptic society. The melancholic wanders among the ruins in a blasé attitude: his nerves don't fire, she is indifferent. For Durkheim the symbolic was shot through with life. The symbolic was the normal set up against the pathological. But here the explosion of the symbolic, of the national symbolic by the cultural commodities of the global information culture, is also the destruction of life, the invasion of the normal by the pathological. Death, and its partner being, are no longer outside us but among us. There is nothing more at stake.

This book has addressed the shift from high modern epistemology to the ontology of the second modernity. Both the late Durkheim and Simmel make this step. The positivist diremption of fact and value is a matter of straightforward epistemology, ruling out of court value questions: extreme positivists even holding that value is superstructural to fact, that fact explains value. But the late Durkheim and Simmel switch this question round. Now value, as *conscience collective*, as classifications, as elementary forms of religious life, becomes the basis, the grounding, for fact. Now, instead of fact explaining value, value *explicates* fact. Now we can speak of a value-structure of fact.

With the rise of the global information culture, ontology comes unstuck. The very speed of the new technological order destroys the horizon, devastates being, paralyses subjectivity in a death-like stasis, to be bombarded by signal-objects in electromagnetic fields. This is the scenario ever repeated in turn-of-the-twenty-first-century popular culture, where there is no longer a constitutive outside, of a swirling vortex of microbes, genes, desire, death, onco-mice, semiconductors, holograms, semen, digitized images, electronic money and hyperspaces in a general economy of indifference. This is the scenario in which even being is reduced to the status of an 'actant', of equal status with the other main types of actants: with subjects, objects and symbols. Here being, like other actants, figures merely as a function in a narrative: figures merely as a player in the construction of actor networks. In this context being, alongside objects, subjects and symbols, works as a mediator, extending the networks over ever greater, increasingly global, stretches. Here being itself becomes technology, as existential actants are digitized, translating, mediating and building the networks.

In the networks, the actor-networks of the information society, objects and symbols are no longer finalities. The object becomes a terminal, a means of extending the networks. Subjectivity for its part loses all singularity. In the sea of indifference it becomes also a terminal indistinguishable from other actants. The subject no longer faces death, losing self-reflexivity on the horizon of time. The subject is now dead itself, reduced to a means, a terminal translating, mediating and extending the networks. The 'network society', reducing all to indifference, destroys ontology. Now all actants stand exposed to one another on the temporal horizon of speed, so that each – including being – becomes fully transparent to the other. In the network society, risks, reflexivity and ontology are dissipated, as technology – destroying the difference between instrumentality and finality – and new modes of capitalist accumulation wreak their revenge.

The network society has exploded limits, between human and non-human, between nation states, between the cultural and the material. But it, under the motive force of the global corporations in the new sectors, has created a new border: between those included and those denied access to the mode of information; a new stratification between those inside and outside 'the loop' of the information and communication structures. Sources of destabilization to the network society will come from both outside and inside the loop. Destabilization will come from the 'communication takers' outside the loop, who can divert and diffract the messages of the network society. And from inside, from the large and increasingly important number of workers in the techno-culture sectors. Both 'techno-artists' and 'techno-scientists' are vastly increasing their proportion of the labour force in the emergent sectors. In printing, graphics, software design, CD-ROM and Web site design, and post-production digital editing – indeed right through the culture industries and the information and biotechnological sectors – the legions of highly educated graduates are increasing. The techno-culture producers are increasing both as employees (techno-scientists and techno-artists in large firms) and through developing flexibly clustered small firms. Thus in multimedia the creators of global network space may be subject to challenge through what may amount to an alternative production of space.

The production of actor-networks and their extension, the production of globally expanding series of terminals, with their logic of mediation and translation, is in the global information culture the characteristic mode of production of space. This brings us back full circle to the opening chapters of this book and to questions of space. It brings us back to the paradigmatic model for the production of space. To Henri Lefebvre's 'spider' extending its body through space, producing space, mimetically, through symmetries and asymmetries, through mimesis and alterity, of its body, weaving a web and producing space. The spider gives us a model for challenging the exclusivist production of space of the network society. Lefebvre's spider weaves a web. And a web is vastly different from a network.

Lefebvre's spider, before the existence of images, prior to the emergence of symbols, weaves its web of a fundamentally *material* space. Like Lefebvre's spider, we in the global information age live not so much in a culture of narratives or images, but in a directly and literally material culture. Lefebvre's spider – with which we began this book – bears a striking resemblance to Walter Benjamin's melancholic, with which the book has come to a close. Both make their way through a culture of the real: through a culture in which we no longer get our fundamental orientations through narrative. In today's material culture we no longer primarily come to terms with our own self-identity through our life narratives. We no longer engage with existential meaning through the encounter with death. We no longer gain our orientation in the world through the encounter with the dominant narratives in the novel, cinema or television. The global information age is not a narrative but an *object* culture. It is a material culture in which technologies, objects of consumption, lifestyles, commodities, software, computer games, CD-ROMs, objects on the Internet come to dominate the cultural landscape. In which the previous narrative texts take their place among the former as just another set of material objects.

Lefebvre's spider is Benjamin's allegorist, operating in the real and weaving webs. Weaving webs of the fragments of narratives, images and symbol in the global information culture. Benjamin's melancholic wanders round the ruins of the city, via the fragments of stone through which he might glimpse redemption, might glimpse being. Benjamin's melancholic excavates the fragments and then recombines them, producing an allegorical space. Operating not by eye, not by ear, her orientation is tactile in the material ruins of the city. She strings together not narratively, but 'connectively', allegorically, the ruins, the objects of the dead and disused material space.

This object space in the real space of body orientation finds its parallel in a prosthetic space, a parallel space that is increasingly virtual. A space that is more interactive than interactivity. In an *inhabited* space. Yet real space, with its increasing ubiquity of international brands as signposts, becomes ever more similar to the parallel space. In both real space and parallel space our culture increasingly consists of finding our way among the objects. Now narratives become one of many types of object-entity in a sea of cultural objects, themselves increasing in proportion to the population of material objects. As we track these virtual and real objects, as we weave them into allegories, we also weave them into webs. Webs reaching back into long ago and far away. Webs that, at work and at play, may link us to other similar subjectivities, as well as tracking and producing objects in real and parallel space. Webs that may help to constitute communities of subjects and technologies. Webs that may once again open up the possibility for the retrieval of ontology. That may once again open up the possibility of redemption.

Notes

Chapter 1   Introduction

1   Michel Foucault, 'What is enlightenment?', in Paul Rabinow (ed.), *The Foucault Reader* (New York: Pantheon, 1984).

2   Ulrich Beck, *Risikogesellschaft, Auf dem Weg in eine andere Moderne* (Frankfurt am Main: Edition Suhrkamp, 1986), p. 16. Translated into English as *Risk Society* (London: Sage, 1992); Alain Touraine, *Critique of Modernity* (Oxford: Blackwell, 1995).

3   Jacques Derrida, *Donner le temps, 1. La fausse monnaie* (Paris: Editions Galilée, 1991), pp. 202–3. Trans. in English as *Given Time: 1. Counterfeit Money* (Chicago: University of Chicago Press, 1992).

4   Immanuel Kant, *The Critique of Judgement* (Oxford: Clarendon Press, 1952), p. 35.

5   Marshall Berman, *All That Is Solid Melts into Air: the Experience of Modernity* (London: Verso, 1982).

6   Anthony Giddens, *Modernity and Self-identity* (Cambridge: Polity Press, 1991).

7   Richard Rorty, *Philosophy and the Mirror of Nature* (Princeton, NJ: Princeton University Press, 1979), pp. 31ff.

8   Vincent Descombes, *Modern French Philosophy* (Cambridge: Cambridge University Press, 1980), pp. 75ff.; John B. Thompson, *Critical Hermeneutics* (Cambridge: Cambridge University Press, 1981), pp. 46–7; Hans Herbert Kögler, *The Power of Dialogue, Critical Hermeneutics after Gadamer and Foucault* (Cambridge, MA: The MIT Press, 1996).

9   Kant, *The Critique of Judgement*, p. 4.

10   Gilles Deleuze, *Francis Bacon, Logique de la sensation* (Paris: Editions de la différence, 1981).

11   Jean-François Lyotard, *Instructions païennes* (Paris: Editions Galilée, 1977).

12   See Georges Lefebvre, *Production de l'éspace*, 3rd edn (Paris: Editions anthropos, 1986), p. 273.

13   Georg Wilhelm Friedrich Hegel, *Grundlinien der Philosophie des Rechts oder Naturrecht und Staatswissenschaft im Grundrisse*, Werke 7 (Frankfurt: Suhrkamp, 1970), pp. 294–5.

14   Gillian Rose, *The Broken Middle* (Oxford: Blackwell, 1992), p. 12.

15   John Milbank, *Theology and Social Theory* (Oxford: Blackwell, 1990).

16   See, for example, Max Weber, *Wirtschaft und Gesellschaft, Grundriss der verstehenden Soziologie* (Tübingen: J. C. B. Mohr, 1960), pp. 317–19.

17 Emile Durkheim, *Les formes élémentaires de la vie réligieuse* (Paris: Presses Universitaires de France, 1968), pp. 557–61.
18 Martin Heidegger, *Sein und Zeit* (Tübingen: Max Niemeyer Verlag, 1986), pp. 252–4.
19 Derrida, *Donner le temps*, pp. 201–2.
20 Gilles Deleuze and Felix Guattari, *Anti-Oedipus, Capitalism and Schizophrenia* (New York: Viking Press, 1977), pp. 25ff.
21 Daniel Bell, *The Cultural Contradictions of Capitalism* (London: Heinemann, 1976), pp. 82–3.
22 Jonathan Friedman, *Cultural Identity and Global Process* (London: Sage, 1994), pp. 42–3.
23 Manuel Castells, *The Information Age: Economy, Society and Culture. Volume 1: The Rise of the Network Society* (Oxford: Blackwell 1996), pp. 337–8.
24 Talcott Parsons, *The Structure of Social Action. Volume I: Marshall, Pareto, Durkheim* (New York: Free Press, 1968), p. 551.
25 Bell, *Cultural Contradictions*, p. 47.
26 Castells, *Network Society*, pp. 61–2.
27 Mark Poster, *The Second Media Age* (Cambridge: Polity, 1995).

Chapter 2   The First Modernity: Humans and Machines

1 Manfredo Tafuri, *The Sphere and the Labyrinth: Avant Gardes and Architecture from Piranesi to the 1970s* (Cambridge, MA: MIT Press, 1987), p. 20.
2 M. Tafuri and Francesco Dal Co, *Modern Architecture, 1* (London: Faber, 1986), pp. 21ff.
3 Ibid., pp. 35–40.
4 Philip Johnson, cited in Peter Eisenman, 'Beyond the mirror: on the writings of Philip Johnson, *Oppositions*, 10, (1977), pp. 1–13, at p. 4.
5 Tafuri and Dal Co, *Modern Architecture*, pp. 47–9.
6 Ibid., pp. 25–7.
7 See Raymond Unwin, *The Gilds and Companies of London: Organisation in the Sixteenth and Seventeenth Centuries* (London: Methuen 1908), pp. 335–9; Tafuri and Dal Co, *Modern Architecture*, pp. 33–4, 51.
8 Herrmann Schwengel, *Der kleine Leviathan, Politische Zivilisation um 1900 und die amerikanische Dialektik von Modernisierung und Moderne* (Frankfurt: Athenaum, 1988), pp. 164ff.
9 Tafuri and Dal Co, *Modern Architecture*, pp. 197, 215.
10 Lewis Mumford, 'The ideal form of the modern city', in D. L. Miller (ed.), *The Lewis Mumford Reader*, pp. 162–75, at pp. 166–72.
11 Mumford, *The Mumford Reader*, pp. 176–7, 180–1, 205.
12 Nikolaus Pevsner, *Pioneers of Modern Design: from William Morris to Walter Gropius* (Harmondsworth: Penguin, 1960).
13 Philip Johnson, 'Reflections: on style and international style; on post-modernism; on architecture', *Oppositions*, 10 (1977), pp. 15–19, at p. 15.
14 Giorgio Ciucci, 'Invention of the modern movement', *Oppositions*, 24 (1982), pp. 68–91, at p.78.

15   Ibid., pp. 85–7.
16   Tafuri and Dal Co, *Modern Architecture*, p. 82.
17   Ibid., pp. 88–90.
18   Barbara Miller Lane, *Architecture and Politics in Germany, 1918–1945* (Cambridge, MA: Harvard University Press, 1968), pp. 8–9, 47, 69.
19   Ibid., pp. 58–9, 60–70.
20   Tafuri, *Sphere and Labyrinth*, pp. 202–3.
21   Lane, *Architecture and Politics*, p. 104.
22   Günter Uhlig, 'Stadtplanung in der Weimarer Republik: sozialistische Reformsaspekte', in *Wem gehört die Welt – Kunst und Gesellschaft in der Weimarer Republik* (Berlin: Neue Gesellschaft für bildende Kunst, 1977), pp. 50–71, at p. 54.
23   Tafuri, *Sphere and Labyrinth*, p. 210.
24   Uhlig, 'Stadtplanung', pp. 58–9; Tafuri, *Sphere and Labyrinth*, pp. 208, 213, 216–17.
25   Tafuri and Dal Co, *Modern Architecture*, p. 52.
26   Mumford, 'The Brooklyn Bridge', *Mumford Reader*, pp. 44–8, at pp. 47–8.
27   David Frisby, *Fragments of Modernity* (Cambridge: Polity Press, 1985), pp. 137ff.
28   Mumford, 'Towards modern architecture', *Mumford Reader*, pp. 49–72, at pp. 49–50; Tafuri and Dal Co, *Modern Architecture*, p. 58.
29   Tafuri and Dal Co, *Modern Architecture*, pp. 54, 58.
30   Bruno Bruognolo, 'Technische Voraussetzungen für den Bau von Hochhäusern', in F. Zimmermann (ed.), *Der Schrei nach dem Turmhaus, Der Ideenwettbewerb Hochhaus am Bahnhof Friedrichstrasse, Berlin 1921/22* (Berlin: Bauhaus-Archiv Museum für Gestaltung, 1988), pp. 227–37; Mumford, 'Towards modern architecture', pp. 56–8.
31   Philip Johnson, *Mies van der Rohe* (London: Secker & Warburg, 1947), p. 210, chapter 3 passim.
32   Ibid., pp. 180–3.
33   Werner Bläser, *Mies van der Rohe, Die Kunst der Struktur* (Stuttgart: Verlag für Architektur, 1965), p. 29.
34   J. Meyer, 'Mies van der Rohe, Berlin, Kennwort: Wabe', in *Schrei nach dem Turmhaus*, pp. 106–11, at p. 106.
35   Bläser, *Mies van der Rohe*, pp. 12–13.
36   Ibid., pp. 6, 8, 10.
37   Johnson, *Mies van der Rohe*, p. 43.
38   Martin Jay, 'Modern Regimes of Vision', in S. Lash and J. Friedman (eds), *Modernity and Identity* (Oxford: Blackwell, 1992).
39   Van der Rohe, quoted in Johnson, *Mies van der Rohe*, p. 50.
40   Johnson, ibid., pp. 9–13, 20, 28–37.
41   Franze Schulze, *Mies van der Rohe: Leben und Werk* (Berlin: Ernst & Sohn, 1986), chapter 3.
42   Richard Sennett, 'Plate glass', *Raritan*, 1987, pp. 1–15, at p. 4.
43   Ibid., p.13.
44   Elaine H. Hochman, 'Confrontation: 1933, Mies van der Rohe and the Third Reich', *Oppositions*, 18, 1979, 49–59.

45   See foreword to W. De Wit (ed.), *Louis Sullivan: The Function of Ornament* (New York: W. W. Norton, 1986), p. 7.

46   Rochelle Berger Elstein, 'Enigma of modern architecture: an introduction to the critics', in ibid., pp. 199–211, at pp. 204, 207.

47   William Jordy, 'The tall buildings', in De Wit, *Louis Sullivan*, pp. 65–158.

48   Ibid., p. 76.

49   Mumford, 'Towards modern architecture', pp. 62–7.

50   See Scott Lash, 'Moderne und bürgerliche Identität: Paris/Wien/Berlin', *Soziale Welt*, 41 (February 1990), pp. 41–67.

51   Jordy, 'Tall buildings', p. 149.

52   Ibid., p. 104.

53   Ibid., pp. 144–8.

54   See S. Lash, 'Modernity or modernism? Weber and contemporary social theory', in S. Whimster and S. Lash (eds), *Max Weber, Rationality and Modernity* (London: Allen & Unwin, 1987), pp. 355–77.

55   Stanford Anderson, 'Modern architecture and industry: Peter Behrens and the AEG factories', *Oppositions*, 23 (1981), pp. 52–83, at pp. 54–6.

56   Ibid., pp. 65–7.

57   Ibid., pp. 62, 77.

58   See S. Lash and J. Urry, *The End of Organized Capitalism* (Cambridge: Polity, 1987).

59   Mumford, 'Towards modern architecture', pp. 68–9; Tafuri and Dal Co, *Modern Architecture*, pp. 65–70.

60   William Curtis, 'Le Corbusier: nature and tradition', in *Le Corbusier, Architect of the Century* (London: Arts Council of Great Britain, 1987), pp. 13–23, p. 14.

61   Christopher Green, 'The architect as artist', in *Le Corbusier, Architect of the Century*, pp. 110–30, at pp. 112, 114.

62   Ibid., p. 112.

63   Tim Benton, 'Six houses', in *Le Corbusier, Architect of the Century*, pp. 44–70, p. 59.

64   Benton, 'Urbanism', in *Le Corbusier, Architect of the Century*, pp. 200–22, at p. 204.

65   Werner Oechslin, 'Critical note', *Oppositions*, 24 (1982), pp. 62–5.

66   Jean-Louis Cohen, 'Die Versuchung des Universellen', *Arch+*, Part 4, 90/91 (August 1987), pp. 93–7.

67   Green, 'Architect as artist', p. 114.

68   J.-T. Kohler and J. Maruhn, 'Wettbewerb der BVG 1929', in *Schrei nach dem Turmhaus*, pp. 167–85, pp. 174–5.

69   Green, 'Urbanism', in *Le Corbusier, Architect of the Century*, p. 201; Curtis, 'Nature and tradition', in ibid., p. 16.

70   Bruno Reichlin, 'l'esprit de Paris', *Arch+*, 90/91 (1987), pp. 47–58.

71   'Postscript to Corbusier: monofunctionalism and architecture', *Oppositions*, 24 (1982), pp. 66–77.

72   Benton, 'Six houses', p. 47.

73   Peter Eisenman, 'Writings of Johnson', p. 9.

74   See Philip Johnson, 'Reflections', *Oppositions*, 24 (1982), p. 17.

75 T. Adorno, 'Functionalism today', *Oppositions*, 17 (1979), pp. 31–44, at pp. 31–3.

76 Ibid., p. 42.

77 Ibid., p. 34.

78 See Herbert Schnädelbach, 'Dialektik als Vernunftkritik. Zur Rekonstruktion des Rationalen bei Adorno', in L. von Friedeburg and J. Habermas (eds), *Adorno-Konferenz* (Frankfurt: Suhrkamp, 1983), pp. 66–93, at pp. 70–1; Richard Kager, *Herrschaft und Versöhnung, Einführung in dem Denken Theodor W. Adornos* (Frankfurt: Campus, 1988), pp. 100–1; Michael Theunißen, 'Negativität bei Adorno', in *Adorno-Konferenz*, pp. 41–65, at pp. 63–4. Theodor W. Adorno, *Negative Dialektik, Jargon der Eigentlichkeit, Gesammelte Schriften, Band 6* (Frankfurt am Main: Suhrkamp, 1973), pp. 50–1. Also see F. Jameson, *The Political Unconscious* (London: Methuen, 1981), pp. 281–3.

79 Lewis Mumford, *The City in History: Its Origins, Its Transformations and Its Prospects* (New York: Harcourt Brace, 1961), p. 444.

80 Ibid., pp. 440ff.

81 Ibid., pp. 463–4. Also on the baroque and space see Hans-Georg Gadamer, 'Bemerkungen über den Barock', in Enrico Castelli (ed.), *Retorica e Barocco* (Rome: Fratelli Bocca Editori, 1955), pp. 61–3, at p. 61. Victor Tapié, *Baroque et classicisme* (Paris: Livres de Poche, 1980), p. 134. Christine Buci-Glucksmann, *La folie du voir* (Paris: Eds Galilée, 1986), pp. 20–1; Hans Sedlmayr, 'Allegorie und Architektur', in *Retorica e Barocco*, pp. 197–207, at p. 198.

82 Ibid., pp. 471–81.

83 Mumford, 'The case against modern architecture', in *Mumford Reader*, pp. 73–83, at p. 75. Also see S. Lash, 'The Politics of a Semiotic Society: Modernization and Politics in a Reunified Berlin', in Paul Knox (ed.), *The Restless Urban Landscape* (Englewood Cliffs, NJ: Prentice Hall, 1992), pp. 173–200.

84 Mumford, 'The case against modern architecture', p. 81.

85 Eisenman, 'The graves of humanism', *Oppositions*, 12 (1978), pp. 21–7, at p. 22.

Chapter 3   Simulated Humanism: Postmodern Architecture

1 Michel Foucault, *Les mots et les choses, une archaeologie des sciences humaines* (Paris: Gallimard, 1966). In *Les mots et les choses*, after the Renaissance episteme there are not one but two modern epistemes. The Renaissance episteme is understood in terms of the 'prose of the world'. The first modern episteme – which Foucault calls 'classical' – comes under the heading of 'representation'. The second modern episteme, basically after the 'Kantian revolution', comes under the heading 'the limits of representation' and is in many ways similar to the second modernity addressed in this book.

2 Max Weber, *Wirtschaft und Gesellschaft, Grundriss der verstehenden Soziologie*, 5th edn (Tübingen: J. C. B. Mohr, 1980), pp. 11–16; Parsons, *The Structure of Social Action, volume 2*, pp. 640ff.

3 Alasdair MacIntyre, *After Virtue: a Study in Moral Theory* (London: Duckworth, 1981), pp. 137ff.

4 Michel Foucault, *Histoire de la sexualité, 2, L'usage des plaisirs* (Paris: Gallimard, 1984), pp. 34–5; Foucault, *Histoire de la sexualité, 3, Le souci de soi* (Paris: Gallimard, 1984), pp. 147ff.

5 Emile Durkheim, *The Elementary Forms of Religious Life* (London: Allen & Unwin, 1915).

6 Max Weber, 'The social psychology of the world religions', in H. Gerth and C. W. Mills (eds), *From Max Weber: Essays in Sociology* (New York: Oxford University Press, 1946), pp. 267–302.

7 Robert A. M. Stern, 'The doubles of post-modernism', *Harvard Architectural Review*, 1 (1980), pp. 75–88, at pp. 86–7.

8 Ibid., pp. 79–80.

9 Maurice Culot and Leon Krier, 'The only path for architecture', *Oppositions*, 14 (1978), pp. 39–50, at p. 39.

10 Krier, 'The consumption of culture', *Oppositions*, 14 (1978), pp. 54–9, at p. 58.

11 Culot and Krier, 'Only path', p. 41.

12 Krier, 'Consumption', p. 57.

13 Culot and Krier, 'Only path', pp. 53, 41.

14 Robert Venturi and Denise Scott-Brown, 'Interview', *Harvard Architectural Review*, 1 (1980), pp. 228–39, at p. 231.

15 Vincent Scully in 'Beaux-Arts Exhibition: Forum', *Oppositions*, 8 (1977), pp. 160–75, at pp. 167–8.

16 S. Lash, 'Modernism and bourgeois identity: Paris, Vienna, Berlin', in Lash, *Sociology of Postmodernism* (London: Routledge, 1990), chapter 9.

17 Paul Rudolph, 'Beaux-Arts forum', pp. 161–2.

18 Alan Colquhoun, 'Three kinds of historicism', *Oppositions*, 27 (1984), pp. 28–39, at pp. 28–31.

19 Denise Scott Brown, 'Beaux-Arts forum', p. 166.

20 Kenneth Frampton, 'In Search of ground', in Ole Bouman and Roemer van Toorn (eds), *The Invisible in Architecture* (London: Academy Editions, 1994), pp. 190–5.

21 Anthony Vidler, 'Academicism, modernism', *Oppositions*, 8 (1977), pp. 1–5.

22 Colquhoun, 'Historicism', p. 138.

23 Wilhelm Hennis, 'Personality and life orders: Max Weber's theme', in Sam Whimster and Scott Lash (eds), *Max Weber, Rationality and Modernity*, pp. 52–74.

24 Eisenman, 'Graves', pp. 23–5.

25 Charles Moore, in 'Beyond the modern movement, forum discussion', *Harvard Architectural Review*, 1 (1980), pp.190–217, at p. 208.

26 Stern, in ibid., p. 214.

27 Rudolph, 'Beaux-Arts forum', p. 165.

28 Colquhoun, 'Sign and substance: reflections on complexity, Las Vegas and Oberlin', *Oppositions*, 14 (1978), pp. 26–37, at p. 27.

29 Krier, 'Debate: Casabella', *Oppositions*, 24 (1982), pp. 93–101, at p. 94.

30 Krier, 'Modern movement, forum', pp. 215–16.

31 Georg Wilhelm Friedrich Hegel, *Werke 8, Enzyklopädie der philosophischen Wissenschaften im Grundrisse (1830), Erster Teil, Die Wissenschaft der Logik* (Frankfurt: Suhrkamp, 1970), pp. 247–52.

32 Colquhoun, 'Sign and substance', pp. 26, 30.
33 Tafuri, *Sphere and Labyrinth*, pp. 285–6.
34 Johnson, 'Reflections', p. 19.
35 Colquhoun, 'From bricolage to myth, or how to put Humpty-Dumpty together again', *Oppositions*, 12 (1978), pp. 1–19, at p. 4.
36 Ibid., pp. 2–3.
37 Ibid., p. 7.
38 Ibid., pp. 16, 18.
39 Tigerman, 'Modern movement forum', p. 217.
40 Scott-Brown, 'Interview', p. 233.
41 Colquhoun, 'Sign and substance', p. 36.
42 Venturi, 'Interview', p. 234.
43 Scott-Brown, 'Interview', pp. 239, 234.
44 Ibid., pp. 229, 238.
45 Charles Moore, 'Conclusion to debate over Venturi and Rauch's Yale Mathematics Building', *Oppositions*, 6 (1976), pp. 20–1, at p. 20.
46 Venturi, 'Interview', p. 237.
47 Moore, 'Conclusion', p. 21.
48 Colin Rowe, 'Robert Venturi and the Yale Mathematics Building', *Oppositions*, 6 (1976), pp. 10–19, at p. 17.
49 Ed Soja, *Third Space* (Oxford: Blackwell, 1996).
50 OMA, Rem Koolhaas and Bruce Mau, *Small, Medium, Large and Extra-Large* (New York: Monacelli, 1995), pp. 764–821.
51 Celia Lury, *Prosthetic Culture* (London: Routledge, 1997).

Chapter 4   Grounding the City

1 Kenneth Frampton, 'In search of ground', in Ole Bouman and Roemer van Toorn (eds), *The Invisible in Architecture* (London: Academy Editions, 1994), pp. 190–5; David Harvey, *Justice, Nature and the Geography of Difference* (Oxford: Blackwell, 1996), pp. 291–326. On 'roots' and 'routes' see Paul Gilroy, *The Black Atlantic* (Cambridge, MA: Harvard University Press, 1993); James Clifford, *Routes* (London: Harvard University Press, 1997).
2 Fredric Jameson, 'Postmodernism, or, the cultural logic of late capitalism', *New Left Review*, 146 (1984), pp. 53–92.
3 Abraham Moles and Elisabeth Rohmer, *Labyrinthes de vécu. L'éspace: matière d'actions* (Paris: Librairie des Meridiens, 1982), p. 9.
4 Pierre Bourdieu, 'Le champs intellectuel: un monde à part', in Bourdieu, *Choses dites* (Paris: Editions de Minuit, 1987), pp. 167–77; Jean-François Lyotard, *Discours, figure* (Paris: Kincksieck, 1971); Maurice Mearleau-Ponty, *The Phenomenology of Perception* (New York: Humanities Press, 1962).
5 Moles and Rohmer, *Labyrinthes*, pp. 167–8.
6 Ibid., pp. iiiff.
7 Ibid., p. 170.
8 Ibid., pp. 30, 33.
9 Ibid., pp. 16–20.
10 Ibid., pp. 69–70.
11 Ibid., p. 76.

12   Kevin Lynch, *Images of the City* (Cambridge, MA: MIT Press, 1960), p. 6.
13   Ibid., p. 8.
14   Ibid., pp. 30, 39, chapter 2.
15   Ibid., pp. 47, 60.
16   Ibid. p. 42.
17   Ibid., pp. 66–70.
18   Ibid., p. 48, 72ff.
19   Ibid., p. 39.
20   Ibid., pp. 62–5.
21   Ibid., p. 48.
22   Dieter Hoffmann-Axthelm, 'Mythos-Stadt-Wahrnehmung', in *Mythos Berlin, Zur Warhrnehmungsgeschichte einer industriellen Metropole*, Katalog zur Ausstellung (Berlin: Aesthetik und Kommunikation, 1987), pp. 41–57, at p. 50. In Berlin the idea of myth and the city was raised on a large and public scale on the occasion of Berlin's 750th birthday in 1987. Large-scale works on building façades were undertaken, especially in the eastern side of the then divided city. The literature on architecture and myth is perhaps even more relevant in the context of today's 'unified' Berlin. In this context see, for example, Dieter Hoffmann-Axthelm's historical account of the Kreuzberg area of Berlin in *Strassenschlachtung, Geschichte, Abriss und Gebrochenes Weiterleben der Admiralstrasse* (Berlin: Nishen, 1984), pp. 87–98. Also worthy consulting by Hoffmann-Axthelm in the context of Berlin as myth is *Baufluchten: Beiträge zur Rekonstruktion der Geschichte Berlin-Kreuzbergs* (Berlin: Transit Buchverlag, 1987), pp. 108–44, and finally his *Die dritte Stadt, Bausteine eines neuen Gründungsvertrages* (Frankfurt: Suhrkamp, 1993), pp. 226–32. Hoffmann-Axthelm is himself something of a myth builder of origins. That is, his writing on the city is at the same time myth building. In this last cited book, his arguments for the reconstruction of the reunified Berlin in terms of a planning for urban density are addressed. Also on historical memory and Kreuzberg see Rainer Graff, 'Mixturen im Zwischenraum', in *Kreuzberger Mischung. Die innerstadtische Verflechtung von Architektur, Kultur und Gewerbe*, Katalog der Internationale Bauaustellung Berlin 1987 (Berlin: Aesthetik und Kommunikation Verlag, 1987), pp. 23–40. See also the debates in the Berlin based architecture journal *Arch+, Zeitschrift für Architektur und Stadtbau*; for example, Nikolaus Kuhnert and Wolfgang Wagener, 'Das Verschwinden der Architektur', *Arch+*, 95, 1988, pp. 78–83.
23   Hoffmann-Axthelm, 'Mythos-Stadt-Wahrnehmung', p. 41.
24   Ibid., pp. 44–52.
25   Ibid., p. 55.
26   See, for example, Rudolf Stegers, 'Das sentimentale Berlin oder die Großstadt als Gute Stube', *Aesthetik und Kommunikation*, 16, Heft 61–62 (1986), pp. 101–6.
27   Eberhard Knödler Bunte, 'Mythos Berlin', in *Mythos Berlin*, pp. 13–16.
28   Henri Lefebvre, *La production de l'espace*, 3rd edn (Paris: Anthropos, 1986), pp. 199–223.
29   Ibid., pp. 229–30.
30   Ibid., pp. 360–5.
31   Ibid, pp. 271ff.

32 Ibid., p. 232. A much fuller and less simplified account of Lefebvre is given in my *Technological Culture* (London: Sage, forthcoming).

33 Peter Eisenman, Introduction to Aldo Rossi, *The Architecture of the City* (Cambridge, MA: MIT Press, 1982), p. 3.

34 Aldo Rossi, ibid., p. 95.

35 Ibid., pp. 30–5.

36 Rossi, cited by Eisenman, p. 8.

37 Rossi, ibid., pp. 72–3.

38 Eisenman, p. 9.

39 Rossi, ibid., p. 86.

40 Lewis Mumford, *The City in History: Its Origins, Its Transformations and Its Prospects* (New York: Harcourt Brace, 1961), p. 47; Rossi, *Architecture of the City*, p. 136.

41 Mumford, *City in History*, pp. 48–9, 160.

42 Rossi, *Architecture of the City*, pp. 68, 93, 137.

43 Mumford, *City in History*, p. 308.

44 Ibid., p. 346.

45 Ibid., pp. 295, 308, 329, 352–7, 380–5. George Unwin, *The Guilds and Companies of London, Organisation in the Sixteenth and Seventeenth Centuries* (London: Methuen, 1925), pp. 28ff.

46 Mumford, *City in History*, pp. 347–9.

47 Ibid., pp. 320–3.

48 Ibid., p. 381.

49 Cited in Erwin Panofsky, *Meaning in the Visual Arts* (Chicago: University of Chicago Press, 1982), p. 177.

50 Ibid., p. 176.

51 Ibid., pp. 4, 5, 42–3, 52. Wilhelm Hennis, 'Max Webers Thema: Die Persönlichkeit und die Lebensordnungen', *Zeitschrift für Politik*, 31, pp. 11–52.

52 Panofsky, *Meaning in the Visual Arts*, pp. 59–61.

53 Ibid., p. 62.

54 Ibid., p. 99.

55 Ibid., p. 57

56 Ibid., pp. 2–3.

57 Sonia Brough, *The Goths and the Concept of Gothic in Germany from 1500 to 1750* (Frankfurt: Verlag Peter Lang, 1985), p. 122.

58 Ibid., pp. 201ff.

59 Please accept the remarks in the following section from an analyst who has no claims to particular expertise in Japan. It is difficult if not impossible for a Westerner to lay claims to an understanding of spatial sensibilities in Japan. Please also forgive the limited amounts of evidence I draw on in making my points. As a social and cultural theorist, I am proceeding by means of ideal types. I am looking at urban space and architecture in this part of this book in an attempt to discern the broad lines of the dimension of the groundedness, roots, particularity, place in what I have called the second modernity. I am drawing on some considerations of spatial sensibility in Japan to try to fill out this idea. In some ways, theorizing by ideal types proceeds more by way of illustration than by evidence. Theorizing by ideal types works – as it did in Weber – through drawing on social configurations that are vastly disparately

located in time and in space. In any event I am not sure that this book works through the amassing of evidence. I am not sure that the legal model of 'making a case' is what I am doing in this book. I see it instead as a set of *explorations* in the second modernity, and in discovering facts and discerning patterns in these explorations that will add depth and breadth to our understanding.

60 Augustin Berque, *Vivre l'espace au Japon* (Paris: Presses Universitaires de France, 1982), p. 119.

61 Ibid., pp. 124–5.

62 Ibid., pp. 118–19.

63 Ibid., pp. 121, 141–5.

64 Ibid., pp. 122, 127, 146.

65 Ibid., pp. 128–38, 152–3.

66 Ibid., pp. 130–2.

67 Ibid., pp. 159–64.

68 Ibid., pp. 32–3, 36–8, 42–3, 152–3.

69 Ibid., pp. 52–3.

70 Robert Wilson, 'Rehearsals', in Robert Wilson and David Byrne, *The Forest* (Berlin: Theater des Freien Volksbuhne, 1988), chapter IX.

71 Berque, *Vivre l'espace*, pp. 50, 61, 63, 66ff.

72 Augustin Berque, *Le Sauvage et l'artifice: les Japonais devant la nature* (Paris: Gallimard, 1986), pp. 48–9, 152, 157.

73 Ibid., pp. 108, 126, 175–6, 207–10.

74 Ibid., pp. 251–5.

75 Rem Koolhaas, *Delirious New York, a Retroactive Manifesto for Manhattan* (New York: Oxford University Press, 1978). The idea of complexity in urban space in this earlier Koolhaas book is based largely on buildings as objects. Compare this with the notion of complexity in Venturi discussed in chapter 3. Koolhaas has subsequently spoken of complexity in contrasting urbanism with architecture. Complexity in this view becomes associated with movement and especially with the movement of people through spaces in Koolhaas's idea of urbanism. See OMA, Rem Koolhaas and Bruce Mau, *Small, Medium, Large, Extra-Large* (Cologne: Benedikt Taschen Verlag, 1997), pp. 764ff.

76 Koolhaas, *Delirious*, pp. 81, 89, 137.

77 Ibid., pp. 98, 200, 215–20.

78 Johann Friedrich Geist, *Arcades: the History of a Building Type* (Cambridge, MA: MIT Press, 1983), pp. vii–viii.

79 Ibid., p. viii.

80 William H. Whyte, *The Social Life of Small Urban Spaces* (Washington, DC: Conservation Foundation, 1980).

81 Geist, *Arcades*, pp. 85–100. The arcade is evoked to great effect in, for example, Werner Fassbinder's video version of Döblin's *Berlin Alexanderplatz*.

82 Jürgen Habermas, *Strukturwandel der Öffentlichkeit* (Neuweid: Luchterhand, 1962). See also Habermas, 'Moderne und postmoderne Architektur', in *Die neue Unübersichtlichkeit* (Frankfurt: Suhrkamp, 1985), pp. 17–18. Geist, *Arcades*, pp. 80–2.

83 Moles and Rohmer, *Labyrinthes*, p. iii. And see Werner Fuld, 'Die Aura, zur

Geschichte eines Begriffes im Werk Walter Benjamins', in Walter Benjamin, *Deutschlands Untergang in zwanzig Thesen* (Münster: Aurin Verlag, 1987), pp. 23–50, at pp. 25–6.

84 Walter Benjamin, Charles Baudelaire, *Ein Lyriker im Zeitalter des Hochkapitalismus*, in Walter Benjamin, *Gesammelte Schriften*, *I-2* (Frankfurt: Suhrkamp, 1991), pp. 509–690, esp. pp. 517ff.

85 Ibid., pp. 525ff.

86 See ibid., pp. 568–9.

87 Ibid., pp. 582–3.

88 Ibid., pp. 588–9.

89 Ibid., pp. 591–2. See discussion of Benjamin and Baudelaire in the context of the notion of the object in chapter 13.

90 On the empirical and the transcendental see Richard Beardsworth, *Derrida and the Political* (London: Routledge, 1996).

Chapter 5   From System to Symbol:
Durkheim and French Sociology

1 Daniel Bell, *The Cultural Contradictions of Capitalism* (London: Heinemann, 1976), pp. 82–3; Marshall Berman, *All That Is Solid Melts into Air: the Experience of Modernity* (London: Verso, 1982).

2 Bruno Latour, *We Have Never Been Modern* (London: Harvester Wheatsheaf, 1993).

3 Pierre Bourdieu, 'Fieldwork et philosophie', in *Choses dites* (Paris: Editions de Minuit, 1987), pp. 13–46.

4 See, for example, Wolf Lepenies, *Die drei Kulturen, Soziologie zwischen Literatur und Wissenschaft* (Munich: Carl Hanser Verlag, 1985), pp. 59–63.

5 Donald N. Levine, *The Flight from Ambiguity, Essays in Social and Cultural Theory* (Chicago: University of Chicago Press, 1985), pp. 2–5.

6 Steven Lukes, *Emile Durkheim, His Life and Work* (Harmondsworth: Penguin, 1975), chapter 2.

7 Anthony Giddens, *New Rules of Sociological Method* (London: Hutchinson, 1976), pp. 142–8.

8 Lukes, *Durkheim*, pp. 378–82.

9 Ibid., pp. 386–9.

10 Michel Foucault, *Les mots et les choses, une archéologie des sciences humaines* (Paris: Gallimard), pp. 262–4.

11 Paul Rabinow, *French Modern, Norms and Forms of the Social Environment* (Cambridge, MA: MIT Press, 1989), pp. 19–20.

12 Ibid., pp. 10–12.

13 Ibid., pp. 25, 32.

14 Ibid., pp. 135ff.

15 Ibid., pp. 130–3.

16 On functional explanation see G. A. Cohen, *Karl Marx's Theory of History: a Defence* (Oxford: Clarendon, 1978), pp. 226–30; Scott Lash and John Urry, The new Marxism of collective action: a critical analysis', *Sociology*, 18 (February 1984), pp. 33–50.

17 Jurgen Habermas, *Theorie des kommunikativen Handels, Band 1, Handlungs-rationalität und gesellschaftliche Rationalisierung* (Frankfurt: Suhrkamp, 1981), pp. 72ff.

18 Rabinow, *French Modern*, pp. 60ff.

19 Friedrich Nietzsche, *Jenseits von Gut und Böse, Vorspiel einer Philosophie der Zukunft*, in Nietzsche, Werke in drei Bänden, zweiter Band (Munich: Carl Hanser Verlag, 1966), pp. 598–601.

20 Emile Durkheim, *Les règles de la méthode sociologique* (Paris: Presses Universitaires de France, 1977), pp. 47–58; Emile Durkheim, *Le suicide, Etude de sociologie* (Paris: Presses Universitaires de France, 1973), p. 434.

21 Rabinow, *French Modern*, p. 66.

22 Emile Durkheim, *De la division du travail social* (Paris: Felix Alcan, 1893).

23 Rabinow, *French Modern*, p. 48. Also see above discussion in chapters 2 and 4.

24 Rabinow, *French Modern*, pp. 50–1.

25 Claude Lévi-Strauss, *Introduction to the Work of Marcel Mauss* (London: Routledge, 1987), pp. 24–5.

26 Ibid., p. 14.

27 Pierre Bourdieu, *Le sens practique* (Paris: Editions de Minuit, 1980).

28 Mauss, cited in Lévi-Strauss, *Mauss*, p. 34.

29 Mauss, *La Magie*, cited in Lévi-Strauss, *Mauss*, p. 56.

30 Lévi-Strauss, ibid., p. 63.

31 By cultural pessimism I am referring to thinkers such as Arnold Gehlen, *Moral und Hypermoral. Eine pluralistische Ethik* (Frankfurt: Athenäum, 1969).

32 Emile Durkheim and Marcel Mauss, 'De quelques formes primitives de la classification, contribution à l'étude des représentations collectives', in Marcel Mauss, *Oeuvres. Volume 2, Représentations collectives et diversité des civilisations* (Paris: Editions de Minuit, 1969), pp. 13–89, at p. 86.

33 Durkheim and Mauss, 'Formes primitives', p. 13.

34 Ibid., p. 14.

35 'Formes primitives', pp. 14–15.

36 Ibid., p. 17.

37 'Formes primitives', p. 20.

38 Ibid., p. 82.

39 Ibid., pp. 19, 83.

40 Ibid., pp. 22, 24–5.

41 'Formes primitives', p. 83.

42 Ibid., p. 86.

43 Ibid., p. 84.

44 Luc Boltanski and Laurent Thevenot, *De la justification. Les économies de la grandeur* (Paris: Gallimard, 1991).

45 Durkheim and Mauss, 'Formes primitives', p. 87.

46 Ibid., p. 88.

47 Ibid., pp. 48–9.

48 Ibid., pp. 70–81.

49 Ibid., pp. 71–2; Anthony Giddens, *The Constitution of Society* (Cambridge: Polity Press, 1984), pp. 258–9.

50 Durkheim and Mauss, 'Formes primitives', pp. 79–80.

Chapter 6   Symbol and Allegory: Simmel

1 Wolf Lepenies, *Die drei Kulturen* (Munich: Hanser, 1985), pp. 16, 51.
2 Ibid., p. 87.
3 Ibid., p. 45.
4 See article by Herbert Schnädelbach on this theme in Adorno's negative dialectics, in L. von Friedeberg and J. Habermas (eds), *Adorno-Konferenz 1983* (Frankfurt: Suhrkamp, 1983) pp. 70–88, at p. 73.
5 Lepenies, *Die drei Kulturen*, pp. 74ff.
6 Levine, *The Flight from Ambiguity: Essays in Social and Cultural Theory* (Chicago: University of Chicago Press, 1985), pp. 66–7.
7 See H. Stuart Hughes, *Consciousness and Society* (New York: Octagon Books, 1976).
8 Benedict Anderson, *Imagined Communities*, 2nd edn (London: Verso, 1991), pp. 42ff. My use of ideographic and nomothetic here is only metaphoric. Clearly Windelband's later introduction of these terms must be understood differently in a strict sense. Windelband was not alluding to the classical ideal in his idea of ideographic. I am indebted to Jonatas Ferreira on this point.
9 W. Lepenies, *Between Literature and Science: the Rise of Sociology* (Cambridge: Cambridge Univesity Press, 1988), p. 48.
10 See Artur Bogner, *Zivilisation und Rationalisierung* (Opladen: Westdeutscher Verlag, 1989), pp. 18ff.
11 On symbol and allegory see Hans Georg Gadamer, *Wahrheit und Methode* (Tübingen: Mohr, 1986), pp. 76ff.
12 See Walter Benjamin's *Goethes Wahlverwandtschaften* in *Abhandlungen, Gesammelte Schriften, Band I-1* (Frankfurt: Suhrkamp, 1974), pp. 123–202, pp. 143ff. I am indebted to Trevor Smith for these points.
13 Michael Landmann, 'Georg Simmel und Stefan George', in H. J. Dahme and O. Rammstedt (eds), *Georg Simmel und die Moderne* (Frankfurt: Suhrkamp, 1984), pp. 147–73, p. 170.
14 H. P. Rickman, *Wilhelm Dilthey* (Berkeley: University of California Press, 1979), pp. 74ff.
15 See, for example, Lepenies, *Literature and Science*, p. 271.
16 Sam Whimster, 'The secular ethic and the culture of modernism', in S. Whimster and S. Lash (eds), *Max Weber, Rationality and Modernity* (London: Allen & Unwin, 1987), pp. 259–90.
17 See, for example, Heinz Petzold, *Ernst Cassirer, von Marburg nach New York, Eine philosophische Biographie* (Darmstadt: Wissenschaftliche Buchgesellschaft, 1995).
18 Although Heinrich Rickert had a unique position in this context. Rickert, proffered a nomothetic *Wissenschaft* of value, based on a highly cognitivist notion of value. See Stephen Turner and Regis Factor, *Max Weber and the Dispute over Reason and Value* (London: Routledge, 1984). See also Jonatas Ferreira, 'Judgement, modernity and classical sociological theory', PhD thesis, Lancaster University, 1998.
19 Lepenies, *Die drei Kulturen*, p. 380ff.
20 Otthein Rammstedt, 'Die Attituden der Klassiker als unsere soziologischen Selbstverständlichkeiten, Durkheim, Simmel, Weber und die Konstitution

der modernen Soziologie', in O. Rammstedt (ed.), *Simmel und die frühen Soziologie* (Frankfurt: Suhrkamp, 1988), pp. 275–307, at p. 295.

21 Wolfgang Mommsen, *Max Weber and German Politics* (Chicago: University of Chicago Press, 1984).

22 Whimster, 'Secular ethic', pp. 270–2.

23 Rammstedt, 'Attituden der Klassiker', pp. 278–9.

24 See Thomas E. Willey, *Back to Kant* (Detroit: Wayne State University Press, 1978), and especially Heinz-Jürgen Dahme, 'Das "Abgrenzungsproblem", Philosophie und Wissenschaft bei Georg Simmel, Zur Genese und Systematik einer Problemstellung', in *Georg Simmel und die Moderne*, pp. 202–30, at p. 207.

25 Louis Althusser, *Lénine et la philosophie* (Paris: Maspéro, 1972).

26 Max Weber, 'The social psychology of the world religions', in H. Gerth and C. W. Mills (eds), *From Max Weber* (New York: Oxford University Press, 1958), pp. 267–301.

27 See Michael Makropolous, *Modernität und Kontingenz* (Munich: Wilhelm Fink, 1997).

28 Alexander Deichsel, 'Das Soziale in der Wechselwirkung, Friedrich Tönnies und Georg Simmel als lebendige Klassiker', in *Simmel und frühen Soziologie*, pp. 164–85, p. 170.

29 Werner Jung, *Georg Simmel zur Einführung* (Hamburg: Junius Verlag, 1990), pp. 31–54.

30 Dahme, 'Abgrenzungsproblem', pp. 212–14; Georg Simmel, 'Stefan George, Eine kunstphilosopische Studie', in Simmel, *Vom Wesen der Moderne, Essays zur Philosophie und Aesthetik* (Hamburg: Sammlung Junius, 1990), pp. 195–214, pp. 201–2.

31 There are important exceptions to this: especially the hermeneutics of retrieval of Dilthey and Gadamer, who work with a very strong notion of the ground. For Dilthey this is in his idea of objective knowledge, for Gadamer through tradition. I address Gadamer in broadly this context in chapter 9. I am grateful to Larry Ray for this point.

32 David Frisby, *Fragments of Modernity* (Cambridge: Polity Press, 1985), p. 94.

33 Klaus Lichtblau, 'Das "Pathos der Distanz". Präliminarien zur Nietzsche-Rezeption bei Georg Simmel', in Dahme and Rammstedt (eds), *Simmel und die Moderne*, pp. 231–81, at pp. 237–8; G. Simmel, 'Friedrich Nietzsche, Eine moralphilosophische Silhouette', in *Wesen der Moderne*, pp. 61–82, at p. 74.

34 Lichtblau, 'Pathos', p. 247.

35 Dahme, 'Abgrenzungsproblem', pp. 226–7.

36 Ibid., pp. 210–11.

37 Lichtblau, 'Pathos', p. 273.

38 Landmann, 'Simmel und George', p. 151.

39 Ibid., pp. 152, 172.

40 Gadamer returns to discussions of the baroque in his article, 'Begriffsgeschichte als Philosophie', published originally in 1970. Cited in the *Eragänzungen Register, Wahrheit und Methode* (Tübingen: Mohr, 1986), pp. 77–91, at pp. 85ff. Landmann, 'Simel und George', p. 169.

41 Landmann, 'Simmel und George', p. 152.

42 Lichtblau, 'Pathos', pp. 250–2.

43 Ibid., pp. 255, 257.

44 Ibid., p. 252

45 Brigitta Nedelmann, 'Georg Simmel als klassiker soziologischer Prozess-analysen', in *Simmel und die Moderne*, pp. 91–115, at p. 109.

46 Georg Simmel, *The Philosophy of Money*, 2nd edn (London: Routledge, 1990), pp. 297ff.; Diechsel, 'Das Soziale', p. 73.

47 Nedelmann, 'Georg Simmel', pp. 106–7.

48 Vergsellschaftung is often translated as 'societalization'. More literally it means the way in which a notion, an idea or a feeling is worked through by a society, by social institutions. For example, Klaus Eder's important book *Die Vergesellschaftung der Natur* (Frankfurt: Suhrkamp, 1987) addresses how different social formations with widely varying institutions work through a given notion of nature.

49 Nedelmann, 'Georg Simmel', pp. 94–5.

50 Ibid., pp. 98–9; Michel Maffesoli, 'Ein Vergleich zwischen Emile Durkheim und Georg Simmel', in *Simmel und die frühen Soziologie*, pp. 163–80, at p. 169.

51 Eder, *Vergesellschaftung der Natur*, pp. 88ff.

52 Nedelmann, 'Georg Simmel', p. 100.

53 Ibid., p. 102.

54 See detailed discussion in chapter 13 below. I am indebted to Hermann Schwengel on this point.

55 Christine Buci-Glucksmann, *La folie du voir, de l'esthétique baroque* (Paris: Editions Galilée, 1986), p. 41.

56 Not just Benjamin but Gadamer spoke of such a 'language of things'. See his 'Die Natur der Sprache und die Sprache der Dinge', in his *Gesammelte Werke, Band 2, Hermeneutik II, Wahrheit und Methode, Ergänzungsregister* (Tübingen: Mohr, 1986), pp. 66–76.

57 David Frisby, 'Georg Simmels Theorie der Moderne', in *Georg Simmel und die Moderne*, pp. 9–79, at p. 20; Georg Simmel, 'The Adventurer', in Georg Simmel, *On Individuality and Social Forms* (Chicago: University of Chicago Press, 1971), pp. 187–98.

Chapter 7   The Natural Attitude and the Reflexive Attitude

1 U. Beck, A. Giddens and S. Lash, *Reflexive Modernization* (Cambridge: Polity, 1994), pp. 116–17.

2 Hans-Georg Gadamer uses this contrast of 'espitemology' and 'ontology' in his 'The phenomenological movement', in Gadamer, *Philosophical Hermeneutics* (Berkeley: University of California Press, 1976), pp. 130–81, at p. 131. I am indebted to Hermann Schwengel for the above point on Hegel.

3 I have learnt the most about the ontological structures of things – in distinction to the understanding of things as nature – as well as the ontological structure of subjectivity from Emmanuel Levinas's often neglected book, *The Theory of Intuition in Husserl's Phenomenology* (Evanston, IL: Northwestern University Press, 1973), pp. 10–13, 113–15.

4 There was a major sociological literature in the 1970s dealing with Schutz and life-world phenomenology. For example, Richard Bernstein, *The Restructuring*

of Social and Political Theory (London: Methuen, 1976); Anthony Giddens's *New Rules of Sociological Method* (London: Hutchinson, 1976); Zygmunt Baumann, *Hermeneutics and Social Science* (London: Hutchinson, 1978); John B. Thompson, *Critical Hermeneutics* (Cambridge: Cambridge University Press, 1981). This was largely in the context of the critique of sociological positivism via interpretive sociology and especially ethnomethodoloy. I am addressing Schutz and life-world phenomenology some twenty years later in the wake of deconstruction and post-structuralism and after study of Heidegger and Gadamer. This treatment of Schutz differs from the seventies treatment in its context of the critique of deconstruction and the critique of the idea of reflexive modernizaton from the ground of the life-world. It is also different in its focus on time. I hope it helps to attest to the lasting value of Schutz's work to a new generation of social theorists.

5   Alfred Schutz, *The Phenomenology of the Social World* (London: Heinemann Educational Books, 1972); *Der Sinnhafte Aufbau der sozialen Welt: Eine Einleitung in die verstehende Soziologie* (Frankfurt: Suhrkamp, 1974). In the pages that follow I will in notes to the English language edition as *PSW*.

6   Georg Simmel, 'Henri Bergson', in *Vom Wesen der Moderne, Essays zur Philosophie und Aesthetik* (Hamburg: Sammlung Junius, 1990), pp. 119–43, at p. 140.

7   See Heidegger on 'Auslegung', and 'explication' in *Sein und Zeit* (Tübingen: Max Niemeyer, 1986), e.g. p. 37.

8   Schutz, *Sinnhafte Aufbau*, pp. 71ff. See also Jean-Luc Marion, *Réduction et donation, Recherches sur Husserl, Heidegger et la phénoménologie* (Paris: Presses Universitaires de France, 1989), pp. 97–103.

9   See Edmund Husserl, *Ideen zu einer reinen Phänomenologie und phänomenologischen Philosophie, Allgemeine Einführung in die reine Phänomenologie*, 5th edn (Tübingen: Max Niemeyer, 1993), pp. 64–5.

10   Here Schutz's observations are based on Husserl, *Ideen*, p. 52.

11   Schutz, *Sinnhafte Aufbau*, p. 95, *PSW*, p. 71.

12   *Sinnhafte Aufbau*, p. 97, *PSW*, p. 73.

13   Schutz, *PSW*, pp. 72–3.

14   *Sinnhafte Aufbau*, p. 98; *PSW*, p. 74; Husserl, *Ideen*, pp. 180ff.

15   Heidegger, *Sein und Zeit*, pp. 142ff.

16   Schutz, *Sinnhafte Aufbau*, p. 62; *PSW*, p. 45.

17   *PSW*, p. 70; *Sinnhafte Aufbau*, p. 93.

18   *Sinnhafte Aufbau*, p. 65; *PSW*, p. 47.

19   *PSW*, pp. 50–1; *Sinnhafte Aufbau*, p. 68. See Husserl, *On the Phenomenology of the Consciousness of Internal Time* (Dordrecht: Kluwer, 1991), p. 42.

20   *PSW*, pp. 48, 51. Husserl, *Texte zur Phänomenologie des inneren Zeitbewußtseins (1893–1917)* (Hamburg: Felix Meiner Verlag, 1985), pp. 125–30.

21   Schutz, *PSW*, p. 48; *Sinnhafte Aufbau*, p. 65. Husserl, *Internal Time*, pp. 44–5.

22   *PSW*, pp. 49, 52. Husserl, *Inneren Zeitbewußtseins*, pp. 177ff.

23   *PSW*, p. 60; *Sinnhafte Aufbau*, pp. 74–5. Husserl, *Internal Time*, p. 54.

24   Heidegger, *Sein und Zeit*, pp. 134–5.

25   Gerhard Schulze, *Die Erlebnisgesellschaft, Kultursoziologie der Gegenwart* (Frankfurt: Campus, 1993), pp. 231ff. Translated in English as *The Experience Society* (London: Sage, 1999).

26 Gadamer, *Truth and Method*, 2nd edn (London: Sheed & Ward, 1989), pp. 246–62. See also Howard Caygill, Walter Benjamin, *The Colour of Experience* (London: Routledge, 1998).

27 In the *Ideen* (p. 139), for example, section 75 is entitled 'Die Phänomenologie als deskriptive Wesenslehre der reinen Erlebnisse'.

28 Yet Husserl speaks of a 'double intentionality of retention', in *Internal Time*, p. 84.

29 Schutz, *Sinnhafte Aufbau*, pp. 102–3; *PSW*, p. 76.

30 *Sinnhafte Aufbau*, p. 104; *PSW*, p. 77.

31 *Sinnhafte Aufbau*, p. 111; *PSW*, p. 83.

32 *Sinnhafte Aufbau*, p. 112; *PSW*, p. 84.

33 This is addressed famously in the section on intersubjectivity in Husserl's *Cartesianische Meditationenen* (Hamburg: Felix Meiner, 1987), pp. 91ff. In this book a number of sections are devoted to the possibility of grasping the experience of the other, where Husserl consistently uses *Erfahrung* and not *Erlebnis* to speak of the experience of the other ('*Fremderfahrung*').

34 *PSW*, pp. 97–9.

35 *PSW*, pp. 102–4.

36 *PSW*, p. 101.

37 Ibid.

38 Ibid., pp. 101, 104n.

39 Schutz, *Sinnhafte Aufbau*, pp. 165–6, *PSW*, pp. 119–21. Also see Umberto Eco, *A Theory of Semiotics* (Bloomington: Indiana University Press, 1976), p. 4.

40 *Sinnhafte Aufbau*, pp. 167–8; *PSW*, pp. 123–4.

41 *Sinnhafte Aufbau*, pp. 186–8; *PSW*, pp. 133–5.

42 *PSW*, p. 127.

43 Ibid., pp. 125–6.

44 Ilja Srubar, *Kosmion, Die Genese der pragmatischen Lebenswelttheorie von Alfred Schütz und ihr anthropologischer Hintergrund* (Frankfurt: Suhrkamp, 1988), p. 272.

45 Niklas Luhmann, *Gesellschaftsstruktur und Semantik, Studien zur Wissenssoziologie der modernen Gesellschaft, Band I* (Frankfurt: Suhrkamp, 1993), pp. 15ff.

46 Srubar, *Kosmion*, p. 273: Bauman, *Hermeneutics and Social Science*, p. 179.

47 Stephen Turner, *The Social Theory of Practices* (Chicago: University of Chicago Press, 1994).

48 Bryan S. Turner, *The Body and Society* (Oxford: Blackwell, 1984), p. 61.

49 Gadamer, 'The philosophical foundations of the twentieth century', in *Philosophical Hermeneutics*, pp. 107–29, at p. 120.

50 Michael Dummett, 'Gottlob Frege', *The Encyclopaedia of Philosophy, volume 3* (New York: Collier Macmillan, 1968), pp. 225–37, at pp. 227–8.

51 Thompson, *Critical Hermeneutics*, pp. 11–15.

52 John Searle, *Speech Acts: Theory and Pragmatics* (Dordrecht: Reidel, 1980), p. 12.

53 Thompson, *Critical Hermeneutics*, p. 21.

54 Ibid., p. 18; Bernstein, *Restructuring*, pp. 138–9.

55 Paul Ricoeur, 'Negativity and primary affirmation', in *History and Truth* (Evanston, IL: Northwestern University Press, 1965), pp. 305–28, at p. 311.

56 See discussion of intentionality in Edmund Husserl, *Logische Untersuchungen, II/*

2, *Elemente einer phänomenologischeschen Aufklärung der Erkenntnis* (Tübingen: Max Niemeyer Verlag, 1993), pp. 8–63.

57 Ibid., p. 309.
58 Paul Ricoeur, 'Phenomenology and hermeneutics', in *Hermeneutics and the Human Sciences: Essays on Language, Action and Interpretation* (Cambridge: Cambridge University Press; Paris: Editions de la Maison des Sciences de l'Homme, 1981), pp. 101–30, at p. 116.
59 Ricoeur, 'Negativity', p. 308.
60 Ricoeur, 'Phenonemology and hermeneutics', p. 118.
61 Ibid., p. 119.
62 Hubert Dreyfus, *Being-in-the-World* (Cambridge, MA: MIT Press, 1991), p. 343.
63 Ricoeur, 'Phenomenology and hermeneutics', p. 126.
64 Ricoeur, 'Negativity', pp. 307–11.
65 Thompson, *Critical Hermeneutics*, p. 46.
66 Charles Kelbley, Translator's introduction to Ricoeur, *History and Truth*, p. xx.
67 Ricoeur, 'Phenomenology and hermeneutics', p. 118.
68 Ricoeur, *La configuration du temps dans le récit de fiction, Tome II, Temps et récit* (Paris: Editions du seuil, 1984), pp. 194ff. See also Ricoeur, 'Hermeneutics and the critique of ideology', in *Hermeneutics and the Human Sciences*, pp. 63–100, at p. 73.
69 Ricoeur, 'Phenomenology and hermeneutics', pp. 110–12.
70 Thompson, *Critical Hermeneutics*, pp. 56–7.
71 Ricoeur, 'Negativity', p. 310.
72 Ibid., p. 315.
73 Ibid., p. 320; Emmanuel Levinas, *De l'existence à l'existant*, 2nd edn (Paris: Librairie Philosophique J. Vrin, 1990), pp. 15–16.
74 Ricoeur, 'Negativity', p. 323.
75 Ibid., p. 326.
76 Ibid., pp. 317, 327.
77 Kelbley, Introduction, pp. xvi–xviii.
78 Ricoeur, Preface to the first edition, *History and Truth*, pp. 6–7.
79 Ibid., p. 13.

Chapter 8 Difference and Infinity: Derrida

1 This chapter draws on Derrida to help further to flesh out the nature of the second modernity's ground. But it is also critical of him and deconstruction for too much forgetting of this ground. It does not constitute a 'critique' *per se* of Derrida. Such a critique is beyond the scope of this book, and, I expect, my scholarship. In this book I draw on only a selection of his work, and especially on a detailed treatment of *Speech and Phenomenon*. A proper critique of Derrida would necessitate chapter length detailed readings from a range of his major texts. It could be argued, for example, that in *Spectres of Marx* (London: Routledge, 1994) there is a notion of memory not far removed from the grounded intersubjectivity of life-world hermeneutics, and especially a strong notion of mourning for this ground. The present book in its discussion of the

global information society largely understands the ground, the missing ground, in terms of such mourning. In part V I have understood the global information culture in terms of the explosion of the space of ontological difference into the flatness, the immanence of a more generalized *indifference*. In response to this it could be shown that Derrida does not only rely on a *space* of difference, but that difference can be 'disseminated' in a sense that suggests the collapse of the distinction between the same and the other, between beings and being. See J. Derrida, *La dissémination* (Paris: Editions du Seuil, 1972), pp. 363ff. Further, Derrida's very recent work with Bernard Stiegler begins to take on the asumptions of the informational order. See Jacques Derrida and Bernard Stiegler, *Echographies de la télévision* (Paris: Galilée, 1996).

2   We will see in chapter 10 the importance of the third, aesthetic critique in this context.

3   Derrida addresses Husserl's reduction and Kantian Ideas of Vernunft in J. Derrida, *Edmund Husserl's Origin of Geometry: an Introduction* (Stony Brook, NY: Nicholas Hays Ltd, 1978), pp. 139–41.

4   W. H. Walsh, *Kant's Criticism of Metaphysics* (Edinburgh: Edinburgh University Press, 1975), p. 41.

5   Immanuel Kant, *Critique of Pure Reason* (London: Macmillan, 1933), pp. 65ff.

6   See, for example, E. Husserl, *Ideen zu einer reinen Phänomenologie und phänomenologischen Philosophie, Allgemeine Einführung in die reine Phänomenologie*, 5th edn (Tübingen: Max Niemeyer, 1993), p. 60.

7   Ibid., pp. 19–20.

8   Ibid., pp. 111–14; I am indebted to Galena Tasheva on this point.

9   Derrida, *Donner le temps, 1. La fausse monnaie* (Paris: Galilée, 1991), pp. 34–7, 202–3.

10 Ibid., pp. 51ff.

11 J. Derrida, *La voix et le phénomène, Introduction au problème du signe dans la phénomenologie de Husserl*, third edition (Paris: Presses Universitaire de France, 1976), p. 85. J. Derrida, *Speech and Phenomena, and Other Essays on Husserl's Theory of Signs* (Evanston, IL: Northwestern University Press, 1973), p. 76.

12 J. Derrida, '"Genèse et structure" et la phénomenologie', in *L'écriture et la différence* (Paris: Editions du Seuil, 1979), pp. 229–53, at p. 234. Translated into English as '"Genesis and structure" and phenomenology' in *Writing and Difference* (London: Routledge, 1978), pp. 154–68, at p. 157.

13 *Voix et phénomène*, p. 26; *Speech and Phenomena*, p. 25; Genèse et structure', p. 232; Genesis and structure, p. 156

14 *Voix et phénomène*, pp. 11–12; *Speech and Phenomena*, pp. 11–12.

15 'Genèse et structure', p. 238; 'Genesis and structure', p. 160.

16 'Genèse et structure', p. 238; 'Genesis and structure', p. 160.

17 'Genesis and structure' pp. 162–3. See also Simon Critchley's insightful commentary on this essay in *The Ethics of Deconstruction, Derrida and Levinas* (Oxford: Blackwell, 1992), pp. 63ff.

18 'Genesis and structure', p. 163. Husserl, *Ideas Pertaining to a Pure Phenomenology and to a Phenomenological Philosophy. First Book, General Introduction to a Pure Phenomenology* (Dordrecht: Kluwer, 1982), pp. 171ff.

19 In *Ideen* (p. 201), Husserl speaks, in the context of the noetic–noematic structure of the pure phenomenological experience of the hyletic and noetic mo-

ments as real and the noematic moment as irreal moments of experience (*Erlebnis*).

20 Husserl, *Ideen*, pp. 67–8.
21 Gayatri Spivak, Translator's preface, to J. Derrida, *Of Grammatology* (Baltimore: Johns Hopkins University Press, 1976), pp. ix–lxxxviii, at p. lxv.
22 Derrida, *Grammatology*, pp. 11–12. On the transcendental signified see also J. Derrida, *Positions* (Editions de Minuit, 1972), p. 31.
23 Hence he speaks of the notion of Being in Heidegger in terms of what is effectively a transcendental signified. See J. Derrida, *Spurs, Nietzsche's Styles, Eperons, Les styles de Nietzsche* (Chicago: University of Chicago Press, 1978), pp. 81–2.
24 I am indebted to a conversation with Richard Beardsworth on this. He is not at all responsible, of course, for any interpretations in this chapter.
25 'Genesis and structure', pp. 164–5.
26 J. Derrida, 'Differance', in *Speech and Phenomena*, pp. 136, 138.
27 Differance', pp. 141, 150.
28 J. Derrida, 'La différance', in *Marges de la philosophie* (Paris: Editions de Minuit, 1972, pp. 1–31, at p. 22.
29 Ibid.
30 Ibid., p. 25.
31 See Richard Beardsworth, *Derrida and the Political* (London: Routledge, 1996).
32 *Voix et phénomène*, pp. 68, 71–2; *Speech and Phenomena*, pp. 60, 63–4.
33 *Speech and Phenomena*, p. 66; Husserl, *Phenomenology of the Consciousness of Internal Time*, pp. 16–20.
34 *Voix et phénomène*, pp. 90–1, *Speech and Phenomena*, p. 83.
35 *Speech and Phenomena*, p. 83.
36 See E. Husserl, *Logische Untersuchungen. Band 2, Untersuchungen zur Phänomenologie und Theorie der Erkenntnis, I. Teil* (Tübingen: Max Niemayer, 1993), pp. 23–4. The whole of part I of this volume of the *Untersuchungen* is devoted to the discussion of expression and meaning.
37 J. Habermas, *Der Philosophische Diskurs der Moderne, Zwölf Vorlesungen* (Frankfurt: Suhrkamp, 1985) pp. 344ff.
38 Derrida, *Speech and Phenomena*, p. 28.
39 Heidegger, *Sein und Zeit*, pp. 45–9.
40 *Voix et phénomène*, p. 59; *Speech and Phenomena*, p. 53.
41 See Husserl's discussion of the idea of pure grammar in *Logische Untersuchungen, Band 2, I. Teil*, pp. 294ff.
42 *Voix et phénomène*, pp. 84–5; *Speech and Phenomena*, p. 76.
43 *Speech and Phenomena*, p. 53
44 *Sein und Zeit*, p. 78.
45 *Speech and Phenomena*, p. 76.
46 *Voix et phénomène*, p. 80; *Speech and Phenomena*, p. 72.
47 See Husserl, *Internal Time*, p. 333.
48 Heidegger, 'The question concerning technology', in *The Question Concerning Technology and Other Essays* (New York: Harper & Row, 1977), pp. 3–35, at p. 17.
49 *Voix et phénomène*, p. 89; *Speech and Phenomena*, p. 79.

50   'La différance', *Marges*, pp. 11–12.
51   'Differance', p. 140.
52   Descombes, *Modern French Philosophy*.
53   Gillian Rose, *Hegel contra Sociology* (London: Athlone, 1995), chapter 2.

Chapter 9   Reflexive Judgement and Aesthetic Subjectivity

1   Michel Foucault, 'What is enlightenment?', in Paul Rabinow (ed.), *The Foucault Reader* (New York: Pantheon, 1984).
2   The idea of 'bridge' is not fully appropriate here. The influence of Kant's third critique, extending from Schelling through Derrida, is very much one in which reflexive judgement is not just a mediator between, but the condition of possibility of, both determinate and indeterminate judgement. See Jonatas Ferreira, 'Judgement, modernity and classical sociological theory', PhD thesis, Lancaster University, 1998. Also on Kant's aesthetics see, for example, Donald W. Crawford, *Kant's Aesthetic Theory* (Madison: University of Wisconsin Press, 1974) for a standard presentation of the third critique. And Clement Greenberg, *Arrogant Purpose, 1945–1949. Volume 2, The Collected Essays and Criticism* (Chicago: University of Chicago Press, 1986), pp. 26–9.
3   Immanuel Kant, *Critique of Practical Reason* (Indianapolis: Bobbs-Merrill, 1956), p. 124–5.
4   Immanuel Kant, *Critique of Pure Reason* (London: MacMillan, 1933), p. 84.
5   Kant, *Pure Reason*, pp. 48–51; W. H. Walsh, *Kant's Criticism of Metaphysics* (Edinburgh: Edinburgh University Press, 1975), pp. 7–11.
6   *Pure Reason*, pp. 142–3 ; Immanuel Kant, *The Critique of Judgement* (Oxford: Clarendon, 1952), p. 91. See discussion of the imagination as Einbildung in conjunction with the schematisms of the first critique and the sublime in Jean-Luc Nancy, 'L'offrande sublime', in *Une pensée finie* (Paris: Editions de Galilée, 1990), pp. 147–96, at pp. 152–5. I am indebted on a number of points in this chapter to discussions I had with Michael Hammond in the context of Lancaster University's Radical Philosophy group, convened by Russell Keat.
7   Kimberly Hutchings, *Kant, Critique and Politics* (London: Routledge, 1995), p. 14.
8   Kant, *Pure Reason*, p. 84.
9   Gilles Deleuze, *Francis Bacon: Logique de la sensation* (Paris: Editions de la différence, 1981); Pierre Bourdieu, *Distinction* (London: Routledge, 1984).
10   Kant, *Pure Reason*, pp. 122–4.
11   *Practical Reason*, pp. 126ff.
12   *Pure Reason*, pp. 135–6.
13   Hans Blumenberg, *Legitimität der Neuzeit* (Frankfurt: Suhrkamp, 1966); Wolfgang Schluchter, *The Rise of Western Rationalism: Max Weber's Developmental History* (Berkeley: University of California Press, 1981); J. Habermas, *Theorie des kommunikativen Handels* (Frankfurt: Suhrkamp, 1981).
14   Howard Caygill, *The Art of Judgement* (Oxford: Blackwell, 1989), p. 12. The treatment of Kant's third critique in the first half of this chapter is

heavily indebted to, and in most important respects consistent with, Caygill's analyses.

15   Gillian Rose, *The Dialectics of Nihilism* (Oxford: Blackwell, 1984).

16   Caygill, *Art of Judgement*, p. 356.

17   Ibid., pp. 12, 15.

18   Hutchings, *Kant, Critique*, pp. 21–3.

19   Kant, *Critique of Judgement*, pp. 5. Here Kant wrote: 'The peculiar principle . . . belonging to the faculty of judgement . . . must not be derived from a priori concepts, seeing that these are the property of understanding and judgement is only directed to their application.' Further, such application would have a principle or 'rule' – 'but not as an objective rule . . . because then 'another faculty of judgement would again be required to enable us to decide whether or not the case was one for the application of the rule or not'.

20   I am indebted to Hermann Schwengel of Freiburg University for points about Benjamin and the 'Lücke' and Hegel and singularity, which I draw on throughout this book. For a discussion of judgement and responsibiity, see Ferreira, *Judgement, Modernity*, chapter 6.

21   Ernst Cassierer, *Kant's Life and Thought* (London: Yale University Press, 1981), pp. 273–5; *Critique of Judgement*, p. 362.

22   *Practical Reason*, p. 96; *Critique of Judgement*, p. 227. In part I of the *Metaphysics of Morals*, Kant approvingly cites Shaftesbury's dictum as to the bechmark of a theory surviving being laughed at. See Kant, *The Metaphysical Elements of Justice* (Indianapolis: Bobbs-Merril, 1965), p. 8.

23   See also Hegel's critical remarks on the classical aesthetics of Wolff and Baumgarten in G. W. F. Hegel, *On Art, Religion and Philosophy, Introductory Lectures to the Realm of Absolute Spirit*, ed. J. Glenn Gray (New York: Harper & Row, 1970), pp. 22–3; G. W. F. Hegel, *Introduction to Aesthetics, Being the Introduction to the Berlin Aesthetics Lectures of the 1820s* (Oxford: Oxford University Press, 1979), p. 1.

24   *Critique of Judgement*, p. 150.

25   Ibid., pp. 83–4.

26   Ibid., p. 6, Kant wrote: the faculty of judgement 'deals with cases in which experience presents a conformity to law in things, which the understanding's general concept of the sensible is no longer adequte to render intelligible or explicable, and in which judgement may have recourse to itself for the principle of the reference of the natural thing to the unknowable supersensible.'

27   Hutchings, *Kant, Critique*, p. 24.

28   *Critique of Judgement*, p. 91.

29   Jean-François Lyotard, *Lessons on the Analytic of the Sublime* (Stanford, CA: Stanford University Press, 1994), pp. 57–60.

30   Emanuel Levinas, *Autrement qu'être ou au delà de l'essence* (Paris: Livre de Poche, 1990), pp. 253–5.

31   Lyotard, *Lessons on the Sublime*, pp. 60–1, 67–8.

32   *Critique of Judgement*, pp. 42–3.

33   Ronald Hitzler, 'Bastelexistenz', in U. Beck and E. Beck-Gernsheim (eds), *Riskante Freiheiten* (Frankfurt: Suhrkamp, 1994), pp. 307–15.

34   W. H. Walsh, *Kant's Criticism of Metaphysics* (Edinburgh: Edinburgh University Press, 1975), pp. 1–4.

35   *Critique of Judgement*, p. 39.

36   *Practical Reason*, p. 42. Lewis Beck, *Studies in the Philosophy of Kant* (Indianapolis: Bobbs-Merril, 1965), p. 44.

37   Max Weber, *Wirtschaft und Gesellschaft, Grundriss der verstehenden Soziologie* (Tübingen: J. C. B. Mohr, 1960), p. 13; Weber, 'Politics as a vocation', in H. Gerth and C. W. Mills (eds), *From Max Weber*, pp. 77–128, at p. 95.

38   Georg Wilhelm Friedrich Hegel, *Grundlinien der Philosophie des Rechts, oder Naturrecht und Staatswissenschaft im Grundrisse, Werke 7* (Frankfurt: Suhrkamp, 1970), p. 80. In the first pages on Selbstbewußtsein in the *Phenomenology of Spirit*, the similarities of the 'Ich' of self-consciousness with the subjectivity of Kantian judgement (i.e. not of the Kantian understanding or reason) are apparent. Hegel keeps speaking of the centrality of 'life' to self-consciousness, and of its difference especially from the universality of Reason. For example: 'Denn da das Wesen der individuellen Gestalt, das allgemeine Leben, und das Fürsichseiende an sich einfach Substanz ist, so hebt es, indem es das Andere in sich setzt, diese seine Einfachheit oder sein Wesen auf, d.h. es entzweit sie, und dies Entzweien der unterschiedslosen Flüssigkeit ist eben das Setzen der Individualität.' G. W. F. Hegel, *Phänomenologie des Geistes, Werke 3* (Frankfurt: Suhrkamp, 1970), p. 142

39   Adorno, *Negative Dialektik, Gesammelte Schriften, vol. 6* (Frankfurt: Suhrkamp, 1973), pp. 172–3, 366–7.

40   Caygill, *Art of Judgement*, pp. 54–7.

41   Cited in ibid., pp. 82–3, 85.

42   See ibid., p. 321.

43   Alasdair MacIntyre, *After Virtue: a Study in Moral Theory* (London: Duckworth, 1981), pp. 109, 169ff.

44   Jean-Luc Nancy, *The Inoperative Community* (Minneapolis: University of Minnesota, 1991), pp. 77–8.

45   Caygill, *Art of Judgement*, p. 299.

46   *Critique of Judgement*, p. 18.

47   Caygill, *Art of Judgement*, p. 316. It is important to keep in mind here that for Kant and philosophy this singular judging subjectivity is always transcendental and never empirical. For sociology, as in Bourdieu's *Distinction*, it is empirical. For me as a sociologist it is only transcendental in late modernity. But this is *empirically* determined.

48   J. Habermas, *Theory and Practice* (London: Heinemann, 1974), pp. 156–7. The above quotes show how much the young Habermas was indebted to the idea of a singular subjectivity introduced in Kant's third critique and developed by Hegel in his Jena writings well before *The Phenomenology*. Habermas insisted that we depart not from an 'absolute beginning' but from 'natural consciousness'. This chapter of *Theory and Practice* appeared in German in 1968 in *Technik und Wissenschaft als Ideologie*. In the same year *Erkenntnis und Interesse* (Frankfurt: Suhrkamp, 1968) was published, in which Habermas underscored that this 'history of the species' as 'self-formative process' was not 'a naturalistic reduction of transcendental-logical properties to empirical ones. Indeed it

is meant to prevent just such a reduction.' Cited from English translation in *Knowledge and Human Interests* (London: Heinemann, 1971), p. 196. Thus Habermas's subjectivity, like Kant's from the third critique, is at the same time singular and transcendental. In *Der philosophische Diskurs der Moderne* (Franfurt: Suhrkamp, 1985) pp. 65ff. many years later Habermas would see the development of what he sees as characteristically modern as starting with the young Hegelians who drew on Hegel's Jena philosophy, and thus broke with the transcendental unity of the 'I' in what I call in this book high modernity. For Habermas this break begins the critique of the philosophy of consciousness and its logic entails the much fuller break of his own discourse theroy of species self-formation. The latter opens up the space for possible completion of modernity's *unvollendete Projekt*.

49 Caygill, *Art of Judgement*, p. 85.
50 Gillian Rose, *The Broken Middle* (Oxford: Blackwell, 1992), p. 5.
51 T. Adorno, *Ästhetische Theorie, Gesammelte Schriften, vol. 7* (Frankfurt: Suhrkamp, 1970).
52 Tzvetan Todorov, *Theories of the Symbol* (Ithica, NY: Cornell University Press, 1982), p. 156.
53 Friedrich Nietzsche, 'Uber Wahrheit und Lüge im Außermoralischen Sinn', in Nietzsche, *Werke in drei Bänden, Band III* (Munich: Carl Hanser Verlag, 1966), pp. 309–22.
54 Todorov, *Symbol*, pp. 170–1.
55 Kant, *Critique of Judgement*, pp. 69–74.
56 Celia Lury, *Prosthetic Culture* (London: Routledge, 1997), pp. 5, 140.
57 Todorov, *Symbol*, pp. 167ff.
58 Ibid., pp. 171, 174ff. The reader should note that this definition of 'motivation' in regard to poesis is opposite to the way I used the term in chapters 7 and 8.
59 Ibid., pp. 202–3; Gadamer, *Truth and Method*, pp. 72–7.
60 Todorov, *Symbol*, p. 205; Charles Taylor, *Sources of the Self: the Making of Modern Identity* (Cambridge: Cambridge University Press, 1989), pp. 377–80.
61 Todorov, *Symbol*, pp. 208–9; Nicky Chu, 'Nihilism and the religious', PhD thesis, Lancaster University, 1995.
62 See the lengthy and learned discussion of the finality of the object in Lyotard, *Lessons on the Sublime*, pp. 3–14, 66–72.
63 Kant, *Practical Reason*, pp. 20–1.
64 This point is underscored by Benhabib with respect to Hegel in her *Critique, Norm, Utopia* and with respect to the neo-Aristotelians and Gilligan's feminism in *Situating the Self*. Benhabib promises to take the argument further in her book on Arendt, but ultimately is unable to. Benhabib seems unaware of the extent to which her notion of situated intersubjectivity constitutes a fundamental break with what Husserl called 'transcendental intersubjectivity' implicit in Habermas's discourse ethics and with straightforward notions of 'deliberative democracy'. In my view she goes far beyond these positions in political theory. See Seyla Benhabib, *Critique, Norm and Utopia: a Study of the Foundations of Critical Theory* (New York: Columbia University Press, 1986), pp. 27–9; *Situating the Self* (Cambridge: Polity Press, 1992); *The Reluctant Modernism of Hannah Arendt* (London: Sage, 1996).

65 Rose, *Broken Middle*, pp. 276–7.
66 See my criticisms of Levinas's and Zygmunt Bauman's postmodern ethics in S. Lash, 'Postmodern ethics: the missing ground', *Theory, Culture and Society*, 13, 2 (1996).
67 Rose, *Broken Middle*, pp. 51–84.
68 Lyotard, *Lessons*, pp. 199ff.
69 Hans Georg Gadamer, 'The relevance of the beautiful' in *The Relevance of the Beautiful and Other Essays* (Cambridge: Cambridge University Press, 1986), pp. 1–56, at p. 14; Gadamer, *Wahrheit und Methode*.
70 Robert Bernasconi, Editor's introduction to *Relevance of the Beautiful*, pp xi–xxi, at p. xii.
71 Gadamer, 'Hermeneutik (1969)', in *Wahrheit und Methode, Ergänzungen Register, Hermeneutik II, Gesammelte Werke, Band 2* (Tübingen: Mohr, 1993), pp. 425–36, at pp. 432–3.
72 Gadamer, 'Relevance', p. 6.
73 Ibid., p. 13
74 Ibid., p. 14.
75 Ibid., p. 17.
76 See chapter 7 above.
77 Gadamer, 'Relevance', p. 46, italics added; Gadamer, *Wahrheit und Methode, Grundzüge einer philosophischen Hermeneutik, Hermeneutik I, Gesammelte Werke, Band 1* (Tübingen: Mohr, 1990), pp. 126 ff. For the rest of this chapter this will be simply refereed to as *Wahrheit und Methode*.
78 'Relevance', p. 23; *Wahrheit und Methode*, pp. 107ff.
79 'Relevance', p. 25.
80 Ibid., pp. 32, 33, 35, 36.
81 Ibid., p. 28; *Wahrheit und Methode*, pp. 270ff.
82 Gadamer, 'Intuition and vividness', in *The Relevance of the Beautiful and Other Essays*, pp. 157–170, at p. 159.
83 Gadamer, 'Intuition', p. 165.

Chapter 10   Discourse, Figure . . . Sensation

1 Levinas, *Totalité et Infini, Essai sur l'extériorité* (Dordrecht: Kluwer, 1971), pp. 5–6; *Totality and Infinity*, trans. Alphonso Lingis (Dordrecht: Kluwer), pp. 35–6.
2 In his discussion of the 'dynamically sublime', Kant spoke of the sublimity of God in a sense that is very close to the Jewish idea of the deity. See *Critique of Practical Judgement*, p. 127. See Derrida, 'Violence et métaphysique: Essai sur la pensée d'Emmanuel Levinas', in *L'écriture et la différence* (Paris: Seuil, 1967), pp. 117–228, at p. 138.
3 *Critique of Judgement*, p. 151.
4 Lessing argued polemically in 'Laokoon' against the painterly tendency of eighteenth-century poetry. For him painting was a medium in the dimension of the spatial, and poetry in the temporal. Poetry of course could work through the effectivity of *Gleichzeitigkeit* (simultaneity), but this was vastly differ-

ent from the temporal fixity which was more the proper domain of painting. See Paul Hoffmann, *Symbolismus* (Munich: Wilhelm Fink, 1987), pp. 66ff.

5   W. J. T. Mitchell, *Iconology* (Chicago: University of Chicago Press, 1986), p. iv. See also Terry Eagleton, *The Ideology of the Aesthetic* (Oxford: Blackwell, 1990), pp. 53–6.

6   Mitchell, *Iconology*, pp. 127, 132. Gadamer likens the Enlightenment's critique of tradition to natural science's critique of the evidence of the senses and speaks of Burke's critique of the Enlightenment in this context. See *Truth and Method*, pp. 272–3.

7   Burke often contrasted the sublime with the didactic. See Norman Bryson, *Word and Image: French Painting in the Ancien Regime* (Cambridge: Cambridge University Press 1981), p. 235.

8   *Critique of Judgement*, pp. 168–9.

9   On the Judaic God as singular, see Gillian Rose, *Judaism and Modernity* (Oxford: Basil Blackwell, 1993), pp. 168ff.

10 See Martin Jay, *Downcast Eyes: the Denigration of Vision in Twentieth Century French Thought* (Berkeley: University of California Press, 1993). Bataille's fragment, 'The pineal eye', posits a progression of evolution through erotic force from the ape's anus to the erect human's head and brain, to that of the pineal eye, a final and deadly erection that blasts through the human skull and sees the sun. See Allan Stoekl, Introduction to Georges Bataille, *Visions of Excess: Selected Writings, 1927–1939* (Minneapolis: University of Minnesota Press, 1993), p. xii; and Bataille, 'The pineal eye', in the same volume, pp. 79–90, at p. 82.

11 See Levinas, *De l'existence à l'existant* (1947) (Paris: Vrin, 1990), pp. 77, 101–2.

12 Nick Land, *The Thirst for Annihilation: Georges Bataille and Virulent Nihilism* (London: Routledge, 1993), pp. 102–3.

13 Jay, *Downcast Eyes*, pp. 216, 228.

14 Ibid., pp. 216–21; Jean Baudrillard, *L'échange symbolique et la mort* (Paris: Gallimard, 1976), pp. 202ff.; Derrida, *Donner le temps, 1. La fausse monnaie* (Paris: Editions Galilée, 1991), pp. 202–3.

15 Heidegger, 'The question concerning technology, in *The Question Concerning Technology and Other Essays* (New York: Harper & Row, 1977), pp. 3–35, at pp. 24–5.

16 Breton wrote: 'The difficulty one has in telling a genuine automoton from a false one has held man's curiosity spellbound for centuries . . . the most troubling ambiguity has always existed between animal life, especially human life, and its mechanical simulacrum. The specific response of our age has been to trsnspose this ambiguity by shifting the automoton from the outer world to the inner world, by letting it develop freely within the mind itself. Psychoanalysis has detected the presence of an anonymous mannequin in the recesses of the mental attic, "without eyes, nose or ears", not unlike the ones Giorgio de Chirico painted around 1916. This mannequin, once the cobwebs that concealed and paralyzed it were brushed away, has proven to be extremely mobile, "superhuman" (it was precisely from this need to give this mobility free rein that Surrealism was born)'; André Breton, 'Raymond Roussell 1877– 1933', in *Anthology of Black Humor* (San Francisco: City Lights, 1997), pp. 226– 36, at p. 226. In contrast, and as opposed to the 'ecriture automatique' of

Breton, Bataille wrote that writing was a 'mask' for a cry and for non-knowledge. See Jean-Luc Nancy's essay on Bataille, 'Excrit', in J. J. Nancy, *Une pensée finie*, pp. 55–64, at p. 58.

17 Jacques Derrida, *The Truth in Painting* (Chicago: University of Chicago Press, 1987).

18 Jay, *Downcast Eyes*, pp. 222, 332.

19 Peter Dews, *Logics of Disintegration, Post-structuralist Thought and the Claims of Critical Theory* (London: Verso, 1987), p. 81.

20 Sigmund Freud, *The Interpretation of Dreams, volume 4*, Pelican Freud Library (Harmondsworth: Penguin, 1976), pp. 650–1. On the relationship betwen the real (sensation) and its figuration in dreams see Maurice Dayan, 'Qu-est-ce que penser en rêve?', in P. Fédida and D. Widlöcher (eds), *Actualité des modèles freudiens, Langage-Image-Pensée* (Paris: Presses Universitaires de France, 1995), pp. 91–106, at p. 98.

21 Freud, *Interpretation of Dreams*, pp. 686ff.

22 Deleuze, *Logique de la sensation* (Paris: Editions de la difference, 1981).

23 Jay, *Downcast Eyes*, pp. 344ff. The convergence here between the young Lacan and philosophical anthropology's notion of human incompleteness and *Instinktarmut* is worth noting. See Arnold Geghen, 'Philosophische Anthropologie: zur Selbstbegegnung und Selbstentdeckung des Menschen', in A. Gehlen (ed.), *Anthropologische und sozialpsychologische Untersuchungen* (Hamburg: Rowohlt, 1986), pp. 7–145, at pp. 69ff.

24 Serge Tisseron, *Psychanalyse de l'Image, de l'imago aux images virtuelles* (Paris: Dunod, 1995), pp. 46–7.

25 Pierre Macherey, 'Lacan avec Kojève, philosophie et psychanalyse', in *Lacan avec les philosophes*, Bibliothèque du Collège international de philosophie (Paris: Albin Michel, 1991), pp. 315–21, pp. 323–4. Frantz Fanon, *Black Skins, White Masks* (New York: Grove Press, 1967), p. 161; Jay, *Downcast Eyes*, p. 345.

26 See the transcendental reading of Lacan in Jean-Claude Milner, *L'Œuvre claire, Lacan, la science, la philosophie* (Paris: Editions du Seuil, 1995), pp. 110–12.

27 Marc Strauss, 'La vrai fonction du père, c'est d'unir un désir à la loi', in Gérard Miller (ed.), *Lacan* (Paris: Bordas, Philosophie Présente, 1987), pp. 59–76, at pp. 66–7.

28 Jay, *Downcast Eyes*, pp. 341, 349.

29 Consider, for example, the relation between sun and mutilation – that is, visuality and sensation – in Bataille's 'Sacrifical mutilation and the severed ear of Vincent Van Gogh', in Bataille, *Visions of Excess*, pp. 61–72, at pp. 61–2.

30 Pat Barker, *Regeneration* (Harmondsworth: Penguin, 1992); Barker, *The Eye in the Door* (Harmondsworth: Penguin, 1994); Barker, *The Ghost Road* (London: Viking, 1995).

31 Nancy, *Inoperative Community*, p. 4.

32 The 'we' relations in Nancy and Levinas presuppose not a self-identical, hence universal subjectivity, but a self-*different*, singular subjectivity.

33 Yet Levinas writes, 'The bible does not begin the building of an ideal city in a void . . . To recognise the necessity of a law is to recognize that humanity cannot be served by at once magically denying its condition . . . To speak of

law is not to remain at the stage surpassed by Redemption. To speak of Redemption in a world that remains without justice is to forget that the soul is not the demand for immortality but the impossibility of assassinating'; Emmanuel Levinas, 'Place and utopia', in *Difficult Freedom, Essays on Judaism* (Baltimore: Johns Hopkins University Press, 1990), pp. 99–102. In this essay Levinas contrasts the 'joy of solitary salvation' of Christianity with the primacy of ethical order and law of Judaism. Its focus is on law and talmud as this worldly justice, in contrast to the other-worldly salvation of Christianity. This essay was a polemic in regard to the esablishment of the Israeli state written in 1950. It is indeed difficult to reconcile with his devaluation of history in *Le temps et l'autre* (Paris: Presses Universitaires de France, 1979) and elsewhere in his work. A unifying factor lies in Levinas's consistent devaluation of the senses. Levinas thus identifies Christian salvation with 'desire', speaking of the 'joy of salvation'. In this sense Levinas identifies the iconic, egoism and desire with Christinaity, the voice and law with Judaism. See also Jay, *Downcast Eyes*, p. 578.

34   Thus Heidegger writes, 'Das entscheidene Wesensmoment der Erfahrung besteht darin daß in ihr dem Bewußtsein der neue wahre Gegenstand entspringt . . . Das Fahren im Erfahren hat die ursprüngliche Bedeutung des Ziehens. Der Zimmermann fährt beim Hausbau mit dem Balken in eine bestimmte Richtung. Das Erfahren ist das auslagend-erlangende Gelangen. Das Erfahren ist eine Weise des Anwesens, d.h. des Seins'; M. Heidegger, 'Hegels Begrif der Erfahrung' in *Holzwege* (Franfurt: Klostermann, 1950), pp. 115–208, at p. 185. See especially Heidegger's late essays such as 'The thing' and 'Building, dwelling, thinking'. I am indebted to discussions with Paul Morris and Nicky Chu on these points.

35   Max Weber thus contrasts the 'plebian' character of the rabbis, who were often also tradesman, with 'aristocratic religious virtuosi' of other world religions. The plebian rabbi is interpreter of the law and is unconcerned with the 'gnostic-mystic pursuit of salvation'. The aristocratic virtuosi tend instead 'to devalue law and ethically correct conduct'. Again as in Levinas above, we see in Weber's analyses of Judaism the coexistence of unusual this-worldiness and extreme other-worldliness. The extraordinary thing for Weber is the contrast of the law of Judaism with 'irrational forms of seeking salvation'. The latter entail a departure from iconicity, from the figure, in the direction of the 'ethical rational content' of the Torah. For Weber the uniqueness of Judaism lay not 'in the substance of religious experience', but instead in 'the compression of this content in such narrow compass'. It lay 'especially in the popular character and absolute understandability of the holy text for everyone'. Note here that ethical rationality is directly related to such popular understandability. Thus Weber refers to a sort of dual nature of Judaism in its 'directly understandable and, at the same time, heaven soaring prophetic conception of God'; Max Weber, *Ancient Judaism* (New York: Free Press, 1967), pp. 393, 396–7.

36   For Levinas, Judaism is the religion of '*discourse*'. In his writings on Judaism immediately after the Second World War, Levinas contrasted 'violence' and 'discourse'. Activities that are somehow 'causal' partake of the realm of vio-

lence. These include knowledge of the object, 'fabrication of a thing, desire of an object, struggle and war'. 'Violence is applied to the thing, it seizes and disposes of the thing.' For Levinas what is not violent is discursive. Like in Judaism, Levinas's idea of discourse, escaping the violence of metaphysics, is as much prosaic as it is immensely elevated. It is the law in the 'voice' of Jahweh. But, as importantly, the law is the very embedded and everyday teachings of the Torah and Talmud handed down to the generations by the rabbis. Levinas's Judaism is rabbinical Judaism. The relationship with the Other for Levinas is at the same time quite prosaic. It is a question of discourse again in the everyday sense; of entering a conversation with your neighbour. This 'face-to-face relationship' is much more important than the 'content communicated'. It is the condition of possibility of communicating a content. The 'Other' is an 'interlocutor'. Levinas refers to the other as 'the face'. Again the idea is quite prosaic. The face is entering the face to face relationship. The face is a 'visage', and the relationship with the Other is most of all not *taking* the other for an interlocutor, but *being* an interlocutor for the other. It consists of being an interlocutor for the other's look which 'aims (*vise*) at you'. Hence the face (*visage*) in the first instance aims (*vise*) at you. The relationship with the Other is not so much recognizing the other – which presumes at first that you do not recognize him and are in a violent relationship with him, that you objectify him. It is instead putting yourself in the position in which the Other can recognize *you*. It is putting the Other not in the position of an entity that you know. That is, 'the Other appears not in the nominative but the vocative'. He appears in the position of speaker and not of a being whom you can know. Here 'you are exposed to the action of the Other'. This is not so much a question of concentration camps and hostages, but most of all of everyday sociality. In greeting (*saluer*) the other I am putting myself in a position to 'be part of society'. (Levinas, 'Ethics and spirit', in *Difficult Freedom*, pp. 7–8).

The Other for Levinas is a 'being with a face'. Beings without a face are things. Judaism is based on the 'I–thou' relationship. Levinas accordingly is disparaging about the 'I–it' relation, the relation with the thing. The I–it relation is always a relation of violence. The I–thou – when the I does not treat the Thou as an it – is non-violent. The 'I', for its part, is also not becoming an object, an 'it' for the 'thou'. The 'I' might be putting himself in the position of being accepted or rejected as an interlocutor. But he is not putting himself in the position of an 'it' *vis-à-vis* the other. Hence Levinas rejects any possibility of beginning from Hegel's master–slave relation. Science (philosophy) is about the 'I–it' relation, 'reason' about the 'I–thou'. Science for Levinas is violent. Reason and language are non-violent. Levinas notes Hegel's rejection of the abstractions of Judaism for the *Sittlichkeit* of the *polis*. Christianity is a bit of a halfway house – between Judaism and 'Greek' philosophy/science – regarding the realization of the abstract in the concrete (see Levinas, 'Hegel and the Jews', *Difficult Freedom*, pp. 235–8). Christian love (*agape*) presupposes a certain object-ness in what one loves. This may be better than knowing the object, but it still presupposes 'violence', as well as a certain irrationality and mysticism. For Levinas, Judaic notions of justice are prior to love. 'Revelation' is based in the I–thou, 'disclosure' in the I–it. 'Things give, they do not offer a face,' he writes. The thing presupposes egoism and violence. 'Violence is applied to the thing, it seizes and disposes of the thing.' This includes the violence of Husserl's reduction, of Heidegger's disconcealment of ontological structures. Hence, 'the face is an irreducible mode'. The 'I' and the 'Other' are beings with faces, not with ontological structures to be reduced, but instead with 'identities'. The thing is perhaps a particularity with an ontological structure. But the 'I' and the Other are *singularities*, in that we cannot be reduced. Through the face, 'the being is open, establishing itself in depth and, in this opening, presenting itself somehow in a personal way' (*Difficult Freedom*, p. 8).

I disagree that we should start from the sort of transcendental intersubjectivity that Levinas proposes. I think it is necessary to begin from the more empirical intersubjectivity of sociality and community (see chapter 7 above). Second, we irredeemably live in a world that comprises objects, including aesthetic objects. Levinas's seeming distrust of art is startling. Things for him 'are beings without a face'. Perhaps, he continues, 'art seeks to give a face to things, and in this its greatness and its deceit simultaneously reside' (ibid., p. 8). Finally, in the context of contemporary technological culture, the sharp dualism of agents and things is no longer tenable: especially no longer tenable as a starting point for an ethics or a politics. Also see Nicky Chu, 'The religious and nihilism', PhD thesis, Lancaster University, 1996.

37   This chapter works from an ideal-type of Judaism or the Hebraic that is close to the notions of Levinas and Weber (see above notes). This highly discursive and rationalist (in the sense of course of ethical and not cognitive rationality) dimension of Judaism is not of course the only one. Susan Handelman, for example, points to the importance of a mystical, cabbalistic Judaism registered in Kafka, Walter Benjamin and systematized in, above all, Gerschom Scholem. She contrasts this with the 'rationalism' of Levinas and Franz Rosenzweig. Here both rationalist and cabbalist begin from the Revelation of law, and ultimately of the law handed down to Moses from God and from Moses to the people of Israel. But whereas the rationalists see this law as accessible and taught in clear language from generation to generation, the cabbalists see it as a 'secret law' that is not directly knowable. Neither rationalists nor cabbalists foreground the iconic in any sense. Language, however, for the rationalist is a clear medium of explanation, whereas for cabbalists language works through 'ruses' and carries mystical meanings. Language for cabbalists is not a means to say something outside of itself, but is a finality carrying its meaning within itself. I address 'the cabbalistic' in chapter 13. The idea was handed down to Benjamin by Protestant theologians and philosohers. Benjamin in turn influenced the understanding of Scholem, who took it quite literally and devoted his life to writing the definitive works in Jewish mysticism. Levinas of course would see language in the cabbalistic sense as too thing-like and hence inscribed in a logic less of discourse than of violence. The more conventional Jewish talmudic teachings given definitive form by eleventh- and twelfth-century European rabbis consists of *halakha* and *aggadah*. *Halakha* consists quite directly of laws, of prescriptions. *Aggadah* is a set

of narratives and parables which refer more or less directly to the laws. Rationalists like Levinas and by implication Weber focused on *halakha*. Scholem and Benjamin understood Kafka's novels and stories in the dimension of *aggadah*. Scholem saw the laws ultimately as secret, Benjamin as regrettably absent. Weber's rationalism partook of an earlier generation's *Gründerjahre* rationalism of *Wissenschaft des Judentums*. Benjamin, Kafka and Scholem reacted against this rationalism and assimilationism of their fathers' generation. Levinas and, for that matter, Habermas write in the wake of the Holocaust, understanding mysticism as violence or strategic. Finally, Weber's and Levinas's views purvey a Pharasiac legal-rationality, of the routinization of rationality and Revelation through the generations. Scholem and Benjamin have much more charismatic, indeed anarchic, notions. In Weberian terminology the rationalists are on the side of routinization and legal-rationality while the cabbalists are on the side of charisma. The rationalists are with the priests, the cabbalists with the prophets. See Susan Handelman, *Fragments of Redemption: Jewish Thought and Literary Theory in Benjamin, Scholem and Levinas* (Bloomington: Indiana University Press, 1991), pp. xix–xxi, 3–14, 47–58, 337–45.

38 Weber, *Ancient Judaism*, pp. 380ff.
39 Bryan Turner, *For Weber* (London: Routledge, 1981); Jonatas Ferreira, 'Judgement, modernity and classical sociological throry', PhD thesis, Lancaster University, 1998, chapter 5.
40 In *Judaism and Modernity*, Gillian Rose contests the predominance of voice in contemporary Judaic thought. She has in mind especially Levinas, although she underscores similarities between Levinas and Rosenzweig and Martin Buber. Rose argues that, despite his focus on *halacha*, the Talmud and law, Levinas and his colleagues are essentially 'antinomian'. This is because the idea of law in their work stands in dualistic opposition to positive and empirical law and the norms governing functioning institutions in everyday life. Indeed, she stresses that their idea of law is on the lines of Kant's 'morality' in its absence of embeddedness in the empirical law and conventions of social life. Rose puts together Levinas with contemporary Christian theologians such as Milbank and Taylor as 'postmodern' theologians. In their antinomian critique of violence and the law of institutions, Rose continues, the postmodern thinkers only repeat the 'diremptions', the dualisms of modernity. Rose instead argues for a 'broken middle'. This is not a third space of difference, which for Derrida is a transcendental. It is instead much more empirical. The broken middle is found in institutions of positive law, which promote freedom and the exercise of reason and thought as well as 'violence'. These institutions are a sort of *mediation* in which we live. This mediation or middle is broken also in being constitutively flawed, and necessarily so. Rose also contests the Jew–Greek antinomy and Levinas's (Rosenzweig's) counterposition of Revelation, on the one hand, and the violence of philosophy, on the other. Philosophy, from the ancient Greeks, is also about 'wonder'. The final diremption for Rose is of philosophy and social theory, a diremption again of the transcendental and the empirical that modernist (positivist) philosphers/sociologists inaugurated and which postmodernists

have only repeated. Rose's 'broken middle' is thus perhaps most importantly simultaneously transcendental *and* empirical. G. Rose, *Judaism and Modernity*, pp. 25–32, 37–51, 127ff.

41 Jean François Lyotard, 'Figure foreclosed', in Andrew Benjamin (ed.), *The Lyotard Reader* (Oxford: Blackwell, 1989).

42 J. F. Lyotard, *Discours, figure* (Paris: Klinseick, 1971).

43 Lyotard, 'Jewish Oedipus', in, *Driftworks* (New York: Semiotexte, 1984).

44 Jay, *Downcast Eyes*, p. 568.

45 'Figure foreclosed', p. 69.

46 Ibid., p. 83.

47 Helmut Berking, *Schenken: zur Anthropologie des Gebens* (Frankfurt: Campus, 1996); translated in English as *Giving* (London: Sage, 1998).

48 Max Weber, 'Die nichtlegitime Herrschaft (Typologie der Städte)', in *Wirtschaft und Gesellschaft* (Tübingen: Mohr, 1972), pp. 727–814, at pp. 744–7.

49 Lyotard, 'Figure foreclosed, p. 75. See in this context also the postwar reflections, indeed 'confessions', on law and the political in Carl Schmitt, *Ex Captivitate Salus* (Plettenburg: Edition Peiran, 1987), pp. 55ff.

50 Levinas, *Difficult Freedom*, pp. 69ff.

51 Cited in Lyotard, 'Figure foreclosed', p. 87.

52 Ibid., pp. 93–4.

53 Ibid., p. 89.

54 Richard Roberts, 'Time, virtualitry and the goddess', in S. Lash, A. Quick and R. Roberts (eds), *Time and Value* (Oxford: Blackwell, 1998); Lyotard, 'Figure foreclosed', p. 96.'

55 'Figure foreclosed', p. 94.

56 Ibid., p. 101.

57 Wolf Lepenies, *Melancholy and Society* (Cambridge: MA: Harvard University Press, 1992).

58 I am indebted to John Urry for this idea.

Chapter 11 Objects that Judge: Latour's Parliament of Things

1 Bruno Latour, *We Have Never Been Modern* (Hemel Hempstead: Harvester Wheatsheaf, 1993). The 'sociology (and anthropology) of things' has a considerable pedigree. There is of course the juxtaposition of use-value and exchange-value in Marx. There is something irreducibly thing-like in Durkheim's 'social fact', which is a thing as much as it is a structure. Mauss's *Gift* in a sense gave the strongest foundations to this analytic of things. Marx's use-value versus exchange-value follows very much in the Kantian frame (chapter 9) of finality versus instrumentality. Indeed, so does the contemporary anthropology of things of Appadurai and Kopytoff in their juxtaposition of 'singularity' versus 'commodity'. See Arjun Appadurai, 'Commodities and the politics of value', in Appadurai (ed.), *The Social Life of Things: Commodities in Cultural Perspective* (Cambridge: Cambridge University Press, 1986); and I. Kopytoff, 'The cultural biography of things: commoditization as process', in

ibid. Yet the anthropological argument very much breaks with the transcendental and universalist assumptions of Marxism and Kant and looks at symbolic values for specific cultures. Thus too can be understood Daniel Miller's
'material culture analyses' in his several books: see, for example, *A Theory of
Shopping* (Cambridge: Polity Press, 1998).

The logic of this section of the present book breaks radically with any such
aporetic juxtaposition, even with the aporia of gift-society versus exchange-
society. Its inspiration is partly Baudrillard. Not Baudrillard's nostalgia for
Maussian symbolic exchange, but instead his theory of the object. And especially his idea of the object, which is, on the one hand, not knowable by the
subject, and hence not an instrumentality; but an object that is also and
emphatically *not a finality*. Hence the importance of the idea of 'reversibility'
for Baudrillard. What is not a finality for him is reversible. Baudrillard's object
seduces. Finalities do not seduce. They are sublime or beautiful but they do
not seduce. To speak of the sublime is still to speak the language of aporetics.
The sublime is part and parcel of the second modernity, not of the global
information culture. 'Sign-value' seduces. Sign-value has nothing to do with
the status associated with consumption. Baudrillard's consumer culture is a
culture of seduction. It is not a culture of commodification. Baudrillard
will refuse critical theory's analyses of mass society based on the
counterposition of commodity and use-value, or alienation and authenticity.
The quasi-objects in Latour's actor-networks are also clearly not finalities. and
also not instrumentalites. They transmit, they judge, they speak. See Jean
Baudrillard, *Seduction* (London: Macmillan, 1990), p. 103; and see 'Dead
symbols', interview with Jean Baudrillard, *Theory, Culture and Society*, 12, 4
(1995).

2   Gayatri Spivak, 'Let the subaltern speak', in Cary Nelson and Lawrence
Grossberg (eds), *Marxism and the interpretation of Culture* (Champaign-Urbana:
University of Illinois Press, 1988), pp. 271–313.

3   Latour, *Never Modern*, p. 138.

4   Ibid. See also Donna Haraway, *Modest Witness@Second_Millennium.Female
Man©_Meets_Oncomouse*™ (London: Routledge, 1997). In her focus on microbes, units of genetic information and the like, Haraway, unlike Latour, ties
her 'non-humanism' to a systematic periodization of what are effectively
frameworks of knowledge. Her contemporary phase, which is derived from
her thinking about microbiology, immunology and genetic engineering,
amounts to a systematic formulation of an episteme, one which clearly is
posterior to Foucault's modern episteme. Philosophers tend to think in terms
of the transcendental and the universal both spatially and temporally. Anthropologists tend often to think in terms of difference and particularities spatially
– that is, across cultures – but tend to think in terms of universals temporally.
In thus sense Latour thinks very anthropologically, arguing that we never
were modern, but just thought we were. And, indeed, how we now are is how
we always were. Haraway, like the general argument in this book, will think
in terms of temporal difference in her periodization. This is a very sociological
mode of analysis. The only problem is that sociologists, and the present
analysis is no exception, tend often to lose sight of spatial difference. They

tend to think temporally but to universalize a sort of Western model across cultures.

5   *Never Modern*, p. 131.

6   Ibid., p. 139.

7   Ibid., p. 141.

8   Ibid., p. 142.

9   Ibid., p. 90. See Emile Benveniste, *Problèmes de la linguistique générale* (Paris: Gallimard, 1966).

10   Latour, *Never Modern*, p. 89.

11   Ibid., p. 42.

12   Ibid., p. 101.

13   Ibid., p. 97.

14   Ibid., p. 53.

15   But see Karin Knorr Cetina, 'Sozialität mit Objekten, Soziale Beziehungen in post-traditionelen Wissengesellschaften', in Werner Rammert (ed.), *Technik und Sozialtheorie* (Frankfurt: Campus, 1998), pp. 83–120; Latour, *Never Modern*, p. 93.

16   Latour, *Never Modern*, p. 102, 63. See the discussions of Latour and Callon and of constructivism in Andrew Pickering (ed.), *Science as Practice and Culture* (Chicago: University of Chicago Press, 1992).

17   See Michel Callon, 'Techno-economic networks and irreversibility', in J. Law (ed.), *A Sociology of Monsters* (London: Routledge, 1991), pp. 132–64. Werner Rammert offers us elements for a general sociological theory of technology. Rammert notes that the refusal of technological determinism has led to a thoroughgoing forgetting of technology (technik) in social science. Like Heidegger he begins with an idea of 'technik' in terms of the fourfold nature of Aristotelian causation. Rammert then rejects Heidegger's definition of the essence of technology in its simultaneous hiding and bringing forth of the meaning of Being. Instead he sociologically argues for the difference of technik in different social situations. Influenced by Latour and the sociology of science, he none the less forgoes radical constructivism for a pragmatic notion of technology. This is a Deweyan, strongly embedded and practice-oriented idea of technology. Rammert notes the historic progression from substantial to functional notions of technology in Western thought. He agrees with neither. He replaces modern functionalist focus on 'ends–means-concept' with his pragmatic focus on 'medium–form-relationship'. Technology here becomes a mediator that is not necessarily only a means. It is instead a medium. And the difference between media in this context is of the utmost importance. This holds especially for the difference between biological bodies, physical things and symbolic signs in today's information societies. This model is of great potential explanatory value in distinguishing technology in industrial society from information society and in analysing biotechnology, high technology and the like in what Rammert notes is our 'increasingly technically mediated social life'. See Rammert, 'Die Form der Technik und die Differenz der Medien: auf dem Weg zu einer pragmatischen Techniktheorie', in Rammert (ed.), *Technik und Sozialtheorie*, pp. 293–320, pp. 293–6, 318–20.

18   Latour, *Never Modern*, pp. 131, 137–8.

19 I am indebted to conversations with Vivian Sobchack on this. See Sobchack (ed.), *Cinema, Television and the Modern Event* (New York: Routledge, 1996).

20 The anthropology of things with its contrast of singularity and commodity tends to repeat the Kantian aporia. Daniel Miller's *Modernity: an Ethnographic Approach, Dualism and Mass Consumption in Trinidad* (Oxford: Berg, 1994) begins to put this dualism into question. Howard Morphy's work on the West and African art radically opens up the categories, understanding the object not just as singularity versus commodity, but also as artefact as art etc. See Howard Morphy, *Aboriginal Art* (London: Phaidon, 1998).

21 Latour, *Never Modern*, pp. 64, 96.

22 Ibid., p. 67.

23 Sherry Turkle, *Life on the Screen* (London: Weidenfeld and Nicholson, 1996).

24 Leo Strauss, *Natural Right and History* (Chicago: University of Chicago Press, 1953); Latour, *Never Modern*, p. 28.

25 Latour, ibid., pp. 31, 143.

26 Ibid., p. 29.

27 Ibid., pp. 23–4.

28 See Roy Boyne, 'Angels in the archive', in S. Lash, A. Quick and R. Roberts (eds), *Time and Value* (Oxford: Blackwell, 1998); Michel Serres, *The Parasite* (Baltimore: Johns Hopkins University Press, 1982), pp. 62–3; Latour, *Never Modern*, pp. 82–4.

29 Luc Boltanski and Laurent Thévenot, *De la justification, les économies de la grandeur* (Paris: Gallimard, 1991); Latour, *Never Modern*, pp. 44–5.

30 Boltanski and Thévenot, *De la justification*; Luc Boltanski, *L'amour et la justice comme compétences* (Paris: Métailié, 1990); Celia Lury, *Prosthetic Culture* (London: Routledge, 1997), pp. 2–3.

31 Latour, *Never Modern*, pp. 41, 116.

32 Ibid., pp. 117–18, 119–20, 121–2.

33 Ibid., pp. 68, 69, 70–1; Habermas, *Theorie des kommunikativen Handels, Band 1, Handlungsrationalität und gesellschaftliche Rationalisierung* (Frankfurt: Suhrkamp, 1981), pp. 72ff.

34 Latour, *Never Modern*, pp. 46, 75, 88, 108–9.

35 Klaus Eder, *Die Vergesellschaftung der Natur* (Frankfurt: Suhrkamp, 1987); Latour, *Never Modern*, p. 19.

36 Latour, *Never Modern*, pp. 106–8.

Chapter 12 Bad Objects: Virilio

1 Paul Virilio and Sylvère Lotringer, *Pure War* (New York: Semiotext(e), 1983), p. 5.

2 Ibid., p. 15.

3 Ibid., pp. 16, 19–20.

4 Ibid., pp. 28, 30, 64.

5 In fact Virilio devotes a great deal more attention to what he calls critical space (*l'espace critique*) than he does to the dialogic space of the city. Indeed, the

collection of books that Virilio edits at the publishers Galilée is called l'espace critique. Espace critique is not the space from which critique can be launched. Virilio seems not to be very interested in critique. It is first and foremost the space of disappearance of the city. It is instructive to look at his *L'insécurité du territoire* (Paris: Galilée, 1991) in this context. This book, first published in 1976, appeared one year later than *Bunker Archaeology* and a year before the French edition of *Speed and Politics* (*Vitesse et politique*). Its first chapters were written as early as 1969. Here the governing theme seems to be the disaggregation of the city and especially the European city. The city as a 'centre that holds' is dissolved. The happily greeted Libération of 1944 was also the destruction of the city walls. Virilio writes, remembering his boyhood: 'Nous sommes prisonniers non seulement des forces d'occupation, mais aussi des mûrs de nos villes . . . la libération serait aussi l'abolition de la ville, de cette cité trompeuse qui pouvait si facilement se retourner contre sa population' (*Insécurité du territoire*, p. 17). But now the 'sky appears in history', 'notre patrie, c'est le mouvement'. Virilio speaks thus of time, or movement, as if it were space. He speaks of how we live in time. From the start, the aeroplane and airport are at centre stage. He speaks of how the gates of our cities are now airports (p. 20). Hence space is 'de-realized' into the 'universal absence' of the blue of the skies.

In the last essay of the book he returns to the metaphor of space as a country ('pays de la vitesse'). He notes that as 'technical vehicles abolish the space of the (human) species', 'administration will now be primarily of time of displacement'. And 'the ministry of the Aménagement [governance] du territoire will be succeeded by that of the governance of duration'. He observes that now we pass less from one place to another than from 'one state of movement to another'. We don't experience places, we experience ('cinétically') sequences, as in the nineteenth century not only the cinema but the train was often compared to a magic lantern (ibid., pp. 243–6).

6   *Bunker Archeology* (New York: Princeton Architectural Press, 1994), pp. 13–14 (first French edition published in 1975); Arthur Kroker, *The Possessed Individual* (London: Macmillan, 1992), pp. 39ff.; Celia Lury, *Prosthetic Culture* (London: Routledge, 1997), pp. 177ff.

7   Paul Virilio, 'Exposer l'accident', *Traverses, 26, Les Rhetoriques de la Technologie* (1982), pp. 36–41, at p. 38; Kroker, *Possessed Individual*, pp. 30–1.

8   Virilio and Lotringer, *Pure War*, pp. 61, 69, 84, 86.

9   Virilio has the greatest regret for the demise of the twentieth-century European city. Indeed, the triumph of the 'pays du mouvement' is 'critical space' itself. Critical space for Virilio is not territory, but the insecurity of territory. It is at the same time movement and the 'overexposed city'. When he speaks of overexposure, the model is overexposed film. When Virilio speaks of our contemporary 'negative horizon', again the model is film negatives. We are overexposed not just to the ubiquity of surveillance machines, but in what is no longer our 'occupation' of a 'marked' and opaque space, but now our 'occupation of transportation and transmission time'. The absence of markers entails a certain transparency. Markers have their own substance, their own opacity. Markers give us an orientation in space, and at the same time they

conceal, they keep secrets, they make myth possible. We now thus occupy a certain transparency. This is found also in the absence of markers and myth in the transparent of the blue skies of the airport. The nature of the facade is changing: from stone to glass and finally to 'interface', in each case more transparent, more exposed. The city is exposed to its hinterland as boundaries between city an countryside dissolve: its citizens exposed in the collapsing distinction between housing, on the one hand, and traffic, on the other. Now traffic – of one sort or another – goes right through housing. See Virilio, *L'espace critique* (Paris: Christian Bourgois, 1984), pp. 19, 28. Virilio's seeming obsession with the airport as city gate is in a sense very well founded. Take, for example, Chicago, whose centre of gravity and population centre has shifted markedly over the past three decades from the old downtown 'Loop' area to O'Hare Airport in the near Northwest suburbs.

10 Virilio, *L'Horizon negatif* (Paris: Galilée, 1984).
11 Virilio and Lotringer, *Pure War*, pp. 140–1.
12 Ibid., pp. 34, 124.
13 Ibid., pp. 27, 127.
14 Ibid., p. 124.
15 Paul Virilio, *War and Cinema: The Logistics of Perception* (1984) (London: Verso, 1989), pp. 2–3.
16 Ibid., pp. 32–3.
17 Ibid., p. 36.
18 Virilio, *The Vision Machine* (London: British Film Institute, 1994), pp. 19–20; Lury, *Prosthetic Culture*, p. 175. The first French edition of *La machine de vision* was published in 1988. The English translation cited here is from the second 1991 edition.
19 *Vision Machine*, p. 20; *War and Cinema*, pp. 92–3.
20 *Vision Machine*, pp. 23, 25.
21 Ibid., p. 28.
22 Ibid.
23 Ibid., pp. 35–6.
24 Dieter Hoffmann-Axthelm, 'Identity and reality: the end of the philosophical immigration officer', in S. Lash and J. Friedman (eds), *Modernity and Identity* (Oxford: Blackwell, 1992), pp. 196–218; Virilio, *Vision Machine*, p. 43.
25 *Vision Machine*, pp. 38, 41, 52.
26 Paul Virilio, 'L'image virtuelle mentale et instrumentale', *Traverses, 44–45, Machines Virtuelles* (1987), pp. 35–9, at p. 39.
27 'Image virtuelle', p. 37.
28 'Image virtuelle', pp. 36, 38; *Vision Machine*, chapter 5, passim.
29 Richard Sennett, *The Fall of Public Man* (Cambridge: Cambridge University Press, 1974), pp. 38–41; 'Image virtuelle', pp. 36, 38; *Vision Machine*, p. 75.
30 *Vision Machine*, p. 67; 'Image virtuelle', p. 38. Virilio writes: 'La fréquence temps de la lumière est devenue un facteur déterminant de l'apperception des phénomènes, au détriment de la fréquence espace de la matière: d'où la possibilité inouïe de ces trucages en temps réels, ces luerres qui affectent moins la nature de l'objet que l'image de sa présence, dans l'instant infinitésimal où

virtuel et actuel se confondent pour le détecteur ou l'observateur humain';
Virilio, 'La déception', in *Les chemins du virtuel, Simulation informatique et création industrielle*, special issue of *Cahiers du CCI* (Paris: Editions du Centre Pompidou, 1989), pp. 175–80, at p. 180. Here Virilio understands transformations in the space and time of representations on the model of deception in war. Also see James Der Derian, *Antidiplomacy, Spies, Terror, Speed and War* (Cambridge, MA: Blackwell, 1992), pp. 130–4.

31   'Image virtuelle', p. 37; *Vision Machine*, pp. 68, 71, 72, 73, 74, 76, 77.
32   Paul Virilio, *Inertie polaire* (Paris: Christian Bourgois, 1990), pp. 16–17.
33   Ibid., pp. 25, 28; Nigel Thrift, *Spatial Formations* (London: Sage, 1995).
34   *Inertie polaire*, p. 147.
35   Ibid., p. 46.
36   Ibid., pp. 43, 49.
37   Ibid., p. 50.
38   Virilio, 'Un cockpit en ville', *Traverses*, *41–42, Voyages* (1987), p. 69; *Inertie polaire*, pp. 55, 58–9.
39   *Inertie polaire*, p. 50.
40   Ulrich Beck, *Democracy without Enemies* (Cambridge: Polity Press, 1998).
41   Virilio, *Inertie polaire*, p. 76.
42   Ibid., p. 81.
43   Ibid., p. 107.
44   Ibid., pp. 138–47.

Chapter 13   The Symbolic in Fragments: Walter Benjamin's Talking Things

1   Susan Buck-Morss, *The Dialectics of Seeing* (Cambridge, MA: MIT Press, 1991), p. 23.
2   Walter Benjamin, 'Der Erzähler, Betrachtungen zum Werk Nikolai Leskows', in *Aufsätze, Essays, Vorträge, Gesammelte Schriften, Band II-2* (Frankfurt: Suhrkamp, 1977) pp. 438–65, at pp. 439–40.
3   Gerhard Schulze, *Die Erlebnisgesellschaft* (Frankfurt: Campus, 1993), pp. 34ff. Translated as *The Experience Society* (London: Sage, 1999); Howard Caygill, *Walter Benjamin: the Colour of Experience* (London: Routledge, 1998). This book has appeared just as the present book is about to go into press. Thus it has been impossible to take account of its contribution.
4   Benjamin, 'Der Erzähler', p. 439.
5   Ibid., p. 447. Translated as 'The storyteller', in Walter Benjamin, *Illuminations* (London: Fontana, 1973), pp. 83–107, at p. 91.
6   'Erzähler', pp. 441–2, 'Storyteller', pp. 84–5.
7   'Erzähler', p. 445, 'Storyteller', p. 89.
8   John B. Thompson, *The Media and Modernity* (Cambridge: Polity Press, 1995).
9   'Erzähler', p. 446, 'Storyteller', p. 90.
10   'Erzähler', p. 464; 'Storyteller', p. 107.
11   'Erzähler', section X.
12   Ibid., section XI.

13 Ibid., section XIX
14 Ibid., sections XVII, XVIII.
15 Benjamin, 'L'oeuvre d'art a l'époque de sa réproduction mécanisée', *Abhandlungen, Gesammelte Schriften, Band I-2* (Franfurt: Suhrkamp, 1974), trans. Pierre Klossowski, pp. 709–39, at pp.713–14.
16 'Erzähler', section XV.
17 Ibid., section V.
18 Ibid., section XIV. Parts of these pages were published in my 'Being after time', in S. Lash, A. Quick and R. Roberts (eds), *Time and Value* (Oxford: Blackwell, 1998), pp. 305–19.
19 Ibid., section XIII.
20 Ibid., section XV.
21 Ibid., section XIV.
22 Ibid., section III.
23 Ibid., section VIII.
24 Ibid., section XIII.
25 Ibid., section XII.
26 Ibid., section XVI.
27 Ibid., sections XVI, XVII. Nicky Chu, 'The religions and nihilism'. PhD thesis, Lancaster University, 1996.
28 Winfried Menninghaus, *Walter Benjamins Theorie der Sprachmagie* (Frankfurt: Suhrkamp, 1980), p. 8.
29 Ibid., p. 11. In this sense too television can be understood as a medium that cannot necessarily be reduced to a means.
30 Menninghaus, *Sprachmagie*, p. 19.
31 Ibid., pp. 24, 32.
32 Ibid., p. 11, 17.
33 Oswald Ducrot, 'Le structuralisme en linguistique', in François Wahl, *Qu'est-ce que le structuralisme?* (Paris: Seuil, 1968), pp. 13–96, at pp. 50–2; Menninghaus, *Sprachmagie*, pp. 23, 232.
34 Benjamin, 'The task of the translator, an introduction to the translation of Baudelaire's *Tableaux parisiens*', in *Illuminations*, pp. 70–82, at pp. 72–3. Menninghaus, *Sprachmagie*, pp. 24, 28, 53, 57.
35 Walter Benjamin, 'Uber Sprache überhaupt und über die Sprache des Menschen', in *Aufsätze, Essays, Vorträge, Gesammelte Schriften, Band II-1* (Frankfurt: Suhrkamp, 1977), pp. 140–57, at pp. 142–4. Menninghaus, *Sprachmagie*, pp. 13, 18, 54–6.
36 Walter Benjamin, 'On the mimetic faculty', in *Reflections* (New York: Schocken Books, 1986), pp. 333–6, at p. 334.
37 Menninghaus, *Sprachmagie*, p. 137.
38 Benjamin, Uber einige Motive bei Baudelaire', in *Abhandlungen, Gesammelte Schriften, Band I-2* (Frankfurt: Suhrkamp, 1974), pp. 607–53, at pp. 622, 630.
39 Benjamin, 'Der Surrealismus, Die letzte Momentaufnahme der europäischen Intelligenz', in *Aufsätze, Essays, Vorträge, II-1*, pp. 295–310, at pp. 297–8.
40 Zygmunt Bauman, *Mortality, Immortality and Other Life Strategies* (Cambridge: Polity Press, 1992).

41 David Frisby, *Fragments of Modernity* (Cambridge: Polity Press, 1985), pp. 202–3.
42 W. Benjamin, 'Uber einige Motive bei Baudelaire', in *Abhandlungen, Gesammelte Schriften, Band I-2* (Frankfurt: Suhrkamp, 1974), pp. 607–53, at pp. 615, 632–3; Menninghaus, *Sprachmagie*.
43 On tragedy see G. Michael Dillon, *Politics of Security* (London: Routledge, 1996). For a sociological portrait of the tragic existence of what Benjamin might have viewed as allegorists of the ghetto, see Philippe Bourgois, *In Search of Respect: Selling Crack in El Barrio* (Cambridge: Cambridge University Press, 1995).
44 W. Benjamin, 'Some motifs in Baudelaire', in *Charles Baudelaire, a Lyric Poet in the Era of High Capitalism* (London: Verso, 1983), pp. 107–54, at pp. 140–3.
45 Benjamin, 'Uber einige Motive', pp. 609–11.
46 Benjamin, 'Some motifs', pp. 138ff.
47 Benjamin, 'Uber einige Motive', pp. 611–12, 615; Christine Buci-Glucksmann, *La rasion baroque, de Baudelaire à Benjamin* (Paris: Galilée, 1984), pp. 53ff., translated as *Baroque Reason: the Aesthetics of Modernity* (London: Sage, 1994).
48 Menninghaus, *Sprachmagie*, p. 155.
49 Walter Benjamin, *Ursprung des deutschen Trauerspiels* (Frankfurt: Suhrkamp, 1963), p. 36; *The Origins of German Tragic Drama*, p. 50.
50 *Trauerspiels*, p. 54; *Tragic Drama*, p. 41.
51 *Trauerspiels*, p. 56; *Tragic Drama*, p. 42.
52 *Trauerspiels*, p. 65.
53 Ibid., p. 69.
54 Ibid., pp. 138–9; *Tragic Drama*, p. 150.
55 *Trauerspiels*, p. 150.
56 *Tragic Drama*, p. 140.
57 Ibid., p. 139.
58 *Trauerspiels*, p. 152.
59 Ibid., pp. 150, 152.
60 Ibid., pp. 144–7, 152.
61 Ibid., 148, 152–3, 155.
62 Ibid., pp. 156–7.
63 Ibid., pp. 161, 165.
64 *Tragic Drama*, p. 167.
65 *Trauerspiels*, p. 189, *Tragic Drama*, pp. 169–70.
66 *Trauerspiels*, p. 182.
67 Ibid., p. 183.
68 Ibid., p. 184.
69 *Tragic Drama*, p. 170.

Index